OUTLAW
COOK

ALSO BY JOHN THORNE

Simple Cooking (1987)

OUTLAW COOK

JOHN THORNE

WITH

MATT LEWIS THORNE

NORTH POINT PRESS

FARRAR STRAUS GIROUX

NEW YORK

North Point Press
A division of Farrar, Straus and Giroux
18 West 18th Street, New York 10011

Printed in the United States of America
Published in 1992 by Farrar, Straus and Giroux
First paperback edition, 1994

Portions of this book first appeared, some in different form, in *Wigwag Magazine*, *American Food & Wine*, *The Journal of Gastronomy*, *Harper's Magazine*, and in the authors' *Simple Cooking* food letters.

Grateful acknowledgment is made to the following for permission to reprint copyrighted material:

William Morrow: Excerpt from *The Complete Book of Pasta*, by Jack Denton Scott. Copyright © 1968 by Jack Denton Scott. Reprinted by permission.

Doubleday: Excerpts from *The Cooking of South-West France*, by Paula Wolfert. Copyright © 1983 by Paula Wolfert.

Chiang Jung-feng and Ellen Schrecker: Excerpt from *Mrs. Chiang's Szechwan Cookbook*, by Chiang Jung-feng and Ellen Schrecker with John Schrecker. Copyright © 1976 by Chiang Jung-feng and Ellen Schrecker. Harper & Row. Reprinted by permission.

A. J. Liebling: Excerpt from *Between Meals*. Copyright © 1962 by A. J. Liebling, renewed in 1987 by Norma Liebling Stonehill. Reprinted by permission of Russell & Volkening as agents for the author.

The New York Times: Excerpt from "Vive la Baguette: As French as Paris," by Patricia Wells. Copyright © 1983 by The New York Times Company. Reprinted by permission.

J. M. Dent & Sons, Ltd.: Excerpt from *The Constance Spry Cookery Book*, by Constance Spry and Rosemary Hume. Copyright © 1956 by J. M. Dent & Sons, Ltd. Reprinted by permission.

Sydney Clark: Excerpt from *All the Best in Italy*, by Sydney Clark. Copyright © 1968 by Dodd, Mead & Co.

Alfred A. Knopf: Excerpt from *Mastering the Art of French Cooking* (Vol. I), by Simone Beck, Louisette Bertholle, and Julia Child; copyright © 1961 by Alfred A. Knopf, Inc.; reprinted by permission. Excerpt from *Beard on Bread*, by James Beard; copyright © 1973 by James A. Beard; reprinted by permission.

Dover Publications, Inc.: Excerpts from *The Complete Book of Pasta*, by Enrica Jarratt and Vernon Jarratt. Copyright © 1969 by Enrica and Vernon Jarratt. Reprinted by permission.

Bill Penzey, Jr.: Excerpt from *Penzey's Spice House Ltd. Winter 1991–92 Price List*, by Bill Penzey, Jr. Reprinted by permission.

Pantheon Books: Excerpt from *The Tin Drum*, by Günter Grass. Copyright © 1963 by Günter Grass. Reprinted by permission.

Janice Biala: Excerpt from *Provence*, by Ford Madox Ford. Copyright 1935 by Ford Madox Ford. Copyright renewed 1962 by Mrs. Janice Biala Brustlein. Reprinted by permission of Janice Biala.

Random House, Inc.: Excerpts from *Speak, Memory*, by Vladimir Nabokov. Copyright 1944 by Vladimir Nabokov. Reprinted by permission.

Dutton: Excerpt from *Jane and Prudence*, by Barbara Pym. Copyright by Barbara Pym. Used by permission of the publisher, Dutton, an imprint of New American Library, a division of Penguin Books USA, Inc.

HarperCollins Publishers: Excerpts from *Honey from a Weed*, by Patience Gray; copyright © 1986 by Patience Gray; reprinted by permission. Excerpt from *The Cook's Encyclopedia*, by Tom Stobart; copyright © 1980 by Cameron & Tayleur (Books) Limited; reprinted by permission. Excerpts from *Paula Wolfert's World of Food*, by Paula Wolfert. Copyright © 1988 by Paula Wolfert. Excerpt from *Italian Food*, by Elizabeth David; copyright 1954, © 1963, 1987 by Elizabeth David; reprinted by permission.

Simon & Schuster: Excerpts from *The Taste of China*, by Ken Hom. Copyright © 1990 by Taurom Incorporated. Reprinted by permission.

Ancel Keys: Excerpts from *How to Eat Well and Stay Well the Mediterranean Way*, by Ancel and Margaret Keys. Copyright © 1975 by Ancel and Margaret Keys. Reprinted by permission.

Pan Books: Excerpt from *Middle Eastern Cookery*, by Arto der Haroutunian. Copyright © 1982 by Arto der Haroutunian. Reprinted by permission.

Grateful acknowledgment is also made to Madeleine Kamman, Colman Andrews, Dr. Edward Wood, and Michael Rosen for permission to reprint material previously published in our food letter, *Simple Cooking*, and to Patience Gray, *carissima amica*, for permission to print excerpts from a letter to the authors regarding Giacomo Castelvetro.

The Library of Congress has cataloged the hardcover edition as follows:
Thorne, John.
    Outlaw Cook / John Thorne ; with Matt Lewis Thorne.—1st ed.
        p.   cm.
    Includes bibliographical references and index.
    1. Cookery.   I. Thorne, Matt Lewis.   II. Title
TX652 .T459 1992
641.5—dc20   92008281

Paperback ISBN: 978-0-86547-479-6

www.fsgbooks.com

For my mother and father
with love

A Note on Authorship

✧ ✧ ✧

It is a pleasant fiction that because the words originated in his or her own brain they are the writer's own creation. The truth is more complex; credit is harder to assign. I only know that I am a different and, in my own eyes, a better writer since I began living with the woman who is now my wife, Martha Lewis Thorne. Matt has considered every word of every draft of the pieces collected in this book, reacting, suggesting, amending, and hence *reshaping* what appears on every page—except the one you're reading now. At such a level of intimacy, reader and writer can only be finally differentiated by the objective fact of who it is that punches out the words on the computer keyboard. The subjective self who gave them their meaning is a larger, braver, much more interesting person—a transformation that deserves a form of recognition more public and more tangible than what usually appears, however sincerely, as a coda to an acknowledgment section.

CONTENTS

✤ ✤ ✤

LIST OF RECIPES

❖ ❖ ❖

pasta
—pan-fried, with olive oil

SALADS

SANDWICHES AND SNACKS

SAUCES

SOUPS AND STEWS

VEGETABLES

PREFACE

✦ ✦ ✦

All I wanted to do was to go into the kitchen and cook. Why did that prove so very difficult?

*O*utlaw Cook is an assembly of pieces that for the most part were first published in *Simple Cooking*, the food letter my wife, Matt, and I write and publish. It has now survived for over a decade, the first issue having been sent out sometime in the fall of 1980. Then it was a single, legal-sized sheet, printed at a local photocopy shop. I sent it out free to approximately fifty people, some of whom had already purchased *A Treatise on Onion Soup* or *Aglio, Oglio, Basilico*, two pamphlets I was then selling through small classified ads in (of all places) *The New Republic* and the *National Review*, and to correspondents to the letters pages of *Gourmet, Bon Appétit,* and *Cuisine* whose full addresses I had been able to find in the collection of telephone books at the Boston Public Library.

This was about as hopeless a method as there is for finding readers but, being completely ignorant of the publishing business, I hadn't yet found that out. In any case, what really mattered was that I had finally begun to sort out what had been happening to me for the six years previous—since 1974, that is, when, after years of teaching at a small private school, I had moved to Boston and begun to cook.

The first gale-force waves from that decade's great storm of culinary discovery were just then beginning to roll into the Hub, and it wasn't long before they washed me away. Every week, it seemed, another exciting cookbook arrived in the bookstores—reporting on the culinary revolution in France, presenting at long last the authentic details of the regional cuisines of Italy, China, Mexico, and India, explaining precisely the making of a genuine croissant, a *pizza margherita*, a cassoulet in the manner of Languedoc or Toulouse.

Kitchen equipment stores were springing up overnight, and the single shelf or two of specialty groceries were expanding into entire shops. Even in Boston, it was now possible to buy virgin olive oil, good wine vinegar, shallots, *crème fraîche*, *pancetta*, and, for a time, unpasteurized French cheeses. It was all so new and, to a freshly awakened palate, so *good*.

Not coincidentally, this was also a time when a journalistic revolution was taking place, emblemized by the larger-than-life presences of Tom Wolfe and Hunter Thompson. Journalists were now propelling themselves directly into the story, as much participants as reporters. No surprise then that in the Boston alternative papers, where even the television listings were *engagé*, a writer named Mark Zanger—under the culinary persona of "Robert Nadeau"—began reviewing local restaurants and producing occasional food columns in the first person political.

I was immediately drawn to Zanger/Nadeau as I had been to no other food writer. He was like me—only he was more honest about it. He was teaching himself eating and drinking and simultaneously wondering out loud what he should be making of it, gnawing away at all pat assumptions.

I had read other writers before him who had claimed neither to be good cooks nor to possess a perfect-pitch palate, but their writing tended to weave an unsteady course between humorous self-deprecation and a relentless flood of just-learned good advice. Zanger was always more than that. He taught me— although I've taken my time in learning the lesson—that honesty means nothing if there's no real risk to it, no genuine self-examination.

I needed that kind of perspective right then, because things had already started to go wrong. The most visible symptom was my conviction that I couldn't have too many recipes. I subscribed to every food publication; I had rummaged every cookbook in the open stacks of the Boston Public Library; weekly, and sometimes daily, I scoured the remainder tables at Barnes & Noble. By 1978, I was amassing recipes at such a rate that at the end of the year I filled a whole trash barrel with those that, on sober reflection, I realized I didn't want or need. But of those that I thought I *did* need, I saw no end in sight.

Always, of course, there are answers within answers, but the simplest reason why I was collecting all those cookbooks, all those recipes, was the same one that explained why I kept bringing home grocery bags full of new, untried ingredients. Even being able to pare things down to the truly good (and this itself, I discovered, is no easy thing) did not necessarily free me from making some hard choices. I was like a child in a candy store, tempted by too many good things all at once.

E. M. Forster once wrote that he didn't know what he thought until he said it, and it's the same with me. Mark Zanger had given me a model—in the beginning I even tried to imitate his prose style—but my own experiences not only were presenting me with my theme but were doing so with such urgency that, when I started to formulate *Simple Cooking*, my mind flooded over with words.

I still have my original working notes, and, looking over them, I can see that, right from the start, what I was trying to do was to formulate an approach to cooking that would get me out of the mess I had gotten myself into . . . without surrendering the great pleasure I felt—and still do feel—when I just go into the kitchen and cook. My thought—much elaborated, first in a set of nine culinary pamphlets and then over the years in *Simple Cooking*—was to concentrate on dishes toward which I felt an immediate and intuitive affinity . . . building up a personal cuisine out of what best suited my own tastes, temperament, and cooking talent.

I was much slower in addressing the conflict that came from my sometimes fighting off and sometimes surrendering to the enormous temptation to use cookbooks to inflate my sense of self as a cook—even though I had begun to see how dependent this made me on recipes and how much it ultimately sapped my self-confidence in the kitchen.

A child who is forced to learn self-control in a candy store is engaged in a very ambiguous project. The poignancy inherent in that ambiguity has always provided the octane on which the *Simple Cooking* engine runs. It explains why I excoriate recipes although I am obviously on intimate terms with countless numbers of them; why I denounce trendy ingredients while remaining willing to give the next one a try; and why I continually voice suspicion about the relevance of foreign cuisines to American cooks although much of my writing is devoted to nothing else.

In other words, from the very beginning, my writing was rife with symptoms of the disease I was struggling to cure myself of. It is all there in full cry in the mushroom-soup recipe that appears in the first issue. Though I say that I vary the recipe to suit "what is in the larder or to whim," the actual details convey a dish whose emphasis, in typical recipe fashion, falls on the lip-smacking persuasion of a very familiar set of ingredients. These start with butter, bacon, and chicken stock. "Then," I continue, "stir in two cups of light cream and a scant teaspoon of cognac or good brandy (or even Madeira)." I like the restraint of that "scant teaspoon."

Still, there were also signs that this same engine might at least take us all for an interesting ride. There were three pieces in the first issue: the one on mushroom soup; another that marveled at the simple ingenuity of *boeuf à la ficelle*, which was later put into my first book, *Simple Cooking*; and, lastly, the feature essay, a rumination on salt. This, with some minor touchings-up, is reprinted below. It still works, I think—despite an unintended but still slightly sourish whiff of male chauvinism—and it examples what for me is the genuinely interesting question about the food we eat: not where it comes from or who grows it or even which of it tastes the best, but why it wants to kill its father and sleep with its mother. . . .

If it's cheering to discover that I was writing things ten years ago at the very beginning of my career that I can reprint today with pleasure, it is also salutary and somewhat sobering to realize that the problems I wrestled with in the eighties are very much the same ones that Matt and I find ourselves facing at the start of the nineties. This, I think, explains the deeper threads of intro- and retrospection that distinguish *Outlaw Cook* from its more youthful predecessor. If these meditations can be said to have a single theme, it appears—with apologies to Hermann Hesse—succinctly stated at the beginning of this preface. I pose it in the form of a question—one that, in the end, may never be adequately answered. Even so, as we used to say in the seventies, *la lutte continue . . .* the struggle continues.

On Salt

(REPRINTED FROM *SIMPLE COOKING* #1)

Salt is the masculine presence in the tabletop constellation, sugar the feminine one. Sugar is not only sweet itself but a flatterer in other foods, heightening and mellowing flavors without intruding any taste of its own. Like sugar, salt is a flavor without quality. Its bitterness has no character, only an effect—it makes you salivate. But, unlike sugar, salt has no respect for other flavors; its savor dominates where it intrudes.

This assertiveness is partly why salt conjures up images of the masculine. But it is also because the body is and tastes salty. Blood and sweat, especially when unmediated by either artifice or soap, both have mostly masculine associations. Tears, of course, are a feminine prerogative, but kissing them away (and in the process enjoying their savor) is a masculine one. Thus, "an old salt" is a tag not usually attached to a woman. The phrase "Oh, you salty dog!" has a definite priapic ring to it, and a salty tongue implies male, not female, cussedness.

Salt, then, has masculine connotations because of its aggressive physicality, whereas sugar is a medium of reverie. As children, we fantasized castles of gingerbread in a candy landscape where even the clouds were spun sugar; as adults, the image of sugar still brings with it a romancing of food . . . it heightens anticipation. But the mere thought of salt can cause the tongue to drool and the stomach to grumble—thus rubbing us against our present hunger. So does the skeptic's pinch of salt also bring illusion to an end.

Salt dehydrates meat tissue, forcing out moisture. This chemical action has its metaphorical ramifications, too. You'd expect to find a recipe for steak seared in salt on a red-hot skillet in James Beard, not Fannie Farmer—and you'd be right. Beard approved the method because the salt crust sealed the steak, holding in the juices, which, in fact, it does not do.

At first glance, this bit of culinary folklore seems contrary even to common sense: after all, salt is used to wick moisture out of meats in the drying of salt cod and the curing of country ham. But extend by analogy the feeling of contraction that comes when the tongue is sprinkled with salt to a raw piece of meat and you can see why Beard might have come to believe it.

You can also see why he might have other reasons to be predisposed to do so. Even the idea of a well-salted steak makes the mouth salivate, priming it to put away larger quantities of meat than appetite would otherwise allow—and also allowing it to wolf the meal down quickly. Both aspects are supposed traits of the masculine hunger that Beard, a hearty trencherman if ever there was one, conspicuously espoused.

In brief, then, sugar seduces—the hand that reaches for the next chocolate does so because of the excess of pleasure from the last—while salt, by compelling salivation, commands: "Mouth, forward *marrrch!*" In masculine parlance, to obey such an order is no sign of weakness. It is a battle cry, the signal for appetite to wade in and begin the fight.

However, precisely because it is so aggressive, salt is also a food to measure and, ultimately, one to control. There's no end to the amount of sugar you can put into a cup of coffee (ask a Turk), but the limits of salt are much more closely defined. This helps explain the presence of salt in hospitality rites of aggressive (i.e., masculine) societies: "There is salt between us," the Arabs say, and we cannot imagine the word "salt" replaced by, say, "sugar" or "a pat of butter." This salt is an expression of generosity but also one that compels control and, hence, restraint, the acknowledgment of which is the first step to trust.

Doubtless, salt is a necessity in the kitchen, especially for food cooked in water, which otherwise leaches out any salts already present. A broiled steak can be enjoyed without salt, but a piece of beef boiled in unsalted water emerges inert and dead, meat cooked but not transformed into food. Even so, salt's presence at the table is a cultural phenomenon related less to food than to dining. It allows us to regulate the speed with which we ingest our food —so as to match the rate of our neighbors at the table and to get the job done within an allotted time. The longer one has to eat and the more attention one can pay to the food itself, the less salt is required as a table condiment.

However, if you do put it there, take a close look at the ingredient list on its original container. If you find anything but salt itself, buy some other brand. Salt is a taste that precedes even a mother's milk, for it is the taste of life itself. No food is as good as it can be if the salt that is eaten with it is not clean and pure.

Perhaps the best salt of all is bay salt, sun-dried from sea water. The crystals form into large and crumbly pyramidal flakes, as nice to touch as they are to taste. Their clean savor is so persuasive that a flake easily finds its way, now and then, straight into the mouth of the cook. A pinch of this salt is a reasonable measure, and it is expensive enough so that moderation is a financial as well as a moral pleasure. British Maldon sea salt is a bay salt widely available in this country, from, for example, Williams-Sonoma and—in that firm's own proprietary packaging—Crabtree and Evelyn.

LEARNING
TO
COOK

The Discovery of
Slowness

❖ ❖ ❖

Most of the time when I was a kid, we lived in Fort Bliss, Texas, an army post on the outskirts of El Paso. But as many summers as we could, the whole family (Mother and Dad, four children) would pile into the Buick Super and head for New England. After a four-day drive, with a stopover in Boston to visit my grandparents, we would arrive at the dock in Portland, Maine. There we caught the boat to Long Island, out in Casco Bay. My father would then leave us at the family cottage until the end of summer, when he'd return to spend what was left of his leave before bringing us all back to Texas.

The cottage existed, like all summer places, in a world of slow time. Perched on a cliff overlooking the bay, it was bounded on all sides not by paved roads or even a sidewalk but by a sea of grass. The drinking water came from a well, the washing water from rain barrels set under the eaves. The food was cooked over a tiny camp stove; perishables were kept in an icebox, cooled with an actual giant chunk of ice. At night, games were played and stories read aloud by kerosene lantern; the last trip to the outhouse was lit by a candle in a jar, because flashlight batteries were expensive and we kids ran them down, shining its light for company all the time we sat there.

We had no radio, no television, no telephone. Here was here; there was somewhere else. Things traversed the distance between the two over the water, by boat, slowly. Even when the *Gurnet* or the *Aucocisco* had been sighted steaming toward us up the bay, there was still plenty of time to push the wheel-barrow through the woods and across the beach to meet it. Boxes of groceries, blocks of ice, visitors' luggage were all wheeled home in it slowly . . . time taken to get used to something new.

Smart, but timid and easily panicked, I was a child who needed this slowness. My mind raced quickly but only really grasped the things it was allowed to take in small bites. This may be why, although I was naturally interested in treats, I wasn't all that drawn to food. Eating was just something else that had to be done too quickly. Lingering at the table or playing with one's food was not allowed. To get dessert, what came before had to be eaten at a rate that was the same as everyone else's, which meant not so much tasting as perform-ing the necessary motions.

Learning to become a socially acceptable table partner is not at all the same thing as learning how to eat. Involvement with what went into the mouth was possible only for such things as cocoa or ice cream, food that was taken in small, contem-plative mouthfuls and—unlike the monotonous plasticity of chewing gum—rewarded such patience by continuing to taste good.

On the island, however, ordinary rules of the table didn't hold. Eating, too, was incorporated into slowness. Blueberries and raspberries, for example, grew everywhere, and were to be picked, examined for bugs, and then eaten one by one. Or a whole leisurely morning could be spent picking them, until there were enough to be made into a pie or, even better, into preserves. Then one could watch their gradual transformation into an astonishingly clear and deep-colored liquid. This, dipped up in a spoon, could be turned by patient blowing into a quivering mass of fragile jelly, lustrous as a jewel.

Digging for clams, I found that they were not slow but sur-prisingly quick—just not quick enough once you learned to outsmart them. In any case, they could only move at all when burrowing through the sand. When fingers clutched them, they gave up like a victim at tag.

This was good, because crabs and lobsters were terrifying even in captivity, scurrying about so quickly, snapping their claws. I was upset by fishing, too, but for a different reason. I knew that the fish wouldn't hurt me, but its convulsive thrashing touched off an inner empathetic agitation. I felt too close to such spasms myself, as when cornered in math class by a word problem, on one side, that needed an hour to sort out and a teacher, on the other, insisting that I solve it that moment, at once, immediately.

Lobsters, at least, were made to be eaten slowly, each leg carefully searched for all hidden morsels before going on to the next. The big, juicy piece of tail meat, I learned, was to be saved for last, like the heart of an artichoke, to finally fill the mouth with as much as it could hold of the flavor that, until now, had been worried out in bits.

Clams were steamed in big pots full of clean seaweed, which gave them plenty of time to decide to open their shells. Those that refused escaped being eaten. Each of the others was taken from its shell, had its rubbery neck pulled off like a dirty undershirt, and was given a bath in hot broth. Then, finally, the soothing dip in melted butter . . . it was like getting them ready for bed.

Although clams are often steamed right on the beach, I liked the fact that our family brought them home to eat. There, at the table, the beach that the clams lived and fed in could be held at a distance and considered with cautious pleasure. Contrarily, what I loved about eating on the beach was how it transformed what was, when we ate it at home, completely ordinary. Meals that would otherwise be made in a minute now took a whole afternoon. Food waited patiently in the big wicker basket while we edged into the icy water, taking our time to work up nerve for that first electric plunge. Then blankets would be spread, creating a room; rocks would be propped together carefully to make a fireplace, driftwood gathered, and a fire started. There could be no cooking done until the wood had burnt down into coals, and, since the fire wasn't started until everyone had come up from swimming, supper proceeded for once with exemplary slowness.

The sun slipped down behind the island. The breeze off the water blew no longer cool but chill. We sat around the burning logs, impatiently picking away the bark from our sharp-

pronged cooking sticks, fashioning them to personal specifi-
cation, until, finally, the last flame flickered away, leaving behind it a bed of glowing embers.

Each of us then impaled a hot dog and got as near to the
fire as we could, dodging the smoke, which made us blind
with tears. By practicing slowness, we could make our hot
dogs first sizzle and then burst, exposing their bright, juicy
innards. All the while, the rolls were being carefully toasted
on a rock propped at the edge of the fire. Success meant a hot
dog that was burnt black only in spots but leaking all over with
steamy juices, slipped into its grilled roll and dressed with Mr.
Mustard and plenty of piccalilli.

By the time we roasted the last of them, the sun had gone.
The beach was dark, and when the coals were prodded with
our sticks, sparks scattered up like fireflies. Now my mother
took out of the picnic basket the makings of her own favorite
part of the meal: Campfire marshmallows, Hershey almond
bars, and Nabisco graham crackers.

Each of the marshmallows, of course, was to be speared and
then rotated cautiously over the fire until its exterior was an
even brown and its interior melted through. The trick was not
only to have the patience to wait for this moment but also to
recognize it when it arrived—so that the marshmallow would
collapse onto a graham cracker, not into the coals. The sandwich was then completed with a chunk of the Hershey bar and
a second graham cracker pressed firmly on top of all. In our
family these were called simply toasted marshmallow sand-
wiches, but, by whatever name they are known, this is the
taste that calls up for countless American kids a certain kind
of summer night—of fire, feeding, and the ragged festivity that
comes from genuine happiness.

Of course, only as adults do we taste all this in the confection;
as children, the thing itself was enough. Melted marshmallow
pressed flat in its still-crisp crust, the softened chocolate, the
salty, crunchy nuts, the dry, crumbly graham cracker . . . it's
on such as this that kids are permitted to get drunk. Soon,
marshmallows are set aflame and waved about to raucous
laughter, mouths get burnt, and adult good humor starts to
wane.

For my mother, the most evocative toasted marshmallow sandwich was the one made exactly right. By showing us, her children, how that could be managed, she might see herself through her own mother's eyes. Here was a moment when my mother understood slowness completely. As I watched her in the darkness, patiently turning one final marshmallow over the dying coals, I was at last able to feel that growing up did not entirely mean speeding up, that ahead of me might also lie the ability to become stronger even in slowness.

Written in memory of my uncle Walter Brooks Favorite (1924–1990), who, of all my mother's generation, loved this place the most.

KITCHEN DIARY: RASPBERRIES

The British make a dessert with fresh strawberries, variously called Clare College Mush or Eton Mess, in which the berries are macerated in Cointreau and stirred into a mixture of whipped cream and crushed meringues. This is good, but I like it even better made instead with raspberries and a raspberry liqueur like Chambord, where the intense sourness of those berries makes a better contrast with the sweetness of the meringues.

RASPBERRY CRUMBLE
(SERVES 4)

3 large egg whites, at room temperature	*Dash of vanilla*
¼ teaspoon cream of tartar	*2 tablespoons raspberry eau-de-vie or Chambord*
Pinch of salt	*1 pint fresh raspberries*
½ cup sugar	*1 cup heavy cream, chilled*

Preheat the oven to 250°F. Put the whites into a mixing bowl, making sure no speck of yolk gets in with them, and whip until frothy with a whisk or electric mixer. Then beat in first the cream of tartar and then the pinch of salt. Continue beating, and add 6 tablespoons of the sugar, one at a time, sprinkling each spoonful in slowly. Do not rush this. Finally, mix in the vanilla. Beating at high speed, whip the mixture until it is glossy and firm enough to hold its shape when the beaters are removed. Drop tablespoons of this mixture onto a lightly greased cookie sheet and bake in a low oven for one hour. Then turn the oven off but do not remove the meringues for another hour. (If not using them immediately, keep tightly sealed in a tin.)

While the meringues are baking, pour the raspberry liqueur and 1 tablespoon of the remaining sugar over the raspberries, stirring gently but well. Leave this mixture to macerate for at least one hour. Before serving, whip the chilled heavy cream with the last tablespoon of sugar. Coarsely crumble the meringues and mix these and the macerated berries together in a large bowl. Fold in the whipped cream and turn equal portions of this mixture out into small chilled bowls. Serve at once.

COOK'S NOTE: If a raspberry liqueur or *eau-de-vie* is unavailable, *crème de cassis* or ordinary black currant syrup can be substituted for the raspberry liqueur, giving the dessert a pleasantly mysterious note. Finally, if making meringues is something that you never seem to get around to, *amaretti di Saronno* can be substituted, using three for each serving.

This cake is extravagant in its use of fresh raspberries, but you'll realize how worth the expense it is when, during the last ten minutes of baking, the kitchen is flooded with that berry's fragrant aroma. And the cake itself lives up to this advance billing, with its deep, spicy raspberry flavor, marvelously set off by the buttery richness and the sweet-sour savor of the brown sugar.

I found the recipe in Haydn S. Pearson's The Countryman's Cookbook, *a very opinionated, very charming collection of New England recipes from the 1940s. The recipe as he gives it calls for canned raspberries and a flavoring mixture of clove, nutmeg, and cinnamon. Matt and I replaced the canned with fresh berries and two of the spices with fresh lemon zest, which we felt better brought out the slightly elusive raspberry flavor.*

FRESH RASPBERRY CAKE

(MAKES ONE 9-INCH LOAF)

¾ cup (1½ sticks) unsalted butter, softened
1 cup brown sugar, packed
2 eggs
2 tablespoons sour cream
Grated zest of 1 small lemon

2 cups all-purpose flour, sifted before and after measuring
1 teaspoon baking soda
⅛ teaspoon cinnamon
1 pint fresh raspberries
Whipped cream for topping

Preheat the oven to 325°F. Lavishly butter a 9 × 5 × 3-inch loaf pan; set aside. In a large bowl, cream the butter well and beat in the sugar. Beat the eggs until frothy in a separate bowl and then beat them into the butter-sugar mixture. When this is light and creamy, beat in the sour cream and the grated lemon zest. Then sift the flour, baking soda, and cinnamon on top, and mix until smooth. Gently fold the raspberries into the batter with a spatula, mixing well but breaking up the berries as little as possible.

Turn the batter into the buttered pan, smoothing it evenly on top. Bake for about 55 minutes or until a cake tester or straw comes out clean. Let the cake cool on a wire rack for about 15 minutes before inverting the pan gently, letting the cake slip out onto the same rack to cool completely. Cut in thick slices and serve with whipped cream.

LEARNING TO EAT

❖ ❖ ❖

1

A man who is rich in his adolescence is almost doomed
to be a dilettante at table. This is not because all millionaires
are stupid but because they are not impelled to experiment.
In learning to eat, as in psychoanalysis, the customer, in
order to profit, must be sensible of the cost.

—A. J. Liebling, *Between Meals*

My first piece of cooking equipment was an 8-inch cast-
iron frying pan. I was in a junk shop on Manhattan's Lower
East Side, rooting around for two used chairs to bring back to
my new apartment at East Ninth Street. I had moved in the
day before and discovered I had inherited three pieces of furniture: a mattress, a vintage-model air conditioner the size of
a refrigerator, and a table. The first two of these were to be
reclaimed that morning by the former tenant's boyfriend. He
didn't take the table, however, perhaps because it stood up
only when propped against a wall.

I was sorry to see the mattress go because, wretched as it
was, without it I was reduced to sleeping on the floor. But it
was even more important to have a table. Using the floor as a
bed is an inconvenience that most of us have suffered at least
once, but using it as a table is to lose all touch with civilized

life and, with it, all hope. The gift of a table, however, means the buying of a chair. I could afford that, and I hoped I could afford two of them. A second chair was a promise of company. I didn't know anyone in New York City right then, but I wanted to.

So I had come to this place where old chairs went to die. Eventually I found two whose demise had been misjudged by a year or so, and as the old proprietor was tying them together so that I could carry them back home, he asked me if I was moving into the neighborhood. I told him that I had just rented my first apartment and that these two chairs would be my first pieces of furniture. He nodded and, when he had finished with them, turned and rummaged through a huge pile of junk that was dumped across the table behind him. He emerged from it with the frying pan. It was a disgusting-looking object, crusted thickly all over—inside and out—with dust caked onto ancient grease. He held it out to me. "With this," he said, "you'll never starve. It's a whole kitchen by itself. Take it." As I hesitated, he thrust it forward and said, "As a moving-in present. Yours for seventy-five cents."

When I still stood there motionless, he set it down on the counter without rancor. "Let me give you a little cooking lesson for free," he said. "This pan is a gem. You don't know why because you've never cooked anything. So, I'll tell you." He leaned a little toward me over the counter and hissed, "*Because it's never been washed*, that's why. And it never should be washed. When you're done using it, throw in some salt and scrub it out with a crumpled piece of newspaper, a paper bag. No soap, no water—no stick." I paid him, balanced it on the two chairs, and brought it home. I didn't believe him about the pan, but I knew he was right about one thing: I didn't know how to cook. The truth was, I hadn't yet even found out how to eat.

❖ ❖ ❖

I lied when I told the junk dealer that this was my first apartment. I had already dropped out of college to share a place in New York City a year earlier, but that time was a lark. This time I had left college for good, committed to becoming a writer. I had arrived in Manhattan the day before at five in the morning, alone, with precious little money and too many expectations: in short, so far as this city was concerned, a rube.

I threw my luggage into a locker at the Port Authority Bus Terminal, picked up a copy of *The New York Times*, and went to an all-night cafeteria on Forty-second Street for steak and eggs. I left my tray at a vacant table to go back for some packets of sugar, and when I returned I found a vagrant polishing off my breakfast. Shaken, I went through the line again and sat somewhere else, spending the next two hours marking off places I thought I could afford. By 9 A.M. I was working my way through the list from East Fourteenth Street down.

The day was gray and bitter cold. Snowflakes floated in the air. The apartments were universally grim. I rejected them, one after another, with growing despair. In some the ends of each hallway were pitch black; in others there was a common toilet shared by the whole floor. The rooms reeked of unwashed bodies and stale food. The one I finally chose, on East Ninth Street between First Avenue and Avenue A, was on the top floor of a five-floor walkup. But the stairwell was brightly lit, the toilet had a closet to itself off the single (windowless) bedroom, and the two windows looked out onto a neatly kept back yard where a large sycamore grew, its bare branches reaching almost as high as the sill.

Thirty years now and I can still remember that apartment almost as if I had just stepped out of it, from the feel of the lock knob to the location of the electric sockets to the shape of the tub, the size of the closet, the pane of glass with a crack shot through it that popped out of its frame during a February blizzard. I can call back up to the mind's eye that first long night spent carefully painting the living-room walls and ceiling a bone white, then scrubbing the floors and rubbing them with paste wax, to coax out of their scuffed wood a reluctant, soon-to-vanish sheen.

The smell of fresh paint barely overlaid a fainter, more pungent odor, the accumulated fear and loneliness and terrified excitement of those who had lived here before me. My immediate successor had simply vanished, leaving her possessions behind. Her boyfriend took what he wanted; the landlord told me to throw the rest out. She was young, or at least her clothing was; I packed it up in her battered fiberboard suitcase. But after a month of keeping it in the closet, I carried it down to the basement and abandoned it. It was too vivid a reminder of my own fear about what might happen to me.

New York is a brutal city, especially if you come there without friends, work, or money, and if your sense of self is buoyed by nothing but the flimsy dreams of youth. It isn't just the eruption of random, sudden violence—the electric iron flung during a family fight out of a third-floor window, the gunshot on the roof overhead—but the brutality of walls and moldings that have been painted over so many times that their outlines are swollen, shapeless . . . layer on layer of fresh hope that has eventually turned as grimy and black as those that lie beneath. The brutality of too much fragile experience crushed together.

I blocked off my windows with long drapes cut from a bolt of burlap dyed royal blue. When I woke in the morning, wrapped up in my living-room rug, the sun streamed in through the loose weave in the coarse-grained color of an early Technicolor movie. Although the room was dark and starkly empty, it was filled with flecks of blue-tinged light, as if it were a closed eyeball and I myself an overstimulated optic nerve.

I had come to New York to become a writer, but the story that was my life was washed out from under me by a violent torrent of sensation—inner impulse and outer stimuli. At my age, that story was my single subject. I was entirely flushed of words. The typewriter took a long slow fade; it was only after someone broke in and stole it that it reappeared in my consciousness, now an ironic symbol. I was a refugee whose forged passport had been stolen and, with it, the fantasy of escaping into a false, safe self. All my dreams at the time were of elevated trains shooting over chromatic cityscapes on roller-coaster trestles. In waking life that ride often left me breathless, but I found that it didn't take my appetite away. In fact, I was very, very hungry.

2

Outside my apartment—that large, shut eye—were Russians, Poles, Ukrainians. A Russian Orthodox church sat on a nearby corner and near it a genuine Russian bathhouse; the single display windows of assorted tiny import stores sported rugs with savage bears wandering in forests or pious religious motifs woven in Day-Glo hues on black backgrounds. Signs promised safe delivery of parcels to behind the Iron Curtain. In other windows had been propped cards that read "Apartment to Let—Polish People Only." This, a super explained, didn't mean me—who could pass as a kind of Pole—but blacks and also the Hispanics encroaching in from Avenues C and D.

It was, in fact, a neighborhood of old people. I did once see a crowd of fresh-faced, well-scrubbed Boy Scouts, a Polish-American troop (in ironed uniforms!) waiting for a bus to camp, but they probably accounted for every Slavic youth on the entire East Side. Mostly I encountered suspicious, wrinkled faces peering from behind chained doors, sagging bodies on withered legs shuffling up the steep flights of stairs in carpet slippers, dragging a shopping cart behind. Now and then I would pass an old woman, dressed entirely in black, down on her hands and knees, scrubbing the sidewalk with a brush and a pail of soapy water.

Once my presence became familiar to these people, I ceased to exist. Exciting no fear or interest, I was not worth seeing. I was the Invisible Man. I passed them on the sidewalk or in the hallway without remark; they barely glanced at me or answered a greeting when I edged past them on the stoop or waited next to them at a counter.

This intensified the dreamlike quality of my life. It also had another effect. Nothing among these puffy, dowdy women and crabby, withered men, these religious shops and churches, the cramped, furniture-stuffed, heavily curtained apartments, echoed back or reflected any part of the intense sexual excitement that my youth and this flood of sensation had sent rushing through my responsive but tightly reined-in flesh.

At the time, I didn't think of it as restrained. On the contrary, my brain reeled with sex. I read Jean Genet, Henry Miller, William Burroughs, Allen Ginsberg, Wilhelm Reich. I absorbed Fellini's *8½*, Kenneth Anger's *Scorpio Rising*, the then budding oeuvre of Andy Warhol's film factory. Even so, all this was in my head—the same head that had locked my body into what would prove to be a near-unbroachable shell. Looking back, I see I had already made a clear if unconscious choice by locating myself not in the permissive Village but on the Lower East Side, a repressed-seeming neighborhood where I would be kept safe from finding—or myself becoming—an object of desire.

At the age of twenty, however, desire is not that easy to avoid. With nothing else to do, I used up my free time walking the city. That first winter, every other Friday—payday—I would find myself walking west, into the Village, to browse the bookstores for a mystery or to see a movie, and end up discovering, once again, that I had somehow managed to brush up against it. My body charged with electric current, I would walk back home, stopping at the Night Owl Grocery on the corner of Tenth Street and First Avenue for a bag of potato chips. Back in my apartment, I would take these and my mystery and go straight to bed.

At the time about which I write, any pretensions I had regarding connoisseurship revolved around tobacco. My cooking, such as it was, came mostly out of cans. I was too intensely inhibited to directly focus on the pleasure of eating in the company of anyone, even myself. Now, lying under the covers, my mind absorbed in a book, I would eat through the bag of chips, producing—like the solitary sex that often followed after—a state of contented oblivion, a self-induced warmth that filled mind and body, wadding it as best as I could against the reality without.

Once let into my life, however, I found it hard to confine this kind of eating to the safety of my bed. As summer approached, I became more and more reluctant to return home. Nightfall came later, my rooms were hot and airless, and I began instead to head south, crossing Houston Street into Little Italy, Chinatown, and the Jewish neighborhoods by the Wil-

liamsburg Bridge. Here were places where I had already seen
food being conspicuously enjoyed; here also were places
where, if I had any change in my pocket, I could afford to eat.

❖ ❖ ❖

Still, if desire urged me forward, repression, shyness, continued to hold me back. I became, at least at first, a gastronomic
voyeur. I stared into shop windows. If the shop was large and
crowded, I might let myself go in and browse, peering into the
display cases, watching, still clinging to my invisibility, the
interplay between counterman and customer. I would hover
about the Essex Street Market, a block-sized building the city
had erected years ago to get the pushcarts off the street, letting
myself be swept in at one end and out the other, safe and
unseen in crowds of every ethnicity and human hue, who
pushed their way through the alleyways between the stands.
These, often no more than planks on sawhorses, displayed hog
maws, plantains, live turtles, rabbits, violent-colored un-
wrapped confections, blocks of halvah, vats of olives, and tubs
of brine-cured onions, cucumbers, and chile peppers.

What little of this that I bought and ate had already been
made eatable—pickles, olives, cheese. Mostly I observed. A
leg of beef was one thing, a plucked and eviscerated duck—
complete with head, bill, and feet—another. I came from a
place where appetite was diffident and picky and didn't want
to know too much. It was a place where supermarkets trimmed
meat into individual portions in the back and wrapped these
in cellophane; where waiters brought out food only after it had
already been chosen; where, that is, appetite was stimulated
by packages, advertisements, menus—by words and pictures,
not by the food itself.

Here, however, appetite was raw aggression, and those who
meant to feed it did so on those terms. Not only were shop
windows full of actual, unpackaged food, but on slow days
shopmen stood in their doorways to urge your custom, street
vendors saluted you as brazenly as beggars. So did their food.
The air was full of appetizing smells: roasted chestnuts, hot
peanuts, hot dogs. Good Humor men, with no scents to waft,

jangled bells. Eateries, in competition, put on their own performances. Peppers, onions, and sausages fried in full view in a whole row of electric frying pans; huge gyros (which for years I believed to be legs from some Greek strain of super-sheep) rotated on vertical skewers, sweating grease; and, of course, solemn pizzaioli flipped and spun large, twirling disks of dough with two clenched fists, as watchers gawked and they themselves stared coolly at nothing at all.

Working as a mail boy for fifty dollars a week, I shared with this crowd its hunger; I was alone in my shame of it. I could not imagine eating hugely, openly; the prickling of appetite was exciting until I reached out my hand to take . . . then it fled. There were times when I could have afforded a whole Sicilian pizza—the kind I coveted: rectangular, thickly crusted, heaped with cheese and sauce—but I could never bring myself to order more than a slice or two.

Even eating that made me self-conscious; I preferred to scoop it up and run. Eating while reading had been my introduction to gastronomic pleasure because the mind was too buried in words to notice what the mouth was up to. Walking and eating, I now discovered, nearly replicated that experience. Paradoxically, eating made me feel less, not more, conspicuous out on the street; like taking out the dog, it was a reason to be there. Those who had previously looked straight through me now looked at what I was doing . . . and responded with a smile. *I* was still unseen—they looked at the eating, not at me—but the warmth inside me drew up a warmth outside as well. Unnoticed, between two warmths, I had found a way into another safe and private place.

Now on the prowl for such pleasure, I began to notice that this was the one form of sensuality my neighbors did explicitly encourage. Up and down First Avenue were food stores. The bakery windows were crammed with bread of every shape, flavor, and texture—plump, round loaves of pumpernickel; elongated, sleek-crusted loaves of rye; rough, heavy, chunky loaves of Polish "corn" (made not with corn at all but coarse-ground rye); and glossy, brown-crusted, braided loaves of challah with a soft, yolk-yellow crumb. Pastry shops offered their own elaborate concoctions: split puffs oozing whipped cream, hazelnut tortes, Black Forest cakes, and fruit tarts sporting impossibly huge, glossy strawberries.

Pork butchers draped long links of sausage across their windows—German bratwurst, mettwurst, blood sausage. With them hung lengths of Polish *wiankowa* and kielbasa; red-faced, fatty hams and whole smoked loins were tucked into the corners. Thick blocks of sweet butter, hefty as cornerstones, sat on the counter of the dairy store. One tiny shop, no more than a door, tucked around a corner on Seventh Street, sold "Farm Fresh Eggs—Thursdays Only." Produce shops burst out onto the sidewalk, their bins overflowing with cabbages, carrots, cauliflowers, leafy greens beyond my capacity to identify or, in some instances, even imagine eating.

Furthermore, entering food stores to take food out, I learned I could linger and still retain that place within. A delicatessen on Houston Street sold potato knishes—large, bright yellow, pillowy squares, deep-fried in chicken fat—for a quarter each. I ate these, washed down with celery tonic, while leaning against the stand-up counter along the wall, watching countermen hand-slice paper-thin cuts of smoked salmon, while bakers, towels tied around their heads, brought out huge trays of bagels and bialys.* All around me, I was starting to see, was food that I could also bring home.

In the Village, on the corner of MacDougal and Bleecker, a thickly mustachioed Chilean sold empanadas out of a booth built from a packing crate. These came two ways (I think his only English was "meat" and "cheese"), fried fresh to order: he would plunge the chosen pastry into boiling oil and prod it with tongs until it was golden and crisp. I had just left the late-night double feature at the Bleecker Street Cinema, and this hot pastry was my company on the long, dark walk home. I carried it gingerly until it was cool enough to eat. Even then,

---

* A bialy is a bagel that got lost inside a Polish joke: its outside is crusty instead of glossy and the hole in the center doesn't make it all the way through. But, fresh from the oven, it is a delicacy unique to itself, crisp and chewy at once, the center dimple stuffed with translucent onion bits and (if wished) garlic. At the time, these were two for a quarter, and some weeks those two were all I could afford—or would want—for lunch.

on a cold night, the first bite released a savory cloud of steam.

I am not, and never have been, a gourmet. I possess no curiosity about world-class restaurants, and while I am more drawn to the idea of exemplary foods—truffles, caviar, goose liver, rack of lamb—the fact that I have never tasted any of these except in the most adulterated form must mean that, finally, they are not all that important to me. It is character, not the tongue, that determines one's gustatory destiny, and that empanada was the key to mine.

I soon knew its physiognomy as well as I knew the contours of my own face. I was drawn to the immediate, enveloping comfort of fat: fried wontons or potatoes or onion rings or pieces of chicken or grilled sausage on a stick. More specifically, it was always something hot, salty, succulent, preferably compact enough to be eaten casually, quickly, standing up, on the go.

This, for better or worse, was to become my chosen form of gastronomic pleasure. Not for me the elegant, massive, public presence of a standing rib roast; I chose instead the single barbecued beef rib, which, with its rebarbative, greasy chunks of flesh, vein, and gristle, claims for its eater a kind of animal privacy. This is a form of enjoyment that, no matter the company, remains deeply solitary, totally absorbing, hurriedly done with, and, let it be said, at times edged with shame.

In New York City, where there was no sense of safety anywhere, I had now found two havens: reading and eating in bed, and walking and eating in the street. But supper remained a can of Campbell's cream of celery soup with a fistful of oyster crackers. Before I could learn to cook, I had to not only learn to eat, but learn to eat at home . . . and in some other place than bed.

KITCHEN DIARY: VEGETABLE BRIEFS

How to Cook an Artichoke. Almost every cookbook instructs the cook to trim away its stem at the base of the globe. This is necessary if the artichoke is to be stuffed, because it has to be stood on end. But, otherwise, the heart is the choicest bit of the artichoke, and the heart is no more than the top of the stem. If your grocer sells them by the piece, rather than by the pound, try choosing ones with a good portion of the stem still attached. I think you'll find, as I do, that they cook as tender and tasty as the heart itself, and nearly double the size of that portion.

How to Eat an Avocado (you think you know how, but you don't). First of all, it must be a perfectly ripe Hass avocado (small, dark green, and with an alligator's crumply skin). Cut it in half and gently pop out the seed. Set each half, cut side up, in a shallow bowl. Now, in a separate dish, mix together (for every two halves) about a spoonful of olive oil, a good squeeze of fresh lime, a few drops of Tabasco, and a pinch of coarse salt. Mix this well and dribble a fair share into each avocado half. Now fall to, eating the avocado out of its skin with a teaspoon, catching a bit of the dressing with each bite. A little buttered bread is good with this; the oil and lime juice can be further enhanced, if you like, with a morsel of crushed garlic and, instead of the Tabasco, a sprinkle of powdered cayenne. God didn't make the avocado just for guacamole.

Belgian Endive. I pull the head apart into its separate leaves, wash and dry these carefully, and then break them into bite-sized pieces. These are quickly dressed with the juices and a bit of the fat from a just-cooked piece of sautéed chicken or steak. Eaten immediately, this produces a crisp and peppery and very good salad all by itself, without any intrusion of lettuce or onion. My only way to cook it is to wilt the separate leaves quickly in the same kind of meat juices or in a little melted, pepper-seasoned butter. Rich people can afford to slowly braise whole heads in butter or cream, which sounds terrific. But any recipe that calls for them to be steamed or boiled is a recipe up to no good.

Cavolini di Brusselle alla Milanese. The Brussels sprout and I might still be going our separate ways if I hadn't come across a recipe in Janet Ross's *Leaves from Our Tuscan Kitchen* for a dish that—despite strong forebodings—sounded just too good not to try. Essentially, the sprouts are boiled for about ten minutes in salted water, drained, and then sautéed in a skillet in which equal portions of butter and fruity olive oil have been heated together. Ross directs that this cooking take place over "a rather fierce heat" until the sprouts begin to brown—at which point they are tossed with a good handful of homemade bread crumbs and a generous sprinkle of freshly grated Parmesan, the cooking continuing just long enough for the cheese to melt and help the now crisped crumbs cling to the sides of the sprouts.

As I say, this *sounded* good—and that the dish didn't live up to that first impression was for a reason at once obvious and yet somehow impervious to understanding. We've been conditioned to think of a single sprout, once pared of its ratty outer leaves, as being itself bite-sized, as perhaps it is for a consenting adult anxious to clean the plate of them. But not for any other reason, since a whole sprout seems to contain the concentrated taste of an entire cabbage . . . a taste that simply mocks the efforts of butter and Parmesan—or whatever—to salve the dish with their moderating presence.

It was by pure accident that I set this right: having purchased too many sprouts to finish the first time around, I set out to make the dish again. Remembering how hard it had been to get a round sprout to brown in the hot butter-oil mixture, I cut them in half, steaming them for about six minutes, or just enough for their color to soften and the leaves to wilt, then adding them to the hot oil.

This time the cut surface did acquire a tasty brown edging. This time the bread crumbs did find nooks and crannies in which to wedge themselves securely enough to not all stay behind in the pan. And best of all, this time the crunchy bread crumbs, the tart, rich taste of cheese, the luscious mixture of butter and oil had the chance they needed to mollify the harsh edge of each half-sprout without drowning out its essential sweetness. In short, not bad at all—which is high praise for the vegetable that, all by itself, has damned by implication the whole of Belgian cuisine to near oblivion.

OUTLAW COOK

✧ ✧ ✧

1

Klepp rolled over on one side and silently, with the assured
movements of a somnambulist, attended to his cookery.
When the spaghetti was done, he drained off the water
into a large empty can, then, without noticeably altering
the position of his body, reached under the bed and produced a plate encrusted with grease and tomato paste.
After what seemed like a moment's hesitation, he reached
again under the bed, fished out a wad of newspaper,
wiped the plate with it, and tossed the paper back under
the bed. . . . After providing me with a fork and spoon
so greasy they stuck to my fingers, he piled an immense
portion of spaghetti on my plate; upon it, with another of
his noble gestures, he squeezed a long worm of tomato
paste, to which, by deft movements of the tube, he succeeded in lending an ornamental line; finally, he poured
on a plentiful portion of oil from the can. He himself ate
out of the pot. He served himself oil and tomato paste,
sprinkled pepper on both helpings, mixed up his share,
and motioned to me to do likewise. . . . Strange to say, I
enjoyed that spaghetti. In fact, Klepp's spaghetti became
for me a culinary ideal, by which from that day on I have
measured every menu that is set before me.

—Günter Grass, *The Tin Drum*

*T*he *Tin Drum* was the first novel I ever bought new, in hardcover, and so I still remember the expedition from the Lower East Side to the Doubleday Book Shop on Fifth Avenue. I produced my (expired) passport as identification (in lieu of a nonexistent driver's license) for my check, then anxiously bore my prize home. I was anxious partly that it wouldn't live up to the expenditure and partly that it would prove too much for me—as, in fact, it did. Thirty years later, images from its pages still fitfully flicker in my memory, but only images from the earlier pages. I never finished *The Tin Drum*. It exhausted me —as novels, especially long novels, tend to do—before I exhausted it.

Even so, I read far enough for Günter Grass to present me with a disconcerting portrait of a deviate cook. It was that of the jazz musician Egon Münzer, aka Klepp, keeper of a self-imposed exile, for weeks at a time, in his own bed. Indeed, his rented room contained no other furniture—he kept at arm's reach all he needed: reading material, a case of beer, an alcohol stove, boxes of spaghetti, cans of olive oil, tubes of tomato paste, lumps of salt wrapped in newspaper, and a pot containing what, at the beginning of each internment, started out as cooking water but, as it was used over and over again, became a dark and murky paste.

It would be silly to write that this passage made me hungry, an easy enough accomplishment in any case. Günter Grass pulled off something much more difficult. He made me aware, against the force of all my upbringing, of a denied appetite, of a repressed and forbidden hunger.

A shy and diffident child, I was self-conscious at all public occasions, shrinking into myself and away from my appetite. I anticipated almost any formal eating occasion—from the nightly family supper to holiday feasts—with a mixture of desire and dread. The moment I sat down, I found myself wanting the meal to be over as soon as possible, so as to be excused from the table and the scrutiny of adults.

My appetite came to life only in privacy, secretly. Like other children, I stole cookies from the cookie jar, squirreled away

Christmas treats to enjoy at my leisure, and spent my allowance on ice cream sundaes and Charleston Chew bars. But the secrecy I mean revolved around eating that was not so much extracurricular or even illegal as outside public knowledge and hence family law, a world in which I could be left completely alone.

Thus, on the nights when my parents gave dinner parties, after the company had finished eating and retired to the living room, I would sneak downstairs and into the kitchen to pick over the leavings of the meal for tidbits of food, leavings from the adult world that—in their own eyes—had now ceased to exist.

Perhaps the single most powerful gastronomic memory of my childhood was the discovery, as I cleared away the remains of a baked ham, of the marrow in the ham bone. So rich and succulent, so entirely ignored. Ever after, I would happily, surreptitiously, dig it out with and then eat it from the handle of the narrowest, most delicate of my mother's silver teaspoons. An even earlier discovery (which perhaps eventually led me to the marrow) was the "oysters"—two delicate-tasting, chicken liver–like morsels—that I found could be gouged out of the inside of the chicken back, the least wanted portion of our Sunday-dinner fried chicken.

By the time I was a teenager, I had expanded this invisible gustatory universe to include trips to the gourmet store for cans of pâté and little crocks of port-wine-flavored cheese. Late at night, alone in my bedroom, I would spread them on exotic crackers, to be eaten in my bed. These midnight feasts were the true beginnings of my culinary education. This was food I anticipated eating and could surrender myself to with excited pleasure. And preparing it remained a distinctly different enterprise from the formal cooking and eating of meals, a task I would find myself taking on in just a few years. Then, even though I lived alone, my ingrained eating patterns continued to make my actual suppers nervous, abstracted affairs, meals that were often over before I noticed they had begun.

This was why I was, at twenty, a person whose happiest home eating took place in bed—usually with a book. Reading absorbed conscious attention; the pleasure that my hand brought to my mouth was all peripheral sensation, the purring of a cat. Most important, perhaps, was the closeness of the food and the mouth. What fiercer culinary taboo than the prohibition against lying on the table with the filled plate right beside the mouth? In bed, sheet and tablecloth become deliciously, even lasciviously, confused.

As we all know, the other face of this confusion is chaos, filth. The child who eats in bed fears being not only caught in the act but discovered afterward. Every escaped crumb that digs into his back, his neck, as he tries to sleep is a goad of guilt as much as of discomfort. Eating is mess making. We are taught to stop making that mess first on our tray, then on our plate, and finally on our face. Some poor souls are forced to pursue the lesson further, keeping even the contents of their stomachs neat and clean. For the rest of us, the lips are the demarcation line; what happens *in* the mouth is nobody's business but our own.

By the same tender age as everyone else, I learned that a sign of mess was a sign of trouble. But I also found myself unable to stop making them—as I'm still unable to now. For me, they remain the signal that a place is private, my own. I did learn, of course, to be ashamed of them. The experience of eating became divided in two: the pleasurable mess; the aftermath of denial and shame. At the time I read *The Tin Drum*, I thought that the denial and shame part was immutable, that the trick was to stay as long as possible in the mess.

My relationship with this mess, however, was strictly that of a passive consumer. Klepp suggested another, much more radical possibility. By making his bed into a kitchen, he pointed the way for me to make my kitchen into a bed. Even today, as I write down this thought, a thrill runs through my body. It was as if Günter Grass had reached deep down inside me, plucked out my most repressed, most volatile taboo, and cheerfully exploded it in my face. Given my preoccupations and fears, it was in Klepp that I found my image of the supreme renegade: not the junkie or the con man or the hired gun, but the outlaw *cook*.

2

He is going back to cook a solitary lunch, thought Jane,
or perhaps it will just be beer and bread and cheese, a
man's meal and the better for being eaten alone.
                    —Barbara Pym, *Jane and Prudence*

Living on my own and without the funds to eat out every
night, I had perforce begun to cook, but my kitchen activities
were perfunctory, mechanical—even the zest was mechanical.
My efforts had a certain ambition to them—I didn't simply eat
out of cans—but I still didn't think of cooking as having anything to do with me . . . the real me, that is, buried within the
armor of my performing self. I made my meals the way I
brushed my teeth, to show that I was a good boy, taking care
of myself. And just as on certain nights I sometimes found
myself too tired, too preoccupied, too drunk to brush them—
and, hence, was a *bad* boy—on other nights (or those same
ones) I ate no supper at all, subsisting instead on potato chips,
pistachio nuts, a bag of pecan sandies.

The closest my formal eating came to taking on this sense
of freedom was on payday, when I would bring home the only
meal from this time which still moves me: a loaf of challah
from the day-old-bread shop and a slab of sweet butter from
the dairy store. I would climb the five flights to my walkup
flat and make a meal of just the two, pulling off whole chunks
of the golden-crusted, eggy loaf, folding them around thick
slabs of the butter, and eating until the loaf was gone. I would
then cut a final piece of butter and use it to pick up all the bits
of flaky crust that had fallen to the table. The last mouthful—
a kind of improvised croissant, a crust-flake-and-butter pastry.

This, although it occurred at the end of the meal and not
before it, was my first real culinary creation, my first—completely unconscious—step in learning to cook.

The next step was equally unpremeditated, although far
more public. Although by day I was clinging to the bottom
rung of respectability by working as a mail boy for W. R. Grace

on Hanover Square, by night and weekend I was trying to defrost the ice of my deeply ingrained New England puritanism. To aid in this project, a friend arrived at my doorstep every Saturday to drag me through the Village bars.

I've forgotten most of them, which is probably just as well —of the two that I do remember, one was a place called something like Dirty Julie's, famous for having never been cleaned. The walls were black; dirt hung from the ceiling in greasy swags. The other place is still around—McSorley's Old Ale House on East Seventh Street. At the time, it was notorious for refusing to allow women on the premises; half the fun of being there was to wait on Saturday night for the inevitable woman who would insist on coming in. A waiter would immediately block her way, ask her to leave, and, if she didn't go quietly, forcibly hustle her out the door to the jeers of the patrons. You can see why McSorley's might appeal to college boys: you didn't even have to hold your liquor to prove you were a man—you had only to not be obviously female.

McSorley's other attraction, the one *we* had ostensibly come for, was the less controversial reputation of its ales—one dark, one light—supposedly brewed on the premises. Boldly—since I had yet to come to terms even with our country's ordinary, light-bodied, uncomplicated beers—I called for a pint of the dark. I found it to be a thick, mildly sweet-and-sour brew that at best summoned out of me a kind of ruminative sipping. My companion, whose image of pub life was one of hearty quaffing, quickly finished off his first mug and hailed the waiter for a second. As a subterfuge to hide my having already fallen from the race, I asked for a plate of crackers and cheese.

I had seen one of these being delivered to a patron at a nearby table and my fingers had immediately begun to ache for one of my own. For a very modest price you got a heap of saltine crackers, paper-thin onion rings, a slice of sharp New York State Cheddar, and a dollop of mustard. You took up a cracker, dabbed it with a little mustard, laid a bit of cheese and onion on it, and ate it—washing it down, of course, with a mouthful of ale.

This, I would learn years later, was their version of the pub meal that, just then in England, was being promoted as a plowman's lunch: ale, bread, pickled onion, and cheese. McSorley's version was a decent replica. The tang of the Cheddar, the bite of the mustard and onion, the salty crispness of the crackers not only rounded off the vegetative richness of the brew but also let me pace my sips, the slow assembly giving mind and hand productive work between the swallows. Until now my idea of great bar food was the free roasted peanuts handed out at yet another Village bar—name forgotten—its floor a compost heap of trodden shells. Here was something different. The mere idea of it lifted me to culinary heaven.

The line over which the eater steps to become a cook is a much finer one than is usually imagined: it is that point at which the eater—and not someone else, not some *cook*—takes control of *making* the dish. Here, at McSorley's, I took over the making of this one. It didn't matter that no actual cooking took place. It didn't matter that someone had already sliced the onion and cheese. If they had just brought me the knife, the Cheddar, and the onion, I would have known what had to be done, and I would have much preferred to do it all myself. The pleasure of knowing just what I wanted to *do* with these things is what made this the moment that, for the first time, I became consciously aware of myself as a cook.

3

In a piece that I believe originally appeared in an early issue of *The Pleasures of Cooking*, Sally Barnes described Gloria Pépin's first attempt to cook for her famous-chef husband. At one point, overcome with nervousness, she fled the kitchen, returning to find that Jacques

> had taken a fork, punctured both yolks, mixed them together and put a piece of ham on top. She describes the result as a "steamed mess. The bottoms of the eggs were crusty and brown, the top was wet and mushy and looked awful." He slid this onto a plate and ate it with gusto.

This isn't a dish that Jacques Pépin teaches his students, nor could he. No one can teach you how to cook like this if the dish isn't already in you; if it is, what you need is not the lesson but permission—even if that permission comes only from the example. However you find it, the dish seems waiting inside you, like a fragment of a former life, for you to recognize its face.

This is why, while I still need a lesson on how to poach an egg, no one has had to teach me how to fry one. When I first went to do it, my eating had already given me a complex grammar of possibility. The subject "egg" and the verb "to fry" I already knew well; they immediately called up an image of a hot skillet, of sputtering fat, of edges crisping and turning brown. The rest is just a matter of fleshing the dish out with whatever modifiers lie at hand in the refrigerator/thesaurus: butter, onion, garlic, sweet or hot pepper, parsley, the leftover lamb roast, the jar of chicken fat. The trick is getting the permission in the first place—or, I should say, *taking* it.

Cooking, we think, is something done for others: even when that other is ourself. This at least is the way we first *experience* cooking and how we unthinkingly come to define it: Mother making meals for us. Mother's cooking can be wonderful but it comes with a price: socialization. Not only is the child stopped just at the moment his own form of cooking is getting interesting—the boiled potato mashed into the peas, the pat of butter floated in the milk—but all the sensory richness of such exploration is denied.

When the grown child goes for the first time into the kitchen to prepare a meal, it isn't mother's cooking that awaits, but the role of *being* mother. To cook is to don a mental apron, a servile garment shed only when the meal is prepared and everyone sits down to eat. No matter how attentive, careful, and interested the cook is in what he or she is doing in the kitchen, he or she is still, first of all, performing a necessary chore. A distinction has been drawn between cook and eater, server and served, work and pleasure.

However, cooking at its most primal is not consciously instructed labor but a flowing, attentive reverie. Spear a chunk

of meat on a skewer and hold it over a bed of smoldering
charcoal. It's not conscious thought but a continual tension
between the fire's hunger and your own that directs the sharp-
eyed turning, keeping sear from turning altogether into char
as the fat bubbles and pops, the juices sizzle and crust, and
the odors of smoke and meat swirl about your head. Flame is
the most sensual of culinary catalysts; it releases aromas, awak-
ens flavors, plasticizes shapes. And, by being dangerous, it
heightens absorption; by its shameless show of hunger, it eggs
us on. Our original, primal relationship with food is forcibly
recalled when the frying pan is made to serve as the dinner
plate.

Or when the dinner plate becomes the frying pan. As small
a first step toward culinary outlawry as it was, my McSorley's
plate of crackers and cheese gave me permission to return to
the wordless, sensual concentration that I had had to abandon
to become civilized. And this feeling intensified and expanded
as I began to incorporate fire into this play—that being, of
course, another childhood prohibition. Utterly absorbed in
peeling, prodding, scraping, cutting, frying, basting—even *eating*, to the point where the meal was half gone before, officially,
it was supposed to begin—I was doing what I had to do to
taste food best. This outlaw cook was, at heart, still a six-year-
old *bandido*, fighting off civility for the pleasure of making himself completely familiar with his dinner . . . before he put it
into his mouth.

The kitchen as bed, cooking as sensual communion, a self-
pleasing, attentive dream state—any stream of instruction flowing through my head at such a moment would have been as
welcome as Miss Manners scurrying over with a sponge to
mop up the crumbs. The purpose of a recipe in my cooking
was to plunge me into a reverie that could be acted out at the
stove, not to interrupt it constantly with well-meaning advice.
So what if it gave me a good meal, if it knocked me out of
connection again with my inner needs and wants?

The problem was—and remained—that I could only enter
this world *alone*. The same timidity that made me cling to a
need for intimacy with my dinner also left me paralyzed by
the specter of childhood notions of propriety. My time alone

in New York was too short, too exceptional by reason of its dire poverty, to blossom into a full-fledged cuisine. Returning, first to college, then to a prep-school teaching career, and finally to a long-term relationship, I found myself dragged out of my kitchen bed and into public view. There I performed as a dutiful, occasionally inspired, recipe-following drudge, cooking for real only at the margin of things: when I was left in the house alone or when I escaped for an evening of barbecuing with a like-minded bachelor friend.

It took me twenty years of instinctively but slowly acquiring the protection of a repertoire of recipe-resistant dishes before I could actively cultivate the persona of the outlaw cook.* Ironically, only as I did so did it begin to occur to me that *all* true cooks might be outside the law—at least civility's law. It isn't by accident that Klepp is a jazz musician; jazz is a primal, earthy, assertive music—a mess of sound improvised into shape in front of other people.

Jazz musicians describe this act, when they've got the motion just right, as "cooking." Klepp wasn't interested merely in squeezing the tomato paste onto his sheets; his concept of pleasure was more focused, seeking a shape, an end, a final

---

* Very few cookbooks abetted me in this endeavor, and those mostly by their example rather than their contents. This is because most cookbook writing has yet to escape from the nineteenth century, where it still oscillates between empty-headed flowery prose and mechanistic explanations whose only human quality is the nagging tone of the schoolmaster or the manic euphoria of the village explainer. The true reasons for our culinary failures are beyond their ken: fear of failure or of getting fat or of not getting enough to eat; rage at Mother for not taking good enough care of us; guilt at treating ourselves well. Nor can they necessarily take credit for success, something which is often due almost entirely to the spontaneous delight that the best cooks take in pleasing. Their dishes glisten with a happy generosity that culinary skill can only hope to gloss. Also, cookbook explanations rarely convey anything of the process by which we absorb and internalize a new dish. Recipe writing is better suited to programming robots than humans, which is why, following a recipe, we often find ourselves acting like one. A reverie-based cuisine need not be entirely without cookbooks, however, or useful instruction; see Daniel Spoerri's *Mythology & Meatballs* or Patience Gray's *Honey from a Weed* (both discussed later in these pages). In my first, never-finished effort, I was trying to write such a book myself . . . and, I guess, I still am. If I ever manage it, the essay that follows, "Plowman's Lunch," might well serve as its prolegomenon.

explosion of delight. Artists do something different to messes than clean them up. And that something subverts observers into accomplices: witness the transformation of Oskar, Günter Grass's diminutive narrator, from revolted witness into delighted participant.

This brings us back to Jacques Pépin. "A recipe tells you nothing," he once told Sarah Fritschner in an interview—which is another way of saying that they get in his way. Chefs are the opposite of epicures: whether men or women, overtly or subvertly, a major component of their creativity is aggression. It may be mastery of technique that makes Pépin a culinary artist, but the force that drives him is his outlaw heart. The cacophony of the restaurant kitchen gets his adrenaline flowing; then he starts to *cook*.

In a suggestive piece written years ago for *The Washington Post*, Steven Raichlen described playing *stagier* to chef Fernand Chambrette. One of the last of the old school of French chefs, Chambrette had once been the owner of Paris's famed La Boule d'Or but was now an instructor at La Varenne—a short, stocky, "grouchy, grumbly old goat with a mean streak a mile wide," who wore an apron flaunting a week's worth of stains, shuffled around without socks in an shabby pair of backless slippers, swore like a sailor, rained blows on the bottoms of his assistants, and spat in the deep-fat fryer to gauge its temperature. "Every morning before class," Raichlen wrote,

> Chambrette went on a rampage, raiding all the refrigerators for wilted vegetables, meat scraps past their prime, chicken's feet, pork rind, minute saucerful of hollandaise, madeira, and velouté sauce, and countless other goodies which he affectionately called his *petits cacas*. With these queer, mismatched piles of leftovers, he concocted divine culinary creations.

While his students were infatuated with the products of their efforts, Chambrette was in love with the act of making itself . . . which is why he, like Jacques Pépin, dismissed the importance of recipes—*they* can't teach you how to cook!—and would sit down with a beaker of ice water to a simple meal of bread and cheese, while his students ate the dishes they had just produced in class. "Then he'd trundle off in his civvies, the leftovers loaded into an old gym bag for his wife and cat."

Raichlen leaves us to imagine what went on in the old chef's mind as he watched his students drinking their fine wines and devouring the terrines *en gelée*, the coulibiacs, the soufflés, and the éclairs. I suspect that he contemplated them with something like bemusement: they had before them only the remains of the real meal, the one that he had just taken his time enjoying right before their astonished, unbelieving eyes.

KITCHEN DIARY: BLACK BEANS AND RICE

Karyl Bannister, who also writes and publishes a food letter—Cook & Tell—out of Maine, often telephones her readers to find out what they're really making for supper.* If she had called us on New Year's Day, 1989, she'd have discovered Matt making black beans and rice with curried egg sauce after a recipe Karyl herself had published, sent in by her subscriber Sally Monroe.

When Matt first read the recipe, she liked the honest ingredients and straightforward preparation: the beans simmered with a ham hock, onion, garlic, and a dose of cumin and oregano. But it was the way Sally suggested serving the soup that drew Matt to think about actually making it.

Most beans have a "fat" quality to their texture that needs only meat or olive oil to make them truly unctuous, but black beans have a meagerness that demands a more substantial richness. This is why a traditional garnish for black bean soup is sliced hard-cooked egg. Sally went that one better, serving the dish with rice and with deviled eggs baked in a curry sauce.

These enrichments had an immediate appeal. We had recently tracked

---

* When Karyl Bannister isn't phoning readers, she's stirring up controversy over the origins of Wellesley fudge cake—or sharing the secret for an easy homemade tortilla chip or the recipe for Uncle Henry's oyster loaf. A rambunctious, very participatory sort of food letter: *Cook & Tell*, Love's Cove, West Southport, ME 04576 ($12 a year for 10 issues—sample issue $1).

down a nearby farm that would sell us fresh-laid eggs. Their distinctive flavor and golden yolks soon had us remembering the pleasures of such homey dishes as soft-cooked eggs in a nest of pulled buttered toast.

Both curry powder and white sauce are familiars in New England cooking; since childhood, Matt has loved dishes that incorporated them. It struck her that to simply mix the chopped hard-cooked eggs into a curry sauce would be less complicated than deviling and baking them.

On hand were some glossy new-crop beans from Walnut Acres and a pink, spectacularly meaty ham hock from Burgers' Smokehouse in California, Missouri. This was how her appetite put it together: these beans cooked with that hock, made into a dish of black beans and rice —with a rich amalgam of curried eggs ladled alongside. Here, in narrative form, is the way we worked it all out.

BLACK BEANS AND RICE
WITH HAM HOCKS AND DEVILED EGGS
BAKED IN CURRY SAUCE

The night before, a pound (2 cups) of the black beans were picked over, rinsed, and put to soak. The next afternoon, they were drained and set in a large pot with 10 cups of fresh water. This was brought to a boil and allowed to bubble for 10 minutes, with any scum skimmed away. Then the ham hock, a bay leaf, 2 celery stalks (cut in large pieces), and a knotted bunch of parsley were added, the heat was turned down, and the pot covered and left to simmer until the beans were tender (in this case, about an hour). Meanwhile, 4 eggs were hard-cooked and let cool. Two onions and 3 large cloves of garlic were minced and sautéed in a couple of tablespoons of olive oil, with about 2 teaspoons each of cumin and Greek oregano, and a pod of dried hot red pepper, seeded and minced.

When the beans were tender, the pot was removed from the heat and the parsley and celery discarded. The ham hock was lifted out, and its meat and rind removed from the bone and cut small (the rind can also be left in a large, separate piece if there is only one who likes it). The meat, rind, denuded bones, and the fresh flavoring mixture were returned to the pot and cautiously salted to taste, a half teaspoon at a time. The soup was then put back to simmer another hour.

About a half hour before supper, some rice was started and the white sauce made. Two tablespoons of butter were melted in a small saucepan. The same amount of flour and a teaspoon of curry powder were whisked in and the mixture was cooked briefly to rid it of its rawness. Then the pan was removed from the heat and a cup of scalded milk beaten in. This sauce was brought close to a boil and simmered until supper, while the eggs were peeled and chopped into big chunks and some parsley was minced.

At the last minute, the eggs were stirred into the curry sauce, the beans tasted again for salt (which they needed) and pepper. A bed of rice was laid into four hot bowls and beans ladled over two-thirds of it, with enough cooking liquid to come almost to the top of the rice. Minced parsley was sprinkled over the beans; the curried eggs were spooned over the remaining rice surface and dusted with paprika and a grating of pepper. Matt served this with a salad of romaine leaves dressed with a sharp vinaigrette—all in all, a delicious and generous supper, with plenty of black beans left over for a soup the next day.

A Note on Sources. Burgers' Smokehouse, Highway 87 South, California, MO 65018; (800) 624-5426. Walnut Acres Organic Farms, Penns Creek, PA 17862; (800) 433-3998. Both enterprises will send a free catalogue on request.

PLOWMAN'S LUNCH

✦ ✦ ✦

The cheese, the onion, and the bread I figured out for myself. They were a start, but only that. It's an American trait, I think, to consider the beverage that accompanies the meal an optional, almost disconnected item, the way that one good overcoat is worn to cover two different wool suits, or over the various mixes of sport jacket, shirt, tie, and slacks. I grew up like everyone else, drinking milk with my meals when I couldn't have a Coke or a ginger ale. At college, pitchers of milk sat on every table. There was no thought of matching meal to beverage; the one was there to wash the other down.

From the vantage point of now, I can see how strange this is. Milk is more food than drink; it's a way of getting children to down more nutrients without knowing it. Beer does the same for adults (and once also did for children); for generations in beer-drinking countries it was a necessary aspect of the diet—which is to say, a part of the meal. Tracts were written in England when tea began to edge out ale as the workingman's friend: ale was rich in nutrients, healthy, and home-brewed; tea was foreign, costly, affected stuff, and at bottom nothing more than flavored water—and that flavor did nothing good to the taste of bread and cheese.

This was important, because bread (carbohydrate), cheese (fat and protein), and ale (more carbohydrates plus vitamins) were an important meal, sometimes made into a dish but more commonly eaten just as they were—an easily portable feast for workers too far away to walk home for lunch. In England, where it is a popular pub snack, this combination, thanks to a national advertising campaign in the 1960s, has come to be known as a plowman's lunch. When the plowman actually ate such a meal—which he simply called "bait"—the piece of cheese would have been more equal in size to the bread, and both would have come from the farm whose fields were being plowed.

The beer would have been home-brewed, and the onion would have been both fresh and raw, eaten like an apple, not a vinegary pickle fished from a jar. In *Gardener's Delight*, John Seymour tells us how:

> As for eating onions—here is my recipe. Sit down under an oak tree and spread a white-spotted red handkerchief on your lap. Place on it a hunk of wholemeal bread, a hunk of cheese, and a raw onion. Pull out your pocketknife, cut off mouthfuls from each of these three articles of sustenance, and put them in your mouth. Wash them down with home-brewed beer.

Bread, cheese, onion, and a fermented brew (ale/beer/wine/cider) make a well-married, even classic, combination in part because it feeds us well. The rest is due to centuries of honing; given the many kinds of bread, beer, and cheese, the number of possible combinations is almost infinite. Here, both cultural conditioning and individual physiology come into play. At about the same time I was discovering the plowman's of saltines and New York Cheddar at McSorley's, a friend who was working his way through college at a deli counter told me that the owner, an enormous individual with a beet-red face and a walrus mustache, would sometimes at closing, after locking the door and pulling the shade, draw him into the back room, produce a loaf of pumpernickel, a jar of Polish horseradish mustard, a creamy slab of Limburger, and a pile of onion rings salvaged from the chopped liver display. Two well-chilled bottles of Beck's appeared, dripping wet, from the pickle tub in the walk-in refrigerator, and they would both fall to.

One of the differences between the universe of cooking as portrayed in beginner's cookbooks and as we acquire it in real

life is that in the former knowledge progresses in an orderly
fashion, while in real life it arrives in unique chunks of experience . . . and those in no particular order. In this regard, it
is more like doing a jigsaw puzzle: putting your hand on just
the right piece can link several other unconnected-seeming
pieces together into a coherent pattern.

This was how that glass of McSorley's ale worked for me: it
vitalized bread, cheese, and onion. All of a sudden they seemed
to emit a kind of magnetic attraction. This sense of mutual
attraction is what made them an ideal introduction to the meditative cooking that is the sole province of the solitary eater-
cook. When cook and eater are one, half the meal's pleasure
is in letting hunger craft an appetizing whole by instinctively
balancing what is really a kind of physiological equation. Consequently, our four ingredients should always be read as if
each were enclosed in brackets—[bread], [cheese], [onion],
[brew]—because each is as much a place holder in a constantly
fluctuating force field as it is an item of food.

The *classic plowman's lunch*, for example, pits the oily, crumbly
richness of a ripe Cheddar or Cheshire against the sharp-sour
bite of onion and the bitter tang of ale, all mellowed together
in the yeasty sweetness of good white bread. But if I pour
myself a glass of milk or sweet apple cider instead of beer, the
onion falls out of the combination. With milk, an apple might
replace it; with cider, a slice of country ham. The exact choice
isn't important; what I need to feel is the shift of appetite,
righting the equilibrium, resolving the equation.

If I reach for a different cheese, the same counterbalancing
is necessary, more challenging still if the cheese has an especially intimidating personality or a particularly subtle one. Con-
fronted with a brassy Roquefort or a delicate Caerphilly,
appetite must show a special agility—matching the Roquefort
with, say, a slice of well-buttered rye, a ripe pear, and a glass
of brandy; or highlighting the sweet tang of the buttermilk in
the Caerphilly with whole-wheat bread, thin slices of celery,
and a dry fermented cider.

Some frown on serving butter with cheese—good cheese
brings its own butter, bad cheese needs none, say the
French—but while its lusciousness can mask the personalities

of some, it enhances that of others. Butter can mellow sourness, offset dryness, and balance excessive saltiness (as occurs in export Roquefort). It is an integral part of the combination with, say, Emmenthaler or Appenzeller served with sour rye bread and a glass of a flowery German Riesling.

If the ingredients aren't themselves fixed entities, neither is the flavor of the ingredient nor the role it plays in the combination. British ales have a bitter complexity generally shunned by other beer-drinking countries, where a crisper, less complex-tasting brew is preferred. The balance of flavor in a German version of the plowman's is maintained by matching a pungently sour *Bierkäse* with rye bread and pickled onion slices. Our brick and (obviously) beer cheese have a similar affinity to our milder American brews.

Handkäse (hand cheese, as the Pennsylvania Dutch version is known) is another pungent cheese associated with lager. Germans cut it into little chunks, swirl these around in the beer until they melt, and drink the mixture down. This same playfulness is expanded into a dish that will leave the eater a little soberer:

KÄSE MIT MUSIK / CHEESE "WITH MUSIC"
(SERVES 1)

A rectangular wedge, ½ inch thick, of Handkäse	1 tablespoon distilled vinegar ½ cup minced onion
2 tablespoons olive oil	A thick buttered slice of rye bread

Set the slice of cheese in a shallow-sided dish. Mix the oil and vinegar together vigorously and pour over the cheese slice. Sprinkle on the minced onion. Let marinate an hour or two at room temperature, gently turning the cheese over midway through the process. Serve with bread and butter and cold imported beer.

The more genteel German beer parlors serve this as an actual dish—the onions on the cheese, the cheese on the buttered bread—to be eaten with a knife and fork. But it is best eaten directly out of the marinade. Scoop up some onion bits with the end of the knife and mash them into a bit of the cheese, spreading that on a piece of buttered rye.

VARIATIONS: Other soft-textured, pungent cheeses such as beer, brick, or Tilsit can be substituted, but none of them melts into the same butter-soft consistency of the looser-formed hand cheese, and this is half the fun of the dish. (Hand cheese, by the way, has a powerful odor; the uninitiated should know that the bark is worse than the bite: the flavor is quite mild.)

When I encountered cheese "with music," I finally grasped how the raw (plowman's) crossed over to the cooked (toasted cheese): not only because this is really a method of melting cheese, even if no heat is used, but also because the ingredients have actually been changed into something else—"a dish." Since cheese by its very nature has already been cooked, whatever I do to it between slicing and eating is only for my pleasure—thus firmly keeping it in the realm of intuitive, meditative cookery. When I grill, toast, or melt cheese, I *mean* to make it taste better, but better here often means more comforting, more personal, not more flavorful.

Consider, for example, *fried cheese*—not the delicate technique by which the Italians turn Scamorza or the Greeks Kasseri into little molten packages with golden crusts, but the brutal method I discovered early in my eater-cook career of frying cheese all by itself into a deliciously greasy crisp. A thick slice of cheese set onto a lightly greased, well-heated frying pan almost at once collapses into a batterlike consistency punctuated with a lacy pattern of air bubbles, like pancake batter. Amazingly, this batter also produces a kind of pancake, or at least its bottom turns golden and crunchy, and can eventually—carefully—be dislodged from the pan.

Once the cheese has been prodded and tugged free, it can be flipped over and browned on the other side or folded over itself like an omelet, leaving a soft center that can itself be enhanced by slipping another sliver of the same cheese inside it, leaving this just long enough for the contents to melt. However it is done, fried cheese has to be eaten at once; it soon loses its crunch and turns rubbery—so quickly, in fact, that the eater has to balance fading crispness against the risk of burning the mouth.

No cheese—with the possible exception of commercial mozzarella—is improved by this treatment; most actually suffer. If the solitary eater-cook insists on treating it this way anyway—as I have treated very good Cheddars—it is because the loss of character in flavor is offset by the visual, aural, and tactile pleasures of making it, the comfort of the heat of the stove and the cheese's own greasy crispness, and the satisfaction of stamping public food with an implacably private brand.

Frying cheese this way gave me an intuitive grasp of a simple dish that I had often read about but had not until then dared to try: *toasted cheese*. This is the fireplace version of the plowman's and surely as venerable, sharing the same ingredients and philosophy. Its rhythms of making and eating are necessarily personal ones, too, no matter how many eater-cooks share the toasting fork. In this instance, however, a good toasting cheese—Cheddar or Cheshire—offers a different, and at least as pleasing, side of its character through toasting, producing a soft, rich, succulent texture in perfect harmony with its buttery taste.

TOASTED CHEESE
(SERVES 1)

"Ten cookes in Wales," quothe he, "one wedding sees."
"True," quothe the other, "each man toasts his cheese."
—*Springes for Woodcockes* (1613)

To toast cheese, you need a good knife, a long-handled fork (such as completes a barbecue set), and a fire in the fireplace that has burnt down to a nice set of coals. Sit yourself down before it with all necessary ingredients at hand: the cheese to be toasted, some paper-thin slices of onion, a pot of mustard or the butter dish, an unsliced loaf of bread, and a mug of beer. Cut a thick slice from the loaf, spear it through the crust with the fork, and toast it on both sides over the coals. Place it on a plate, spread it with a little mustard or butter, and set it on the hearth to keep warm.

Now cut a block of cheese about the size of a toothpick box and spear it through one side with a fork, taking care not to let it crumble. Hold the cheese over the coals, not too close, watching carefully. Turn the fork regularly, slowly, so that the heat penetrates all sides at approximately the same rate. The surface will begin to sag as the cheese melts; twirl the fork to keep runny cheese from falling into the fire. The moment the whole piece begins to collapse, slip it onto the piece of toast, spreading it over the surface with the blade of the knife. Top with onion rings and eat when it has cooled a little, washing it down with the beer.

The cheese toaster needs elbow room and time to concentrate and is rewarded with the drama of expectation and risk—the cheese can, and sometimes does, drop into the fire, especially until the skill is mastered. In Britain, when every lodger had a fireplace, toasting cheese was a convivial bachelor meal—as readers of *Great Expectations* may remember. In more modern times, rented rooms have changed, and the dish has evolved with them into what we now call Welsh rabbit.

Welsh rabbit is a joke name on the order of calling watermelon "Georgia ham"; in *The Art of Cookery Made Plain and Easy* (1747), Hannah Glasse's recipe calls simply for toasted cheese to be set on toast spread with mustard (her recipe for "Scotch rabbit" sets it on buttered toast). The version we now know is the logical consequence of distancing the cook from the eater, and the eater from the fireplace.

Really, though, it might be more accurately argued that the dish evolved into *two* distinct dishes, the first being "Welsh rarebit"—that chafing dish specialty rechristened to assuage the snobbery of economy-minded hostesses. It is the "rarebit" that has gradually worked its way into the common vernacular as the dish of cheese-sauce-soaked toast points served up in some households the night before payday—at least until Kraft macaroni dinners arrived upon the scene.

The other version, still called Welsh rabbit, lingers on in England in the rented rooms of retired military men on half pension who make it up on their hot plates and extract the necessary moiety of self-respect and satisfaction by whisking in a few drops of good whiskey or Worcestershire and by using a fine old Cheddar they keep in the wardrobe wrapped in a vinegar-dampened tea cloth . . . coaxing from the mixture some vestigial recollection of fireplace and toasting fork.

WELSH RABBIT
(SERVES 1)

4 ounces Cheddar or Cheshire cheese
½ small onion
1 to 2 tablespoons sweet butter
2 tablespoons ale (or port, whiskey, stout)

A thick slice of buttered toast (kept warm)
Black pepper

Grate the cheese and mince the onion. Melt the butter in a saucepan and sauté the onion over medium-low heat until amber and soft, but not brown. Add the cheese and ale, turn the heat down to low, and stir gently until the cheese is melted and the mixture smooth and creamy. Set the thick slice of buttered toast in a shallow bowl, pour the cheese mixture over, grind some black pepper over the top, and eat at once, perhaps with a grilled tomato set at the side.

VARIATIONS: "Like every other cook, my own recipe for Welsh rarebit [sic] exceeds all others in quality," writes Sarah Tyson Rorer in *Mrs. Rorer's New Cook Book* (1902). "There is not a dish in the whole list that has so many methods of making, all more or less alike, but the simple change of seasoning gives different results." And to prove her point, she goes on to name them: a pinch of cayenne, a dash of Worcestershire, a grating of horseradish or garlic to point up the flavors, or an egg beaten into the ale to make the mixture richer (or richer still with two egg yolks). If you try the yolk, be sure to beat it (or them) into the mixture with the pan off the heat, lest you cook the yolks rather than thicken with them.

Now, if we had Gruyère in the larder instead of Cheddar, and white wine instead of beer . . . A fondue, of course, is a dish of melted cheese into which the bread is dunked, so it is made more like a cheese soup. (In fact, the great French gourmet Brillat-Savarin, who was born on the Swiss border at Belley, wrote in 1795 that the elderly of the district still chuckled over the memory of the local bishop eating his fondue with a spoon.) In the same way, more ale can be added to a Welsh rabbit to give it, too, a fondue-like consistency. Here is a dish from Gloucestershire that does so, although the mixture is still poured onto toast, not scooped up with it.

SOUSED CHEESE
(SERVES 1)

4 ounces Double Gloucester or
   Cotswold cheese
1 tablespoon coarse-textured, full-
   flavored mustard

¼ cup ale
Hot buttered toast

Crumble the cheese into a buttered ovenproof pot. Beat the mustard into the ale and gently stir this mixture into the cheese. Bake in a preheated 350°F oven until the mixture is melted, hot, and bubbling—about 15 minutes. Meanwhile, make the toast, butter it well, and cut it into bite-sized croutons. Spread these in a shallow bowl. Remove the soused cheese from the oven and use a buttered heatproof rubber spatula to scrape it over the toast. Eat at once, with some grilled slivered scallions on the side.

COOK'S NOTE: The British market a Double Gloucester in the U.S.A. that is peppered with chives and called Cotswold. If neither can be found, a Cheddar, Cheshire, or other toasting cheese can be substituted.

Toasted cheese and toasted bread . . . you would think that the simplest method to combine them would be to put the one between two slices of the other and slap the result onto a well-greased grill. However, if you follow the evolution of toasted cheese as I have pursued it here, you can begin to understand why, familiar as it is to us, the grilled (or toasted) cheese sandwich is a relatively recent innovation. A search of my old cookbooks failed to unearth a single recipe for it before—or even early into—the twentieth century. For example, Mrs. Rorer, in the book already mentioned above, while she devotes four pages to cheese dishes in general and "rarebits" in particular, never mentions the grilled cheese sandwich. Nor is she alone.

A common argument for this kind of omission is that cookbook writers in those days thought no one needed instructions for such easy dishes—to see one is to know how to make it—but Mrs. Rorer is nitpicky about the obvious elsewhere. I believe the grilled cheese sandwich is, at least as a common dish, a creation of our century. All the adaptations of toasted cheese that we've considered up to now are strategies that evolved from the fireplace, adapted to the stove. The grilled cheese sandwich has no suggestion of this at all; it is as modern as the truck-stop grill.

For me, coming to cooking from my mother's planned home meals, the grilled cheese sandwich was already there, a familiar Wednesday night supper eaten with (and surreptitiously dunked into) Campbell's tomato soup. But it would only be much later, after I had passed along this path, that I was able to take it into the domain of the solitary eater-cook, by deconstructing it into the two separate dishes that were joined together in order to create it: toasted cheese and "bread and drip."

Germans eat something they call a *bread sandwich*—a slice of pumpernickel spread on both sides with bacon drippings or fresh lard, salted, and then clamped between two slices of sour rye. Most of us, however, eating grease with bread want heat applied somewhere in the equation. I wrote a whole chapter of my first book, *Simple Cooking*, on *bruschetta*, a slab of peasant bread toasted over a fire, rubbed with garlic, and drizzled with freshly pressed olive oil. The bread is also delicious rubbed with garlic and then fried—this time in ordinary olive oil.

This is, in effect, a new culinary concept: buttering the bread *before* toasting it. It is a strategy that comes naturally to the eater-cook who, having just fried an egg or some chicken thighs or onions and peppers, can easily see the advantage of adding a square of bread to mop up the residue, and then to brown and crisp. *Texas toast*, for example, made by dusting a thick slice of bread on both sides with powdered chile and frying this in the remnants of the broiler pan, goes better with a steak than a serving of French fries. (For those who like a simple, savory breakfast, melt some butter, punch a hole in the center of the slice with a biscuit cutter, and fry an egg there while you fry the bread.)

In one of his mystery novels—I forget which—Douglas Clark has a policeman fondly reminisce as he watches schoolchildren hurrying home after school:

> "Lord, how I used to like it. Scarpering home for tea. And if it wasn't ready I used to get a slice of bread and dripping. Pork dripping was best, with the brown bottoms and a scatter of salt. I don't suppose any of those kids has ever tasted anything half so good as a slice of bread and drip."

The British eat their dripping spread on bread, but that phrase "brown bottoms and a scatter of salt" inspired me to fry my bread in it instead, producing a crunchy slice dotted all over with bits of pan scrapings.

DRIPPING-FRIED BREAD
(SERVES 1)

Some good meat broth
2 to 3 tablespoons meat fat, congealed juices, pan scrapings

1 or 2 thick slices of stale bread
Pepper and salt if needed

Put the broth in a wide bowl. Heat the drip in a frying pan and spread it with a heatproof spatula so that the juices and browned bits are evenly distributed. When the fat is hot, take each piece of bread and dunk it in the broth. The bread should be wet but not soaked or it will fall apart. Set each slice in the hot fat, turning it over when the bottom is golden brown. The outside of the bread will fry to a greasy crispness, embedded with savory bits; the inside will turn into a broth-flavored custard. Since the drip will probably be salted and peppered already, season carefully.

VARIATIONS: These pretty much depend on what happens to be around. I remember one feast when I had both chicken fat and chopped chicken liver in the refrigerator. I spread the bread with the latter after I turned over the first side. The British sometimes spread their bread and drip with Bovril or a similar meat concentrate; another, more localized, favorite is a "chip butty"—fresh, crisp-fried potatoes sandwiched between two slices of drip-fried bread—Cheshire's answer to the New Orleans fried-potato po' boy.

Once I began to perceive the grilled cheese sandwich as a marriage between fried bread and toasted cheese, I found it amenable to a much wider range of play than just dunking the finished product into a bowl of tomato soup. Most versions of a plowman's work well when grilled—the one combining Caerphilly, whole-wheat bread, and celery is especially good—and new versions become possible. My own favorite is to take a slab of roasted sweet red pepper and grill it with the Cheddar between two slices of good white bread. But best of all, perhaps, is to eat a plain grilled cheese sandwich with a bowl of homemade bread-and-butter pickles—into which plenty of the sweet-sour-and-spicy pickling juices have been poured for dunking.

Innovation can wander further afield than this. The best grilled cheese sandwich I ever made was concocted of Brie and paper-thin slices of Westphalian ham, put between slices of pumpernickel that were then spread with sweet butter and grilled. The bread can also be dipped into egg and milk that have been lightly beaten together and seasoned with paprika or cayenne (for Cheddar) or nutmeg (for Gruyère). If ham is added to the cheese, you have what the French call a *croque-monsieur*. Ale can be substituted for the milk and toasted onion bits for the ham to make a grilled plowman's.

The grilled cheese sandwich introduces the third intuitive culinary technique that the solitary eater-cook requires no lessons to master: the art of dunking. Eating dunked or sopped bread is as old as cooking itself, and the notion of dunking and *then* cooking the bread follows as easily from the idea of dunking bread as frying bread dipped in grease follows from buttered toast. Hannah Glasse, again in *The Art of Cookery Made Plain and Easy*, does exactly this, giving an inverse twist to the recipe for soused cheese. Her recipe for an "English rabbit" calls for toast to be moistened with red wine or ale and covered with an ample amount of thinly sliced cheese. This dish is baked in a hot (350°F) oven until the cheese is melted and the toast crisp (about twenty minutes).

By combining dunked (or sopped) bread, fried bread, and Welsh rabbit, we could spread a thick blend of melted cheese and ale between two slices of bread dipped in beaten egg and milk and produce—well—a sandwich that lies at the far edge of the ordinary eater-cook's ambitions. It's too much of a production . . . almost a chore. Perhaps it is no accident that the fondue-like mixture of cheese and wine grilled between two slices of egg-and-milk-sopped bread is called a *croque-madame*. They must mean a *croque-maman*.

So far as the solitary eater-cook is concerned, we've come to the end of the line. Beyond this point there are only recipes. But let us notice that these are recipes built up out of our now-familiar kitchen play. To give a final example: of all the combinations through which we've put our four ingredients—cheese, bread, beer, and onion—the one thing we haven't done is to cook them up together in one big mess. This, essentially, is how you go about making a bread and cheese pudding:

BREAD AND CHEESE PUDDING
(SERVES 4)

8 slices of good white bread	1 bottle (12 ounces) ale or beer
8 ounces Cheddar or its like	½ teaspoon cayenne
2 eggs	Salt and pepper
1 small onion, minced	4 tablespoons butter

Slice the bread thick, toast it lightly, and set it to one side to cool. Grate the cheese in a large bowl, break in the eggs, and stir in the minced onion and the ale. Mix this together until the eggs are well combined with the other ingredients. Season with the cayenne and salt and pepper to taste. Tear the toast into small pieces, tossing them into the bowl. With the hands or a wooden spoon, mix all this together. Let the bowl sit so that the bread can absorb some of the liquid while the oven preheats to 375°F. Grease a 6-cup soufflé dish with half the butter. Add the pudding mixture, compressing it a little if necessary to make it fit. Dot the top evenly with small pieces of the remaining butter. Bake for about 45 minutes or until the top is puffed and golden and a knife blade comes out clean.

VARIATIONS: Use whole-wheat, rye, or pumpernickel bread, altering the cheese, liquid, and seasonings accordingly.

Having traversed this distance, we are better placed to define the transition point between the solitary and the public cook. The eater-cook doesn't necessarily cook without recipes; rather, he or she tends to be drawn to those that fall together—as does the bread and cheese pudding recipe above—into familiar chunks of tactile and sensory play.

What more natural way than this kind of kitchen pleasure to absorb and develop culinary technique? Toasting and buttering bread, dunking it to sop up juices from our plate, melting cheese, eating bread and onion and cheese and ale—all untaught activities, but as we begin to articulate them, we find how easy it is to shuffle and deal them into different culinary hands.

For example: dice up some onions and sauté them in butter or drip until they are caramelized, add some ale or wine mixed with water to make a broth, toss in a handful of cheese, grated or cut into cubes, float toasted bread on top, and we have onion soup. Our four staples shift suddenly into a new sensory pattern, a starting point for another round of dishes, a whole new area of exploration . . . and another chapter of our imaginary book.

Maybe what all this means is that we don't really start learning how to cook until we begin noticing what gives us pleasure in the kitchen. Cooking is about eating, of course, but it's also about doing, and recipes are as fairly judged by the quality of experiences that they offer to the cook as by those that they offer to the eater.

For the eater-cook, dishes made up out of familiar handwork

are that much more owned. Each time we connect these sensory activities together in another way, we elaborate a little more the map of our own particular culinary place. Such dishes possess—just as they do when made from vegetables picked from our own garden or from clams raked up out of the beach just down the road—not only the tang of our labor but the specific flavor of our life.

A personal cuisine built up out of such a repertoire does have its limitations. It develops slowly. Because it depends on one person's palate and personality, it is necessarily selective and may seem to others unnecessarily arbitrary, even unbalanced—especially before time has been given a chance to round out harsh edges and mellow prejudice.

But this same narrowing of focus also brings with it greater depth of field. A love of bread, cheese, and onions has not only led me to the dishes mentioned here but also, to give a single instance, helped me understand that onion soup is not so much a dish as a *method*, used in the Mediterranean to make garlic and herb pottages and, in Tuscany, *panzanella*, an uncooked salad-soup of fresh basil, tomato, onion, and bread (to which, not surprisingly but unconventionally, I add some mozzarella).

The best response to such criticism, however, is that no one should have to spend a lifetime cooking alone. The commingling of two different personal cuisines in a single household brings an unimaginable sensual enhancement to the relationship and a freshening of experience that comes from sharing with another. This, however, is a very different kind of culinary adventure—one that for me, at the age of forty-eight, has only just begun.

"Papa doesn't care what he has, if it's only ready. He would take bread-and-cheese, if cook would only send it in instead of dinner."

"Bread-and-cheese! Does Mr. Gibson eat cheese?"

"Yes; he's very fond of it," said Molly innocently. "I've known him eat toasted cheese when he has been too tired to fancy anything else."

"Oh! but, my dear, we must change all that. I shouldn't like to think of your father eating cheese; it's such a strong-smelling, coarse kind of thing. We must get him a cook who can toss him up an omelette, or something elegant. Cheese is only fit for the kitchen."

"Papa is very fond of it," persevered Molly.

"Oh! but we will cure him of that. I couldn't bear the smell of cheese; and I'm sure he would be sorry to annoy me."

—Mrs. Gaskell, *Wives and Daughters*

KITCHEN DIARY: TWO AUTUMN SALADS

An End-of-Season Grill. Here in Maine, long after the weather turns too cold for cooking meat, we keep the barbecue grill out for roasting peppers, a very pleasant pastime on a nippy but sunny November afternoon. The seared flesh and sweet, meaty aroma of roasting red peppers are so suggestive of grilled steak that the only surprise is why a dish that combined the two hadn't composed itself sooner in my mind. As it turned out, the deep autumnal colors and simple but rich-tasting mix of taste and texture proved a persuasive reason to keep the grill out of the garage until the first snow arrived, a few weeks later.

A SALAD OF STEAK, KALAMATA OLIVES, AND ROASTED PEPPERS
(SERVES 4)

4 *large sweet red peppers*	2 *teaspoons fresh lemon juice*
2 *(12-ounce) sirloin shell steaks*	4 *tablespoons virgin olive oil*
1 *small onion*	1 *clove garlic, minced*
10 *to* 12 *Kalamata (or other brine-*	1 *tablespoon capers, chopped*
cured black) olives	*Salt and pepper to taste*

Heat charcoal in an outdoor charcoal grill until red hot and a white ash forms. Grill the peppers, turning with tongs as needed, until they are charred on all sides. Remove the peppers and place them in a large paper bag. Fold the bag over to loosely seal and let the peppers steam in their own heat for 15 minutes. Meanwhile, place the two shell steaks over the coals and grill to rare, about 5 minutes on the first side and 3 to 4 minutes on the second. Remove and set aside to cool.

Peel the charred skin from the peppers. Then stem them carefully, removing all seeds. With a sharp knife, slice the peppers into narrow strips, each about as long as the steaks are wide. Put the slices, as cut, into a large bowl. When the steaks have cooled, cut them into thin (but not paper-thin) strips, slicing widthwise and discarding any scrim of fat.

Set out a large platter and interleave the strips of pepper and steak, each resting on the one before, so that each piece is visible. (Don't discard the pepper juices.) Slice the onion as thin as possible into rings. Set it into a colander and pour a kettle of boiling water over it. Shake away excess water, turn the onion rings onto paper toweling, and pat dry. Spread these in a fine web over the slices of meat and pepper.

Pit the olives and, with your fingers, tear the olive meat into small bits and scatter these also over the platter. Pour the lemon juice and olive oil into the pepper juices that remain in the bowl that held the pepper slices. Stir in the garlic and capers. Mix this dressing well and spoon evenly over the collation. Finally, season it with plenty of freshly ground pepper and sprinkle with a pinch or two of salt.

Cover with plastic wrap and let sit for about half an hour before eating, to allow the flavors to mingle (but do not refrigerate—it should be eaten at room temperature). Serve with good crusty bread and a simple lettuce salad.

A Cajun Corn-and-Tomato Medley. *The following recipe is actually for a* macque choux: *a Cajun cooked corn-and-tomato dish, here transformed into a (quite wonderful) salad by the simple expedient of not cooking the tomatoes.*

A SALAD OF TOMATOES AND CORN
(SERVES 4)

6 ears of fresh corn (or about 3 cups kernels)

2 teaspoons each butter and corn oil

1 small onion, cut into small pieces

1 small bell pepper, seeded and chopped fine

1 clove garlic, minced

2 or 3 dashes Tabasco

4 red ripe tomatoes, coarsely chopped

2 tablespoons heavy cream

Salt and pepper to taste

Cut the corn kernels from the cobs with a sharp knife, scraping each cob with the back of the knife afterward to rub away as much pulp as possible. Collect in a bowl. Heat the butter and oil together in a skillet and, when butter is melted, stir in the onion bits. Cook these until just translucent, stirring often.

Mix together the pepper pieces, garlic, and corn kernels and pulp; season with the Tabasco; and add all this to the onions. Cook for about 5 minutes, just until the kernels are soft and the pepper pieces tender (they should still have a little crunch). Remove from the stove and turn out into a large bowl. When the mixture has reached room temperature, add the tomatoes and stir in the cream. Taste for seasoning, adding salt and freshly ground pepper to taste. Serve at room temperature.

FORTY CLOVES
OF GARLIC

✧ ✧ ✧

1

The time: Thanksgiving Day, 1970. The place: the Massachusetts Berkshires. Snow had been falling all morning. It had stopped by the time I came out to shovel a path to my car, but storm clouds still hung darkly over the deserted campus of the private school where I was then a teacher. The students and most of the faculty had already left for the holiday, and the only building with any lights on was the school dining hall. There, Alice Brock—just recently made famous by Arlo Guthrie's song "Alice's Restaurant"—was cooking a Thanksgiving dinner with all the trimmings for the hip folk of the Lenox-Stockbridge area. Alice had once been a faculty member at the school (as Arlo had been a student), and in consequence, any teachers staying over the holiday, hip or no, were also invited.

As my friend Dave Bremer and I got into my little Triumph Herald, a tandem of Land Rovers came plowing up the drive: the first guests, already arriving. We went down their tracks and turned right onto the icy surface of Route 183, heading for town. I drove off not unconscious of a historic moment being missed—and not without real pangs of regret at missing it. For while Alice didn't yet actually run a restaurant, she already was a legendary cook in the area, and there were rumors that she was about to ride her newfound notoriety to high places in the big-time culinary world.

Dave and I, however, were going to have supper with a young couple, Jim and Judy Mendel (not their real names), who had promised us something different for Thanksgiving— something with lots of garlic and no turkey. And even the allure of a meal cooked by Alice Brock didn't overcome my lack of enthusiasm for that bird and all its tedious accompaniments.

In other words, there had been, there still was, a wrestling match going on within. Part of me wanted to go where it had already sniffed out a genuinely good feed; another part, bolstered by the excuse of icy roads and threat of storm, insisted on staying where it could rub shoulders with famous people and get to eat famous food. This time, my stomach won.

As it turned out, there was no reason to be sorry. Alice Brock wrote a not-very-memorable cookbook and has otherwise remained a celebrity relic of the sixties . . . but that night I ate a dish that had a powerfully subversive effect on my notions of fine cooking. I ate chicken cooked with forty cloves of garlic.

❖ ❖ ❖

I was twenty-seven at the time; Judy Mendel was the first serious cook I had encountered. I had thought, until I met her, that *I* was a serious cook. The truth was that neither of us had had any real culinary training, and it may be that I knew as many recipes and techniques as she did. The difference between us was that Judy was aggressively honest about what she wanted to eat, whereas my cooking suffered, without my realizing it, from an essential failure of nerve.

Even with foods that I liked and was confident that I cooked well, there was something slyly passive in my claims to pleasure. I was unable, for example, to go to a good butcher, buy a two-inch-thick slab of prime porterhouse, coat it with olive oil, and grill it over chunks of real charcoal. Such extravagance of appetite seemed too terrifyingly conspicuous.

So instead I would go to Adams Market, buy a scant inch-thick sirloin of dubious grade, rub it with charcoal-seasoned salt, grill it under the broiler, and eat it topped with thick "coins" of maître d' butter made with dried garlic bits, dehydrated parsley flakes, and minced frozen chives. I ignored the bogusness of all this because it allowed me to produce the dish's enrichments at the last possible moment—as if otherwise, somehow, I risked being caught and exposed.

Judy had no time for such "gourmet" touches. Her approach to extravagance was fearless and direct. Although she had lived in the Berkshires a year less than I, she had already persuaded a mushroom enthusiast to share the secret places where morels grew in early spring. She had convinced an old Italian couple with a large herb garden to supply her all summer with bunches of fresh basil. And she'd found a tiny grocery store in Pittsfield that sold real Parmesan, plump heads of garlic, *pignoli*, imported DeCecco pasta, and a rich-tasting, deep-colored Sicilian olive oil.

The dishes that she made from these ingredients agitated me by the openness of their pleasure. The morels were gently sautéed in sweet butter. The basil was pulverized with the garlic, *pignoli*, olive oil, and Parmesan into *pesto alla genovese*, a dish I had never heard of before. Such astonishing stuff it was, too: a mouthful of aggressive flavors, each—like the colors of an Expressionist painting—retaining a coarse vibrancy while still somehow melding into a single, ravishing whole.

What I didn't understand then was that these dishes also composed a portrait of Judy. If you are what you eat, you are even more what you cook. But what I found compelling in her cooking, I found pushy and coercive in *her*. I wanted those baskets of morels, those bunches of fresh basil, too, but I was incapable of the bullying and cajoling that would get me them. It was like putting down a buddy for the way he chatted up the girls but still wanting him to set me up with a date.

Nor is this simile at all inappropriate. Garlic is one of the most directly sexual of foods—which is perhaps why, until Judy, I had desired it greatly but approached it very circumspectly. I still found it daring to mince a whole clove into a pasta sauce—in fact, I kept returning to dehydrated garlic precisely because desiccation absolved it of its pervasive suggestiveness.

Recipes for chicken with forty cloves of garlic often make much of the fact that the long cooking mutes that bulb's sometimes harsh-seeming pungency, as indeed it does. But nothing suppresses that throaty muskiness—and in this dish it is present in breathtaking abandon. After all, at its purest, it consists of nothing but pieces of chicken and the unpeeled bulbs of four whole heads of garlic, thoroughly braised in olive oil. You pick up a clove, suck off the juices that cling to it, bite away the husk at one end, squeeze the succulent mash into the mouth, and then follow this with a bite of the rich, greasy, garlicky chicken.

If there is nothing sexually forward about this dish, then food and love have no common ground at all. I have come to think otherwise, and certainly this explains why, despite the fact that both pesto and *poulet aux quarante gousses d'ail* became flashing beacons for me in what was still a great darkness, my navigation toward them remained uncertain and slow. This was, I think, because for a very long time both of these dishes seemed to me as secret as sex.

Food writers have for so long acted as if they knew about pesto forever that it is hard to remember in how very few cookbooks it appeared before 1970—and how much it was ignored in those in which it did appear. The same was even truer of *poulet aux quarante gousses d'ail*. If it appears among the hundreds of chicken recipes in the 1961 edition of the *Larousse Gastronomique*, I can't find it, and that situation is no different with several other now-venerable French cookbooks, including Anne Willan's *French Regional Cooking* and, surprisingly, *Mastering the Art of French Cooking*.

I didn't encounter it in a book myself until 1973, when I first read Ford Madox Ford's quirkily appealing meditation-cum-travelogue, *Provence*. There it figures in an oft-quoted tale about a French model in London who found it impossible to reconcile her trade and her passion for garlic. In despair, she decided to chuck the job and went home and made herself a *poulet béarnais*, "the main garniture of which is a kilo—two lbs.—of garlic per chicken, you eating the stewed cloves as if they were *haricots blancs*." Instead of firing her when she returned to work, her employers found her suffused with a new and mysterious attractiveness.

This story is sometimes used as evidence of the harmlessness of cooked garlic. But Ford is, I think, saying something very different—something you will now understand. I picked that up right away. What it took me longer to notice—partly because Ford had become a kind of literary father figure for me and partly because, simply, this part of the story is told only when he picks up its thread again after an intervening two hundred pages—was that Ford could not in fact bring *himself* to eat those garlic cloves "as if they were *haricots blancs*" . . . because, he said, he wasn't that much a hero.

2

> It appeared that her kind Grace . . . had had a couple of capons cooked and had them stuffed each with twenty-five cloves. . . . She was under the impression that she would thus be giving me *poulet béarnais*, but she was a little mistaken. The dish of Henri Quatre has the garlic stewed under the fowl.
>
> —Ford Madox Ford, *Provence*

It's not her Grace who has got things wrong, but Ford, who confuses *poulet aux quarante gousses d'ail* with *poulet béarnais*, also called *poule au pot d'Henri IV*. This is a dish in which a fat hen is stuffed and then stewed on a bed of pot vegetables. It is not, in any version I know, especially garlicky, although a modest amount is always present among the ingredients. Either Ford once knew a French cook who thought otherwise, or else the two dishes got somehow muddled in his memory.

No one doubts that *poule au pot* is a Béarnais specialty, but if that region also claims *poulet aux quarante gousses d'ail*, it's only one pretender in a rather long line. Jean-Noël Escudier includes it in *The Wonderful Food of Provence*, Paul-Louis Couchod appropriates it for the Dauphiné in *La France à table*, James Bentley has it in *Life and Food in the Dordogne*, and André Daguin sets it among *Foie Gras, Magret, and Other Good Food from Gascony*.

Provence, Béarn, Gascony, the Dauphiné, Dordogne—the more pins one pushes into the map, the more one comes to suspect that the dish originated in the culinary area that they surround and which has influenced much of their cooking: Catalonia. For while all the South of France loves garlic, it is simply impossible to imagine *la cuina catalana* without it.

Allioli, a Catalan sauce made essentially of olive oil and garlic, might be called, Colman Andrews writes in *Catalan Cuisine*, "the Catalan catsup." Another famous Catalan dish, called *pistache de mouton*, is a leg of mutton prepared with a garnish —not of pistachio but—of *fifty* cloves of garlic (called *pistache* maybe because the cloves look like fresh pistachio nuts). Made with a whole chicken, this dish would be very much like Ford's *poulet béarnais*.

Writing about a popular Catalan dish of lamb and garlic (a recipe for which is given below), Elisabeth Lambert Ortiz, in *The Food of Spain and Portugal*, describes it as "the first cousin to the Provençal *Poulet aux Quatre Clous d'Ail*." But this is as close as we can get, at least with the sources I have at hand —so for the moment, this notion, however suggestive, must remain unproven.

Fortunately, however much dispersed, the dish everywhere has remained true to its peasant roots—it is so simply made that the regional touches are modest indeed. If in the Dordogne they use goose fat instead of olive oil, or in Gascony duck fat—well, these are choices easy enough for any cook to sort out for herself.

As for Matt and me, our boldest step was a substantial reduction in the amount of olive oil. For the quantity of chicken we used, recipes can be found that call for as much as three-quarters cup of oil. Why so much? One thought is that the stewing hens originally used were relatively lean; another is simply that the people who made the dish liked it that way. Times change, however, and we find that, given the fattiness of American poultry, the dish is quite rich and flavorful enough with a couple of spoonfuls.

Another major departure was to dispense with the traditional seal of flour-and-water paste the dish required. It was customarily made in an earthenware casserole with a poorly fitting lid and baked in a communal bread oven where the heat could not be controlled. At a steady, moderate cooking temperature, any covered casserole will produce tender, juicy chicken, well permeated with garlic essence.

Some recipes call for cooking the chicken whole; others, for cutting it up into pieces. We favor the latter because the cloves are more evenly distributed. Besides, carving a braised chicken is a very different matter from carving a roasted one. Finally, we are of two minds about peeling the cloves. It is more work for the cook to do this and less fun for the eater. But they are such appealing little morsels, *sans chemise* . . . and how else can you get a whole forkful? Like already-shelled pistachio nuts, this may seem altogether too much of a good thing. But this is a matter of taste, even morals, rather than of technique.

CHICKEN WITH FORTY CLOVES OF GARLIC
(SERVES 4)

3½- to 4-pound chicken, cut into serving pieces
Salt and freshly ground pepper
40 cloves of garlic (about 4 heads)
1 to 2 tablespoons fruity olive oil

Several sprigs of parsley and one of thyme
Thick slices of country bread, fried in olive oil

Preheat the oven to 325°F. Season the pieces of chicken with salt and pepper. Examine the cloves of garlic. If they are fresh and firm—and if you care to—use them unpeeled. Otherwise, peel them carefully, discarding any soft or moldy ones and cutting away any brown spots and assertive green sprouts. Choose a flameproof casserole with a tight-fitting lid, just large enough to hold the chicken pieces comfortably. Heat the olive oil in it over medium-high heat and, when it is hot, quickly brown the chicken pieces on all sides. Do this in batches, removing each piece to a platter as soon as it is done. When all the pieces have been browned, put the garlic cloves into the hot oil and sauté these, stirring constantly, for 2 or 3 minutes, until they soften and begin to brown a little at the edges.

Remove the casserole from the heat and return the chicken pieces, stirring so that they and the garlic cloves are well mixed.

Tie the sprigs of parsley and the sprig of thyme together with string to make a bouquet garni. Work this down among the chicken pieces, cover the pot tightly with foil, and press on the lid. Bake for 1½ hours. The chicken will be meltingly tender and suffused with the garlic. Serve with the fried crusts of bread, to be spread with the soft garlic.

COOK'S NOTE: An attractive version of Ginette Mathiot's in *À Table avec Édouard de Pomiane* replaces ten of the garlic cloves with shallots, which are peeled and chopped fine. The dish is prepared as directed above, with the addition of a generous half-cup of dry white wine. This is poured in just before the pot is covered and boiled off over high heat when the dish is done. The chicken and garlic are then served at the table from the pan.

Afterword from our subscriber Michael Rosen (Oberlin, Ohio). "Concerning chicken with 40 cloves of garlic (which my family just finished eating): I've always used the recipe from a Provençal cookbook called *Cuisine Provençale*, by Michel Barberousse. There is no date in the book and it seems as though the author published it himself. French friends tell me it is rare and, at the same time, reputable. I prefer his version because he leaves the chicken whole. It fills up a rather high earthenware casserole I found at a rummage sale. I tuck a bouquet garni inside the feckless bird and cook it on its bed of garlic in the pot. A whole chicken makes for a more festive event as I carve (or rather divide) the final product at the table."

Here, as Matt and I transposed it from the original, is:

MICHEL BARBEROUSSE'S CHICKEN WITH FORTY CLOVES OF GARLIC

Take a plump young chicken of, say, 2½ pounds and clean it. Salt and pepper its cavity, put in a bouquet garni, and sear it all over. Choose an earthenware casserole into which the bird can be comfortably nestled. Into this put ¾ cup of olive oil and 40 unpeeled cloves of garlic. Add a large bouquet of rosemary, thyme, sage, bay, parsley, and celery. Place the prepared chicken on this bed of seasonings and turn it so that it is covered with the aromatic oil. Cover the pot and seal the lid shut with a strip of dough made of flour and water. Cook this in the oven for about 1½ hours at 325°F (a smaller chicken will take less time). Remove the pot from the oven and break off the seal. Bring the pot to the table, removing its lid only at the moment of serving. . . . The air is filled with suggestive aroma, the chicken golden, tender, and deliciously scented. Serve with toasted French bread for the eaters to spread with purée squeezed from the garlic cloves.

LAMB WITH FORTY CLOVES OF GARLIC
(SERVES 4)

40 cloves of garlic (about 4 heads)	*1 to 2 teaspoons paprika*
2 pounds boneless lamb	*1 to 2 tablespoons red-wine*
2 tablespoons olive oil	*vinegar*
1 medium onion, finely chopped	*Salt and pepper to taste*
1 bay leaf	

Preheat the oven to 325°F. Prepare the garlic as described in the recipe for chicken with forty cloves of garlic above. Cut the lamb into bite-sized pieces. Choose a flameproof casserole with a tightly fitting lid, just large enough to hold the lamb pieces comfortably. Heat the olive oil in it over medium-high heat and, when it is hot, quickly brown the pieces of lamb on all sides. Do this in batches, removing each one to a platter as soon as it is done. When all the pieces have been browned, put the garlic cloves and chopped onion into the hot oil and cook these, stirring constantly, for 2 or 3 minutes, until they soften and begin to brown a little at the edges.

Remove the casserole from the heat and return the lamb, stirring until it and the garlic and onion are well mixed. Add the bay leaf, paprika, vinegar, and salt and pepper. Cover tightly with foil, top with the lid, and cook for about 2 hours. The cooking vegetables should weep sufficient liquid to keep the contents of the pot moist. Check after an hour to make sure this is so—if the pot is dry, add ¼ cup of water. Reseal the pot carefully and cook until the lamb is fork-tender and the garlic meltingly soft. Rice goes well with this meal, as does a lightly dressed salad of pungent greens.

COOK'S NOTE: In a similar dish in *Catalan Cuisine*, Colman Andrews omits the vinegar and flavorings, substituting instead a cup of a Catalan fortified wine not unlike a dry sherry. Elisabeth Lambert Ortiz, in *The Food of Spain and Portugal*, suggests dropping the unpeeled garlic cloves into boiling water for half a minute to make them easier to peel.

☛ For further exploration, see Patricia Wells's *Bistro Cooking* for a pan-sautéed version of chicken with forty cloves of garlic; Geraldene Holt's *French Country Kitchen* for a turkey casserole with twenty; André Daguin's *Foie Gras, Magret, and Other Good Food from Gascony* for a version served with a garlic-clove confit; and Colman Andrews's *Catalan Cuisine* for a spectacular roast-lamb casserole with twelve heads of garlic, half of them left whole.

KITCHEN DIARY: A WEDDING PUNCH

Winging my way down to Florida. David Bremer, one of my closest friends, is getting married and I'm best man. I've managed to evade all attached duties except giving the wedding toast and concocting a champagne punch for the reception. Slight as it is, this responsibility has been weighing on my mind. A search through my cookbooks turned up nothing that immediately soothed my unease by perfect appropriateness— champagne punches are pretty much cut from the same cloth, and those that strive for originality teeter instead toward disaster. Weeding out such impostors and weighing the merits of the rest have left me more or less decided on a version from the old *Picayune's Creole Cook Book*.

CHAMPAGNE PUNCH À LA CRÉOLE. 1 lb. sugar; 1 pint fresh lemon juice; 1 quart champagne; 1 quart best white wine; ¼ cup of Curaçao; 2 quarts seltzer; 1 pineapple, half grated and half sliced small; a large piece of ice; and 3 dozen strawberries. Take a large punch bowl and dissolve in it one pound of sugar, one pint of lemon juice, one quart of White Wine, one quart bottle of Champagne, two quarts of Seltzer Water, one-quarter cup of Curaçao, and one-half of a grated pineapple. Mix well. Put in a large piece of ice, decorate with strawberries and sliced pineapple, let it cool, and serve in small cup glasses. The above quantity will serve twenty-five people.

But the piece of paper on which I've copied the recipe is already scribbled with nervous queries: what purpose the white wine? what good is a champagne punch that's half seltzer? And—what's *really* bothering me—how could I hope to judge the merit of a recipe I've never tasted? Literally as well as figuratively (for the sun had long set by the time we arrived at Orlando International), I was flying blind.

No surprise that champagne punch was not the first thing on Dave and Sharran's list of worries, and Dave kindly but firmly let me know, after listening to some of this, that the thing was entirely in my hands. Then he informed me that Sharran's mother had brought a bottle of peach wine back from a visit to California many years ago and wanted to contribute it to the punch for good luck.

This bottle, on being produced, appeared to be not only decades old but *open*—apparently it had been sampled on their return, been declared too good for casual drinking, and had thus been put away in the closet for the right special occasion. I gathered my courage and tasted: it had turned, not to vinegar, but into VSOP—very stale old peach-water. Palatable, yes, if barely—but palate is not the only judge. This was that moment the bottle had been patiently waiting for, and into the punch it would have to go.

An even more unnerving challenge was yet to come. The town's one big supermarket offered plenty of white cornmeal to stuff into my suitcase for the trip home, but a distressingly anemic produce section. The state being Florida, there was some good citrus, but there were no strawberries at all, and their few pineapples were suspiciously without aroma.

What to do? I hovered over the small fruit selection in a panic of indecision. Morbid thoughts of frozen strawberries in syrup roiling in my brain, I began to pick over the peaches, having already decided to freshen the dusty frailty of that old peach wine with a generous portion of real fruit pulp.

Here was a ripe one, there another. Suddenly the obvious began to dawn: give *them* the leading role. Peach was a presence that was as pleasing in champagne as any strawberry, and the peaches were *here*.

Well, some were anyway—after I had picked through them all, I found out there weren't really enough. However, my panic was fading, and a decisive shift had somehow happened, moving the punch's making from the *Picayune*'s imagination to mine. If there weren't enough ripe peaches, I decided, I'd augment them with kiwi fruit.

Having railed against that fruit in *Simple Cooking*, I'm sure the California Kiwi Growers' Association would have loved a photograph of me stuffing handfuls into a paper bag. But floating in a punch bowl, their brilliant color would be only an asset, and with the peaches and pineapple, their indecisive flavor no handicap. A couple of lemons and limes went in after them, and I was through.

As it happened, we did find some strawberries a little later at a fruit stand, but the image of the peaches' luscious flesh had already given me confidence to work up *my* punch— brightly flavored, swimming with fresh bits of glistening fruit, bubbling with lots and lots of champagne. A different beast indeed from the subtler-flavored, stately Creole concoction, this version had a livelier commingling of flavor and aroma . . . and quite a bit more kick.

A lovely presentation it made set out in the huge, clear punchbowl (in many multiples of the original recipe to accommodate a half case of champagne). How did it taste? All I know is that I drank my share and more with complete unselfconscious pleasure. Once the celebrating began, the effort of preparation faded before the meaning of the event—all I had done was mix the ingredients; the wedding made the punch.

TAKING STOCK

❖ ❖ ❖

It is said that stock is the foundation of great cuisine. It is essential to flavorful soups, rich sauces, and boiled or braised meats, not to mention risotto. —Robert Nadeau

Stock is everything. —Escoffier

The sensation of the 1898 Salon des Artistes Français was Joseph-Ferdinand Gueldry's painting "The Blood Drinkers." It depicts the stark interior of a French slaughterhouse. A newly slain ox sprawls in the foreground. One of its slaughterers, his arm dripping with gore, lifts a glass of steaming blood, just filled from the stream still spurting from the animal's heart, to the first of a shambling queue of well-to-do invalids—men, women, children—each waiting a turn to drink.

French doctors then believed such treatment strengthened the weak blood of their patients, and the public fascination with the painting sprang from the same macabre irony as today's organ transplant dramas, where the seriously ill wait for the death of a healthy body so that they might inherit its organs. Gueldry contrasts the vitality of the dead steer with the pallid frailty of the invalids—and contrasts as well their palpable disgust at the drink they are forced to down with their equally palpable desire for the life they hope it promises.

Gueldry's painting still disturbs, but only vicariously, for it can no longer draw us into the scene it portrays. The blood drinkers merely revolt us; we cannot put ourselves in their places. And time has given the graphic depiction of the act of slaughter a patina of nostalgia that was not there when the artist painted it, a feeling, even, of intimacy.

Although the room itself, large and floored with concrete, has a modern impersonality, the carcasses that hang from the overhead rails are not numerous and their slaughterers only two. The victim was led to its death by a rope. The sledge-hammer that stunned it lies in full view—a single, simple instrument.

And then there is the beast itself. The eye is immediately drawn to it—especially the modern eye, for it is this, not the invalids, that has become the real object of its curiosity. The mind—except that of the very squeamish or the resolutely vegetarian—does not balk at the sight of one dead ox.

The original viewers of this painting, especially, knew where meat comes from. They had seen whole carcasses suspended from their butcher's ceiling; they had heard the bellowing from the local abattoir. All that Gueldry removed from the equation was the cook, intermediary between the raw and the roast. For a moment, the curtain was pulled back and appetite suddenly saw itself in the nude.

This is the fulcrum by which Gueldry's painting works. If the idea of that mouthful of hot blood only revolts you, the theme becomes mere sentiment: poor ox, poor invalids, poor viewer. But if a flicker of desire also stirs within, then your reactions become more complex, your understanding more difficult, the painting—for all its limitations as genre—art.

Today, our eyes see but do not comprehend. Our appetite does not know the way back to the ox, for it balks before the workings of the modern slaughtering plant. It cannot imagine a whole herd of bawling cattle, strung by their hind legs, swinging down the conveyor belts, one after another, to meet their death from the blow of a pneumatic jackhammer.

We cannot respond to such an image, not because it is so horrible, but because carnage at this scale is immediately anes-thetizing. If anything, the slaughtering of a single animal with hammer and knife is more horrible because we *can* imagine it.

But what cannot be imagined cannot be experienced. Our slaughterhouses no longer offer experience and so we learn nothing—we are given nothing—from the death of the animals we eat.

✤ ✤ ✤

The essential premise of stock is a good one: letting nothing go to waste. This means, first, finding a way to eat animals that, while edible, have not been raised strictly to be eaten. Once, not so long ago, much of the meat served on all but the tables of the rich came from animals that had already led useful lives as beasts of burden or wool producers, or careerists who had sent eggs and milk to the table before arriving there themselves.

Furthermore, in those days, because of the vexing problems of spoilage, animals were slaughtered locally, sometimes even at home, supplying ample trimmings and bones (not to mention offal). A cuisine based on stock begins with such butcher's leavings—bones, especially, but also cuts of meat too tough to eat. Butchers then had whole carcasses to contend with, not cartons of selected parts. To keep the profitable cuts moving they had to shift all the rest, too, for such price as they could get.

A cuisine based on stock also requires gardinage in plentiful supply: vegetables that come home with all their parts attached; herbs sold not dried in little expensive bottles but fresh in big fragrant penny bunches.

Finally, a cuisine based on stock is a cuisine faced with the problem of kitchen waste. It is a part of the cooking of families that are large and rarely nuclear—of maiden aunts and bachelor uncles, aged grandparents, nephews from the country looking for a job, all crowded round the supper table.

Stock speaks of a time when the good housekeeper served the tops she had cut off from the turnips and the poached beef out of which she had made her broth, and then she scraped the serving platters clean. She cut away the bits of meat that might make up a shepherd's pie and divided the rest between the stockpot and the dripping jar.

Our kitchens do not see this kind of wastage. Today, the

disposal of such garbage is not put into our hands. Except for fruit and the most durable vegetables, everything we now buy has already been trimmed of nature's generous lagniappe. The appeal of meat stock or broth has always been that it is a richness come from nowhere, made from scraps and bones that the careless throw away. Although its public face is frugality, its private one is glee: something good for nothing; meat for free.

This is no longer true. Decent meat is relatively cheap and we can get as much of it as we want. We are stock poor because we are so meat rich. No self-respecting butcher in America today would sell the meat you need to make a true bouillon, and, even if he would, he'd be hard pressed to find any. Genuine mutton, real stewing hens, tough old goat: none of this exists except for those who raise it. Many markets refuse even to carry the unfamiliar, tougher cuts—tail, neck, feet, tongue—of the tender animals we eat.

I don't make stock. But when I was in my early twenties, I lived in a place where people did, a Russian-Ukrainian neighborhood on New York City's Lower East Side. The local meat shop still had sawdust strewn on the floor; a suckling pig was often displayed in the window. The butcher laughed and gossiped with his customers while he cut, trimmed, and packaged the cuts they requested—small orders mostly, a couple of chops for one, a little ground meat for another, a brace of hocks for a third.

Standing behind the others, waiting my turn, I watched with fascination the communal scrutiny every individual transaction received. When a special cut was required, the butcher would go into the meat locker and bring out the part of the carcass from which it would be taken.

The customer followed every motion as the butcher began to slice, a certain tension in her demeanor suggesting that if the job were done one whit less carefully, she was not above snatching the knife away and doing it herself. And once the piece had been cut and weighed, she would insist that all the trimmings be wrapped up with it in the butcher's paper.

The butcher bore such requests with equanimity. Often his red, beefy hands would dip into the large waste can by his side to pluck out a massive, meaty bone "for the dog." It was only after I had lived in the neighborhood for some time that I realized that the dog for whom these frail old ladies were toting home bones was a fictive beast: they were feeding their soup pots instead.

When the butcher showed me my piece of meat, I also inspected it—but only to ensure it was what he said. I could distinguish one cut from another, but with no sense of the anatomy of the animal from which it came, I knew nothing about its relationship to the whole. That was the difference between the cooking of my neighbors and my own—they possessed a culinary imagination that could still confront Gueldry's dead ox. Sharp as a blade, it could peel back the pelt to reveal appetite lurking in the darkness that lay beneath.

A culture's appetite always springs from its poor, and these were poor whose fingers still knew their way into every crevice and cranny of the animals they ate. Stock is the foundation of so many dishes of "grand" cuisine because these were created at a time when boys became chefs for food, not fame. Born hungry, they wove dishes for the rich in which their own appetite ran wild. They stuffed meat with more meat, enriched their gravies with the sweetest of suets, sought to distill out of bone and gristle a concentrate that would imbue any dish with what most propelled their hunger.

This kind of intimate connection between eater and eaten has almost vanished from our cooking, despite the scattered remnants that remain behind to hold its memory. Today's young chefs may be trained in stocks and sauces, but as much as they draw on personal experience their culinary instincts flower most easily at the grill, with its focus on drawing flavor from a particular piece of meat. Theirs is no longer a cuisine of the carcass; it is a cuisine of the *cut*.

Rich and poor alike, none of us likes being reminded of the whole from which our meat is cut; even less do we wish to consider edible the framing that holds it all in place. The only carcass that we regularly encounter is that of the chicken, and even here most of us prefer to buy that bird already cut into parts—though it would take only a few moments to cut it up ourselves so as to have the trimmings to do with as we please. If we don't bother, it is because our honest impulse is to throw all that away.

❖ ❖ ❖

If we don't care enough about broth to make it a matter-of-fact part of our lives, why do we bother with it at all? What makes us cling to our Knorr-Swiss bouillon cubes, our cans of Swanson or College Inn? If such stuff is only a little worse than what we can make for ourselves, why don't we give up cooking with it at all? It isn't, I think, because we love its taste. It's because that bubbling stockpot has remained a compelling symbol, long after the cooking it emblemized has fled.

American cooking, tumbling as fast as it is toward a totally take-out cuisine, retains two potent images that can still revivify our appetite for good, homemade food: baked goods, which stand for the gift of pleasure, and meat-based broths, from which all the kitchen's healing goodness flows.

Not too long ago, this image reflected a truth: a continuous river of broth spilled from the stockpot to inspirit soups, enhance pasta and rice, baste the roast, sauce the vegetables, and provide a sop for bread. And, most important of all, its aroma filled the house, cosseting all who inhaled it with deep well-being, as if the very air were filled with nurture. The chef may have transmogrified his meat waters into gold; the housewife transmuted them into a far more essential nutrient: love.

To understand the power of such broths over our collective unconscious, we must remember that until very recently they were thought to contain—whether stock, broth, or bouillon—an essential, life-enhancing *goodness*. It was not simply minerals, protein, vitamins that the home cook sought to extract from the stuff of the stockpot but the actual vigor and good health of the animal whose parts these were.

We don't seek to consume them, after all, in sickness or old age but, as much as possible, in their prime. We drink their health: and that glass of blood from Gueldry's ox, transmuted by the cook, becomes the cup of broth, of stock. As one is to living meat the other is to cooked—the vital fluid, reduced and concentrated.

However, it was the animal's *body* that oriented appetite, centering what it searched for and giving every part it found a role. By the time the brains were scrambled, the sweetbreads poached, the bones sucked dry of marrow—the vitals of the animal devoured—its *vitality* was totally absorbed. But as fewer and fewer of us have held the hot, soft body of a freshly slain hen or stunned a wildly flapping fish, our cuisine has recoiled that much further from any intimacy with the bodies we eat and their sacrifice has lost all its imaginative weight.

In response to our appetite's disorientation, our culture's metaphors of wellness are shifting. Although we continue to pay lip service to the healthfulness of liver and chicken stock, the truth is that the phrase "health food" now conjures up images that are becoming entirely *anti*-meat. Today, we seek our magic potions in oat bran and canola oil; the noxious concoctions we force ourselves to drink for the sake of health are made of torula yeast, of "tiger's milk," not bull's blood.

Why then aren't we turning to wholesome vegetable broths? Although they exist, they remain an anomaly, a minority concern. Nourishing, yes, but there is no blood in them, no gift of life. If there were anything compelling to the imagination in the vegetable's sacrifice to provision us we would by now all be vegetarians. But there isn't—and we're not.

Instead, in the country of surfeit, the half measure is king. If we can't bear to push our meat plate entirely aside, we can't quite take pleasure in it either. We want beef that is at once fatless and tender; we want chicken that is all breast. And we have the pallid stews, the watery chicken soups, and the pot roasts flavored with onion-soup mix to prove it. We're clinging, as a culture, to a cooking that is no longer possible. As appetite has lost its hold on the necessary ingredients, those ingredients have changed . . . or gone away.

A few years ago—this time in Boston—I was heading home from a visit to the local A&P when I saw a giant garbage truck pulling away from the rear loading dock, its maw stuffed with beef bones, blotchy red with gobbets of flesh. The head butcher told me, when I went back in to protest, that there was almost no demand for such bones and so no profit to be got in selling them; the few he still put out hardly paid for their space in the meat case.

Nor did he have time to bundle them up to give away—and anyway, most people didn't want them like that, all meaty and gristly. They liked bones clean and white, so their dog wouldn't make a mess with them on the carpet. "Soup bones," he said, "are really pet bones—except people don't like seeing the word 'pet' near anything they themselves are going to eat."

In the past few decades, a complete reversal of meaning has taken place. Before, "something for the dog" meant soup bones; now, "soup bones" means something for the dog. Why else, if good homemade stock is as central to our cooking as we still pretend it to be, isn't the stuff sold in bottles in the grocer's dairy case—put up daily at the local free-range chicken farm, wholesome, tasty, sweetly fresh?

Instead, we've become a nation of culinary hypocrites. "When calling for chicken or beef broth," writes the author of a recently acclaimed cookbook, "I specify 'excellent' quality. That means don't use powders or cubes as a base. . . . I rarely have time to make broths from scratch, but certainly homemade is ideal. I use canned 'ready-to-serve' (i.e., not condensed) which I find remarkably close to homemade. I hesitate to give brand names. . . ."

The truth is that, made out of the flavorless chickens that flood our market, the best homemade broth still tastes flat and thin; made out of a rare and pricey free-range hen, the object of the exercise is lost. So we pour it out of a can. Its label reads "chicken," but it might as well say "golden broth." Indeed, it would do better to say that. Its contents may be made from a chicken—or some of its unspecified parts—but who of us would want to know that bird, let alone transmute its wretched life into our own? Drink its health? We wouldn't dare. For us broth is only flavored water. Now that the life has left it, the goodness has flown.

KITCHEN DIARY: CHICKEN IN A CRUST

Is there anything one can do to give our battery-raised chickens more flavor? Recently leafing through Nathalie Hambro's *Particular Delights*, I came across a method for baking a chicken wrapped in a salt-and-flour dough. This cleverly combines two disparate strategies that have long been used to cook a chicken so that it remains moist and tender. The Chinese bury it in a bed of salt, which lets steam escape but seals in the juices. Other cuisines wrap the bird in a sealed wrap of moist clay, which keeps in the steam but traps some of the juices between the clay and the skin. A wrapping of salt-and-flour dough promised to cauterize the juices before they escaped and to absorb those that did, leaving the bird with a crusty skin.

Besides intensifying flavor, this technique interested me for two other reasons. The first is that I had become convinced that the best way to roast chicken is to roast it quickly over high heat (500°F—following Barbara Kafka's lead in *Food for Friends*). I hoped the crust might allow me to do this to a chicken smaller than the usual roaster (5 to 7 pounds), without drying the bird out. (Since we are two, the smaller bird is more suitable for our table.) Secondly, I wondered if, so confined, the meat would taste more of any seasonings placed in the bird's cavity or rubbed into its skin.

So I chose a relatively small chicken, about 3½ pounds, and rubbed it inside and out with a mixture of crushed fresh leaf of thyme and rosemary and a minced clove of garlic, all of which I had let marinate awhile in about 2 tablespoons of olive oil. Then I set it aside, turned on the oven to 500°F, and began to make the dough.

This was done by mixing together a pound and a half each of kosher salt and flour (or about 4½ cups each). A generous cup of water was then kneaded in to make a firm but pliable dough. The first impression was one of far more dough than I would need, but it proved fragile and tore easily if stretched too thin. I rolled it out on a lightly floured board to what I guessed was a size large enough to cover the chicken. I then shifted it to the cooking pan before the first fitting session. This proved a wise choice, for I had to do a little patching at points where, despite my caution, parts of the bird broke through. The result was a solid but ungainly-looking parcel.

All this was actually accomplished in a very short time: the dough, not being edible, could be treated with scant courtesy, poked, pinched, and patched as occasion requires; the chicken was ready for the oven almost by the time the oven was ready for it. I put it in and set the timer for an hour.

I was happy to note the absence of any cooking smell (other than a toastily delicious salt-and-flour aroma) until the last ten minutes or so, when the rich and concentrated smell of chicken suddenly filled the kitchen. At the hour point, the crust had turned a dark, crusty brown and had shrunk to fit the bird. It was impossible, of course, to wiggle a leg to test for doneness: I plunged a skewer in the breast, which released a copious flow of clear, sweet-smelling juices. I decided it was done.

Hambro suggests bringing the chicken to table *en chemise*, as it were, which I would not suggest unless you mean to give your guests a few laughs before feeding them. The dough is truculently hard and I had to rip it away, chunk by chunk, with a well-mitted hand. The bird inside was a lovely gold. The meat was moist and unsalty, the dark meat as succulent as a dream and the breast meat, for the first time in memory, full of juices and mouth-meltingly tender. The meat at the bone, however, was just done—the next time I'll give it another good ten minutes.

The downside, such as it was: first, the skin was tasty but quite salty and not at all crisp, which may prove a boon to those who think they ought to avoid it. Also, despite being trapped in with the bird, the taste of the flavorings was not noticeably enhanced. Worst of all, however, was the effect of that inedible crust—baked a rich biscuit-brown, dotted all over inside with bits of herbs and flecks of chicken skin, and sopped

with drippings. For a fleeting moment, I cursed Nathalie Hambro for getting it all wrong. What was wanted was to wrap up
the bird in a brioche dough, bake it until the bundle was a
tender, golden brown—and then throw away the bird and
devour the crust.

On Not Being
a Good Cook

❖ ❖ ❖

I'm not a good cook. Not that I don't have my moments—like anyone who has spent thirty years happily cooking, I have absorbed something along the way. And in its casual way, it pays off—God knows I eat well enough. However, if our criterion for goodness is whether I possess anything like a genuinely well-rounded repertoire of dishes I consistently prepare well, then my credentials are nothing much to boast about. Quite honestly, this has never bothered me much at all.

It's my experience that truly good cooks are born. I was not born to be one, and I don't like being trained, especially if the result is going to be mere competency. I've generally found life a lot more interesting learning to use my limitations than struggling to overcome them.

For example, since I have little patience in getting things just right, I tend to avoid dishes that require a calculated perfection. I'm a compulsive fiddler, so I steer clear of foods that must be set up to run and then left to cook strictly on their own. And since I can't abide following someone else's directions, I rarely prepare anything that I can't get a good mental fix on before I start.

Given such strictures, there is still a lot of cooking I can do that doesn't involve opening cans and defrosting TV dinners —only I've had to go out and find it for myself. I've acquired my cooking know-how on a very ad-hoc, need-to-know basis, which leaves my culinary knowledge full of gaping holes.

For instance, I have no idea of how to make a béchamel sauce, and if I hadn't become a food writer, I probably still wouldn't even know what one was. I waffle on simple things like custards and crepe batters, food I don't much get around to making. (I once spent a good month at perfecting the one-handed flip-and-jerk that turns the perfect omelet over on itself, eating omelets for supper every night. By the time I acquired the knack I was so sick of them I didn't eat another for fifteen years. Now that I've started again, I'm back to folding them over with a spatula.)

In other words, I've learned to cook the way most people do—or did before there were cooking schools—by following my appetite and fulfilling my obligations, picking up what I needed to please myself and anyone else I was cooking for. My personal cuisine had obvious limits, but boundaries can challenge even as they restrict . . . and within the culinary range I had defined for myself, I found much to enthrall me.

But therein lies the rub. As I've come to earn my living writing about food, I regularly have to fend off the assumption that I'm a good cook. Often, I'm not even asked, it being somehow self-evident that if I write about a subject I'm an expert at it (or at least have convinced myself that I am). Implicit in this expectation is its opposite: if I'm not a good cook, then I'm a fraud—or at least something of a capon (one of those armchair appetites who lovingly detail dishes they've conned their wives into confecting).

Professional food folk, especially, are confused and sometimes upset by my lack of interest in the sorts of competencies that most interest them. Why do I write about food at all if I'm not an expert in the art of good cooking, nor do I want my readers to be? Because I think you don't have to be a good cook, or even aspire to be one, to be an *interested* cook.

There's a distinction begging to made here, and to start in at it let's first note that the opposite of a good cook isn't necessarily a bad one. No more am I a good cook than am I a gifted talker, but I still manage to get my points across in an intelligent conversation—not only keeping tabs on such minimal graces as getting my tenses straight and my nouns and verbs in agreement, but also, on occasion, even managing to utter a genuine (and genuinely unrehearsed) *bon mot.*

Even so, just as I anguish over amounts and kinds of seasoning for dishes I've cooked countless times before, fall into confusion over roasting temperatures, and lapse into a blind reverie just as the broth I'm reducing turns into a black, burnt mass, so, too, do I speak with a nasal wheeze, enunciate poorly, mispronounce (and misuse) more words than I care to know, and have the maddening habit of leaping from subject to subject in the course of a single phrase.

Still, I'm not aware that my friends—or students, when I had them—have ever felt I was in desperate need of a public-speaking course. Since I manage to operate within the range of generally accepted competency, such idiosyncrasies are seen as nuances of character, as flavors more than deficits—as consider the general fondness for Truman Capote's *truly* bizarre vocal deportment: it rounded out the whole. And there, on a much more modest scale, go I.

It's also worth noting in this regard that as the years have gone by, my talk has not much improved from what it was when my "style" firmed up in my late teens and early twenties. All sorts of ambitious ideas have gone tumbling through my brain and out of my mouth between then and now, improving my intellect immensely. But none seems to have done much to improve the medium that actually expressed it. My talk is me: my verbal strategies, such as they are, reflect strengths and weaknesses in my character. They are part of my way of being in the world, and I tamper with them at the peril of owning a voice that is a stranger to my soul.

All this is just as true of my cooking. I don't consider myself a poor cook, even less a lazy and self-indulgent one. Very often, I spend days, even weeks, thinking out a dish before I make it and, if I'm unhappy with the results, resolutely go work it out all over again. If I do find myself chafing at some limitation in my knowledge, I'm happy to consult a cookbook—or an expert—for advice.

Of course, just as with my talk, there have been moments when I've had to seize my cooking by the throat and make it perform at a level far beyond its ordinary limits, producing for a special occasion a meal I would serve unashamed to Fernand Point. But then, with a great and heartfelt sigh, I shrink away from the edge . . . back into the person that is me.

For what delights me about cooking is not getting things right but the simple pleasure of getting to know them in the first place. Today, on my daily visit to market, I came across a cabbage—an ordinary plain green one—but one so small and round and appetizingly demure that I had to immediately seize it up. Cradling its smooth, firm, compact form in my hand, I began to whisper in its ear the sweet nothings that would coax it into dinner.

My expectations were nothing complicated or demanding. I would simmer it in some rich broth with lots of sweet tender green peas, season it with flecks of freshly ground pepper and bits of tarragon, stir in a handful of rice to thicken it, maybe with a pat of butter to enrich it. A simple meal, but one to look forward to, even to mentally play with as the day went on, adding something more, removing something else.

For me, this is enough. To pick up some fresh piece of produce or meat and have a dish naturally cohere around it—to lure my appetite into unfolding itself into a satisfactory scheme—all this is what my cooking tries to be about.

The major difference that I see between myself and the good cook is not so much a matter of skill as of architecture. When it comes to food, I like structures that are simple, sturdy, and easily comprehensible, made of substances with direct sensual resonance, all fitted together with a forthright joinery—honest shapes that I can conceive of in their entirety.

Good cooks can entertain more complex culinary architectures in their minds than I, fitting together sophisticated dishes with instructive ease and grace. I admire that: occasionally, presented with some superbly structured dish, I can even grasp it in all its complexity, just as, during one memorable moment, I managed to hear each separate voice in a Bach fugue sounding out its cohering but resolutely contrapuntal song.

For myself, I'm most content when building a meal from a set of simple building blocks, in easily grasped shapes and appetizing primary colors, blocks that can suffer being occa-

sionally knocked over, misplaced, or misused and still be happy
to be played with next time around. I am too clumsy-fisted,
too slow-witted at the stove to attempt much more, and lucky
in an appetite that demands no less.

✦ ✦ ✦

And what's the connection with conversation? Only this: In
my own experience, what makes conversation good, once basic
expectations are met, has very little to do with skill and very
much to do with one's sense—and enjoyment—of the person
or persons being talked to. The more I like you and like talking
to you, the less I find myself talking down—or up—to you.
We simply connect. The best conversation, no matter the subject, lights up two selves at once.

Cooking should be like that, too: done not *for* someone but
with them. For me, there is no happier moment than when I
share a dish with a person who not only enjoys it but who
also understands it—grasps it just as they would a joke or a
thought that I had been anxious to share. For this reason I like
having company in the kitchen while I cook, someone with
whom I can unfold—and discuss—the logic of my making. So
are appetites entwined.

This isn't to say that I don't want to surprise and delight
those I cook for, but that it is their understanding, not their
praise, I truly want. When friends eat together, food should
be as accessible as it is good, just like the conversation. A meal
cooked brilliantly but in a style beyond those who share it sets
up a table where each eater is isolated with his or her own
pleasure—an audience, not company.

In a restaurant, being part of an audience is expected and
right, which is why we all order for ourselves: restaurants are
to cooking as theaters are to talk. But among family and friends,
being even a happy audience is not enough. Talking a meal is
half the fun of eating it . . . and anyone who wants to should
be able to join in.

So there we are. Some good friends are coming over for
supper, the sort of friends who—no matter how many—can
always manage to squeeze in around the kitchen table. The
conversation starts even at the market as we pick out the

shrimp and the hot peppers for the gumbo, and continues around the stove, beer in hand, as we take turns stirring the roux and gamble on how dark we really dare cook it before throwing in the onions and celery and chopped pepper.

The shrimp may not be as tender as they could be, but they will not be tough either—for if we're not good cooks, we know enough to keep from being bad ones. The glass or two of beer will make us a little light-headed, and we will talk louder than we should and thus make more obvious the sudden pauses when we discover, to mild astonishment, that our subject has completely escaped us.

But our friends, who have come simply to partake and enjoy, will worry about none of these things. And, because this is a sharing and not a performance, neither will we. There's a lot more to cooking than being good at it.

KITCHEN DIARY: SOME THOUGHTS ON OMELETS

As an Egg Pudding. It may come as good news to those who, like myself, lack the knack of flipping an omelet and must ignominiously fold it over with a fork, that there is an omelet heresy put forth by Colonel A. Kenney-Herbert in his *Fifty Luncheons* (circa 1895). He argues that an omelet should not be folded at all. "Books that counsel you to turn an omelet, to fold it, to let it brown on one side, to let it fry for five minutes, etc., are not to be trusted. If you follow such advice you will produce, at best, a neat-looking egg pudding." I like this, for it is not merely an opinion that is being calmly flung into the face of received culinary wisdom. Given that omelets by nature are egg puddings of *some* sort, the Colonel's must have differed from the ordinary kind most obviously in their singular untidiness.

As Sent Straight to Hell. There's also a story attached to that short period in my life when I actually did manage by dint of fanatical practice to master an omelet-flipping wrist snap. My

Lower East Side apartment, like many such, had the bathtub in the kitchen. One evening, making my nightly omelet supper (for, having no food to waste in idle practice, I made a meal of each of my efforts, night after night), I gave the flip a little too much wrist. The omelet flew out of the pan and soared across the room to the furthermost corner, where it landed with a soft plop on the rim of the tub. It hesitated there a second and then, with the barest discernible sigh, slid down the wall out of sight.

I realized at once there was no way to retrieve it. No arm would fit down the crack between wall and tub. Its ungainly size and giant feet prohibited any omelet-fishing with broom handle from below. Suddenly, the pedestrian act of supper-making was transformed into a theological demonstration of the irreversible nature of a sinful act, where redemption was possible only through the intervention of divine grace. In this instance, however, no epiphany occurred. It stayed where it fell and for all I know is there still. And rather than repentance, after the astonishment and disbelief, I have to confess that I felt instead an unholy but truly delicious sense of glee. One omelet sent straight to hell.

As My Introduction to Julia Child. The source of inspiration for this bout of omelet-making was a gift from my grandmother of the just-published *Mastering the Art of French Cooking*, by Simone Beck, Louisette Bertholle, and Julia Child—which celebrated its thirtieth anniversary on October 16, 1991. (Knopf must have realized it was issuing a classic: I've never seen a book before or since with the exact *day* of publication printed on the copyright page.)

Mastering the Art of French Cooking was then (1961)—and for some years afterward—one of just four cookbooks that made up my entire culinary library. (For the record, the other three were Ann Rogers's *Cookbook for Poor Poets (and Others)*, Joyce Chen's Chinese cookbook, and a battered paperback copy of the 11th edition of Fannie Farmer's *Boston Cooking School Cook Book*.)

Julia Child. With all due respect to the other two authors, hers was the voice that spoke to me out of its pages and so it is by her name that I remember that book. Of course, her television persona helped with the task of name recognition, but even before that, there was no question that it was not so much the contents of the book that made me treasure it as the voice that spoke to me out of it.

Before her, as after, there were food writers who knew as much about French cooking as she did—some, unquestionably, even more. But she was the first who was able to write about French cooking in resolutely American speech and with unabashed and unembarrassed American enthusiasm and appetite.

She not only broke through the snob barrier—for without her, haute cuisine would have remained in the possession of such culinary mandarins as Roy Andries de Groot—but she also showed the way for American sensibilities to play with the possibilities inherent in French cuisine without surrendering their own native tastes and voices. All good reasons to take this opportunity to say, again, thank you. No one else in the world could have got me, at nineteen, to add a tin-lined copper omelet pan to my neolithic *batterie de cuisine*, or to then pour into it a bag of navy beans and spend a whole weekend in my primitive kitchen using them as a means of practicing the flip.

MADE
TO
TASTE

MANGIAMACCHERONI

✦ ✦ ✦

1

Before we started the CIT man straightened his tie, looked severely at us, and said: "Please, as a favor, do not disgrace the pasta and use a spoon!" . . . I am not certain, however, that the spoon in some cases isn't preferable to the manner in which many supposedly sophisticated Italians handle their pasta; somewhat like the Chinese with chopsticks, they push their faces close to the plate, sending in a continuous stream of pasta. A most unappetizing sight, even if it is done with gusto.

—Jack Denton Scott, *The Complete Book of Pasta*

One special word about the fine art of eating spaghetti. . . . You will note that many Italians, at least in the less elegant restaurants, do not cut these "little strings." They take up a few strands on the fork, plant the tines of the fork securely in the bowl of a large spoon and twist (clockwise) until the spaghetti is wound up into a little ball of yarn, so to speak, then pop it in and start winding up the next mouthful. No, it is not dainty, and I am told by Italian Emily Posts that nowadays "the best people" are not doing it any more. Against this I must register my alien protest. It is impossible to be dainty eating spaghetti.

—Sydney Clark, *All the Best in Italy*

Riffle through the pages of any illustrated pasta cookbook with even a modest historical perspective—Vincenzo Buonassisi's *Pasta*, Massimo Alberini's introduction to Anna Martini's *Pasta & Pizza*, Anna Del Conte's *Portrait of Pasta*, and especially Julia della Croce's lovely *Pasta Classica*—and concentrate entirely on the pictures. You'll see something to thrill and astonish the small child who still lingers deep within you: scene after scene of people eating pasta, alone and in groups, young and old, men, women, and children, at home and in the street . . . and each and every one of them *eating it with their fingers*.

Although often good-humored, these drawings are not meant to be taken as merely humorous. Dating from as late as the beginning of this century, they are straightforward depictions of fact. Pasta was originally eaten, at least by the poor, in exactly the way we still naïvely intuit it should be: by plucking a generous pinch of sauce-soaked strands and raising them up high enough—which is very high indeed—so that the lips can grasp them and the mouth suck them down in a series of voluptuous gulps.

Since Marco Polo did not, as we are insistently instructed in all these volumes, bring pasta back from China, he might have done his fellow Italians a good turn instead and brought them chopsticks—those simple, useful, egalitarian eating tools, so perfect for catching up and conveying noodles to the mouth, as the customers of countless Chinese noodle stalls demonstrate every day. But if neatness and efficiency go to the Chinese, sheer fun belongs to the Italians—looking at any of those old pictures, you can't help but smile.

Unlike our other two familiar supper starches, rice and potatoes, pasta is an *invention*, created at a time when manners were less inhibited, the relationship to food more intimate and vital. We find the idea of eating pasta with our fingers vulgar, but *vulgaris* means "common"—and for the longest time pasta was anything but. Its single ingredient, white flour, was affordable only by the privileged few. The Italian nobility found nothing wrong with eating pasta with their fingers—after all, there was always the tablecloth to wipe them on.

Eventually, the upper classes did find this way of eating pasta a tad churlish, but only because the churls had begun eating pasta, too. Class distinctions had to be maintained. As flour became cheap and noodle vendors fought for street space in Italian cities, the educated classes took to eating their pasta with utensils, thus abandoning to the *ignoranti* the pleasurable task of preserving the original gusto—and the original logic— of this wonderful invention.

Of course, in Italy it was not quite seen this way. My favorite picture in *Pasta Classica* shows a baffled monk, knife in one hand and fork in the other, who has hoisted up a mass of pasta between them and has no idea what to do next. Here is the classic *mangiamaccheroni*—someone who doesn't know how to eat pasta except with his fingers. When, much more recently, the poor became able to afford eating utensils and were shamed into using them, the *eleganzia* one-upped them again and pro- hibited the use of spoons.

Children take great delight in eating spaghetti, grasping the squirmy strands and cramming them into their mouths, coating hands and faces with the sauce. Adults who have been table trained, however, can be unnerved by this experience. Italians claim that the fork was invented because noble visitors to the Bourbon court in Naples in the time of Ferdinand II were discomfited by the idea of eating pasta with their fingers—but were they any less nonplussed when presented with a fork? Strands are always wriggling free from it, escaping back to the plate, and scattering as they do bits of sauce on napkin, shirt- front, tablecloth.

Shame, as we all know, has two faces: both hide themselves behind the hands—but one of them peeps out between the fingers. The same impulse that has coerced you into twiddling those pasta strands around the fork tines can suddenly invert itself. Then you find yourself wrestling, not with the pasta, but with the temptation to rip off the tight collar, to shove away the delicate little pile of pasta on its elegant china plate, and to rush into the kitchen and plunge your hands right into the pot.

This tension—as much a struggle between rich and poor as it is between appetite and restraint—is the reason that almost every pasta book feels compelled to explain how pasta should be eaten . . . which is to say, how it should *not* be eaten. There are two essential rules. The first is: eat your pasta with a fork. (Don't use your fingers; don't use a spoon.) "When it comes to eating utensils you only need a fork," says Fred Plotkin in a section called "Some Thoughts on Eating Pasta" in his *Authentic Pasta Book*. Then, afraid you might not have gotten the point, he repeats it in the next paragraph: "The fork is the basic implement for eating pasta." Don't *you*, these books say over and over again, be a *mangiamaccheroni*.

2

> In Italian art as much space has been given to the joys of pasta eating as Hogarth, Rowlandson, Gilray, and all their lesser imitators devoted to beer, gin, and wine. From Naples, in particular, came an almost endless stream of colored lithographs showing the Neapolitan lazzaroni—who were literally born, lived, and died in the streets—enjoying their daily portion of pasta. Many of these, although astonishingly vivid and controlled in their line and colour, are the work of anonymous artists. . . .
> —Enrica and Vernon Jarratt, *The Complete Book of Pasta*

The second rule for eating pasta—don't eat too much!—likewise serves to drive home this all-encompassing, anti-*mangiamaccheroni* admonition. If, in Italian, a *maccherone* is a blockhead, a dolt, a numskull, a *maccheronata* is a beanfeast—a big feed. Macaroni, the primal Italian food, has become their synonym for appetite, for hunger and its satiety. But like all of us, Italians are both drawn to and repelled by what inspires their own carnality, an ambivalence made all the stronger by macaroni's *élan vital*.

Consequently, at the same time that Italian mamas scold their children, and, for that matter, recalcitrant papas, to use their forks, and to not gorge themselves as if they were starving, they decorate their dining rooms with colorful lithographs

showing *lazzaroni*—street urchins—enjoying themselves in just
this prohibited way. Appetite is cute in the young, understandable in the poor: combine the two images and the result is
irresistible: pure Italian kitsch.

In all these pictures, the scene is very much the same. The
spaghetti vendor stands over a large shallow pan, resting on
a brazier, in which a huge mound of pasta steams; sometimes,
a reserve pile of cooked pasta waits in a bowl nearby, from
which he can replenish the pan. Behind him, their necks inverted into a rack, are the small round flasks of wine he also
sells. And, lastly, by his side, is another bowl—this one full
of grated cheese, occasionally decorated with a tastefully placed
carnation.

The emphasis in all these illustrations is on the pasta. There
is always plenty of it, and it is always dispensed with a generous hand. Although these vendors usually offered a simple
tomato sauce for another penny, it is almost never shown.
These pictures are all variations on a single theme, and that
theme is having enough to eat—enough *pasta* to eat.

Furthermore, such pictures—and their number is legion—
tell only half the story. Italy is traditionally a fuel-poor country,
and our romantic image of that cuisine's rich, meaty, long-
simmered pasta sauces ignores what, for the poor, was and is
a very different reality. Helen Campbell writes in *In Foreign
Kitchens* (1893):

> Fuel is costly and the price of prepared food the merest trifle
> beyond its value uncooked; and thus many a family relies al-
> together upon cook-shops, from which ascends the smell of
> ever-boiling broth bubbling in huge caldrons. In the windows
> are mountains of smoking-hot, golden polenta; heaps of fried
> minnows, crisp and brown; mounds of rice; great dishes of
> stewed snails, dear to all Italians. . . . Here come the gondoliers
> to bargain for dinner with the cooks, whose huge ladles indicate
> what may be skimmed from those bubbling depths.

This was in Venice; in Naples and elsewhere, the starch was
pasta, not corn or rice, and these same pasta stalls also served
as cookshops for the poor and not-so-poor alike, many cus-

tomers whisking their purchases home to dress them as they pleased.

Such saucing was inevitably quick and simple. The pasta dishes of the humble, whether wolfed down on the street or consumed at home, were a thing apart from the complexly dressed pastas made in kitchens that could afford not only such luxuries as cream and meat, but the stove and the fuel required to cook them.

Indeed, it might be suggested—adopting for a moment Lorenza de Medici's terminology in *The Renaissance of Italian Cooking*—that, quite apart from the regional variations in pasta dishes, Italy has two essentially distinct pasta cuisines: that of the poor (*pasta povera*), heavy in pasta and light in sauce, and that of the rich (*pasta alto-borghese*), in which the sauce predominates, if not in quantity, at least in culinary importance.*

In his book *Sweetness and Power*, Sidney Mintz quotes from a monograph on a Southern Bantu people called the Bemba, whose preferred starch, *ubwali* (thick balls of cooked millet), is, as he puts it in a luminous phrase, "the nutritive anchor of an entire culture." Bemba cuisine is divided between food and relishes, with the food being the *ubwali* and the relish— *umunani*—being what is eaten with it to give it flavor: meat, caterpillars, locusts, ants, vegetables, mushrooms, etc. No matter how much *umunani* comes with the meal, it is the *ubwali* that is the food. Mintz describes some Bantu eating roasted grain off four or five corncobs, only to shout to their fellows later, "We have not had a bite to eat all day. . . ."

This distinction is one that appears again and again in human culture. It is as familiar to us as bread and butter—which is one of the few foods that we still *do* eat with our fingers, even at formal dinners. A fresh-baked loaf of bread, still hot from the oven, is something that we can easily imagine eating in

---

* If there is any merit to these distinctions, then still another might be extrapolated from them—that of Italian-American pasta dishes, made out of the *povera* tradition of generous servings of pasta, but sauced with plenty of meat and cheese from a newfound *abbondanza*. This third category—let's call it *pasta contadini*—is one that is understandably unsettling to rich and poor *Italian* Italians alike, but no less valid (and no less "authentic") for all that.

almost unlimited quantities, given enough butter to "grease its way down."

When poor people prosper, their first impulse is to have as much food as they can eat, and enough relish to dress it well. They then learn to redefine "food" to embrace a larger category of eatables, although the original, basic food retains an honored place at the meal. And always, *with that food alone*, the sense of the defining original balance remains. Just as we look askance at someone who puts too much butter on their bread, Italians abhor the idea of heaping sauce onto a dish of pasta. For them, rich or poor, it is still the spaghetti, not the sauce, that is the food.

3

When we first went to Naples . . . Italy was poor, Naples was very poor, and some areas, including the San Lorenzo Quarter where we worked in the medical school, were truly poverty stricken. But every day . . . we saw little heaps of spaghetti and macaroni on the street curbs put out by the local families for the neighborhood cats to demolish.
—Ancel and Margaret Keys, *How to Eat Well and Stay Well the Mediterranean Way*

How much pasta *should* we eat? Let Corby Kummer—in his piece on that subject in the July 1986 *Atlantic*—speak for all: "The standard portion in Italy, and the size recommended on packages, is two ounces. This is fine for a first course to cut the appetite without killing it. I find three ounces an ideal portion for a main course, but hungry people might prefer four."

Such recommended portion sizes may be provided in the spirit of public information, but they have a subtext that serves equally as a threat. What if a hungry person prefers *five* ounces? Well, they had better keep their mouth shut. What else is Anna Del Conte saying when she writes in *Pasta Perfect*: "I am often asked if my quantities [generally three ounces per person] are for first or main courses, but in fact I find it makes surprisingly little difference, and that people eat the same amount whether there is a main course of meat or fish, or just a salad, to follow"?*

People, of course, eat what they are given. But who is it exactly who decided—once and for all, it seems—how much that amount should be? Or perhaps we should ask who set the standard portion in *Italy*, for it is upon this unnamed authority that all our own pasta writers seem to lean. Strangely, in the ten books whose sole subject is pasta—and in the many others that treat it in some detail—consulted in the preparation of this piece, not one attempts to answer this question, or whether this standard portion really is the amount of pasta that Italians really eat when they sit down at the table.

The notion of Italians, an anarchistic tribe of eaters if ever there was one, all carefully measuring out their little 125-gram portions is so ridiculous that perhaps it need only be mentioned to be dismissed. But it is good to know for sure about such things, and, as it happens, Ancel and Margaret Keys were interested in this question and, contrary to the usual practice, went out and asked around—in homes, restaurants, and taxicabs—all over central and southern Italy. They report their answer in *How to Eat Well and Stay Well the Mediterranean Way* (the earliest and still the best book on that topic):

> In private homes in Italy the size of the pasta portion depends on the physical activity of the family and the make-up of the rest of the meal. For the farm laborer or stone mason the portion may be 200 grams (almost 7 ounces) or more. A farmer, his wife, and teenage child will use a half-kilogram package of pasta (roughly 18 ounces) for a meal—even more during the planting or harvesting seasons.

* How many readers have *ever* encountered—outside a restaurant—pasta served as a first course? Food writers toss this off so casually that it must be a regular occurrence in their lives. Not in mine—nor in anyone else's I know. Americans don't generally eat pasta as a first course. Why, then, do these books keep mentioning it as if we did? Because the notion of pasta as an *appetizer* lends more credence to the doctrine of small portions—and genteel pasta eating—just as Anna Del Conte uses it here.

In other words, Italians eat as much pasta as they want and need. Until recently, most Italian housewives bought their pasta loose. When they cooked it, they tossed in a handful for every eater, plus a handful for the pot. Papa might get a bigger handful than peckish Aunt Sophia, but the rule was always that there must be plenty for everybody, which is why those poor Neapolitans set out the remains of last night's supper for the kitties. No matter how poor a family was, it prided itself on having enough pasta for everyone to eat their fill—which meant that there would always be a little left over that no one could be convinced to eat.

What the Keyses also discovered was that after everyone, young and old, large and small, rich and poor, had had his fill, the *average* consumption of pasta was between four and five ounces per person per meal. Once pasta is put up in packages, however, that "average" portion is transformed into the "recommended" portion . . . a very different thing. A handful for everyone at the table and one more for the pot is no longer possible. This is the tyranny of prepackaged food: enforced portion control. Once a family is convinced to buy its pasta by the package, servings become divisible not by appetite but by the amount in the box.

All but the smallest-sized pasta is sold in Italy in 500-gram packages, a weight just a fraction over a pound. This means that standardized—hence "official"—Italian pasta recipes translate easily into American ones. We accept this assigned amount without question, partly because such portioning has long been part of our way of eating, partly because it has become tacitly understood that only the worst sort of glutton would break this social code and ask for more than his or her fair share.

"Fatso," "slob," "pig"—this is *our* translation of *mangiamaccheroni*, and it explains why food writers are so reluctant to reveal that many Italian families still do not let cookbooks, or any pasta package, dictate the amount of spaghetti that they are going to eat. Whatever else these writers picked up about pasta in Italy, they learned that to have too much of an appetite for it is to appear slovenly and gross; genteel people eat it delicately, in modest quantities—the more modest, the more genteel . . . and that last word, in America, means, especially, the more thin.

Such snobbism, alas, is infinitely contagious. Waverley Root, a man not noted for his abstinence, wrote in *The Cooking of Italy*: "In poorer homes, the main course is sometimes skipped and an abundant helping of pasta serves to blunt, if not to satisfy, the appetite. . . ." If anyone knew that an abundant helping of pasta can itself be a main course, entirely satisfying to the appetite, it was he—but to admit such a thing must have come too close to declaring himself a common glutton.

About eight years ago, I noticed that the G. B. Ratto catalogue sold five-pound cartons of various kinds of pasta made by D. Merlino & Sons, an Oakland firm (for a tasting note on these, see page 108 below). I had only to see a picture of that bigger box of spaghetti for a sense of sweet illumination to spread through my consciousness. I took an empty tin, filled it with the contents of half a dozen linguine packages, and from then on just reached in and took out a fistful when the pasta pot was set to boil.

Being able to take as much as you want makes you notice what it is that you hold in your hand. Now, no longer squinting to see if I had taken exactly a quarter of the box, I was able to concentrate on the feel of the pasta, to notice its solidity, its accumulated heft. I learned that those dry, fragile, slightly nubbly strands are nice to hold. There's something pleasant in letting them slip through the fingers until you find that good weight. And if I took too much . . . well, in those days, I had a dog.

Perhaps not uncoincidentally, this same period saw the growth in my interest in simple pasta sauces, if "sauce" is the right word for spaghetti tossed with some olive oil and a spoonful of *olivada*, or minced parsley, garlic, and anchovy bits. But whether it was sauced or merely seasoned with flavorful condiments, the result produced a filling, satisfying meal.

And how much pasta did I eat? I honestly don't know. But I do know that I've eaten steaks—not counting the garnish of fried onions or the baked potato—that carried more calories than a whole pound of pasta. I found I could take all the spaghetti I wanted, cook it, dress it to taste, and have a filling supper that, with a glass of wine, was, as my suppers went, a relatively moderate one.

Even so, even so . . . after about a year of this, without my really noticing it, the light was snuffed out. I found myself back to carefully eyeballing the contents of individual packages, measuring each portion to make sure I wasn't taking more than I ought. It's not easy to find permission to help yourself when every pasta box and every pasta book—for that matter, every book that gives a pasta recipe—tells you that your portion should never be larger than four ounces—preferably less—or you're nothing but a pig.

Pasta prudery. One price we pay for it is an overemphasis on sauce. Because we don't eat pasta like bread, we can't imagine it as being like bread—something that might be good by itself, with just a little butter. How could we, when we depend on what is *on* the pasta to fill us up? It is as much this as anything that makes us skip through Italian pasta cookbooks for the richest sauces—pesto, carbonara, bolognese, alfredo— and why, to the consternation of Italians, we want to grate cheese on *every* pasta dish.

What appear on the following pages are some ways of eating pasta that give permission to clearly experience the pasta, not the sauce, as the food that makes the meal—and to discover that eating it to a pleasant surfeit on occasion will not necessarily make you fat. It may also tempt you to momentarily liberate yourself from a cultural conditioning even more strongly engrained than the one that forbids drinking soup from the bowl, and eat some with your fingers.

In *An Omelette and a Glass of Wine*, Elizabeth David describes how she used to meet that old rascal Norman Douglas for a meal of pasta at a small, seedy café in Antibes. "At the restaurant he would produce from his pocket a hunk of Parmesan cheese. 'Ask Pascal to be so good as to grate this at our table. Poor stuff, my dear, that Gruyère they give you in France. Useless for macaroni.' And a bunch of fresh basil for the sauce. 'Tear the leaves, mind. Don't chop them. Spoils the flavour.' "

I suppose that when Elizabeth David writes "for the sauce" she means that these two ingredients were to be added to it, not that they would make it up. Even so, when I first read this passage, I saw a terrace flooded with Mediterranean light, two glasses of that astringent, thin, yet surprisingly potent Provençal wine already set on the small, round table, and Pascal himself bringing out a heaping bowl of pasta, shimmering in a dressing of oil and cheese, flecked with bits of pepper and torn basil leaf. This misreading was immediate and convincing: it was exactly the meal I was just learning I would have wanted there myself.

CHEESE

The original "two-cents plain" (*al due*) of the Neapolitan street vendors was a plate of pasta sprinkled with grated cheese. (According to Vincenzo Buonassisi, sauce—made from tomatoes cooked down in their own juices and seasoned only with a little pepper and basil—was strictly extra [*al tre*].) Any grating cheese may be used to dress pasta, but most versions calling for Parmesan add butter as well.

SPAGHETTI WITH CHEESE AND PEPPER
(ADAPTED FROM *PASTA & PIZZA*, BY ANNA MARTINI)

Spaghetti   *Black pepper*
Pecorino Romano

Cook the pasta and drain it, but not too well. Dress at once with a handful of grated cheese per person and plenty of freshly grated black pepper, sprinkling over a tablespoon or so of the cooking water, if necessary, to transform the melted cheese into a "lovely creamy sauce." Vernon Jarratt notes in *The Complete Book of Pasta* that "in Lazio, whence this dish comes, the peppercorns are pounded in a mortar rather than ground, adding to the rustic simplicity of the dish."

Afterword. Colman Andrews wrote when the above recipe originally appeared in *Simple Cooking* to offer the following amendment: "Though the method you give seems to be more or less agreed upon, I got another opinion from a well-known Roman-born restaurateur in Los Angeles named Mauro Vincenti, who is something of an amateur historian/philosopher of food. Rather than letting some water remain to help form a creamy coating with the cheese, he says, the real Roman way of doing it is to drain the pasta very, very well, so that it is as dry as possible, and then bathe it in a bit of fat rendered from *guanciale* (cured, unsmoked pork jowl—the favored pork accent for pasta in Lazio) or at least from pancetta to coat all the strands before tossing it with the cheese and pepper. The spaghetti should be cooked, Vincenti adds, *filo de ferro* or 'iron string,' which is firmer than *al dente*. That's the way the chef makes the *spaghetti cacio e pepe* at one of his restaurants here (both the iron string and the pancetta part), and it is indeed superb."

HERBS

One of the simplest pasta sauces is made by tearing some fresh herb into small bits and tossing these with a good olive oil into a bowl of steaming pasta. A small quantity of almost any likely herb—oregano, thyme, marjoram, chive—used before the subtler notes of its aroma have had a chance to evaporate, is usually enough to give the dish the right amount of savor; only basil and parsley should be used in larger quantities than a sprig. Even an herb as potent as sage (again, only if fresh) can make a surprisingly delicious sauce when a leaf or two is minced and heated in melted butter with plenty of ground pepper. Here is another herbal sauce, made from parsley, which Sicilian coachmen once prepared for themselves at curbside while waiting for a fare.

COACHMAN'S SPAGHETTI (SICILY)
(ADAPTED FROM *THE ART OF SICILIAN COOKING*,
BY ANNA MUFFOLETTO)

Several sprigs parsley	*Pasta*
Garlic	*Olive oil*
Pecorino Romano	*Freshly ground black pepper*

Use a lot of parsley, mincing it together with the garlic. Grate
some Romano. While the pasta cooks, heat a little olive oil in
a frying pan. Sprinkle in the minced herb and remove the pan
from the heat. Drain the pasta, return it to the pot, and turn
into it the herb-garlic-oil mixture and the cheese. Mix this well,
season generously with pepper, and serve. Since the Romano
is salty, you may find no additional salt is necessary.

VARIATION: In *The Regional Italian Kitchen*, Nika Hazelton
gives a Tuscan green sauce which is made similarly, but with
butter instead of olive oil and Parmesan instead of Romano
(and using rather a bit more of both!). Here the pasta emerges
from the pot bathed "in a sort of creamy green sauce."

LEMONS

VERMICELLI WITH LEMON AND OLIVE OIL
(ADAPTED FROM *THE COMPLETE BOOK OF PASTA*,
BY ENRICA AND VERNON JARRATT)

Vermicelli	*Fruity olive oil*
A few leaves of parsley	*Freshly squeezed lemon juice*
A large sprig of basil	*Salt and white pepper*

While the pasta is cooking, tear the parsley and basil leaves
into little bits. Drain the pasta, but not too well. Toss the pasta
with the torn herbs. When this is well mixed, add olive oil,

lemon juice, and salt and pepper, as if dressing a salad. This is one of the few pasta dishes Italians actually eat cold.

VARIATIONS: Fred Plotkin adds a little minced garlic. Also a very ripe tomato, skinned, seeded, and sliced, might be tossed in.

CANNED FISH

There are many Italian pasta recipes utilizing canned anchovies and tuna, but almost none that allows for the use of anything but fresh sardines. Why? Possibly because fresh sardines (in Italy a species different from our own) are quite delicate in flavor and texture; if the same dish were made with canned ones, the effect would become hopelessly oily and fishy. However, the olive oil alone from a sardine can—plus lemon juice, minced garlic and parsley, and ground pepper—makes a delicious pasta dressing by itself, and one of my very favorite impromptu pasta dishes came from the remains of a can of smoked oysters (using all of the liquid and mincing the last of the oysters), tossed into hot cooked pasta with lots of minced parsley.

SPAGHETTI COUNTRY-STYLE (SARDINIA)
(ADAPTED FROM *ITALIAN REGIONAL COOKING*, BY ADA BONI)

Fresh garlic
Sprig of fresh oregano
Spaghetti
Olive oil

Anchovy fillets preserved in olive oil
Pecorino Romano or Parmesan

Mince some garlic and the sprig of fresh oregano together. While the pasta cooks, heat some olive oil in a skillet. Drain the anchovy fillets. When the oil is hot, lower the heat and put in the fillets (one per serving), gradually working them into a paste with the tines of a fork. Then stir in the minced garlic and oregano and remove from the heat. Drain the cooked pasta, return to the pot, and toss with the oil, anchovy, garlic, and herb mixture. Let sit for 2 or 3 minutes before serving with the grated cheese.

VARIATION: Marcella Hazan, in *Marcella's Italian Kitchen*, offers a version made as above but including as well black olives and toasted bread crumbs (about which see "Stale Bread" just below).

STALE BREAD

SPAGHETTI WITH CROUTONS AND PROSCIUTTO
(ADAPTED FROM *PASTA*, BY VINCENZO BUONASSISI)

Spaghetti
Butter
Minced salt pork or pork fat
Prosciutto (or country ham), cut
   into strips

Small croutons of good stale bread
Black pepper

While the pasta cooks, melt some butter in a skillet. When hot, fry the bits of salt pork until crisp, then add the prosciutto and croutons, turning them with a spatula so that the ham is wilted and the croutons lightly toasted. Toss with the cooked, drained pasta, grating in plenty of pepper.

VARIATIONS: The simplest form of pasta made with stale bread involves tearing the bread into coarse crumbs, toasting these in a richly flavored olive oil until golden brown, and tossing this mixture, along with some minced parsley, into hot spaghetti. Season with salt and black pepper. Giuliano Bugialli, in his pasta book, offers a Tuscan version that also incorporates a crushed clove of fresh garlic.

EGGS

SPAGHETTI WITH FRIED EGGS
(ADAPTED FROM *PASTA*, BY VINCENZO BUONASSISI)

Thin spaghetti   Salt
Butter (olive oil)   Parmesan
Egg(s)   Black pepper

While the pasta cooks, heat some butter (or a mixture of butter and olive oil) in a skillet. When it is hot, slip in one egg per person and fry until the white has set but not the yolk. Salt and remove from the heat. Drain the pasta when done and divide into portions. Place a fried egg and a share of the pan butter on each. Serve with the grated Parmesan. The egg should be broken up and stirred into the pasta with the cheese before it is eaten, and the dish seasoned with salt and pepper.

VARIATION: Anna Del Conte gives a similar version in *Pasta Perfect* made with garlic, hot pepper flakes, olive oil, and Romano.

OLIVES

SPAGHETTI WITH CAPERS AND BLACK OLIVES (APULIA)
(ADAPTED FROM *THE MONDADORI REGIONAL ITALIAN COOKBOOK*, BY ANNA MARTINI)

Spaghetti   Red pepper flakes
Capers   Olive oil
Black Mediterranean-style olives   Tomato paste

While the pasta is cooking, drain and chop the capers. Pit the olives, tear the flesh into pieces, and put these with the capers in a bowl with a pinch of red pepper flakes and some olive oil. Stir in just enough tomato paste to add some flavor—in the same proportion as vinegar to oil in a vinaigrette. Drain the cooked pasta, return to the pot, and toss with the sauce. Let sit for a few minutes before serving.

VARIATION: Instead of the olives, use a spoonful of *olivada* —which *condimento*, of course, serves as a fine sauce by itself.

OLIVE OIL

Of course, the simplest way with pasta is to sauce it with some good olive oil and to eat it with a pepper mill and a bowl of coarse salt by your elbow. Pasta and olive oil . . . like bread and butter, you never know how good it is until you make a meal of it, all alone—that is, all by itself and all by yourself. Both the olive oil and the pasta should be as good as you can get, if only because eating them like this is the best way to discover how good they can be—to know, once again, the satisfaction of that most primordial of combinations, starch and fat. Of all the 653 pasta recipes in Vincenzo Buonassisi's superlative codex, *Pasta*, the humblest of them all is #35. It is called simply "fried pasta" and is described as an old Neapolitan dish. To say the name is to know the recipe: you take any kind of leftover pasta set aside for the cat, fry it in hot olive oil, salt it, and eat it.

A plate of pan-fried pasta! It immediately calls up the image of a midnight meal, of doors locked, shutters fastened, of the hot stove, the moist steam of the pasta water, the rich smell of heating oil. Bread and butter, even toasted bread and butter, is one thing, fried bread is another . . . and the same is true here. Crisp, yielding, everywhere greasy, fried pasta is messy, vulgar, and almost feral in its need for privacy. All cuisines have a dish like this at their very heart, food that simply, fiercely, says: Eat.

☛ For further exploration, try Fred Plotkin's Calabrese pasta sauce of sliced raw onion, olive oil, and hot pepper flakes in *The Authentic Pasta Book*; Mary Taylor Simeti's Sicilian pesto of basil, almonds, and raw tomatoes in *Pomp and Sustenance*; and, for the truly adventurous, the spaghetti with basil and whole cloves of uncooked garlic in *Bugialli on Pasta*.

A NOTE ON *AGLIO E OLIO*

Those who are particularly addicted to spaghetti and to garlic will find this dish excellent, others will probably abominate it.   —Elizabeth David, *Italian Food*

Garlic mixed with olive oil is very possibly the most ancient and primitive of all the condiments of the poor. And, at least before olive oil became the relatively expensive commodity it now is in Italy, *spaghetti con aglio e olio* was one of the last resorts of the hungry—and thus, in that special sense, it is in the minds of many Italians the very first sauce of all. As Giuliano Bugialli wrote in *Bugialli on Pasta*:

> *Aglio e olio* is the simplest of vegetable or herb dressings for pasta, and it is still the most used, in many small variations, all over Italy. It seems reasonable to regard it as possibly the oldest of all dressings.

Because it is good, filling, and quick to make, all Italians, poor or not, turn to *spaghetti con aglio e olio* when they are simply ravenous, something that must have been communicated to Fred Plotkin, since this is the one dish where (in his *Authentic*

Pasta Book) he admits to eating more than the standard pasta ration—a third, rather than a quarter, of a pound. ("This recipe is for a *very copious* serving, but people like to eat a *great deal* of this [italics mine]"—really a lot of noise for only one and a third more ounces of spaghetti.)

The simplest version of *spaghetti con aglio e olio* calls for the garlic to be minced or crushed and mixed with the oil into hot pasta, still damp from a strictly cursory draining. This is the method to follow for those who want the strongest contrast of flavors, and some seek to enhance the polarity further by using a fruity, sediment-rich oil and grating or crushing the garlic directly into the pasta.

A mellower effect may be obtained by mincing the garlic and then warming (but not frying) it in the oil over a very low flame, to which mixture can be added, if one desires, some minced herb—usually parsley, cilantro, or fresh basil—with the amounts of all these ingredients to be judged by one's own appetite and taste.

Possibly the most popular variation on this dish is *spaghetti con aglio, olio, e peperoncino*, in which a small (or not so small!) amount of fresh or dried hot pepper is added, enriching the flavor of the sauce and enhancing the sense of heat already provided by the garlic. This unabating, lubricious warmth, so soothing to the appetite, is surely one of the subliminal attractions of the mixture. This dish comes from the Abruzzi mountains, but it has been adopted by Italians everywhere, often prepared, note Enrica and Vernon Jarratt, "by the husband for himself and a few surviving cronies when they get home at one in the morning after a serious night's drinking to find the lady of the house fast asleep."

The version in Carlo Middione's *The Food of Southern Italy*—from Basilicata, the province that makes up the instep of the Italian boot—pounds together whole dried chile peppers and cloves of garlic in a mortar to produce a sauce of compelling pungency (see adaptation below) . . . so much so that, Middione claims, compared to it, the hot dishes of the American South and Southwest are "mere embers compared to roaring flames."

The more elegant versions of *spaghetti con aglio, olio, e pepe-*

roncino direct that both the garlic and hot pepper be strained out of the oil before the pasta is dressed. But as Ada Boni comments in *Italian Regional Cooking*, "this, curiously enough, does not happen when the dish is served in a *trattoria*. . . . On the contrary, there is a great willingness to provide both extra garlic and chili . . . ," showing that in Italy, as in this country, such dishes find in these establishments their last bastion against encroaching gentility.

Instead, if elegance is desired, incorporate some fresh butter. In *Honey from a Weed*, Patience Gray describes the evolution of this version. The first, the Mantuan School, insists that the garlic be sliced and fried a moment in hot olive oil—just until the slices turn color. Then, retrieved from the pan, these pieces are used with fresh butter to flavor *al dente* spaghetti, with or without chopped parsley and/or grated Parmesan.* "The other school of thought," she writes:

> cherishes the fragrance which emanates from sliced cloves of fresh garlic, particularly when . . . newly pulled in June, coming in contact with hot spaghetti in a heated white china bowl in which a tablespoon of olive oil is warming. In this case, butter is lavishly added, and chopped parsley or basil, with plenty of Parmesan mixed in.

MACCHERONI DI FUOCO/FIERY MACARONI
(ADAPTED FROM CARLO MIDDIONE'S
THE FOOD OF SOUTHERN ITALY)

¼ cup good fruity olive oil plus 1 tablespoon
3 or 4 cloves of garlic, peeled
4 to 6 dried small chile pods, stemmed and (if wished) seeded

Salt
1 pound spaghetti

Heat the quarter cup of oil in a small skillet over medium heat. Add the garlic and peppers. Stir until the garlic turns gold.

---

* This puts to the lie, by the by, Giuliano Bugialli's flat dictum in *Bugialli on Pasta*: "I cannot state strongly enough that grated cheese is *never* added to any *aglio-olio* preparation."

Turn this into a mortar with a teaspoon of salt and pound into a paste. Thin this to a thick sauce with a spoonful or so of pasta water. Cook the pasta in salted water *al dente*. Drain not too well and toss with the remaining oil. Serve in warmed bowls with a portion of sauce spooned on top.

TASTING NOTES: CALIFORNIA PASTA, OLIVE OIL, AND GRATING CHEESE

These days, even here in Maine, there are gourmet stores that offer fine imported Italian foods—but at a price. It's hard to have a casual hand in dispensing ingredients that are always costly and sometimes difficult to come by, and we are always on the lookout for reliable domestic sources for good-quality, not-too-expensive pasta, olive oil, and grating cheese. Pasta might seem to be the least of our worries, our local supermarket now carrying at least three imported varieties. But the brand we like the best—DeCecco—is often in short supply and, at its cheapest, $1.49 the pound box.

This is why we were delighted to discover D. Merlino & Sons, in Oakland, New World pasta makers perpetuating Old World traditions, making eighty-seven varieties of pasta from 100 percent durum semolina. Their spaghetti is still available in continuous strands, bent over and over onto themselves in 13-inch folds. Their linguine has the fresh wheat taste and resilient texture we like, and the price, around $5 for 10 pounds (even with the additional shipping), was more than acceptable. Call or write for a price list and a photocopy of their pasta chart. D. Merlino & Sons, 1001 83rd Avenue, Oakland, CA 94621; (510) 568-2151.

❖ ❖ ❖

There is a simple fascination in sampling the family of aged dry Monterey Jacks made by Ig Vella and experiencing a very decent, honest American cheese as it develops character, authority, and an exciting depth of flavor. We tasted three cheeses: the regular dry Jack, aged seven months; the special select, aged one year; and, finally, a piece of the "California Gold." This last is aged at least two years (our wheel, bought in 1990, was dated July 1987!). Good Monterey Jack has a fresh sweetness, and drying it enrobes this quality with an increasingly nutty tang. By the time it is two years old, it has achieved a deep golden color, a wonderful granular texture, and a unique, intense flavor that still retains the sweet dairy freshness of the original cheese. We thought this final version as excellent for eating as it was for grating, very fairly priced at $7.25 per pound for an 8-pound wheel. At the time of writing, their gold medal–winning dry Jack was $6.25 per pound (with a 4-pound minimum). Vella Cheese Company, P.O. Box 191, Sonoma, CA 95476; (800) 848-0505. A descriptive brochure is available.

My experience with California virgin olive oils has been a ho-hum affair at best, and I approached the Sciabica family's collection of varietal extra-virgin olive oils with a little skepticism. However, after the first tasting, we decided to change our house oil to Sciabica's Mission variety natural olive oil, a sweet, clean, golden oil with a deliciously lingering olive flavor (there is a similar-tasting organic version). The care the Sciabicas take in producing all these first-pressing, extra-virgin oils is evident in their artisanal character; the mouth does not feel manipulated by clever blending but is allowed to encounter the character of the year's harvest of each particular variety.

The Sciabicas actually offer pressings from some of their varieties picked at different times of the year. Their "fall harvest" varietals are made from olives gathered early in the season, producing oils with a distinctive green tint and an earthier taste. This presence was a bit too raw for us in the Mission variety fall harvest, but the Manzanillo variety fall harvest had the full character of some Italian peasant-style oils, with a fruity flavor and a throaty burn. Finally, there is the Sevillano variety fall harvest oil: deep gold-green, fruity, very fragrant, with a surprisingly artichoke-like sweetness that sets it apart from any other olive oils we've ever tasted—the perfect present for the olive oil connoisseur. At the time of writing, Sciabica oils run about $25 a gallon, with small sizes available. A tasting pack of six 6-ounce bottles can be ordered for $36. All prices are exclusive of shipping. Write to Nick Sciabica & Sons, P.O. Box 1246, Modesto, CA 95353; (800) 346-5483. Their catalogue and price list are free.

MEATBALL
METAPHYSICS

❖ ❖ ❖

The meatball is a food with "permanent culinary refugee status" stamped on its passport. It is at ease in almost any cuisine but rarely made to feel at home there, for either too big a fuss is made over it or else it is snubbed entirely. I'll bet, for example, that no *French* meatball dish springs to mind. Italians do make meatballs but rarely boast of it: they claim spaghetti and meatballs is a slander against their cuisine. Likewise, the Swedes are mortified that their cooking is known to us almost entirely through an ersatz appetizer to which we have given the name of Swedish meatballs.

Perhaps it's because meatballs aren't used to polite society. Stanley Kunitz helped me place them when I read in his essay "Seedcorn and Windfall" about a young student revolutionary, Konstantin Paustovsky, who, during the reign of Nicholas II, shot Minister Stolypin dead at the Kiev opera and was sentenced to be hanged. He accepted his fate with equanimity: "What possible difference can it make to me if I eat two thousand fewer meatballs in my life?"

This is where the meatball belongs, feeding students and revolutionaries. The imagination quickly sketches out the rest: the seedy, back-street bistro in some Middle European city, windows steamed over, air thick with the fumes of cigarette smoke, strong tea, and boiled cabbage, the atmosphere heady with political passion and melancholic irony. And a menu that features meatballs as its only meat dish.

That's the meatball on its own turf: mocking eyes under an unruly shock of hair, a worn cloth coat belted tightly around the waist, a sheaf of *samizdat* crushed deep in its one good pocket. Little wonder that around us, even after all the passing years, the meatball is still a stranger in a strange land. And we, in turn, go on thinking of it as still wearing its immigrant tag, the point of origin written in indelible ink: what American meatball dish have we allowed to forget its foreign provenance?

Because, familiar as they are, there's still something a little embarrassing about meatballs, something not quite *comme il faut*. They confuse us by being vulgar and delicate all at once, and a little defiant besides. Originally made mostly of sinew and gristle and the least bits of meat and fat, meatballs were willed into existence by determined eaters whom fate had denied any right to meat—but who themselves determined otherwise.

Don't confuse them, then, with the delicate rissoles and forcemeat dishes that amuse the mouths of the wealthy while they wait for the roast suckling pig to be brought to table; meatballs are a food eaten by people who believe they deserve more than they are given. Meatballs are a dish of the aspiring poor and the displaced genteel—and especially, the food of artists, students, dreamers, and other malcontents who have taught themselves to wear their poverty with a flourish. In the meatball they find an insouciance that matches their own. What is a meatball, after all, if not a triumph of quick wit over brute reality?

All this is why we Americans—for whom the lowest imaginable common denominator in meat is ground chuck—have found it hard to take the meatball's measure, or it ours. Here, where its traditional makings are processed into dog food, it has had a hard struggle to find an identity. It beefed itself up into a meatloaf, only to discover it had become fat and stupid—and no more understood than before. And it watched its children grow up to be hamburgers—wholesome, juicy, and utterly bland.

That doesn't mean that the only good meatball is made out of the butcher's scrap pail, but to know them at their best, you do have to taste the crunch of that original gristle in the back of—if not your mouth—at least your mind. Otherwise, that hard-won tenderness becomes mere mildness and mush. This isn't sentimentality speaking, either, but the logic of their making. Because her hoard of meaty oddments were so tough and gristly, a cook had to run them through the grinder twice, and took advantage of that to use the first grinding to work in some extra fat (the meat being not only tough but lean) and the next to grind in some flavorings—garlic, onion, lemon peel—which not only lent flavor but helped tenderize. Hence, each batch of meatballs was unique, with its own textures and flavors.

These days, however, there are no recipes that encourage you to grind your own meatballs. Ground meat is so readily available that it seems an impossible undertaking to convince anyone that the result might be worth the effort. But most recipes—including the ones that follow—*can* easily be adapted so to make the meatballs from scratch. Simply put the meat through a grinder or process it in a food processor fitted with a steel blade. Not only will that give you the superior texture of a knife-cut grind, but it will allow you to combine, say, the trimmings of leftover veal breast with some pork shoulder, working in some shallots and a sprig of summer savory.

Nor should you hesitate to throw in a handful or two of bread crumbs. Their purpose, besides serving as a meat extender, is to give the meatballs lightness and grace. They soften the texture, retain the juices, and help each keep shape in the cooking pot. And a little beaten egg can provide both binding and an appetizing gloss. Neither should be overdone. The main ingredient in a meatball must be meat.

A final caution. Chopped raw onion mixed into ground meat will weep moisture into the meatballs while cooking, giving them a sour taste and often causing them to fall apart. This is why the directions below call for sweating the onions in a hot skillet before adding them to the meatball mixture. But if you grind everything together yourself, you can omit this step. This is why traditional recipes allow the raw onion to be mixed with the meat: ground together, the onion mixture is evenly spread through the mixture and its vapors escape while cooking.

KEFTEDES ON SKEWERS
(SERVES 4 TO 6)

Olive oil
1 medium onion, minced
1½ pounds lean ground lamb
1 teaspoon fresh mint, rosemary,
  or Greek oregano, minced

2 tablespoons parsley, minced
1 egg, beaten
½ cup pine nuts, minced
Salt and black pepper to taste

Soak six 10-inch bamboo skewers in water. Heat a little olive oil in a small skillet and sauté the minced onion until it is just translucent. Remove from the heat. Combine meat, herbs, egg, sautéed onion, and pine nuts in a mixing bowl and, using your hands, mix them into a coarse paste, seasoning this with salt and pepper. Cover the bowl with plastic wrap and set aside for about 30 minutes so the flavors will commingle.

Preheat the broiler or heat charcoal in a grill. Divide the mixture roughly into two halves, and those into two halves again. With damp hands, mold the meat mixture around each skewer into fat finger-shaped sausages, roughly 2 inches in length, fitting four per skewer, with each of the four mounds of seasoned lamb making six *keftedes* (one and one-half skewers).

Grill over the hot coals or in the broiler, turning often, for about 5 to 6 minutes (don't overcook them, or they'll be dry and tasteless). Serve on a bed of hot rice.

SPANISH MEATBALL SOUP
(SERVES 4 TO 6 AS A MEAL)

3 to 4 scallions, minced
3 cloves garlic, minced
Olive oil
1 pound ground pork
1 cup fresh bread crumbs
2 eggs, beaten
¼ cup pine nuts, chopped
⅛ teaspoon cinnamon

Salt and black pepper to taste
Flour for coating
4 cups water
3 to 4 sprigs of fresh parsley,
  minced
Toasted bread squares brushed
  with olive oil

Sauté the minced scallion and garlic in a skillet in a little olive oil until the scallion is wilted and the garlic translucent. In a mixing bowl combine the pork, bread crumbs, eggs, sautéed garlic and scallion, chopped pine nuts, cinnamon, and salt and pepper to taste. Beat with a wooden spoon until the mixture is light.

With moistened hands, shape the mixture into meatballs the size of walnuts, lightly coating each with flour as it is finished. Heat a few tablespoons of olive oil in a large cooking pot with a cover. When the oil is hot, sauté the meatballs, gently turning them as necessary, until they are golden brown. Add the water and the parsley. Bring the water to a gentle simmer and cook—never boiling—for 15 minutes. Taste for seasoning, adding salt and pepper as necessary. Serve with the toasted bread squares as a garnish.

MEATBALLS IN TOMATO SAUCE

(ADAPTED FROM *THE FINE ART OF ITALIAN COOKING*

BY GIULIANO BUGIALLI)

(SERVES 4 WITH PASTA OR BOILED RICE)

1 pound ground lean sirloin
¼ cup pine nuts, chopped fine
¼ cup freshly grated Parmesan
¼ cup plus 2 tablespoons olive oil
Flour for coating
1 or 2 fresh sage leaves

1 clove garlic, minced
1 cup imported canned tomatoes,
* drained and coarsely chopped,*
* with the drained liquid reserved*
Salt and black pepper

If possible, grind the beef yourself in a meat grinder or food processor fitted with a steel blade so that it retains a slightly coarse texture. Put the ground meat in a bowl with the pine nuts, Parmesan, and 2 tablespoons of olive oil. Beat with a wooden spoon until well mixed. Divide the mixture in half and then in half again, into four equal amounts. Divide each of these into four oval-shaped meatballs, coating each one lightly with flour as it is made.

Heat the remaining ¼ cup of olive oil in a large flat saucepan. When the oil is hot, add the sage, the minced garlic, and the meatballs and sauté these over medium heat, turning them gently so they will brown on all sides. Then add the chopped tomatoes to the pan with the meatballs, cover, and simmer over low heat for about 10 minutes.

Taste for seasoning, adding salt and pepper to taste. If the sauce seems too thick, thin it cautiously with a little of the reserved tomato liquid. Cover again and continue to simmer, checking occasionally for threat of scorching, until the sauce is almost completely absorbed, or for about another 15 minutes. Pick out the sage leaves before serving.

RUSSIAN *BITKI* WITH DILL SAUCE
(SERVES 4 WITH NOODLES OR RICE)

For the meatballs

1 small onion, minced	*½ pound ground veal*
2 tablespoons unsalted butter	*1 egg, beaten*
½ cup fresh bread crumbs	*Salt and black pepper to taste*
¼ cup milk	*Flour for coating*
½ pound lean ground beef	

For the dill sauce

Up to 2 tablespoons butter	*2 tablespoons fresh lemon juice*
2 tablespoons flour	*2 tablespoons minced fresh dill*
1 cup chicken stock	*1 egg yolk*
1 cup milk	*Salt and black pepper to taste*

To make the meatballs: Sauté the minced onion in a tiny bit of the butter until it is translucent. Remove from the heat. Soak the bread crumbs in the milk, squeeze out the excess, and then mix with the ground meats, onion, and beaten egg. Season to taste with salt and pepper and then beat with a wooden spoon until mixture is smooth and light. Hands damp, form the mixture into meatballs the size of walnuts, dusting each with flour as it is formed. In a large skillet, melt the remaining butter and fry the meatballs until brown and cooked, about 10 minutes. Remove meatballs and keep warm.

To make the dill sauce: Add enough butter to that already in the skillet to make 2 tablespoons (if the meat was fatty, you may prefer to pour out the accumulated grease and begin afresh). When this has melted, stir in the flour gradually until it is all absorbed. Pour in the stock and milk gradually, stirring all the while, until the flour cooks and the mixture thickens. Then mix in the lemon juice and dill. Remove the pot from the heat for a minute, and then whisk in the egg yolk. Finally, add the meatballs to the sauce and return to the heat—the sauce must *not* boil—for about 3 minutes, or until the taste is smooth and the sauce nicely thick. Add salt and pepper if needed. Serve over rice or buttered egg noodles.

COOK'S NOTE: Russians like dill very much, and recipes call for twice the amount given above; feel free to adjust this to your taste. If need be, 2 teaspoons of dried dill leaf may be used instead of the fresh leaf.

DANISH *FRIKADELLER* IN BEER
(SERVES 6 TO 8 AS A MEAL WITH NOODLES)

4 tablespoons butter	1 pound ground pork
1 medium onion, minced	1 egg, beaten
Salt and black pepper	Flour for coating
1/8 teaspoon nutmeg	1 bottle (12 ounces) Danish beer
4 slices stale bread	2 teaspoons lemon juice
1 pound ground beef	

Melt 2 tablespoons butter in a large saucepan. Add the onion and sauté until translucent. Add the salt, pepper, and nutmeg, mix well, and remove from the heat. With determined fingers or a food processor fitted with the steel blade, crush the stale bread into fine crumbs. Put these and the meat into a mixing bowl and, with your hands or a wooden spoon, work into a soft paste. Mix in the seasoned onion bits and, lastly, the beaten egg. With damp hands, roll this mixture into meatballs about the size of a walnut, giving each, when formed, a light dusting of flour.

Melt the remaining butter in the same saucepan. Add the meatballs and cook these over medium heat until nicely browned. Then add the beer and the lemon juice. Bring just to a boil, reduce the heat so that the liquid barely simmers, and cook for 20 to 25 minutes. Serve with buttered noodles sprinkled with toasted rye bread crumbs.

MEATBALLS WITH SPINACH AND CHICKPEAS

(ADAPTED FROM *A BOOK OF MIDDLE EASTERN FOOD*
BY CLAUDIA RODEN)

(SERVES 4 TO 6 WITH BOILED RICE)

1 medium onion, minced
3 tablespoons olive oil
1½ pounds ground lamb
Salt and black pepper
2 (10-ounce) packages fresh
  spinach

1 can (20 ounces) chickpeas,
  drained
2 cloves garlic, crushed
1 teaspoon ground coriander

Sauté the minced onion in a little of the olive oil until it just turns translucent. Remove from the heat. When cool enough to handle, mix with the ground meat and season to taste with salt and black pepper. Form into meatballs the size of walnuts. Add the rest of the olive oil to the same pan used to cook the onions and sauté the meatballs for a few minutes, or until they are browned.

Wash the spinach well to remove all grit, discarding stems and any damaged leaves. Remove leaves from water but do not drain. Put the spinach in a large saucepan. Cover, lower heat, and let it stew just until the leaves wilt and turn tender (the moisture clinging to the leaves should be sufficient cooking liquid). Put the spinach into a colander set over a bowl. Gently press to remove excess moisture and then turn the spinach onto a cutting board, reserving the liquid. Coarsely chop it with a knife.

Return the chopped spinach and liquid to the pot. Stir in the drained chickpeas and meatballs, along with any remaining olive oil, cover again, and simmer for a half hour, adding a little water if necessary. While this cooks, blend the crushed garlic with a pinch of coarse salt and fry this with the coriander in a few more drops of olive oil until the garlic softens and the coriander releases its aroma. Stir this final seasoning into the dish just as it goes to table. Serve over or with boiled rice.

GARLIC SOUP

✦ ✦ ✦

Along the Mediterranean, an aïgo bouïdo is considered to be very good indeed for the liver, blood circulation, general physical tone, and spiritual health. A head of garlic is not at all too much for two quarts of soup. For some addicts, it is not even enough.
> —Beck, Bertholle, and Child, *Mastering the Art of French Cooking* (Vol. I)

"And the bread, does it get dry?"
"Hard as a stone to kill a dog. Too hard to eat without grinding teeth. But at night if there is no cooked food, one boils water with a little garlic and dips in the bread. That is good."
> —Eliza Putnam Heaton, *By-Paths in Sicily*

Why is garlic soup, which is so similar to onion soup, being equally as tasty and possibly even more soul-satisfying, comparatively so little known? The answer, I think—which is interesting not only in its own right but because it helps explain the power this soup still manages to exert over the imagination of those who are drawn to it—lies in the powerful sexual overtones that garlic exudes, and more particularly still in the difference between the sexual overtones of garlic and onion.

These overtones are, of course, metaphoric and this comparison can only be drawn so far. But it is no less real for that.

Like the sexual parts themselves, garlic bulbs have the ability to overpower our senses and pervade our body with sensation. Unlike other foods, whose capacity to stimulate is generally limited to the nose and the mouth, onion and—especially—garlic can pervade our entire sensual being with its presence, an experience, also like sexuality, that can be exhilarating but also disturbing, even profoundly distressing.

The onion, although it might superficially appear the more powerful, since it is the most awkward to handle—its juices alone make us weep—is actually the weaker of the two, being the one more amenable to control. With cooking it becomes sweet and tame, its aroma reduced to a mere husky-throated whisper.

Garlic, on the other hand, has a power at once more intimate and more muscular, for it attracts us through an act of aggressive seduction. Cooking may smooth its roughest edges, but that it is thus tamed is nothing but an illusion, for once ingested it suffuses our body with its musky scent, announcing its presence to the world through all our bodily exhalations, both sweat and breath.

In other words, where the onion allows itself to be seduced and its charms to yield to the desire of the eater, garlic is the ravisher, dominating those who would eat it, and then crowing that subjugation to the world through the body's every pore. It allows only two possible responses, apart from shunning it entirely: we can rub it raw on our chest and shamelessly swagger our predilection* or use it in pathetic homeopathic doses in hopes that we will not be caught out.

Although I don't doubt that garlic possesses all the healthful qualities claimed for it, these would have been invented anyway if they did not already exist—as they *were* invented for tobacco, and for the same reason. Exactly what disgusts us about garlic and tobacco (for both of these have earned the epithet "filthy") is also what draws us to them: they are at

---

* This is no idle fancy. In *The Unprejudiced Palate*, Angelo Pellegrini writes of working with "a powerful son of Athens whose reverence for garlic left nothing to be desired. He used it daily internally and externally. He ate it regularly raw and rubbed it on his chest and in his nostrils."

once so pervasive and so comforting. They drench us with their presence, satiate us beyond hunger, as if we consumed not only their substance but their spirit as well. It is only to others that we stink: we ourselves feel as if intoxicated in a heady perfume. It's not for nothing that a nineteenth-century commentator wrote of the effect of garlic that it "works upon you like haschisch." And of all dishes in which garlic plays a part, this is most true of garlic soup.

I'm no food historian, but I'd be willing to put a small wager to the effect that garlic soup—at least in the form that I'm about to describe it—originated in Catalonia, that former Spanish kingdom, now a region, that once included a goodly portion of Mediterranean France. The Catalans were and still are brilliant cooks, adept in dishes conjured from olive oil, garlic, and brightly fragrant herbs and spices, all of which are the very essence of this dish. And while it is, in one form or another, everywhere available in Spain and Portugal and has also percolated through southern France, it has not spread much farther. My casual researches located no Latin American version nor any around the Mediterranean, at least not beyond Italy; there are several Arabic and North African garlic soups, but they are of a quite different composition.

In any case, the common origins of the Spanish *sopa de ajo* and the Provençal *aïgo bouïdo* (or *aïgo bolido*, as some have it) are unmistakable, especially in their simplest and no doubt original form, built out of nothing more than a crust of dried bread, some boiling water, a handful of herbs, and the garlic itself. Indeed, *aïgo bouïdo* means simply "boiled water." Boiled water . . . it doesn't sound very satisfying at all, and yet the Provençals also say of it, *"L'aïgo bouïdo sauvo la vido,"* which roughly translates as *"aïgo bouïdo,* saver of lives."

How can this be? Like onion soup, the origins of garlic soup are that it was used as a sop. Until recently, and especially in areas where wood was at a premium, the bread ovens in small communities were not fired every day—often not every week. Consequently, you had either to learn to do without bread or to make do with stale. When it became too hard to chew (especially when one had only a few bad teeth), it was dipped into a hot liquid to soften it and make a meal.

The focus, then, is on the bread, the staff of life: the water, seasoned with garlic and herbs, was a means, not an end. The bread provided both the substance and some of the savor, for a good peasant bread would have the tang of sour and salt and the sweet taste of wheat. If a chunk of bread does have all these things, and if it is really and truly dried out, you'll be surprised both at how much flavor it can give to simple water . . . and at how much texture it has, even after the sopping.

Even so, appetite is not sparked by the idea of dunking the bread into potato or carrot or cabbage water. The two things are not equal; the liquid insults the bread. On the other hand, meat broth is also not right. It is too rich; it condescends. If you can afford meat broth, you don't put stale bread in it.

Herbs and garlic, however, like stale bread, are at once less and more than ordinary food. They work together to perform an act of magic. Here is the original, true stone soup of the folktale, the one that is made of nothing but the faith that we are not meant to starve. A dried crust, a few bits of grass and weed, a bulb of garlic, a little water, a pinch of salt: heat them together and they produce an aroma of such intensity that you inhale it through your pores as much as your nostrils, a flavor that ravishes your mouth and fills and soothes your stomach, a presence that pervades every atom of your body and intoxicates your mind. There is no meat soup, no other kind of soup at all, that works such miracles . . . let alone out of nothing much at all. *L'aïgo bouïdo sauvo la vido.*

Knowing this much about garlic soup, you already see that a recipe is superfluous for making it. For each eater, take two or three cloves of garlic, peel and crush them, and then stir them into a cupful of boiling water. Set this to simmer and add a pinch of aromatic herb or two—the Provençals add fresh sage with wanton abandon and a goodly amount of thyme, while the Catalans add a generous pinch of paprika and maybe a coarsely chopped tomato. In either instance, float a splash of olive oil over the top. Let this simmer for a good half hour and then pour it over a hard slab of stale bread. Stir in a portion of freshly minced parsley and fall to.

Even at this simple level there is much toying with the formula, and you should consider nothing in it fixed. Other herbs can be used, like bay leaf or oregano, such spices as nutmeg or clove, or an aromatic piece of lemon or orange peel. (I also feel that a few drops of good wine vinegar enhance the flavor of a bread broth.) If you prefer a less pungent herbal presence, consider some minced fresh fennel, both bulb and root. Either potatoes or vermicelli can be used instead of the bread. And many like to sprinkle over a handful of grated Parmesan at the same time as (or instead of) the parsley.

I give this version in proportions to feed a single person because it's unlikely you'll want to serve it to anyone but yourself. It is too rude to be anything more than a solitary repast, a self-administered analeptic meant to get the blood stirring again after a hike through a blizzard or a drenching from a summer thunderburst. It is, as claimed, an amazing restorative and at the same time a great soother of nerves . . . just the thing to lull your aching soul and coax you back to bed when a bout of anxiety has tumbled you out of sleep.

But to serve it to others, the soup needs . . . not improvement exactly, but a little socialization—and a little adaptation, not at all to obscure the dish's rustic origins but to compensate for aspects of it that we cannot easily hope to duplicate in our modern kitchens.

For example, while ordinary French bread is famous for its staling ability (what's bought for breakfast can be too much rusk for supper), it still lacks both the deep savor of the sourer rustic loaf and its density of texture. This robs the broth. So the bread is toasted to give it more flavor. Possibly, in this case, chicken or meat broth is used as well. (Another argument for meat broth is the quality of one's tap water, since the aftertaste of chlorine can muddy a mouthful of flavor that should be full of bright edges all around.) And since the soup is too emphatic to serve as a first course and so must do as a meal, it is enhanced with such additional nourishment as cheese and—particularly—eggs, for when the yolks are used to thicken this soup they give it a rich and velvety consistency, perfect foil to the garlic's urgent presence.

The following recipes pick up this theme, working garlic soup through some of its more attractive modern adaptations: hearty, savory, soul-satisfying, and yet still suitable for company. But in each of them lingers the old enchantment, if you dare let your tongue set it free.

SOUPE À L'AIL

(ADAPTED FROM *MONET'S TABLE* BY CLAIRE JOYES)
(SERVES 6)

12 cloves of garlic	*6 eggs*
½ loaf stale French bread	*Salt and black pepper*
6 tablespoons unsalted butter	*Minced parsley for garnish*

Heat 6 cups of water in a cooking pot. When it comes to a boil, reduce to a simmer and add the garlic cloves. Cook until these are tender, about 15 minutes. Remove the pot from the heat. Fish out the garlic with a strainer and, with a mortar and pestle, work it into a smooth paste. Stir this back into the cooking liquid.

Cut the bread into croutons, each about a half-inch square. Reserve 2 tablespoons of butter and melt the rest in a large skillet. Stir in the croutons and, over medium heat, turn them with a spatula until they are evenly browned on all sides. Distribute these evenly among six warmed soup bowls.

Break the eggs into a mixing bowl and whisk into this ½ cup of the soup liquid, adding it in a thin but steady stream. When it is well blended, whisk this mixture into the soup liquid that remains in the cooking pot. Add the remaining 2 tablespoons of butter and, over very low heat, stir until the butter has melted. Do not let the soup come to a boil or the eggs will curdle. Add salt and freshly ground pepper to taste. Pour the hot soup into the soup bowls over the croutons and sprinkle generously with minced parsley. Serve at once.

SOUPE À L'AIL BONNE FEMME
(SERVES 4 TO 6)

2 leeks
2 or 3 fat, ripe tomatoes
2 large potatoes
¼ cup olive oil
4 large garlic cloves, peeled

A few strands of saffron
Salt and black pepper to taste
½ loaf stale French bread
½ cup grated Gruyère cheese

Preheat the oven to 425°F. Trim, wash, and chop the leeks. Peel, seed, and coarsely chop the tomatoes, reserving all juice. Peel the potatoes and cut them into small dice. Heat half the olive oil in a large saucepan, add the leeks, and sauté them until they just turn translucent. Crush 3 of the garlic cloves and add, then stir in the tomatoes with their juice, the potatoes, the saffron, and 3½ cups of water. Season to taste with salt and pepper, bring to a simmer, and let cook for 30 minutes. Meanwhile, crush the remaining clove of garlic into the remaining olive oil and mix well. Cut a thick slice of bread for each eater and rub each side with the garlic/olive oil mixture. Sprinkle one side of each with an equal portion of the cheese and bake these in the preheated oven for 10 minutes, or until a light golden brown. Set a slice in each soup bowl. When the soup is done, ladle it over the slices.

AÏGO BOUÏDO
(A MEDITERRANEAN FRENCH BROTH OF GARLIC AND HERBS)
(SERVES 4)

8 garlic cloves, peeled
1 small bay leaf
1 sprig fresh thyme (or ½ teaspoon dried)
2 fresh sage leaves
1- to 2-inch strip dried orange rind

3 large eggs
4 thick slices peasant-style bread
2 tablespoons olive oil
Salt and black pepper to taste
Minced parsley

Preheat the oven to 450°F. Bring 3½ cups of water to a boil in a large pot. Add the whole garlic cloves, herbs, and orange rind and let simmer for 20 minutes. While this cooks, separate the eggs. Using a pastry brush, coat the slices of bread with some of the egg whites, discarding the rest. Set these on a wire rack placed on a cookie sheet and toast in the preheated oven. (This doesn't take long—don't let them burn!) Remove from the oven and set aside.

When the liquid has simmered its 20 minutes, pour it through a strainer. Pick out and discard the fresh herbs and orange peel, reserving the garlic (and, of course, the liquid!). When the garlic cloves are cool enough to handle, put them and the olive oil into a mortar or the bowl of a food processor set with the steel blade, and pound them to a pulp. Beat this mixture into the egg yolks.

Return the garlic stock to the pot. Stir in the egg yolk/oil/garlic mixture until well blended and reheat over a gentle flame for a few moments, until the soup is hot (but not boiling) and thick. Season to taste with salt and pepper. Put a piece of toast in each of four soup bowls and ladle in the soup. Garnish with a little minced fresh parsley and serve at once.

COOK'S NOTES: The technique of beating the cooked mashed garlic cloves and olive oil into the egg yolks is Paula Wolfert's (from *Mediterranean Cooking*), a terrific improvement over discarding the garlic and just stirring the oil in. She and Robert Courtine (in *Real French Cooking*) both suggest brushing the bread with the egg whites: it makes good use of what might be otherwise wasted and gives the bread an attractive gloss. Another option, suggested by Suzanne McLucas (in *A Provençal Kitchen in America*), is to poach the whites in the soup during the last few minutes of cooking. (Although how does one do this without making a terrible mess? Perhaps better to poach a whole egg for each eater in the broth, then thicken that with a simple amalgam of garlic and oil.) Also, a single crumbled leaf of dried sage can be substituted for the fresh amount, making sure it is not too medicinal-tasting. If so, it would be better just to do without.

SOPA DE AJO

(ONE VERSION OF SPAIN'S NATIONAL GARLIC SOUP)

3 *tablespoons olive oil*	*A few strands of saffron (optional)*
6 *cloves garlic, peeled*	*Salt and black pepper to taste*
½ *loaf stale French bread*	4 *eggs*
1 *tablespoon mild paprika*	*Minced parsley for garnish*
4 *cups good chicken broth*	

Preheat the oven to 450°F. Heat the oil in a large saucepan over medium heat. Add the cloves of garlic and sauté them gently, turning often, until they are golden all over. Remove them and set aside. Pull the bread apart into walnut-sized bits, discarding the crust. Add these to the hot oil and sauté these also until golden on all sides. Remove and reserve. Sprinkle the paprika into the small amount of oil remaining in the pan and stir it, heating it enough to remove its raw taste. Then add the chicken broth and the saffron and bring to a simmer. As the broth heats, finely mince the garlic cloves and stir into the soup along with all the bits of bread. Season with salt and pepper and let simmer for about 15 minutes until the bread is very soft but still holding together.

Set four ovenproof soup bowls or individual-sized casserole dishes (such as small soufflé molds) onto a cookie sheet and equally divide the soup into them, being as careful as possible not to break up the bread. Then quickly but carefully break the eggs and slip them, one apiece, into each of the bowls. Put these, still on their cookie sheet, into the preheated oven and bake just until the eggs are set, about 4 minutes. Serve at once, sprinkling each bowl with a pinch of minced parsley as garnish.

COOK'S NOTES: Often Spanish recipes call for the addition of 2 or 3 ripe tomatoes, seeded, peeled, and coarsely chopped, to be added at the same time as the paprika; the recipe is otherwise prepared exactly the same. Other versions omit the eggs entirely. A piece of lemon zest can be substituted for the saffron and discarded when the soup is divided among the individual bowls. Of course, the soup can be finished in a single large casserole—or the pot, if so designed, can be put straight in the oven. The only problem is serving the soup without making a muddle of the eggs.

GARLIC AND WALNUT SOUP
WITH FRESH GOAT CHEESE
(A COLD SUMMER SOUP)
(SERVES 4)

½ cup walnut meats
3 large cloves garlic, peeled
3 tablespoons olive oil
½ cup light cream

2 ounces fresh goat cheese
3 cups homemade chicken broth
Salt and black pepper to taste

Heat the walnut meats in an ungreased skillet over medium heat, stirring constantly for a few minutes until they release a nutty smell. Turn them into the bowl of a food processor fitted with the steel blade. Crush the garlic and add it to the walnuts; pulse-process the mixture until it is well blended. Then, the machine running constantly, dribble in the olive oil drop by drop to make a thick emulsion. Into this process the cream and finally the goat cheese, producing one cup of a pungent but unctuously rich sauce. Taste—you may decide to do something more interesting with it than making it into a soup.

If not, heat the broth in a small saucepan, whisking in the sauce bit by bit once it gets hot. Do not let it boil. When the sauce is well incorporated, let simmer for a few minutes. Taste for seasoning and then remove from the heat. Let cool and then place in the refrigerator. Serve well chilled, whisking it well first and garnishing it, if you wish, with a tiny amount of minced fresh herb like cilantro or watercress.

COOK'S NOTES: I concocted this soup out of a garlic and walnut sauce in Mireille Johnston's *The Cuisine of the Sun*. It's not quite as interesting served hot, although it helps if you toss into each bowl a slice of toasted bread on which some more of the goat cheese has been spread.

At the time I originally worked on this piece, I had just bought a food processor. That machine now languishes in a cardboard box in the storage room, and if I were making this soup today I would use the large Thai composite-stone mortar on the kitchen counter, switching from pestle to table fork when I mixed in the oil, the cream, and then the goat cheese.

Finally, don't bother making this dish with canned chicken broth; it is simply too salty for this soup. In fact, you should undersalt it when seasoning it at the stove. However, it's quite amenable to plenty of freshly ground black pepper.

☞ Those who would like to explore more elaborate versions of garlic soup should turn especially to the recipes for the dry soup of garlic and fresh coriander in Jean Anderson's *The Food of Portugal*; soupe à l'ail et au vin in Madeleine Kamman's *When French Women Cook*; ajo blanco de Málaga (a garlic gazpacho) in Marimar Torres's *The Spanish Table*; and the evening garlic soup in the manner of Corrèze in Paula Wolfert's *The Cooking of South-West France*. Several further variants are available in Barbara Batcheller's *Lilies of the Kitchen*.

KITCHEN DIARY: LEMON
ICE CREAM

This is perhaps the simplest possible ice cream—sugar, cream, and fresh lemon stirred together and frozen. It has a soft, smooth texture and a delicious flavor, and the pleasure in eating it is only heightened by its being so surprisingly easy to make. It is the sort of thing where you think there must be a trick to it, but what is magical is that there are not any tricks at all.

We first saw the recipe in *Maida Heatter's Book of Great Desserts*, where it is called "Jean Hewitt's Old-Fashioned Lemon Ice Cream." But we later found versions in several other places, including an earlier but nearly identical recipe in Clementine Paddleford's *How America Eats* (1960).

The Paddleford version (to serve six) calls for the juice and grated zest of a single medium lemon, a cup of sugar, two cups of light cream, and two drops of yellow food coloring.

The lemon juice and zest are thoroughly mixed with the sugar. The cream and food coloring are carefully stirred in and this mixture is poured into an ice-cube tray and frozen for at least three hours ("do not stir and it freezes smooth"). The Heatter-Hewitt version ignores the food coloring, adds a pinch of salt, and stirs the mixture in the freezer just before it firms up. Otherwise it is the same.

We took everyone's advice—so far as it simplified. We omitted the food coloring, the salt, *and* the stirring. What appealed to us most was that we could treat it so casually—no whipping the cream or stirring the mixture once in the freezer—and still have it emerge, not only a real ice cream, but "smooth as a petal, a joy to eat."

The proportions of the ingredients can also be varied to suit different tastes or different purposes. Madeleine Kamman gives a recipe for lemon "sherbet" in an old issue of *The Pleasures of Cooking* (Vol. 4, No. 1) in which she calls for a cup *each* of heavy cream, sugar, and lemon juice (plus a pinch of salt). This is because she means the dish, served with little splashes of *marc de Bourgogne* and *crème de cassis*, not as a dessert but as an *entremets*—to wake up the mouth between courses.

We ourselves were more interested in lulling it into a snoozy contented state, but we did want something that would delight and satisfy in smallish portions. Heightening the lemon presence made us pause at each bite and wait until the initial mouth-puckering taste was softly enrobed and sweetened by the cream.

These are our final proportions (to serve two): the juice and zest of 1 medium lemon, ⅓ cup of superfine sugar, and ⅔ cup of non-ultrapasteurized all-purpose cream. In other words, we've tripled the amount of lemon in the Paddleford/Hewitt/ Heatter recipe that was our starting point.

We followed the method as we explain it above except that we substituted superfine for regular sugar. This eliminates all hint of grittiness. We also discovered that stirring the cream during freezing really didn't improve it any, but that whipping it beforehand did give the ice cream a lighter texture. However, we decided we liked the compact smoothness of the unwhipped version better. The ice cream freezes best in a shallow container; we used a wide-bottomed stainless-steel bowl.

For some reason, all the recipes we've seen for this sort of simple ice cream have required lemon or some other citrus fruit. (When we made it with lime, however, the texture was right, but the cream and coldness muted and fragmented that fruit's delicate, flowery flavor.) Could a similarly smooth-textured version be made with a non-citrus flavoring like banana or coffee? We haven't yet been *quite* curious enough to try bananas, but we did make it a few times with an extract of ground coffee beans.

COFFEE ICE CREAM

This is best made with freshly ground, distinctive-tasting coffee beans; the more ordinary the coffee used, the more the result tastes like, well, coffee ice cream. A nice choice is a bean with chocolaty overtones like Mexican Maragogipe or a rich-flavored, aromatic coffee like Hawaiian Kona. We also liked it made with an espresso-roast bean.

Our method, to serve four, requires 2 coffee scoops (or a single quarter cup) of roasted beans, ground finely and then infused in ¾ cup of boiling water. This was allowed to cool and then filtered through a coffee filter, yielding ⅔ cup of extract. This was blended in a large shallow bowl with 1½ cups non-ultrapasteurized all-purpose cream, ¾ cup ultrafine sugar, and a pinch of salt. These were combined and frozen in the same manner as the lemon ice cream. While not as spectacular a concoction as the lemon version, our coffee ice cream was sophisticated-tasting and good—another decidedly adult dessert.

And this final note: If you make this ice cream our way, we think you'll find it best eaten in the company of one or two short, not-too-sweet cookies.

FUL MEDAMES

❖ ❖ ❖

I well remember my childhood, when for a halfpenny I
used to get a bowl of *ful* and a crust of bread at the "*ful*
shop" near my school. Naturally one had to queue, sometimes up to fifteen minutes, then gobble the food and
depart quickly. . . . If a host is to honour a guest he orders
a bowl of *el-ful* from the nearest shop and to refuse to eat
would be tantamount to insult.

—Arto der Haroutunian, *Middle Eastern Cookery*

*F*ul *medames* (or *ful mesdames*, *fool midamess*, *foul midammis*,
etc.), which is no more than small brown fava beans* simmered
to melting softness, dressed simply with oil, lemon juice, and
(usually) garlic, and served with a few choice additions, is
Egypt's national dish. It is generally described as a breakfast
food, since it is eaten then by rich and poor alike, and at its
least adorned. But this is to misrepresent what is really a food
for all hours. Many Egyptians—and not only poor ones—will

---

* Arabella Boxer, in her *Mediterranean Cookbook*, calls them "*foul beans*"—
which seems an unfortunate way of putting it, especially since *ful* itself
means "bean," the phrase thus translating into the not-very-explanatory
"bean beans." The word *medames* is colloquial Egyptian and is simply the
dish's name, probably deriving from the *dammasa*, or stewpot, it is made
in.

have it again for lunch and possibly as a side (or even a featured) dish at dinner, not to mention a couple of plates of it in between.

Almost every street has its vendor selling *ful medames*. Some buyers scoop it up in fresh pita bread and eat it on the run. Children bring empty pots from home, sent by their mothers to purchase the family meal. And since this is only first among many passionately devoured legume dishes, it is hardly surprising that Egyptians are known among the Arabs as the children of *el-ful* ("of the bean").

But it isn't only *el-ful* that they are passionate about. Egyptians are renowned for the appreciative pleasure they bring to the table—as well they should, for theirs is a cooking as varied and interesting as you might expect from a country with so old and complex a history, and a populace whose culture, at least in cosmopolitan areas, is a subtle intertwining of many presences: Mediterranean, Arabic, and African. The reason that *ful medames* can hold the continued interest of such eaters is that it combines simplicity of preparation with endless possibilities of variation—a dish that all Egyptians can hold in common and yet each prepares to the dictates of a very individualized taste.

You can get some sense of the imaginative resources of the Egyptian cook when you compare *ful medames* with *hummus-bi-tahini*—the familiar chickpea spread found throughout the Middle East. For while this latter is a tasty preparation and its flavorings many, it has none of the richness of association that belongs to *ful medames*. You can eat the latter for breakfast seasoned with cumin and mixed with chopped tomatoes; have it again for lunch sprinkled with parsley and mint and accompanied by olives, slices of green pepper, and hard-boiled eggs; and snack on it from a vendor that afternoon, strongly seasoned with spicy condiments—and think of each version as something entirely different from the one before.

If it is analogous to anything in our own American cuisine, it is to peanut butter—or at least would be if our use of peanut butter were half as imaginative as it should be. Like peanut butter, *ful medames* isn't simply a bulk food made palatable with seasoning. It has a flavor and an integrity entirely its own. Whatever is added, there is never a doubt as to the central attraction of the *ful*. Also like peanut butter, *ful medames*—especially in combination with the foods eaten with it—is very nutritious: mixed with yogurt it is used to sustain Egyptians from sunrise to sunset during the month of Ramadan, the yearly Islamic period of fast.

Delicious, sustaining, inexpensive, and (apart from the actual cooking of the beans) quick to assemble, *ful medames* is especially right on a hot summer's day, a cool and leisurely repast whose fresh flavors soothe a palate dulled by sultry heat and whose bright and various colors delight the glare-dulled eye. All that is needed is plenty of pita bread and an icy, water-beaded pitcher full of sweetened, mint-scented iced tea.

❖ ❖ ❖

Egyptian cooks agree only about the basic preparation. Although any fava or broad bean can be used to make *ful medames*, the preferred one is *ful hamam*, a small, round, dark brown bean that turns a deep purple when cooked. Traditionally, these were soaked overnight and then lengthily simmered in a *dammasa*, a narrow-necked metal cooking pot that rested on a charcoal brazier (or electric element). The beans are cooked until tender but not to disintegration, a process that can take several hours. At this point, depending on the cook, they are either tossed or mashed in a mixture of oil (traditionally olive but more recently [edible] linseed, cottonseed, or corn oil), lemon juice, garlic, and salt, and then served with a variety of accompaniments.

Holding this general notion in mind, consider the following recipe as no more than a guide. The proportions are meant only as a mean from which to vary as taste dictates or circumstances require.

FUL MEDAMES
(SERVES 4 AS A MEAL OR 6 TO 8 AS AN APPETIZER)

To prepare the beans

2 cups uncooked small fava beans (see sources, page 137), soaked overnight or for at least 6 hours
½ cup lentils (optional)

¼ cup olive (or other vegetable) oil
Juice of 1 lemon (scant ¼ cup)
Salt and pepper to taste

Wash the fava beans well in cold water, picking them over carefully for any small pebbles. Cover them with water and let them soak overnight or for at least 6 hours. (Note: a larger amount of beans can be prepared and those not used in the recipe frozen.)

When ready to prepare them, pour 2 quarts of water into a heavy, tight-lidded pot and bring to a boil over medium-high heat. Add the beans and cover. Return to a boil and cook the beans for 10 minutes. Now reduce the heat, stir in the lentils (if using), and simmer about 2 hours or so, or until the beans are tender all through. (Do not add salt during this cooking process or it will make the beans tough. If the beans begin to cook dry, wet them with more *boiling* water.)

When they are done, drain them well and let cool. Then combine the olive oil, lemon juice, salt, and pepper. (Note: The amounts given are only suggested: recipes using the same amount of beans call for as much as ⅔ cup of oil and the juice of 2 lemons—almost ½ cup—or as little as 3 tablespoons of oil and 1 tablespoon of lemon juice.) Either mix this in with the beans or mash them into it to make a smooth, spreadable paste.

Suggested flavorings

Mix into the prepared beans any one or a selection of: 1 clove or 2 or 3 of finely minced garlic; some chopped scallion or onion; a coarsely chopped, fully ripe tomato; a tablespoon of minced fresh parsley, mint, and/or coriander (cilantro); and/or a generous pinch of dried cumin.

Suggested accompaniments

One or several of: sliced green pepper; black Mediterranean olives; sliced red onion; hard-boiled eggs or *hamine* eggs (see below); feta cheese; lemon quarters (if lemon juice is not mixed into the *ful*); tahini sauce (see below); and plenty of pita bread.

To serve

Place the *ful medames* in a bowl, sprinkle with a bit more of the fresh chopped herb(s), and set out with the bread and accompaniments for each to choose to taste. Serve with mint-scented iced tea.

HAMINE EGGS

Fresh eggs   *Brown skins from several onions*

Put the eggs and onion skins in a large pot and fill the pot with water. Bring this to a very gentle simmer—it should barely quiver—and cover. Cook for at least 6 hours (or overnight). This extended cooking produces boiled eggs with a soft, smooth texture, very delicious with *ful medames*. In Egypt, they are also eaten plain, as an appetizer, dipped in salt seasoned with cumin, coriander, and cinnamon.

The onion skins, by the way, are to provide color more than flavor. The method is very similar to that for making Chinese tea eggs.

TAHINI SAUCE
(MAKES ½ CUP)

½ cup tahini *(sesame paste)*   ½ *teaspoon cumin*
Juice of 2 lemons (a scant ½ cup)   *A sprig of fresh parsley, minced*
2 *to* 3 *cloves of garlic, crushed*

Blend the first 4 ingredients into a creamy sauce, adding more lemon juice or water if necessary. Garnish with the minced parsley.

A Note on Sources. The only cookbook I know devoted entirely to Egyptian cooking is Samia Abdennour's *Egyptian Cooking: A Practical Guide.* A 160-page spiral-bound volume published by the American University in Cairo, it is usable and authentic, and can be obtained from Kitchen Arts & Letters (1435 Lexington Avenue, New York, NY 10128) for $14.95 plus postage. Our source for the small brown Egyptian fava beans is Sultan's Delight, P.O. Box 140253, 25 Croton Avenue, Staten Island, NY 10314-0014; (718) 720-1557.

Russians and Mushrooms

✧ ✧ ✧

"Yes, yes, yes! with onion, and you know with bay leaf and all kinds of spices. When you open the pot and the steamy mushroom smell rises, it sometimes even brings tears to your eyes. . . ." "Devil take it! Only thinking about eating," growled Milkin the philosopher contemptuously. "Aren't there any more interesting things in life besides mushrooms . . . ?"   —Anton Chekhov, "The Siren"

Attempting, in a recent issue of *Mushroom: The Journal of Wild Mushrooming*, to explain his compatriots' obsession with gathering wild mushrooms, Alexander ("Sasha") Viazmensky tells how, during the peak of the season, Russians drive their cars right off the roads into the forests, in single-minded determination to cover as much ground as possible. This image has its downside—from the perspective of both the ecologist and the foot-borne mushroom gatherer—but from a distance it also has a certain perverse, surrealistic charm: black-beetle Soviet automobiles, like a swarm of 1948 DeSotos, their headlights glowing in the murk, weaving between the tree trunks of a forest that extends as far as the eye can see.

This image also captures something of what the landscape of western Russia is like: immense—and immensely flat. Its forests dwarf the imagination without themselves being all that impressive, for the ground is often damp, the soil poor, and the trees aspen, pine, and birch. They provide the Russian wanderer not with dramatic vistas or a sense of savage charm, but with an intimate, protective privacy—healingly cool and sweet-smelling. Boris Pasternak spoke for all native Russians when he wrote: "Included in the saintly order of pines/We become immortal for a while."

Mushrooms, of course, grow in many places, but for Russians they have an immediate association with these woods; they might be considered, more even than the Russian black bear, their country's emblem. Mushroom hunting appears in Pasternak's poems, in Chekhov's short stories, in Tolstoy's *Anna Karenina*. A recent Russian novel by Zinovy Zinik called *The Mushroom-Picker* tells of an expatriate who comes to define what a Russian is—and what the rest of the world is not—in terms of his nostalgia for the commingling of sensual and sensory pleasure that is the mushroom hunt.

To understand this relationship between Russians and mushrooms, you must first grasp that the latter are, before anything else, a *gift*. Like Easter eggs, they are something put there to be discovered, hidden for the pleasure of being found. Adults are not immune to the happiness that children take in finding things: the delight in the gift is enhanced by that contradictory feeling that simultaneously celebrates one's cleverness and good luck. The wild mushroom becomes a gift not only to the stomach but also to the spirit, all the more so because—unlike wild fruit, which has its predictable season—mushrooms appear magically, overnight, anywhere, following no discernible rhyme or reason. Thus in Russia the approach of the mushroom season is not unlike—to vary the metaphor a little—going to look under the Christmas tree every morning from Advent on to see if any presents are yet hidden beneath its boughs.

However, the moment for *hodit' po griby*—finding the mushroom—arrives neither at Christmas nor at Easter, but sometime in the middle of July. Morels are not much hunted, nor any spring mushroom, the forests being then infested with an encephalitis-spreading tick. You hardly encounter a hiker there until the rumor spreads that someone has found the year's first clump of boletes—whether tawny *edulis*, brown *scaber*, or red *aurantiacus*—and mushroomers start heading for the woods. When these mushrooms actually appear in the farmers' markets, the real rush is on. Morning trains are jammed with hunters clutching baskets, knapsacks, satchels, pails; some foragers—the most devoted—leave the night before. Groups organize expeditions, rent buses through their factories, and spend Friday night getting what sleep they can on the road; individuals catch the last train of the evening and doze fitfully beside a campfire, to get that much of a head start.

All agree that the best time to find mushrooms is at dawn's first light. Mushrooms are the freshest then and competitors the fewest. "You get into the forest and you know instinctively if the conditions are right for them," a young hitchhiker told Colin Thubron in *Where Nights Are Longest*. "You can sense it. It gives you a strange thrill. Perhaps the grass is growing at the right thickness, or there's the right amount of sun. You can even smell them. So you go forwards into the shadows. . . ." Vladimir Nabokov captures, in *Speak, Memory*, the many nuances of that evocative scent. In rainy weather, the shady recesses under the old firs, birches, and aspens in the family park would "harbor that special boletic reek which makes a Russian's nostrils dilate—a dark, dank, satisfying blend of damp moss, rich earth, rotting leaves."

By August, when slow, warm rains start soaking the vast Russian forests, everyone takes part in the feast. A huge billboard identifying the more common varieties of mushrooms is erected in Moscow's central market to help shoppers identify their purchases, and the state sets up multiple "mushroom points," or collection areas, where mushroom hunters can sell their catch and others can take a working holiday to help clean and dry them. Most hunters, however, bring their finds home, some vaunting their success and others keeping it hidden. "A totally open basket with beautiful mushrooms draws everybody's jealous glances," remarks Sasha Viazmensky, "but it looks shockingly immodest." Better to pick a few of your prize finds and lay them on top, and at least partially cover the rest with pretty branches.

Vladimir Nabokov's mother took the opposite ploy. As she emerged from under the dripping trees, "her face would show an odd, cheerless expression, which might have spelled poor luck, but which I knew was the jealously contained beatitude of the successful hunter. Just before reaching me, with an abrupt, drooping movement of the arm and shoulder and a 'Pouf!' of magnified exhaustion, she would let her basket sag, in order to stress its weight, its fabulous fullness."

And what was that basket full of? Volodya, Thubron's young informant, waxes lyrical about the possibilities: "delicate white mushrooms with umbrellaed hats . . . in the pine forests; red, strong-tasting birch mushrooms with whitish stems and feverish black specks; the yellow 'little foxes'; and the sticky, dark-tipped mushroom called 'butter-covered,' delicate and sweet. Then there was the *apyata* which multiplied on shrubs . . . and at last, in late autumn . . . a beautiful green cap which it was a sacrilege to fry." Lesley Chamberlain, in *The Food and Cooking of Russia*, conveys something of how the names and lore of such mushrooms can bring a Russian forest to enchanted life:

> These strange and wonderful growths have names that locate them in a fungous elfin kingdom of old men with ear trumpets, little women with long-stemmed umbrellas, men wearing hoods in the rain, Caesar's favorites, little foxes, little pigs, little hawks and cows and goats with beards, those that live under the birch tree and those that prefer the pine. Always lurking under some tree or other is the devil.

Russians claim that their cuisine makes the greatest and most varied use of mushrooms: they dress them with herbs and eat them raw; they fry them up with butter and serve them mixed with sour cream; they simmer them in soups and bake them in pastry. They pickle them or salt them and wash the result down with vodka. And, after all else, they thread them into long chains and dry them, and cook with these the whole winter through. Still, there is something all of a piece about native Russian cooking (as opposed to the several cuisines of the new Russian federation); it is really a collection of variations on a relatively small number of simple themes. Although there are many dishes that utilize them, at bottom there seems to be a single Russian mushroom dish—or, at least, one basic way of preparing them. Fortunately, it is also the *best* way, as the following version and some of its simpler permutations may suggest.

> Mushrooms are eaten fried, boiled or pickled, while their season endures, by all classes. . . . They are fried on hot ashes, or in a frying-pan; they are boiled alone; they are boiled with shchi or cabbage soup; they are roasted with butter alone, or oftener with butter and smetana or sour cream. They also enter into the composition of some puddings and pies. The latter are generally eaten with soup or with shchi. Mushrooms are often served up with beef-steak, or roast beef sliced, either alone or mixed with potatoes, carrots, turnips, cabbage, asparagus &c., and sauce. They are excellent when prepared with cutlets and rich sauce, duly seasoned.
> —Robert Lyall, *The Character of the Russians* (1823)

MAKING DO WITH
AGARICUS BISPORUS

Mushroom fanciers scorn the familiar commercial mushroom and often make the point that it isn't even a true *champignon* (*Agaricus campestris*)—a tastier but harder-to-grow cousin. The store or "button" mushroom (*Agaricus bisporus*) was easy to domesticate because it thrives in domestic circumstances. It particularly loves horse manure, for which reason Russian peasants shunned it, thinking it unclean. Russians in general shun it for its lack of flavor. As Zinovy Zinik has the narrator exclaim in *The Mushroom-Picker*:

> Nobody in Moscow even bothers to eat them; they grow in Gorky Street between the cracks in the pavement and the people tread them underfoot. Because they don't taste like mushrooms—they taste like rubber galoshes!

Well, *chacun à son goût*. The button mushroom is always available, still reasonably cheap, and, if you know how to cook it, does have *some* mushroom taste. The trick, as Edna Lewis explains in *The Edna Lewis Cookbook*, is to cook them "over high heat, as this seems to seal in their moisture and keep them plump and firm. If the heat is too low, they will stew and become wrinkled and rubbery . . ." and taste like galoshes. It need only be added that to keep them moist, plump, *and* firm, slice them thick; to make them crisp and buttery, slice them thin. Either way, they should then be sautéed in quite hot butter and/or oil until their edges are brown.

As a final enhancement, we finish these mushrooms in a flavor concentrate prepared in advance by pouring a cup of *boiling* water over a half ounce or so of dried boletes or inexpensive Chilean mushrooms (for sources, see the taster's guide on page 149), and letting this mixture steep for a half hour. The liquid is strained off and reduced in a small pot over high heat to about a quarter cup. (The dried mushrooms, having surrendered their flavor, are discarded.) This reduction is stirred into the mushrooms during their last few minutes of cooking until completely absorbed.

Note: Commercial mushrooms are enclosed in airtight plastic containers to ensure that no moisture (and hence weight) is lost. This means that even though you pay more, you *get* more buying them loose. Mushrooms keep longest when stored in the refrigerator in a closed paper bag: in plastic, they rot; in paper, they dehydrate instead.

Fried in butter and thickened with sour cream, her delicious finds appeared regularly on the dinner table.
—Vladimir Nabokov, *Speak, Memory*

MUSHROOMS SAUTÉED IN THE OLD STYLE
(ADAPTED FROM A RECIPE BY BORIS ZABOROV IN
NADINE HAIM'S *THE ARTIST'S PALATE*)

1 pound fresh boletes (porcini,   *1 medium onion, diced small*
    cèpes, etc.) (see note below)   *2 tablespoons sour cream*
4 tablespoons butter   *Salt and pepper to taste*

Clean the mushrooms carefully with a soft-bristled brush. If they are small, leave them whole, otherwise slice them thick. Melt 1 tablespoon of the butter in a skillet over medium heat and add the onion pieces. Cook these until edged with brown, then remove and reserve. Wipe the skillet with a paper towel and put in the last 3 tablespoons of butter. When this is hot and bubbling, add the mushrooms. Cook these over medium-high heat until they are firm-textured and start to brown. Return the sautéed onions to the pan and mix into the mushrooms. Remove the pan from the heat, stir in the sour cream, season to taste with salt and pepper, and serve at once.

COOK'S NOTE: Wild mushrooms don't come by the pound; the proportions in this recipe should be taken as a guideline: the more mushrooms, the more butter and sour cream. Olive oil—or, for a genuine Russian flavor note, sunflower oil—can be substituted for half the butter; a clove or two of minced garlic can replace the onion. Fresh boletes are rarely in the market and are hard to find in the woods. Last fall I received as a gift a single large field mushroom. I cooked it this way and ate it out of the pan; it was delicious. The dish is just as tasty (and authentic) made with a mix of different types. This last is a good course to follow if using commercially grown mushrooms, combining some shiitake and/or oyster mushrooms with a larger amount of plain button mushrooms, enhancing them as described in the box on pages 142–43.

Mushrooms prepared this way can be tossed with minced fresh dill and/or parsley and eaten hot on buttered toast. We prepare a simple meal by cooking a pound or so of commercial mushrooms, mixing in a more exotic type as described above, and cooking these with several chopped scallions, seasoning the dish with minced garlic, some lemon juice, and a small amount of ground chile pepper. We eat this over steaming rice or kasha.

Although it is a fine appetizer made as above, Russian cooks also adapt this dish to make a kind of poor man's caviar:

> "But best of all, kind sir, are yellow-capped saffron mushrooms, chopped finely like caviar, if you know what I mean, with onion and olive oil—delicious!"
> —Anton Chekhov, "The Siren"

MUSHROOM CAVIAR

(ADAPTED FROM JEAN REDWOOD'S *RUSSIAN FOOD*)

1 pound fresh mushrooms
4 to 6 scallions
4 tablespoons olive oil
1 to 2 tablespoons lemon juice

½ cup sour cream
Salt and black and cayenne pepper
Several sprigs of fresh dill

Clean the mushrooms carefully with a soft-bristled brush. Slice thick. Mince the scallions, including all the green except damaged or wilted ends, and sauté them over medium heat in 1 tablespoon of the oil. Scrape into a small bowl and reserve. Add the rest of the oil to the same skillet and sauté the mushrooms over medium-high heat until all the liquid has boiled off or been reabsorbed and the mushroom pieces are firm and lightly browned.

Stir in the sautéed scallion bits, add lemon juice to taste (the amount will depend on the type of mushroom), and scrape the mixture out onto a cutting board. Chop it into a coarse-textured "caviar" and turn into a bowl. Stir in the sour cream and season to taste with salt, black pepper, and a generous pinch of cayenne. The mixture should be served at room temperature. Just before, mince the dill and mix in, reserving some to sprinkle decoratively over the top. Delicious with pieces of toasted, buttered rye or pumpernickel bread.

COOK'S NOTE: In *Please to the Table*, Anya von Bremzen and John Welchman give a recipe for a mushroom and egg salad that is essentially this mushroom caviar blended with chopped egg and mayonnaise. It would be better still, I think, with some crisp, crumbled pieces of bacon as well.

Although she also calls it a "mushroom caviare," Lesley Chamberlain's take on this appetizer in *The Food and Cooking of Russia* is to prepare it uncooked. The raw mushrooms are coarsely chopped, mixed with finely minced garlic and the juice of an onion, and seasoned with salt and black pepper. The mixture is placed under a weighted plate in a large bowl and left for several hours to "cook" in its own juices. It is then tossed with olive or sunflower oil, lemon juice, and a minced fresh herb—dill or a very small amount of tarragon—just before serving.

Our basic mushroom sauté can be transformed into a delicious soup by adding a quart of hot homemade beef or chicken stock and serving it up. Good meat stock is not always available, however, and the Russians have an inspired alternative using dried mushrooms, a method we use to make our own mushroom and barley soup.

MUSHROOM STOCK

½ ounce or so dried boletes (porcini, cèpes)

Although rinsing dried mushrooms washes away flavor, unless you dry your own there's no sure way to tell whether they are free of grit. The strategy is this: *First* soak the mushrooms in water for about 30 minutes (whole dried mushrooms—if you can find them—are said to require much longer), then strain the resulting stock through a paper coffee filter. At this point —and only if you actually plan to use the reconstituted mushrooms—you rinse them. More often, we squeeze out every drop of liquid and discard them. The amount of water depends on the planned use of the stock—it can range from a cup to a quart or more. Hot water extracts the maximum flavor and softens the tougher mushrooms; cold water pampers the more delicate ones and leaves them all with more taste. Any dried mushroom can be reconstituted this way, but not all will provide a flavorful stock—Chinese cloud (or tree) ears, for example, release almost no flavor at all.

MUSHROOM AND BARLEY SOUP
(SERVES 2 TO 4)

Mushroom stock made as above,
   with 1 quart water
½ cup (4 ounces) barley
1 bay leaf
2 teaspoons salt (or to taste)
1 large onion
1 or 2 carrots
2 stalks of celery (with leaves)
1 pound fresh mushrooms

3 tablespoons olive oil
½ teaspoon paprika
2 cloves garlic, minced
1 tablespoon lemon juice
A few sprigs fresh parsley or dill,
   minced
Large dollop of sour cream for
   each serving

Put the mushroom stock in a pot and bring to a simmer. Add the barley, the bay leaf, and 1 teaspoon salt. Bring the stock back to a simmer, cover, and let cook. Chop the onion and cut the carrots and celery into small dice. Slice the mushrooms thick.

Heat 1 tablespoon of the olive oil in a medium skillet and add the onion. Cook this, stirring, over medium-high heat until translucent, then add the carrots and celery. When these have softened and the onion is edged with brown, turn all this into the simmering soup pot. Pour the remaining 2 tablespoons of olive oil into the skillet, and sprinkle this with the paprika and 1 teaspoon salt. Heat over a medium-hot flame; when the pan is hot, add the mushrooms and sauté, stirring often, until they are firm-textured and at least some pieces are beginning to brown. Add the minced garlic. Cook, still stirring, a few more minutes, and turn this mixture into the soup pot too.

The soup is ready to serve when the barley is done—in about an hour. Stir in the lemon juice and minced herb and discard the bay leaf. Serve the soup in warm bowls, topping each with a generous scoop of sour cream. This serves four as part of a meal, two or three as a whole one.

❖ ❖ ❖

Russian cooks have had to find a way to mask frugality behind the appearance of generosity, because to give everybody as many mushrooms as they want at a meal would mean none left over to pickle or salt or dry. So they devised the simple trick of cooking up the mushrooms in a fry—or braise—of potatoes. The delicious result, according to Anya von Bremzen in Please to the Table, *is*

> . . . the quintessential Russian *dacha* dish, and many a Russian would kill for it away from home. . . . For me the dish never fails to evoke the happiest memories of childhood—of my last summer days at the *dacha*, a lingering sadness at twilight on Sunday evening with the prospect of returning to Moscow drawing near.

BRAISE OF MUSHROOMS AND POTATOES
(SERVES 2 OR 3 AS A MEAL, MORE AS A SIDE DISH)

4 to 6 (about 2 pounds) all-
   purpose potatoes
Mushroom stock
2 cloves garlic
½ teaspoon dried thyme
1 pound fresh mushrooms
2 tablespoons each butter and olive
   oil

½ teaspoon hot paprika
1 medium onion, chopped
Salt and pepper to taste
A few sprigs of minced fresh dill
   and/or parsley
Sour cream (optional)

Peel the potatoes and keep them in a bowl of cold water. Prepare the mushroom stock as directed on page 146, using half an ounce of dried mushrooms and about 2 cups of water. Cut up and put aside the reconstituted mushroom pieces from the stock if they are appetizing and grit-free. Mince the garlic and thyme together. Clean the fresh mushrooms and cut into thick (half-inch) pieces, slicing down from cap to stem. Put the butter–olive oil combination into a large (12-inch) skillet over medium-high heat. Stir in the paprika. Add the mushroom pieces and sauté these, turning them often with a spatula, until they begin to brown. Stir in the chopped onion (and, if saved, the pieces of dried mushroom). Continue sautéing until the onion begins to color. Stir in the garlic-thyme mixture.

Chop up the potatoes into large bite-sized pieces. Put them in the skillet and let them cook, turning with the spatula, until they take on some color. Now add the strained mushroom stock and salt to taste. Cover the skillet and simmer 30 to 45 minutes, until the potatoes are tender and most of the liquid has been absorbed. Season with pepper, stir in the fresh herbs, and serve, if you like, with dollops of sour cream.

COOK'S NOTE: This version of the recipe gets the most from store-bought mushrooms; it's our favorite way of eating them. If you have fresh wild mushrooms, the dish can also be made as a straightforward sauté. Prepare it to the point where the potatoes are added. Remove the contents of the skillet and reserve. Heat another tablespoon or so each of butter and olive oil in the skillet and cook the potatoes until they are crisp and deeply golden, about 30 minutes. Return the mushroom-onion-garlic mixture to the skillet, mix well, season to taste, stir in the fresh herb(s), and serve.

TASTING NOTES: DRIED WILD MUSHROOMS

One autumn, a few years back, the pine woods near home were teeming with painted jacks (*Suillus pictus*), a situation too rare and tempting to pass up. So, knowing nothing about it, I decided to try drying a bunch of them. I spent an evening brushing them free of debris, cutting them into chunks, and then stringing them into long chains with a needle and a length of sturdy thread—each piece of mushroom tied an inch apart. I draped these in long swags in front of the living room window. In a few days they had turned into small, firm, fragrant pieces of dried mushroom that, sealed up tightly in preserving jars, kept for well over a year. Drying, if anything, improved the flavor of what is not, when all is said, a choice find.

I tell this not to recommend the method but simply to encourage the attempt. The hard part is getting the mushrooms in the first place. According to Antonio Carluccio in *A Passion for Mushrooms*, the best mushroom for drying is the *Boletus edulis* (king boletes; in Italian: *porcini*; in French: *cèpes*), for the process actually intensifies its flavor. But there are many others worth the effort—I recommend you turn to my favorite mushroom guide, David Arora's *Mushrooms Demystified*, for suggestions and proper identification.

Some food writers suggest drying mushrooms in the oven, but what is really needed is a flow of warm, dry air. They should be cleaned carefully with a brush (an unused, soft-bristled paintbrush is ideal), and the larger specimens should be cut into slices about a half-inch thick. These should then be spread out in a single layer on a clean window screen. On hot, sunny days, they can be covered with cheesecloth and brought outside. Otherwise, leave them in a well-ventilated room, in a sunny—or at least warm—place. Turn them over now and then to ensure thorough drying. Then, when they're completely dried, store them in airtight jars or plastic bags.

The traditional Slavic method is to string the mushrooms up and hang them in garlands before the fire, so that the smoke can add its special savor. Such mushrooms, says Lesley Chamberlain, "yield a rich stock and all the fragrance of the Russian forest in early autumn." However, visions of some future harvest of boletes turning a rich mahogany in my electric meat smoker faded somewhat when we traced a source for smoked Polish mushrooms and found that the woodsy tang carried a little too much of the tar pot for us, at least for our simple mushroom and potato dishes. (We suspect their traditional use is to stretch—and thus enhance—the presence of smoked sausage or ham hocks.) In any case, we preferred the more straightforward mushroom flavor of the unsmoked version.

This was not our only disappointment. Mushroom drying is an art, not a science—and still very much a cottage industry. That little half-ounce of dried *cèpes* you buy at the gourmet store may contain mushrooms picked in different places under entirely different conditions—in some instances in entirely different *countries*. Given that two mushrooms of the same species picked fresh (even in the same spot!) can vary widely in taste—which is one reason why Jane Grigson can describe the horn of plenty (*Craterellus cornucopioides*) as "disappointing" while David Arora begins a two-paragraph rave by calling its flavor "superb"—buying them dried is pretty much a crapshoot.

After tasting several varieties of dried mushrooms over the

past year or so, we still find it hard to sort out any useful advice except that as a general rule we prefer fresh mushrooms for eating and dried mushrooms for adding flavor to dishes in which they themselves then play little or no part. This, of course, is no radical discovery; what might be is our feeling that when flavor is held to firmly as the sole criterion, we find little use for the dried chanterelle, oyster mushroom, horn of plenty, or shiitake. (The pricey but delicious dried morel is outside our brief.) Ignore evocative catalogue prose and stick to dried boletes or the generic "Chilean" mushroom that—though near inedible itself and sometimes full of grit—produces a murky but highly flavorful broth. These last are sold by G. B. Ratto, 821 Washington Street, Oakland, CA 94607; (800) 325-3483, at a price that can't be beat: one *pound* for $10.

For all other dried mushrooms, we suggest Festive Foods, 9420 Arroya Lane, Colorado Springs, CO 80908; (719) 495-2339. They have the best prices—and pretty nearly the best selection—of all the mail-order sources we consulted. See their catalogue for the full list; what interested us were the dried *porcini* from Italy, at $5.50 for two ounces, and smoked Polish boletes—an acquired taste—at $6 for two ounces. These are the ones we would choose for the dishes discussed above.

☞ *Mushroom: The Journal of Wild Mushrooming* is full of useful and up-to-date information on finding, identifying, avoiding being poisoned by, and even growing wild mushrooms, along with book reviews and a roundup of mushroom-news-of-the-world. Some of the publication is aimed at those whose interest in fungi lies at a higher level than merely finding and eating them, but each issue has its share of good recipes and the occasional offbeat culinary tip (to make chanterelle-flavored vodka, slip a small thin *dry* specimen into any bottled vodka and let it sit, the longer the better). This illustrated 42-page quarterly is $16 a year from: P.O. Box 3156, University Station, Moscow, ID 83843.

DANDAN NOODLES

❖ ❖ ❖

Noodles, the cheapest of all foods, allow every man to be
a gourmet. Such is the glory of the food of Szechwan.
—Ellen Schrecker, *Mrs. Chiang's Szechwan Cookbook*

Nels introduced me to the Hong Hing. Spending his days
at a publishing job and his nights working on his art—which
at that time consisted of lithographs of fried eggs and bead
curtains with razor blades replacing the beads—he had neither
time nor inclination to cook and, although he didn't have any
money either, ate all his meals in restaurants. I don't know
what kind of an artist he was, but at locating cheap eats he
was a master.

That summer I was cutting costs myself, saving subway fare
by bicycling back and forth between my apartment on East
Ninth Street and the financial district and my job on Hanover
Square. Some evenings I would meet Nels and go with him to
his latest discovery. Even with the way I was cooking then it
was hard for me to get supper on the table for the cost of some
of the bargain meals turned out at some of his hole-in-the-wall
finds.

Of all of these, as far as I was concerned, the Hong Hing
was best. It was nothing like my previous experiences of
Chinese restaurants. For one thing, the patrons were almost
entirely Chinese and the atmosphere was noisy and full of

camaraderie. Every now and again, one of the chefs would strike a hanging pan cover with the back of his cleaver with a clang and the whole kitchen would break out into song. Waiters intercepted intruding "foreign devils" at the door and attempted to dissuade them—me—from entering by reciting "no spare rib, no chicken finger, no pork fried rice."

If you persisted, your presence was tolerated, but little effort was made at accommodation. The menu was only in Chinese and the welcoming litany about as much English as the waiters knew. The only way to order was to point at something that another patron was being served. Sometimes this required wandering up and down the entire restaurant, waiter in tow, searching the tables until a dish was recognized or looked affordable and good.

This method had its pitfalls, to be sure, but the results were worth it, for the Hong Hing was a noodle house, serving a rich and extremely inexpensive array of China's superlative wheat and rice noodle dishes, prepared with a freshness and savory perfection that I have never experienced since. And a plate of meatless but vegetable-rich *chow fun*, a feast for a king, was only sixty-five cents!

So, when the cold weather came around again, making supper at the Hong Hing a more arduous excursion, I decided to devote myself to mastering Chinese cooking. I would learn to prepare these dishes myself at home. To that end, I threw out most of my tatty collection of cooking implements, including all my silverware—except spoons—so I wouldn't be tempted to backslide. I then went to Chinatown and purchased a wok (of genuine provenance, carbon steel thickly coated with axle grease), a wickedly edged cleaver, a handful of chopsticks—and plunged in.

Although I refused to admit it for several months, this experiment turned out a monumental failure. Part of the reason was the lack of a reliable guide. I had the *Joyce Chen Cook Book*, about the best there was at the time (1965), but Joyce Chen was writing for middle-class cooks, not poor poets. In any case, it was an endeavor that would have required far greater devotion and ingenuity than I was capable of, at least to succeed in making the food I had come to love at the Hong Hing.

Chinese restaurant cooking is a labor-intensive and highly skilled craft, the raw foodstuffs being precisely prepared and then cooked instantly, with astounding precision, over a burst of searing heat.* It is a cooking that works wonders with the least expensive of ingredients—but a price must be paid in the coin of dexterity, concentration, and long apprenticeship before it can be successfully mastered.

I produced any number of dishes *à la chinoise*, redolent of sesame oil, sour of soy, and tangy of bean paste—but nothing that even nearly approached those delicate, complex, sumptuously textured yet clean-tasting noodle feasts I had set as my goal. And so, at home at least, my allegiance turned elsewhere . . . the wok rusted, the cleaver accustomed itself to dicing slab bacon for rice and beans.

However, my interest in eating Chinese food never slackened, and I began having thoughts of trying to cook it again when the Szechuan boom introduced me to an entirely different style of noodle dish. Here, in the form of *dandan* noodles and other cold, spicy-flavored, street-vendor-style noodle dishes, I discovered a more impromptu-seeming saucing, boldly and variously textured, but still not nearly so elaborate in its architecture as the Hong Hing dishes had been. The ingredients were fewer, the dishes themselves much simpler. Here was something I *could* make in my own kitchen.

This, as it turned out, was because they had first been sold from pushcarts or tiny stalls by vendors who possessed only the most rudimentary cooking equipment. The noodles were heaped on the customer's plate and the sauce made right there: by seasoning the noodles to the eater's taste with an array of pungent condiments and garnishing them with simple but well-chosen toppings, a wide variety of separate dishes were composed from a limited number of set ingredients.

The foundation of all these variations was the same simple sauce, a combination of the most familiar of Chinese season-

---

* Also an important limitation: As anyone who has tried to cook with a wok over an American range will know from bitter experience, our gas burners just don't generate sufficient heat for the instantaneous cooking that true stir-frying requires—a fact most Chinese cookbooks don't go especially out of their way to explain.

ings: soy sauce, sesame oil, vinegar, and a sweetening agent, the flavors usually heightened and rendered still more pungent with fresh garlic, ginger, hot peppers, and scallions, and a minced fresh herb such as coriander. In *dandan* noodles, this sauce reaches its perfection through the addition of sesame or peanut paste, imbuing it with a smooth, savory richness that counterbalances the mouth-filling pungency of the seasonings.

The recipes below—prefaced with a few words about the less familiar essential ingredients—example the making of that sauce and its variations, from which, in one form or another, springs a whole family (though, of course, not the *only* family) of Chinese noodle vendor dishes.

A NOTE ON INGREDIENTS

Chinese black vinegar. A rice vinegar with a distinctive mellow flavor and dark color, it is made in different versions that are well worth exploring. There is no exact substitute. Barbara Tropp, in *The Modern Art of Chinese Cooking*, suggests using balsamic vinegar; Nina Simonds, in *Classic Chinese Cuisine*, a third less Worcestershire sauce.

Chinese fresh egg noodles. These are increasingly available in the produce section of many supermarkets, although the locally made product found in Chinese markets is superior. If you have access to one, the flat but very thinly rolled *kuan dan mian* is a good choice for these dishes. Freshly made Italian pasta is the best substitute—otherwise, use a dried durum-wheat spaghettini. Instructions for making your own can be found in Barbara Tropp's *The Modern Art of Chinese Cooking*.

To prepare: The only trick is to separate out the strands before cooking, discarding any doughy clumps. Plunge the noodles into a large pot of boiling (unsalted) water—they will be cooked seconds after the water returns to a boil. Drain them in a colander immediately, shaking out as much water as possible. As with any cold pasta dish, "temperate" is the better word. Sauce and noodles should be at room temperature, not chilled.

Sesame paste. Unlike tahini, the Middle Eastern sesame paste, the Chinese version is made from *toasted* sesame seeds and is thus richer in flavor and more aromatic (imagine peanut butter made from unroasted peanuts and you'll get some sense of the difference). If you don't have access to an Oriental market, you can toast sesame seeds in a hot, ungreased frying pan and then make your own paste in a food processor fitted with the steel blade. *Sesame oil*, for fullest flavor, should also be pressed from toasted seeds.

Traditionally, these sauces were made in a mortar, the ingredients added in an order allowing them to simultaneously reach a fine but textured sauce. I simply mince the ingredients of the more complex sauces with a cleaver before pounding them together in our large stone Thai mortar, bought at a Vietnamese grocery. A food processor fitted with its steel blade will do the job in a snap. Finally, all proportions in the following recipes are only suggestions and should be varied to personal taste.

BASIC COLD-TOSSED NOODLES
(SERVES 3 OR 4 AS A LIGHT MAIN DISH)

1 pound Chinese fresh egg
 noodles (see page 155)

For the sauce

4 tablespoons soy sauce
1 tablespoon brown sugar
2 tablespoons sesame oil
3 tablespoons black vinegar

1 teaspoon chile powder
1 tablespoon minced fresh
 coriander

For the garnish

Chopped scallions or Chinese
 chives (these are like ordinary

chives but have a garlicky
 undertone)

For the accompaniments

Any or all of: bean sprouts, briefly
 parboiled and slivered; slivered
 green beans, carrots, and/or
 peeled, seeded, and lightly

salted cucumbers; chopped peanuts; and boiled shrimp or
 shredded cooked chicken

Mix ingredients for the sauce well and allow the flavors to set—preferably for an hour or two, but for at least 15 minutes—before using. Cook noodles as directed on page 155, draining and shaking off all excess water immediately. Toss the noodles thoroughly in the sauce and set in a large serving bowl. Sprinkle with the garnish. Set out the accompaniments in small separate bowls to surround the noodles.

This Szechuan dish takes its name from the street on which the vendors originally sold it. Its sauce is similar to the one above, but adds garlic, ginger, toasted sesame seeds, and Szechuan peppercorns (which give it a pleasing, menthol-tinged savor).

T'UNG CHING STREET NOODLES
(SERVES 3 OR 4 AS A LIGHT MEAL)

1 pound Chinese fresh egg noodles
 (see page 155)

For the sauce

2 tablespoons toasted sesame seeds   *3 or 4 cloves garlic, minced*
4 to 6 Szechuan peppercorns   *1 teaspoon chile powder*
3 or 4 finely minced scallions   *3 tablespoons soy sauce*
1 tablespoon dark brown sugar   *1 tablespoon minced fresh ginger*
2 tablespoons sesame oil   *1 tablespoon Chinese black vinegar*

For the garnish

Chinese chives (see page 156) or   *Whole toasted sesame seeds*
 scallions, finely chopped

First make the sauce. Pound the toasted sesame seeds and the Szechuan peppercorns into a powder in a mortar. To bring out the flavors, mix this with the rest of the sauce ingredients and set the result to rest—preferably for an hour or two, but for at least 15 minutes—before using.

Cook noodles as directed on page 155, draining and shaking off all excess water immediately. Toss the noodles thoroughly in the sauce and set in a large serving bowl. Sprinkle with the garnish.

Traditionally, these cold-sauced noodles are eaten without any accompaniment, but cold, cooked, slivered chicken is a delicious addition. Tofu is another possibility.

DANDAN NOODLES

At first encounter, the sauce for dandan *noodles seems a wild concatenation of ingredients, but following our progression into complexity, you can see it consists of three basic elements artfully commingled: the noodles themselves, the sauce, and the paste of sesame or peanut, which thickens and enriches it. Dandan noodles are the archetypal street-vendor noodle, since the seed paste adds nutrition and flavor, and gives the sauce a smoother, creamier texture and more luscious flavor, but hardly increases its cost. Two versions are given, since a slightly different harmony is required to accommodate the different taste notes of the sesame seed and the peanut.*

DANDAN NOODLES WITH PEANUT SAUCE
(SERVES 3 OR 4)

1 pound Chinese fresh egg noodles
  (see page 155)

For the sauce

5 or 6 cloves of garlic, minced
1 tablespoon minced fresh ginger
½ cup chunky peanut butter
1 tablespoon dark brown sugar
2 tablespoons sesame oil

1 tablespoon peanut oil
½ teaspoon chile powder
3 tablespoons soy sauce
2 teaspoons Chinese black vinegar
½ cup chicken broth

For the accompaniments

4 scallions, finely minced (including the green)

¼ cup finely chopped roasted peanuts

Put all the ingredients for the sauce except the chicken broth into a food processor fitted with the steel blade. Pulsing the blade, blend the mixture into a sauce the thickness of light cream, thinning it with the chicken broth (or water) until it reaches this consistency. Remove from the processor and let sit for at least 15 minutes to allow the flavors to mingle before cooking the noodles. Prepare the noodles as directed on page 155. Drain well, divide into bowls, and spoon over each a generous amount of the sauce. Let each eater add from the accompaniments as desired. (See the cook's note on page 160.)

DANDAN NOODLES WITH SESAME SAUCE
(SERVES 3 OR 4)

1 pound Chinese fresh egg noodles
  (see page 155)

For the sauce

3 or 4 cloves garlic, minced
1 tablespoon minced fresh ginger
1/4 cup sesame paste
3 tablespoons soy sauce
1/4 cup minced fresh coriander
1 tablespoon dark brown sugar

1/2 teaspoon chile powder
2 teaspoons Chinese black vinegar
A grinding of Szechuan pepper
1/2 cup chicken broth
1 tablespoon toasted sesame seeds

For the accompaniments

4 scallions, finely minced (including the green)

1 cucumber, peeled, halved,
  seeded, and cut into fine strips

Put all the ingredients for the sauce except the chicken broth and sesame seeds into a food processor fitted with the steel blade. Pulsing the blade, blend the mixture into a sauce the thickness of light cream, thinning it with the chicken broth (or water) until it reaches this consistency. Remove from the processor and stir in the sesame seeds. Let this sauce sit for at least 15 minutes to allow the flavors to mingle before cooking the noodles. Prepare the noodles as directed on page 155. Drain well, divide into bowls, and spoon over each a generous amount of the sauce. Let each eater add from the accompaniments as desired.

COOK'S NOTE: In both of these versions of *dandan* noodles, the number of accompaniments recommended is a bare minimum. The actual range of possible additions is quite wide. Szechuan preserved turnip (or vegetables), a spicy-hot Chinese condiment, is popularly recommended, as are any of the accompaniments mentioned with the other sauces. However, no meat is needed and the dish can be made strictly vegetarian by substituting a vegetable broth or water for the chicken broth in either of these recipes.

☞ For further exploration, see the chapter "Snacks and Street Foods" in Ken Hom's *The Taste of China*, Fu Pei-Mei's *Chinese Snacks & Desserts*, and the chapter "Noodle Dishes (for Lunch, Snack, or Evening Meal)" in Mai Leung's *The Chinese People's Cookbook*, as well as the books by Nina Simonds and Barbara Tropp already mentioned above.

BOEUF AUX CAROTTES

❖ ❖ ❖

Reading Rudolph Chelminski's *The French at Table* (a book perhaps better titled *Chelminski à Table*), I came across the following passage in praise of France's original women chefs, "the mothers of Lyon":

> They were a hardy, truculent lot, these women, independent, self-reliant and utterly unimpressed by titles, money or the reputations they had made for themselves. No staff, no décor, no apprentices, no pretension and, usually, not even any written menus: just the *pot-au-feu* bubbling on the back burner, next to the *boeuf aux carottes*, the *poule-au-pot* or the *blanquette de veau*.

For reasons I'm still not sure I understand, the simple name of one of those dishes—*boeuf aux carottes*, or, simply, beef with carrots—prosaic though it was, resonated so deeply in my appetite that when I had finished and closed the book—which is in large part devoted to bite-by-bite accounts of meals eaten in some of the best restaurants in France—it was the single culinary image that lingered.

So vivid was my imagining of it, moreover, that when a search into the usual French sources failed to yield a clue as to its exact composition, those three words were enough to summon up not only the dish but all its individual components, assembling together in a burst of flavor that obediently clustered round the two central players: a gentle braise of chunks

of beef, carrot, and onion, slowly simmering in no more liquid
than they cared themselves to exude, fragrant with browned
beef and onion, plus parsley, garlic, and thyme.

So the first time I made it, that's how I went about it. I took
a couple of pounds of boneless short ribs and ever-so-lightly
dredged them in flour seasoned with salt and freshly ground
pepper. These pieces of meat were browned in batches in a
skillet in olive oil heated almost to smoking and transferred to
a large cast-iron casserole. Then, in the same oil, I sautéed
some onions, cut in fairly good-sized pieces, until they were
translucent and edged with brown—scraping up with them
any tasty, charred bits of flour and meat still clinging to the
skillet.

All this went into the pot with the beef, and so did a generous
pound of carrots (or more—this is a dish that can't have too
many of them), peeled and cut into random-shaped, bite-sized
chunks. Finally, a small handful of parsley was minced and
scattered over, along with a sprinkling of thyme and some
minced cloves of garlic, and the seasoning was adjusted with
a generous pinch of salt and more grindings of the peppermill.

I cooked the dish very slowly—about four hours at 300°F—
enough heat to sweat out a copious supply of juices that bathed
the contents in a rich-tasting, gently thickened gravy, but still
leaving the beef juicy and tender, the carrots moist and sweet
and, without being in the least mushy, as soft and succulent
as a dream.

Good? Yes, even almost delicious. But like many a dish
pulled into being by a moment of appetite, it wanted something
to be remembered by. It needed . . . not savor exactly, for it
had that in its garlic, pepper, and thyme, but rather some clear
flavor-note that would remind me, when I was hungry again,
how much I had enjoyed that dish.

The answer came only after I had cast off spurious but insistent solutions such as reductions of wine or beer (too sour-
edged and diffuse in flavor) and such *gestes* as black olives or
chunks of bacon that wrenched the tongue too far from the
dish's original inspiration.

Returning to the carrots and beef, the soft, sweet flavor of
the one and the rich, gelatinous texture of the other, I found

at once what I was looking for: the sharp, citric bite of lemon, to refresh the mouth and keep it interested, even when hunger had started to abate.

And so my finished version uses not only the juice of half a lemon but a bit of the peel (some strips of zest, cut from the rind and not too finely minced). The results—given that this is, after all, a very simple dish—were all I could have hoped for: a meal, in this household at least, whose name still, after several makings, inspires anticipation.

Later, when I did find an actual French recipe for the dish in the English edition of *La Cuisine: The Complete Book of French Cooking* (by the food editors of *Elle* magazine), I was not in the least put out by the fact that their version was only cursorily similar, a kind of poor man's *boeuf à la mode*. I knew that if I had found this recipe during my original search, the dish would have been made just that once—or even never at all. Appetite knows best. *Les mères* might not agree with my version of the dish, but they would, I think, agree entirely with the course of its inspiration.

BEEF WITH CARROTS
(SERVES 4 TO 6)

1 pound or more carrots
2 to 3 medium onions
Flour for dredging
Salt and black pepper
½ teaspoon plus a pinch of dried thyme

¼ cup olive oil
2 pounds boneless beef short ribs
2 or 3 sprigs fresh parsley, minced
2 cloves of garlic, minced
1 teaspoon minced lemon zest
Juice of ½ lemon

Preheat the oven to 300°F. Scrub the carrots and, if you like, peel them, trimming away the tops. Cut them into bite-sized but not uniform chunks. Put them into a lightly oiled 3-quart casserole. Peel the onions and cut them into bite-sized chunks. Set aside. Take a half-cup or so of flour and season with a generous pinch each of salt, pepper, and dried thyme. Heat the olive oil in a large sauté pan until it starts to smoke. Dredge strips of short ribs (or any inexpensive, rich-textured stewing beef) in the seasoned flour, shaking away any excess. Put the meat in the hot oil and turn with tongs to sear on all sides, transferring each piece as it is finished into the casserole.

When all the meat has been seared, put the onion in the pan, adding more oil if necessary to keep it from burning. Cook until the pieces are translucent and edged with brown, turning them often with a spatula while at the same time scraping up any burnt bits of meat and flour. Scrape all this into the casserole onto the meat and carrots.

Add the minced parsley, garlic, and lemon zest to the casserole, pour the lemon juice over, and generously season with more salt and pepper and the reserved ½ teaspoon of thyme. Toss well with a spatula to mix the seasonings throughout the casserole. Cover, place in the preheated oven, and cook for about 4 hours, checking occasionally to make sure that the contents remain at a bare simmer and to taste for seasoning, adding more salt and pepper as needed. Serve over cooked rice or egg noodles with a small salad of greens, lots of crusty bread, and cold beer.

Afterword from Madeleine Kamman. After this piece appeared in *Simple Cooking*, I received a spirited communiqué from the author of *When French Women Cook* and *Madeleine Kamman's Savoie*, remembering the *boeuf aux carottes* of her childhood:

John!
    The reason you cannot find *boeuf aux carottes* too many places is because that was our *one* protein dish during the war. Your rendition of it is *way off*. It went like this: poorly defrosted stringy beef, all natural juices lost, browned in beef suet; plus one onion (the Germans loved onions so they all went to Berlin . . .); plus one clove garlic because what we raised had to last the year and so was kept like a museum piece for months . . . it was bitter because sprouting; plus lousy old stringy carrots that the Germans exchanged for our lovely little beauties, which went on to relieve the bombed Berlin hunger. Water, period, added as needed. Very little salt because we were also rationed on that essential.
    That was *boeuf aux carottes*. Since we had no heat, you had to swallow it fast or it would just coagulate and congeal on your plate. My poor mother, who is a National Cooking Treasure,

made it by mistake after 1945 and endured the jokes of the whole
family. Leave it to *Elle* to give a recipe for France's most hated
dish, which made the Spam donated by the U.S. Forces taste like
manna from heaven! So much for the history of this one.

> —Madeleine Kamman (who is made
> of the *boeuf aux carottes* she ate once a
> week between June 1940 and May
> 1945!!)

KITCHEN DIARY: GINGER PEAR CAKE

Reading Sheila Hibben's 1946 compendium, American Regional
Cookery, *Matt noticed that the author seemed to be finding variations
of the same cake recipe all over the country. First, it was a ginger loaf
from Alabama; next, it was a ginger spice cake from North Carolina.
Then the Alabama loaf wandered up North to put in an appearance as
a Connecticut ginger cake with stewed apples, baked in a ring mold
and served with a whipped cream border and a filling of warm spiced
fruit.*

*There was something touching and funny about the way it kept
popping up, as if the usually reserved Miss Hibben couldn't keep her
excitement about the cake from bursting into recipe no matter where
in the country she happened to be. And rightly so—for the cake proved
both unusual and good.*

*It was clearly of gingerbread stock, but more delicately sweetened
and with only a dollop of the requisite molasses; the usual spicing was
given depth and heat with lots of crystallized ginger. Finally, it was
moistened with unsweetened applesauce instead of the familiar boiling
water or sour milk.*

*Matt first made the cake as Sheila Hibben directed, using Wolf River
apples from my parents' orchard. We liked it, but we thought its distinct
ginger presence might work better still with pear. So we tried it again,
using puréed canned pears as a simple "pearsauce." That version produced a moist, tender, and delicious cake, but with only the fragrance
of the fruit, not its flavor. Next time, since the canned pears Matt was
using were put up in their own juice, she decided to use that liquid as
well, to see if it would pull out the flavor. It didn't, but it did produce*

a wonderfully sticky crust—and we got the pear taste we were looking for when, soon after, we added some pieces of fresh pear to the batter.

The result was a delicately fruity cake with that chewy crust and real ginger panache. The flavor of the fruit is only hinted at until you bite into an actual chunk: then there it is, rising out of the choir of flavors—the small, sweet voice of pear.

GINGER PEAR CAKE

½ cup (1 stick) unsalted butter
½ cup granulated sugar
½ cup light brown sugar, packed
2 tablespoons molasses
1 extra-large egg
1 can (16 ounces) pears in un-
    sweetened juice
2 cups all-purpose flour
1 teaspoon baking soda

½ teaspoon salt
2 teaspoons powdered ginger
½ teaspoon allspice
¼ cup crystallized ginger, finely
    minced
2 not-quite-ripe pears, quartered,
    cored, peeled, and cut into
    ½-inch pieces

Preheat the oven to 325°F. Generously butter a 9 × 5-inch loaf pan. Cream butter well with sugars; stir in molasses and lightly beaten egg. Mash canned pears into a purée (using fork, food mill, coarse sieve, etc.) and add this to the creamed mixture with the can juices. (This mixture will appear curdled.)

Sift the flour, soda, salt, and dry spices into another bowl and toss in the crystallized ginger. Add the wet ingredients to the dry and stir gently but thoroughly to blend. Fold in the pieces of fresh pear. Turn the batter into the loaf pan with a rubber scraper, smooth the surface, and place on a rack set in the middle of the oven.

Bake for about 1½ hours, or until a straw inserted in the center of the cake comes out clean. Let it cool 15 minutes in the pan, then turn it out onto a rack. Serve slices of the cake warm with lightly sweetened whipped cream. Leftover cake reheats nicely and is delicious sliced, toasted, and served with butter for breakfast or tea.

POTATO PANCAKE
PRIMER

✧ ✧ ✧

There's something so sheerly appetite-inspiring about potato pancakes that their appeal must touch something very
primal, a culinary nerve whose roots lie deep within. And my
guess is that it connects us to that moment in childhood when
we first became conscious of the fact that eating was more than
mouth pleasure but instead a whole sea of sensation into which
we could happily plunge and splash about.

I don't mean by this to suggest that potato pancakes are
something we all share in common from childhood—for one
thing, I didn't encounter them myself until later on in life. But
I do think they are able, more than almost any other food, to
evoke an anticipation richly resonant of childhood appetite in
all its simplicity and intensity. They are so uncomplicatedly
desirable, with their sweetly tender aroma, their gold and glistening presence in the frying pan, a presence that turns to all
crunch and tenderness on the tongue, leaving behind it a wake
of butter and warmth. Certainly this is the motif that appears,
again and again, in passages such as this one, in E. Œ. Somer-
ville and M. Ross's *The Holy Island*:

> While I live I shall not forget her potato cakes. They came in
> hot . . . from the pot oven, they were speckled with caraway
> seed, they swam in salt butter, and we ate them shamelessly
> and greasily, and washed them down with hot whiskey and
> water.

Just as important, they are a dish where appetite and recipe become so entangled that it is almost impossible to know where the one ends and the other begins. The making of potato pancakes is a polymorphous pleasure, an invitation to spontaneous inspiration. The potatoes may be raw or cooked, whole or part, and we can do with them as we will: mash, shred, grate, sliver, or chop, working each particular batch to meet the shape of that night's (or morning's) particular hunger.

For instance, one of the more satisfying batches I ever made was concocted from the leftover husks of a platter of baked potatoes, skins abandoned by eaters too finicky to pick them up and eat them. Their loss was my gain. The next morning I spread the skins, mouth down, on the cutting board and flattened each with the heel of my fist. I then fried them up, all squat and split-edged, in lots of sizzling butter. Chunky, chewy, crisp, and crunchy, they were, every one, a mouthful of delight.

As adaptable in content as in form, no sooner have they set the hand to play than do they urge the mind's tongue to go a-tasting, too, choosing among such options as might be rooted out from the back of the refrigerator or the pantry shelf: tiny cubes of carrot or Cheddar cheese, a scattering of parsley, a diced handful of fatty bits left over from Sunday's roast beef. It might fleck them with thyme, dot them with poppy seed or caraway, plump up their savor with garlic or any member of the onion tribe—or, for that matter, with a whole grated apple, enhancing those two famously harmonizing flavors still further with a generous grate of nutmeg.

All that remains is to cook them up, into whatever fashion appetite has this time worked their protean shape, whether fat mashed-potato burgers or thin, lacy-edged crisps. But do heed this final caution from H. Pearl Adam:

> The way to eat them is almost as potent a reason as their economy for their exclusion from polite tea-parties. They must be served so hot that a piece of cold butter placed between two of them begins to run out before there is time to eat them. The real way, of course, is to have them in the kitchen, straight from

the pan, at an honest-to-God kitchen table scrubbed to snow-colour, with a tower of golden Irish half-salted butter whose pet name is Cut-and-Come-Again Primrose, and hot plates large enough to catch the butter-drip from extended chins. Drawing-room editions of this fine work are feeble things.

We may not be able to serve our potato pancakes with a tower of Cut-and-Come-Again Primrose, but we can move our potato pancakes directly from griddle to heated plate and then eat them at once, with pots of applesauce and sour cream pushed within easy reach. Their magic fades even as it blossoms, melting faster than the butter for which you have paused to slather them. The mouth must seize for enchantment while it can, in hungry, wolfish bites, restrained by no false *politesse*.

IRISH POTATO CAKES #1
(ADAPTED FROM *KITCHEN RANGING*, BY H. PEARL ADAM)

Cold boiled potatoes	Salt
Flour	Butter

Mash the cold (and peeled) potatoes on a well-floured pastry board. Knead into them as much flour as they can absorb, along with enough salt to season to taste (a scant teaspoon for every four potatoes is ample). Roll this potato dough out quite thin (an eighth of an inch) and cut into 2-inch circles. Heat an ungreased griddle over medium-high heat, and lay out on it as many as will fit. Gently but firmly shaking the griddle now and then to keep them from sticking, cook them on the first side until a tinge of brown appears, then turn and do the same to the second (about 3 to 4 minutes a side). Serve them with ample butter the moment they come off the griddle.

COOK'S NOTE: This is the simplest possible potato cake, with a gentle flavor and delicate texture. Its success depends entirely on the quality of the ingredients, especially the freshness of the potatoes, which if old and dry can't absorb much flour at all. Leftover mashed potatoes can be used, but the result will be different, since most mashed potatoes already have milk and butter in them. So, this alternative: Take a gob of leftover mash, pat it into a fat, flat patty, and gently press it into a dish of fresh bread crumbs, lightly coating each side. Then fry it up in plenty of butter until golden brown on both sides. Serve at once.

IRISH POTATO CAKES #2
(SERVES 3 OR 4 AS A LIGHT MAIN DISH)

2 eggs
2 tablespoons flour
1 teaspoon salt
4 large (about 2 pounds) potatoes

¼ teaspoon baking powder
Bacon fat or lard
Plenty of fresh, sweet butter

Beat the eggs together lightly in a mixing bowl, and mix in the flour and salt. Peel the potatoes and grate them into this mixture, stirring occasionally so all the potato bits are covered (this keeps them from turning black). When the potatoes are all grated, mix in the baking powder thoroughly. Heat a skillet over medium heat and grease it with bacon fat or lard (or vegetable oil). When hot, lower the heat and drop the potato mixture onto the skillet by the tablespoonful, pressing each firmly with a spatula. Cook until both sides are crisp and golden. Serve right off the griddle with plenty of butter.

COOK'S NOTE: There are several secrets for perfect potato pancakes, but the most important is to use a heavy cast-iron skillet or griddle, preferably two, and to have them just hot enough to cook the pancakes quickly, but not hot enough to burn them. This takes a little practice, and it's better to start a little low and adjust upward rather than the reverse. Another nice trick is to grate them very fine by using the smallest holes on the grater. This is tedious, but the pancakes emerge lacy-edged and very crisp.

REIBEKUCHEN
(SERVES 3 OR 4 AS A LIGHT MAIN DISH)

4 large (about 2 pounds) baking
  potatoes
4 scallions, minced
2 eggs, beaten
1 teaspoon cornstarch

1 teaspoon salt
¼ teaspoon grated nutmeg
¼ cup bacon fat or lard
Sour cream
Applesauce

Peel the potatoes and coarsely grate them into about a quart of cold water, then let them sit about half an hour. Set a dish towel into a large sieve and set this into a large bowl. Pour the potato-water mixture into this and wring out as much liquid from the potatoes as possible, reserving it in the bowl. Empty the potatoes into another bowl and mix with the minced scallion, beaten eggs, cornstarch, salt, and nutmeg. Pour off all the potato water and discard, saving only the sludge of potato starch that by now should have settled to the bottom of the bowl. With a rubber spatula, scrape this into the bowl with the potato batter, and blend in well.

Heat the fat (vegetable shortening can be substituted) in a large, heavy skillet over medium heat. Use a 2-tablespoon coffee measure to ladle in the batter for each pancake and, with the back of the same measure, gently flatten each cake. Cook to a deep golden brown on each side, turning once. Serve each batch from the skillet as cooked, with plenty of sour cream and applesauce.

COOK'S NOTE: For lovers of truly crisp potato pancakes, this German version may well be unbeatable, since the process of soaking out the starch and then wringing out the moisture makes them lighter and crisper, there being that much less residual moisture in the batter. If you like, the scallion can be omitted and a small peeled apple grated into the potato-water mixture, the recipe otherwise remaining the same. For a slightly more complicated but even more delicate version, see the recipe for *Kartoffelpuffer* in Mimi Sheraton's *The German Cookbook*.

OVEN-BAKED POTATO AND BUTTERMILK PANCAKE
(SERVES 2 OR 3 AS A LIGHT MAIN DISH)

2 large (about 1 pound) baking
    potatoes
2 eggs, beaten
½ cup flour
¾ cup buttermilk

1 teaspoon salt
Generous dash Tabasco
4 to 6 slices thick-cut bacon
Applesauce
Butter

Preheat the oven to 400°F. While the oven heats, peel and grate the potatoes into a mixing bowl. Stir in the eggs, flour, buttermilk, salt, and Tabasco, working together well with a wooden spoon. Cook the bacon in (by preference) a 12-inch ovenproof cast-iron skillet until it just starts to brown. Remove and crumble the bacon, and pour off all but a tablespoon or so of the fat. Pour the potato batter into the still hot skillet, scatter the bacon bits evenly over the top, and bake in the preheated oven for about 45 minutes, or until the pancake is a deep gold and a straw or cake tester inserted in the center comes out clean. Serve cut in wedges, with applesauce and plenty of butter. (If you can, invert the pancake onto a platter before serving so the bottom crust emerges crisp; if left underneath, it softens almost at once.)

COOK'S NOTE: My favorite way to make this is with lots of tiny cubes of fat trimmed from a country ham. Also, I quarter the spuds longitudinally, skin and all, and feed them down the tube of the food processor into its finest grating blade, otherwise proceeding as above. This pancake always takes five minutes more than you think it should to cook—especially since the last half hour is sheer torture. The kitchen fills with an indescribably delicious aroma; every waiting stomach growls in frustrated unison. It's worth the wait.

Tasting Notes: Greek Olives

"When the [olive] harvest begins in late autumn," writes Robin Howe in *The Mediterranean Diet*, "streets are lined with great tubs of olives of all shapes, sizes and colours. There are splendid olives from the island of Lesbos, black and bitter; purple-black olives from Amphissa; mauve, sour-sweet, heart-shaped Kalamata olives; and the celebrated full-flavoured black olives from Kalavala. Chios, the birthplace of Homer, produces a drab-looking dark variety, but appearances are deceptive, for it has a smoky rich and memorable flavor like that of the equally unprepossessing Sicilian wrinkled olive."

Just before I began to copy out this passage, I took one such Amphissa olive into my mouth. As you bite through its skin, your tongue encounters a buttery and juicy flesh, one that is meatier and softer in flavor than a Kalamata and without that latter's sharp-edged sourness. Not delicate enough to be confused with an American olive—for it has a distinct olive flavor—it spreads the pungency through a rich-flavored mouthful that makes it mellow; you can easily imagine enjoying a small plateful with some bread and a wedge of Kasseri cheese.

The miracle is not how good it was but how, living in Maine, I ever got to taste it at all. That is thanks to Sotiris Kitrilakis, who, under the Peloponnese label, imports specialty-cured Greek olives into this country, along with *Kalamata kopanistí*, a knee-weakeningly delicious *olivada*-like spread made of Kalamata olives and wild herbs, and several other items that I will mention in a moment.

But, first, especially, there are the olives: for here from a single source are eight superbly different types of Greek olives, ranging in color from the blackest of purples to the lightest of greens, representing in their textures and flavors a whole education as to how various—and variously good—the Mediterranean olive can be. No matter that this sample is but a fifth of the different olives produced in Greece—or that one artisan's

Kalamata and another's are almost as different as two vintners' versions of Zinfandel. Once you get these olives into your mouth, a set of blinkers falls away—and the olive, any olive, will never be the same.

That is to say, instead of a series of isolated flavor experiences, you begin to notice how these tastes and textures—and the colors—fit into a discernible range. It is this sense of variations on a theme that allows us to begin to discriminate and compare, as well as simply admire.

For example, it was knowing the flavor of an Amphissa that allowed me, when tasting a Kalamata, to actually taste the olive itself apart from its vinegar-flavored brine, and to understand why, because of the Kalamata's bitter sharpness, that other, sourer, presence is necessary: each balancing the intensity of the other. The result is a flood of bitter-sour notes—a pungency of pleasure and not of pain. Because of this, the olive has an intensity of flavor the Amphissa lacks: add a few flecks of Kalamata and their presence is made known in a dish of tomatoes or roasted peppers—especially when sprinkled with the brine instead of the usual vinegar.

On the other hand, the interesting and very labor-intensive Nafplion, a cracked green olive, has a bright tart bitterness unmodulated by any sour agency. I found it too intense for out-of-hand eating, but excellent when pitted and mixed with garlic, olive oil, a little lemon juice, and a pinch of thyme and then spread on chunks of crusty bread. Whereas, almost impossible *not* to devour from the jar were the dry, oil-cured olives of Thasos, whose slow curing removes all the bitterness, leaving only a melt-in-the-mouth texture and a sweet pure flavor that never wavers at its edges, like other, harsher-flavored oil-cured olives I have tried.

The Atalanti, a huge cracked green olive dappled in the lightest of purple shades, had a juicy, chewy texture and a complex flavor that began with a surprisingly intense fruity note. It made an interesting contrast when eaten with the Ionian green. Those were likewise stupendously meaty and sour, yet possessed the purest and simplest olive flavor imaginable (and without the tinny edges—indicating a rushed or careless cure—that flaw so many of this tribe).

Finally, what is perhaps my favorite of all of them, the tiny Elitses (the name itself means just "little olives"). Grown in central Crete for their flavorful oil, they are delicious when left to ripen and then cured in a simple salt-and-vinegar brine that accentuates their fruity richness. The perfect olive for eating out of hand.

As I say, an education . . . and even better, an education in pleasure. Other Peloponnese products also proved very fine. I was so taken with their extra-virgin olive oil that at first I kept my supply hidden in the bedroom closet next to the bottle of twenty-five-year-old Calvados. Their aged wine vinegar is also choice; their roasted red peppers are simply the best ever taken from a jar; and the hand-picked and dried Greek herbs have intense fragrance and taste. Their country olive mix puts all eight olives together in one jar. Consider draining, pitting, and coarsely chopping the contents of this sampler, and then mixing the result with some olive oil, crumbled oregano, and a little of the drained brine. Spoon this heady mixture generously onto garlic-rubbed slices of crusty Italian bread.

Happily, Peloponnese sells its products by mail. Contact The Ægean Trader, 2227 Poplar Street, Oakland, CA 94607; (415) 839-8153, for a free catalogue. It contains other Greek delicacies not mentioned here, including honey, preserves, *meze*, marinades, cookies, and a variety of Greek cheeses.

SOUP WITHOUT STOCK

❖ ❖ ❖

I've mostly ducked the issue of stock by trying not to make dishes that call for it. I don't question that these can be very good, but there is much good eating in this world that doesn't require the time, labor, and raw materials that stock-based cooking does. I might feel differently about this if my way of eating automatically generated the tasty leavings that other kitchens are said to always have on hand—but it doesn't. A roast has become a rare enough treat in my life to send me slipping back to the platter after the company's left to gnaw away the last bits of meat and gristle from the bone and finish up its marrow on some buttered toast.

Even so, no one serious about their cooking can long remain ignorant of—or unaffected by—certain assertions about stock. It seems all a food writer has to do is taste a mouthful of the stuff to start spouting that old-time culinary religion. So, at least, does Stella Standard, who writes in *Stella Standard's Soup Book*: "If a soup is made with care, it is made with stock." And, fearing the sting of her moral flail might not be enough to effect a conversion, she follows with a homily, unblinkingly insisting that "all western soups are French in origin"—and all of them based on carefully simmered stock.

Maybe they are, but it is well to remember that French cooking was not codified by the housewives who invented it but by the chefs who "perfected" it. Stockmaking requires kitchens with an abattoir of bones at hand and plenty of slaveys to crack them—who can then be ordered to simmer and skim, skim and simmer, until the air is dank and the garbage pail full. All this for a quart or two of something that is the means to a still distant end: "Poach the chicken in stock," begins, rather than ends, the classic sort of recipe for which it is the ultimate necessity.

Stock, in other words, is not something immediately, deliciously edible. Its proselytizers have their stick of guilt, but they have their carrot, too—the promised taste of a whole roast beef in a cup. The idea has sold a million bottles of Bovril, but it happens to be untrue. If you ignore the aroma and guard yourself against the glossy texture, what you find in your mouth when you taste stock is not magic but meat water. Stock is meant to enhance a dish with the *presence* of meat, not its actual flavor.

The home cook wants something more at the end of all that work than this: she wants something to *eat*. And so she makes broth instead. Intended from the start to be a meal, or part of one, broth—unlike stock—is salted and, often as not, contains pot vegetables as well as herbs. It requires not a stockpot full of hacked bones but a casserole fitted with a fowl. All that is cooked is meant to be eaten—*bouilli* as well as *bouillon*.

One of the most delicious soups I ever had in my life was a simple chicken broth flavored with tarragon. It was silky smooth in texture and buttery rich in flavor; I remember it still. But that is a tribute to its maker, who knew that a lot of chicken is needed to make broth good. There is no quart of it to be gotten from any carcass, and cooks who claim they do, no matter how much they brag about their fresh parsley, whole peppercorns, and gelatinous wingtips, really owe their success to the salt jar. The result might almost as well be turned out of a can.

We *know* good broth does not come easy. This is why we make it for the rare demanding occasion and use canned broth for all the rest. And although stock and broth originate in very different kinds of kitchens, their use becomes as one when it is not flavor the cook seeks but a smoothing finish to a sauce, gravy, or soup. Says a restaurant chef (quoted in Jim Quinn's *Never Eat Out on a Saturday Night*): "Chicken soup is our MSG.

Some of it goes in every sauce. It is the base of all our soups."

Those three sentences are epitaph to too much of today's home cooking. Used in such unthinking, profligate abandon, broth might as well be MSG, so much alike is their effect (which is why canned broths contain that chemical and bouillon cubes are flavored with little else). They make all things taste good —but make them all taste good in the same blurry way.

Such knee-jerk use of broth should long ago have been allowed to fade into disuse, and other strategies evolved to take its place. Our culinary sages would have provided our cuisine with the better service if, rather than touting stock past its natural lifespan, they had encouraged a turn to food that could be made without it.

Contrary to Stella Standard, there are many good soups that can be prepared without stock, including such traditional French ones as leek and potato, *soupe au pistou*, and *potage bonne femme*. But as the presence of meat broth became the sole criterion of a soup's worth, it has now crept into these, too. The result is the current perverse state of affairs, where almost no one makes broth but almost everyone is busy adding it where it doesn't belong, because cooks have come to rely on its plummy presence to provide *the* requisite guarantee of quality to their cooking.

❖ ❖ ❖

I discovered this for myself when I set out to make some simple vegetable soups to provide a meatless interlude to what at the time was a rather carnivorous diet. These soups did not need to be substantial, but they had to involve my appetite in an immediate, spontaneous way—I wanted to be able to just go into the kitchen and make them up out of whatever happened to be on hand.

This did not, at first glance, seem a very difficult stricture. However, my previous reliance on canned broth (broth + carrot + onion = carrot soup) had dulled my culinary instincts. Without it, for far longer than I ever expected, I found myself at sea.

When I took those same carrots and went to make a soup

out of them with nothing but water and seasonings, I found not only that that liquid was flavorless (at best) but that it also deadened the taste of what it diluted. The carrots' sweet, delicate flavor faded into vegetable water as soon as I thinned the sautéed pieces into soup.

Unnerved by this phenomenon, I tried at first to replicate the mouth-coating effect of broth by adding little drops of potions from the flavoring shelf: tamari, Tabasco, cognac, gumbo filé. I succeeded, but at the cost also of reproducing canned broth's familiar muddiness.

This is the simple truth: No other soup pampers the mouth like a broth- or stock-based one. The tongue needs do nothing but loll on its satin pillow. A simple water broth built up of vegetables has its pleasures to offer, but they will not spoil the tongue. It must learn to work for them.

At first my mouth took umbrage at such a suggestion: "Water, water, everywhere," it snorted, turning away. But I persevered—and learned. Canned-broth–based soups tend toward measliness, using their ingredients as flavoring agents or to add some minimal bulk. But a vegetable soup built from scratch requires an abundance of quality material in the same way that a good meat broth needs meat: heads not leaves of lettuce; bunches of carrots; bags of spinach. . . .

Even so, it still requires salt and pepper to bring back the flavor and often a pinch of sugar to restore the original sweetness. The question then arises as to why bother making such a simple soup at all. If a bowl of the same steamed vegetable has equal nutrition and more inherent flavor, why dilute it with water just so it can be spooned from a bowl?

My answer is that while a bowl of vegetables is just a bowl of vegetables, a simple soup is often a busy day's only enjoyable culinary challenge: to feed ourselves something warm, filling, and nourishing, on a moment's notice and out of nothing much at all.

It teaches you to use your tongue. No vegetable tastes just like the one that rests beside it in the bin. You must hover over, tasting, thinking, seasoning, until the delicate, fragile flavor of your charge—cucumber . . . bell pepper . . . celery

. . . onion—lies there, fragrant and savory in the mouth.

The recipes that follow were originally improvised out of stuff from the cupboard; they represent no classic cuisine. But they are good and honest, with a simple structure that will, I hope, encourage you to try a couple—and then go match them with similar efforts of your own.

FRESH PEA AND POTATO SOUP
(SERVES 3 OR 4)

1 pound fresh peas in the pod
Salt
1½ pounds all-purpose potatoes
1 medium onion
1 tablespoon olive oil
1 tablespoon unsalted butter

½ teaspoon crushed hot red pepper
2 cloves of garlic
1 small head of romaine or escarole
Freshly ground black pepper

Rinse the pods and then pod the peas. Put the empty pods in a large pot with 5 cups of water and 1 teaspoon of salt. Bring the water to a boil, let the pods simmer for 1 minute, and then immediately remove the pot from the stove. When the contents are cool enough to handle, pour the liquid through a strainer into a heatproof mixing bowl. Discard the cooked pods.

Peel the potatoes. Quarter each peeled potato and cut each quarter into bite-sized wedges. As each potato is cut up, put it into the pea broth in the mixing bowl. When the potatoes are all cut up, chop the onion into large-sized dice. Then wipe out the pot with a paper towel and put in the olive oil and butter. Let this warm up over medium heat. Sprinkle in the hot red pepper and ½ teaspoon salt. When the oil is hot, turn in the diced onion. Stir this occasionally with a spatula until the pieces are soft and translucent.

While the onion sautés in the seasoned butter and oil mixture, mince the garlic. Wash the lettuce and chop or tear it into bite-sized pieces. When the onion turns translucent, stir in the minced garlic. Let this cook for 2 more minutes, then pour in the potato and pea broth mixture and the peas themselves. Bring to a simmer and cook for 10 minutes. Add the lettuce pieces. Continue cooking until the potatoes are done and the lettuce soft. Taste the broth for seasoning, adding more salt to taste and plenty of freshly ground pepper. Serve and eat at once.

CUCUMBER, LEMON, AND DILL SOUP
(SERVES 4)

3 or 4 small, firm cucumbers	*Sugar*
1 tablespoon unsalted butter	*2 cups milk*
2 medium onions, chopped fine	*2 tablespoons fresh lemon juice*
1 tablespoon fresh dill, minced	*Freshly ground black pepper*
Salt	

Peel the cucumbers and cut in quarters lengthwise. With a spoon, scrape out the seeds. If these are few and tender, reserve—otherwise discard. Cut the cucumber into bite-sized pieces.

Melt the butter in a skillet. Add the onions and cook until translucent. Do not brown. Add the cucumber and, gently stirring, sauté this for a minute or two. Then pour in 2 cups of water to make a broth. Stir in the minced dill, reserving 1 teaspoonful. Add the reserved cucumber seeds (if any) and small amounts of salt and sugar to bring out the taste of the cucumber. Cover and gently simmer for 15 minutes. Then pour in the milk to complete the broth and, when this has heated, stir in the lemon juice, a teaspoon at a time, until the broth acquires a mouth-pleasing zest. Add the reserved minced dill, grind pepper over, and let soup rest on lowest heat for 5 minutes before ladling out.

COOK'S NOTE: The soup must simmer without ever boiling or the milk will curdle. (But don't worry if it does—the soup will still taste fine.) The milk broth serves to accentuate the rather elusive cucumber flavor, but the soup can be made with water alone for a more tart, herbal taste—or all milk, for a richer, more delicate one.

SWEET PEPPER AND OLIVE SOUP

Red and green bell peppers   *Salt and freshly ground black*
Onions   *pepper*
Olive oil   *Sugar (optional)*
Garlic cloves   *Tabasco*
Kalamata olives plus their liquid

Choose a pepper and a half to two peppers for each eater. Stem, seed, and cut them coarsely into large chunks. Take a medium onion per eater and cut that also into large chunks. Heat a small amount of olive oil in a pot. Sauté the peppers and onions in it for a few minutes, until both vegetables are soft. During the last minute of cooking, add a little minced garlic (about a quarter to a half a clove per eater). Meanwhile, stone and tear into pieces four Kalamata olives per eater (see note).

Remove the pot from the heat and turn the contents out onto a cutting board or into a mortar. Add the olives and chop with a knife or pound with a pestle until the mass is a very coarse-textured purée. Return this to the cooking pot. Add enough water to make a smooth broth and then blend in 1 to 2 table-spoons of the olive liquid for each eater (see note). Season with salt, pepper, sugar (if necessary), and a few drops of Tabasco. Bring just to a simmer, reduce heat, and let flavors meld for 10 minutes before serving, accompanied by a plain, unsweetened cornbread.

COOK'S NOTE: The balance of red to green peppers will affect the flavor of the soup. I prefer two red peppers for each green pepper. Yellow peppers can also be used, as might a small fresh jalapeño. Kalamata olives come packed in a pungently flavored wine vinegar. If another black olive is used, substitute red wine vinegar, adding a few teaspoons of the ordinary olive brine, if palatable.

SPINACH IN CHICKPEA PURÉE
(SERVES 4 TO 6)

2 (10-ounce) packages of spinach
2 (20-ounce) cans of chickpeas
  with liquid
Olive oil

10 to 12 scallions
Tabasco
Salt and black pepper

Stem the spinach and wash the leaves carefully to remove all grit. Shake the leaves well to remove as much moisture as possible and set them to drain in a colander. Pour the chickpeas and their liquid into a bowl and, with a potato masher or the back of a perforated spoon, mash them into a coarse purée.

Heat about 2 tablespoons of the olive oil in a medium-sized pot. Trim away the tops of the scallions and clean the rest, cutting them into small pieces. Put these into the hot olive oil and sauté until tender. Add the chickpea purée and enough water to make a thick broth. Taste for seasoning and add a few drops of Tabasco. Bring this up just to a simmer and let the flavors mellow while the spinach is prepared.

Heat a small amount of olive oil in a large skillet over medium heat. When hot, spread the spinach leaves over the surface of the skillet and, turning with a spatula, cook until they have shrunk into a wet mass of bright jade green. Put this into a colander set over a bowl. Using a potato masher or the back of a spoon, press as much moisture out of the spinach as possible. Turn the pressed spinach onto a cutting board and slice it into strips with a knife. Pour the spinach juices from the bowl into a small mug, season, and enjoy (cook's treat!). In any case, put the sliced spinach leaves into the soup, minus their liquid. Stir well, taste for seasoning, and, before serving, leave on the heat another 5 minutes so the flavors can meld.

CORN, RICE, AND CHICKPEA SOUP
WITH SALSA
(SERVES 2 TO 4)

½ cup raw white rice
1 (20-ounce) can of chickpeas with
   liquid
2 tablespoons olive oil

1 cup corn kernels
Salt and pepper
½ cup or more fresh salsa (see
   note)

Put a generous cup of salted water into a small pot, bring to a boil, add the rice, return to a simmer, cover, and cook the rice (about 20 minutes). Meanwhile, pour the chickpeas and their liquid into a bowl and, with a potato ricer or the back of a perforated spoon, mash them into a coarse purée.

Heat the olive oil in a medium-sized pot. Add the chickpea purée and stir until the mixture just begins to bubble. Mix in the corn kernels and enough water (about a scant cup) to turn the mixture into a thick soup. Let this mellow over very low heat until the rice is done. Just before serving, stir the rice into the soup and taste for seasoning, adding salt and plenty of pepper. Serve in heated bowls, with the salsa offered separately to each eater to spoon onto the soup.

COOK'S NOTE: This amount will serve four adequately or two very generously. The chickpea purée makes a wonderfully rich but delicate-textured base, whose flavor is nicely picked up by the corn and rice. The salsa should be served cool to heighten the contrast between the two (bland/hot against spicy/cool).

Since finding red ripe tomatoes is almost impossible in Maine ten months of the year, we use a salsa out of a jar. (Several fiery, all-natural blends vie for attention these days in most natural food stores.) However, on the rare occasions when we can make our salsa fresh, here is the version we turn to: as good and simple as the soup it is to be added to.

SALSA

(MAKES ABOUT 3 CUPS)

4 *large, dead-ripe tomatoes*	*Salt*
3 *or* 4 *scallions, minced*	*Juice of* 1 *lime*
2 *or* 3 *jalapeño chiles*	*Black pepper*
2 *cloves of garlic*	*Fresh cilantro leaves*

Coarsely chop the tomatoes, saving all juice. If you have a problem digesting the skins or seeds, feel free to remove and discard them. Stir the tomatoes, their juice, and the minced scallions together in a small bowl. Cut the chiles in half and use the tip of a teaspoon to scrape out the seeds (or, for a hotter salsa, leave these be). Mince together the chile halves, the garlic cloves, and ½ teaspoon of salt. When this is cut down to a molecular consistency, stir the resulting mash into the tomatoes and scallions. Blend in the lime juice and season to taste with more salt and grindings of black pepper. Let the flavors meld for a few hours before serving, at which time stir in a sprig or so of cilantro leaves, freshly minced.

COOK'S NOTE: This is, of course, more than you will need for the corn, rice, and chickpea soup. However, the remainder will keep for several days in the refrigerator.

A NOTE ON PEA SOUP

No discussion of soups without stock can afford to ignore the question of dried peas. These make a rich-flavored soup without the use of any meat or meat stock, and yet they can also make good use of a liquid that isn't ordinarily thought of as stock, but which is still produced in many contemporary home kitchens—that used for poaching preserved meat. This is usually too briny and pungent-tasting to put to other culinary purpose, but it tastes so good when used as a pea-soup base that it would be hard to name a Northern European cuisine that utilizes a specific salt meat that doesn't also have a split pea soup recipe specifically conceived to make the best of its remains.

The examples are legion. In *A Taste of Ireland*, Theodora FitzGibbon explains how to make one from the cooking liquid of corned beef and cabbage; in *Spices, Salt and Aromatics in the English Kitchen*, Elizabeth David does the same, utilizing pickled pork liquor, and in *European Peasant Cookery*, Elisabeth Luard describes the Norwegian *ertesuppe*, which is based on the leavings of salt mutton.

Understand this and you also understand why, when such cooking liquid is already at hand, pea soup is so attractive to cooks: it is delicious to eat and both economical and easy to make. The cook just puts in the peas along with any leftover bones or meat scraps and adds a few pot herbs to freshen it all up. The only problem here, if it *is* a problem, is that this tradition tends to pull the imagination—and hence the cook—in one particular direction. At the mention of pea soup, the knee-jerk reaction is—salted meat, smoked meat, and especially salted smoked *fatty* meat.

Once started in that direction, the ultimate destination might as well be *erwtensoep*, a Dutch concoction containing *all* of them. For at its most elaborate it is made with a pig's ears and feet, smoked sausage, and bacon, as well as leeks, celeriac, and potatoes. The Dutch are a prosperous people; they have gone on adding good things to that soup and never taking one of them away. Now it is eaten with a spoon—and knife and fork as well.

What all this ignores is that split pea soup is, all by itself, hearty, thick, and nourishing. It asks for fat—but no more insistently than bread demands butter, or, for that matter, cake, frosting. A very starchy dish allows a great deal of fat to be comfortably eaten with it . . . which is sometimes a good thing, but this is not the same as law.

Certainly, if you take *all* the unctuousness out of pea soup you are left with pea gruel. Appetite can still be asked to accept that idea—but not necessarily persuaded to cross the road for it. However, season this same purée with salt and pepper and float a pat of butter on top—preferably one in which some fresh leaves of marjoram or thyme have been minced—and appetite may at least condescend to pick up a spoon.

A little fat and a little fresh herb: this is the secret to the best of all simple split pea soups. As peas grow old, they quickly lose that faint, sweet, floral note that makes baby peas so delicious; the herb restores not so much the missing freshness as the missing pleasure—which is why a good dried herb can be used, although fresh leaf herb is better still. Mint may be most commonly associated with peas, but there are other herbs worth considering—notably thyme, rosemary, basil, and marjoram.

We've chosen to share here three traditional split pea soups that make this particular point, for their flavor is characterized as much by their pot herbs as by their salt meat (one of them, in fact, contains no meat at all). Here is winter soup that, unlike canned pea soup, is not at all wintery, for each is well seasoned with bits of bright color and brighter taste.

Once set on this track, imagination can pick up the thread for itself, substituting—say—olive oil for butter and then working up a split pea soup out of fresh thyme, minced scallion, sweet potato, and red pepper—or whatever. Freed of the *necessity* of smoked meat, the flavor permutations pea soup makes possible become many—and not at all difficult to compute.

Good plain fare in Sweden is called husmankost, *and this in recent years has experienced a revival, as the Swedes who grew up in postwar affluence now discover a yearning to reestablish a connection with their more frugal culinary roots. Salmon pudding, potato dumplings stuffed with pork, seaman's stew, and baked Swedish brown beans all epitomize this cooking, but none more than* ärter med fläsk, *or yellow pea soup with meat, a thick, rib-sticking gruel that is still eaten every Thursday night by everyone, it is said, from the king on down. The meal is traditionally finished with buttery, crisp-edged pancakes served with lingonberries (see the Kitchen Diary recipe on page 192).*

The familiar Swedish version is made with whole dried yellow peas (which makes for a longer-cooking soup) and a piece of lightly cured lean salt pork. Most adaptations call for American salt pork, which is

*often too salty and too fatty to work well. We suggest trying a lightly
cured piece of pork shoulder instead, especially if it still clings to its
bone. Lacking that, you might do as we do here and use a meaty smoked
country-style ham hock.*

SWEDISH PEA SOUP
(SERVES 4 TO 6)

*2 cups (1 pound) split yellow peas
2 medium onions, finely chopped
½ teaspoon dried marjoram
1 teaspoon ground ginger*

*1 cured pork hock, bone in (about
  2 pounds)
A coarse-textured mustard*

Wash and pick over the split peas carefully, discarding any
suspicious characters. Put them in a large pot and cover with
5 cups of cold water. Bring this to a simmer. Add the onion,
dried marjoram, ginger, and pork.

Cover the pan and simmer gently for about 2 hours, or until
the meat is tender. If fresh marjoram is used, chop it fine and
add it during the last 15 minutes of cooking. Remove the pork
and slice it thin, discarding the bone and—if no one will eat
it—the rind. Serve a portion of meat with each bowl of soup.
If the meat is very tender, it can be served right in the bowl
with a dab of strong, spicy mustard floated in with it; otherwise
it—and the mustard—should be set on a separate plate.

COOK'S NOTES: The authentic dish is made with whole dried
yellow peas. Use them—if you can find them—after an overnight soaking and then a preliminary 15-minute simmer before
the soup is made, discarding any husks that float to the surface.

Swedish cooks disagree about every ingredient in this soup
except the peas and pork. For some it is the marjoram that is
sacrosanct, for others the ginger. Thyme and cloves can be
used also. Because of the soup's simplicity, however, the best
seasoning choice is the herb with the freshest flavor—better
thyme alone, if the marjoram has turned tired and dusty-tasting
in a rarely opened jar.

Split pea soup might not immediately spring to mind as a New Orleans dish, but Creole cooks have long prided themselves on the excellence of their Lenten potages maigres—*several of which are built on a foundation of dried peas. Although meatless, these soups are far from meager—the recipe for "Winter Fast-Day Soup" in* The Picayune's Creole Cook Book *calls for dried peas, a head each of lettuce and celery, carrots, turnips, onions, and spinach, plus fresh mint, thyme, and parsley!*

This is that book's split pea soup (with some additional touches taken from a similar recipe in the twelfth edition of Gourmet's Guide to New Orleans, *by Natalie Scott and Caroline Merrick Jones)—and, if your mother used to dilute Campbell's green pea soup with milk instead of water, you'll find this hearty Creole soup strikes a surprisingly familiar chord.*

CREOLE LENTEN SPLIT PEA SOUP
(SERVES 4 TO 6)

1 cup split yellow or green peas
3 to 4 stalks of celery with leaves
1 carrot
1 medium onion
4 to 5 sprigs of parsley
4 tablespoons butter

1 bay leaf
4 to 6 slices of stale French bread, cut into cubes
2 cups milk
Salt and pepper

Wash and pick over the split peas carefully. Chop the celery, carrot, and onion fine, mincing the celery leaf separately with the parsley. Melt 2 tablespoons of the butter in a small frying pan and sauté the minced vegetables until the onion and celery turn translucent. Put the split peas, the sautéed vegetables, the bay leaf, and the minced parsley and celery leaf into a pot and pour in 3 cups of water. Bring to a simmer and cook gently for 40 minutes, or until the peas and carrot are quite tender.

While the soup cooks, melt the rest of the butter in a frying pan and sauté the bread cubes until they are toasted on all sides. Remove the soup from the heat. Pluck out and discard the bay leaf. Use the back of a wooden spoon to work the remaining mixture through a wide-mesh sieve to form a coarse purée. (This can also be done in a food mill or, in small batches, in a food processor fitted with the steel blade.) Return this purée to the pot and stir in the milk. Season to taste with salt and plenty of freshly ground pepper. Gently reheat the soup and serve at once, each bowl generously garnished with the croutons.

❖ ❖ ❖

Although the following peppery pottage is—despite its name—made with beans, not peas, we've included it here anyway because it's obviously an English pea soup reworked to island taste and circumstance. This soup is very popular in Jamaica, and there are many recipes for it, some very simple, others more complicated. The red peas by themselves are what make it Jamaican, but the addition of fresh hot red pepper is what makes it unique. Our own version has been worked out of recipes—especially those in Jessica Harris's Iron Pots and Wooden Spoons *and Elisabeth Lambert Ortiz's* Caribbean Cooking—*that also call for the addition of fresh herbs.*

Red peas, known in this country as red beans, are available in West Indian and Hispanic groceries. Most cookbooks suggest substituting kidney beans if red beans are unavailable, but kidney beans have a strong, distinctive flavor that is entirely their own. Consider using yellow split peas instead. The resulting soup is very good and visually appealing, the soft yellow of the bean purée flecked all through with bright green herb and hot red pepper.

JAMAICAN RED PEA SOUP
(SERVES 6)

1 pound red peas (red beans)
¼ pound salt pork
1 bunch (6 to 8) scallions
1 small hot red pepper

2 or 3 leafy celery stalks
6 large sprigs of parsley
½ teaspoon dried or 1 sprig fresh
*   thyme*

If you are using red beans, these should be picked over, washed, and set to soak the night before. When you begin making the soup, they should be drained, the soaking water discarded, and the beans put in a large pot. Add 2 quarts of water and bring it to a simmer, skimming away any scum that rises to the surface. Let the beans simmer unseasoned while the rest of the ingredients are prepared.

Cut the salt pork into small cubes. Coarsely chop the scallions, including all of the green except any tired, tough, or soggy ends. Seed, stem, and finely dice the hot pepper. Dice the celery stalks and then mince their leaves with the parsley. Put ¼ cup of water in a small frying pan and set it over medium heat. When the water steams, add the bits of salt pork and fry until the fat is translucent and beginning to color. Add the chopped celery, hot pepper, and scallions and cook with the pork for a few more minutes, to let them soften. Add all this to the beans, plus the minced parsley and celery leaf and the thyme—crumbling this last in if dried or adding whole if a sprig.

Stir well and continue to cook slowly for about an hour, or until the beans are very tender. Remove and discard the sprig of thyme (if used) and purée the rest of the soup either through a food mill or in small batches in a food processor fitted with the steel blade. Do not overprocess—the soup should retain the texture of the peas. Taste for salt and season with a generous amount of bottled hot sauce if a hot pepper has not been used. Reheat and serve.

COOK'S NOTES: If split peas are used instead of red peas, the preliminary soaking of the beans is not necessary, and the cooking time will be less. Although any Caribbean hot sauce goes well with this soup, if you can find a bottle of Westlow's Bonney Pepper Sauce from Barbados, its mustardy, fiery taste is a perfect flavor match.

Jessica Harris's book also offers a recipe for "spinners," simple flour and cornmeal dumplings to be cooked in and eaten with the soup. They're a good reason for searching out this intriguing exploration of the marriage between African and New World cooking.

KITCHEN DIARY: SWEDISH PANCAKES

"Swedish pancakes" is the usual translation, but an even better name is the one they use in Sweden: *tunna pannkakor*, or "thin pancakes." For thin these dessert pancakes certainly are—even more than crepes, which they otherwise resemble, being buttery, delicate, and supple enough for easy folding. They are usually made simply of melted butter, egg, flour, and milk, although a little sugar is sometimes added. Recipes vary widely as to the number of eggs and the amount of butter, but—as Tore Wretman puts it in *The Swedish Smörgåsbord*—"the main rule is that the quantity of liquid should be twice that of flour."

Our own version, fitting for a dessert following a hearty bowl of pea soup, is—as the recipes go—rather lean. But since the purpose of the melted butter is to keep the very wet batter from sticking, the quantity may need adjustment to suit the pan. The amount given here is what works in our nonstick skillet. The pancakes are lacy-edged, dapple-brown, and delicious. Although we first tried them with their traditional companion, *ärter med fläsk* (Swedish pea soup), we find that they make a light and welcome last mouthful to almost any supper, especially when varied as described below.

In Sweden, these can be made in blini-sized rounds (called *plättar*) in a specially indented griddle, which produces a serving at a time. Otherwise, for the sake of convenience, they are made in crepe-sized rounds, one by one, in a small skillet, kept warm and safe on a plate in the oven, and then served folded in quarters. Here is our recipe.

TUNNA PANNKAKOR
(SERVES 4)

¼ teaspoon salt
1 cup all-purpose flour
2 eggs
2 cups milk

1 to 2 teaspoons sugar (optional)
2 tablespoons (or more) unsalted
butter

Sift the salt and flour together through a sieve into a small bowl. Mix the eggs and milk (and sugar, if wanted) together in another bowl and whisk gradually into the flour until you have a smooth, thin batter. Do not beat. If possible, let the mixture rest, covered, for an hour or two.

Melt the butter in a small skillet and whisk it into the batter, which should have the consistency of medium cream (you may need to add a little extra milk). Reheat the still buttery skillet until it is hot enough to send a drop of water skipping. Pour in 2 tablespoons of batter. Tilt the pan to spread the batter into a 6-inch round. When it is no longer liquid on top, flip the pancake over and finish on the other side. Remove this pancake to a platter in a warm oven and make the rest following the same procedure. Because of the melted butter in the batter, the skillet should not require additional greasing. Makes 24 pancakes.

COOK'S NOTES: These are traditionally served with a spoonful of lingonberries preserved in sugar syrup; their tartness nicely complements the buttery but bland flavor of the pancakes. Tore Wretman makes up a torte by layering the pancakes with fresh, sweetened berries and topping this with a generous amount of whipped cream.

We ourselves like them folded into quarters around a small dab of a choice jam (apricot, cherry, raspberry), sprinkled with fresh lemon juice, dusted with sugar, and eaten with our fingers.

BREAKFAST CLAFOUTIS

❖ ❖ ❖

It's the first week of autumn, and Matt and I are on our hands and knees in a boulder-strewn Maine field that overlooks the tidal estuaries at the end of Pigeon Hill Bay. This place is a short walk down the dirt road that runs past our house, and Matt has already come here in late summer to pick blueberries. There are, in fact, a few dried and wizened blueberries still to be found here . . . the few never uncovered by the pickers or the birds. But we're here for wild mountain cranberries.

The mid-morning sky is that pure, translucent blue that in Maine portends the arrival of cold weather, being bright without any hint of warmth. But it is not yet cold, even though a brisk wind blows in off the water. It brings with it what I think are seabird calls and then realize are nothing more than the children playing in the farmyard farther down the road. I also realize, my eyes coming to rest on Matt's bent back, that I am running on idle, looking about and listening, not picking. With a sigh, I bend over and find my hat on the ground, waiting for me. Its bottom is scattered—but far from covered—with tiny crimson berries.

Wild mountain cranberries. Despite their color, they aren't all that easy to find. This is partly because the blueberry leaves are turning a brilliant scarlet themselves, and partly because the leaves of the tiny cranberry bushes are as deeply and intensely green as holly. As conflicting primary colors do, these vivid reds and greens are struggling to cancel each other out.

You only see their individual brightness when you hold them separately in your hand.

I shift, and notice with chagrin that some equally visible crimson stains have appeared on the knees of my pants. As a boy I was a berrying fool; at forty-eight, the thrill of the hunt has pretty much evaporated. Still, no one hereabouts has yet thought of selling wild cranberries in pint cartons by the roadside. If we want to eat them, we have to pick them ourselves. Fortunately, all we need is a modest amount to make next morning's breakfast. We're going to have a cranberry clafoutis.

Clafoutis (more and more spelled "clafouti" these days—perhaps because the "s" makes the word look plural to American eyes) is usually considered a dessert. From the Limousin region of France, it is traditionally made by filling the bottom of a buttered baking dish with stemmed but unpitted black cherries, covering these with a batter, and baking this in an oven. The result is a custardy, slightly puffed, lightly browned confection, dotted with pieces of the soft, fresh fruit. It is eaten warm or cool, dusted with powdered sugar.

According to the new edition of the *Larousse Gastronomique*, the Académie Française originally defined clafoutis as "a kind of fruit flan." This drew protests from the good *citoyens* of Limoges; it was then *re*defined as "a cake with black cherries." Neither definition, really, is very helpful. A clafoutis is not a flan or a cake, nor for that matter is it a pancake—as American cookbooks sometimes define it. You come closest to it if you think of it as a very custardy popover, or perhaps as a puffy, crisp-edged custard.

I should pause here to mention that food writers often appropriate the name and the idea of fresh fruit baked in a custardy batter to work out *fantasy* clafoutis that have only a tenuous connection to the real thing. For example, in *The Way to Cook*, Julia Child makes a "Pear Clafouti" by setting poached pears in a custard-filled prebaked pastry shell and glazing the result with apricot jam. Jacques Pépin's "Blackberry Clafoutis," in the second volume of his *Art of Cooking*, is a mixture of beaten eggs, blackberry purée, slivered almonds, and raspberry brandy, baked in a cream cheese dough.

There are many other examples of this, but they have not

yet managed to corrupt the original clafoutis, which remains, as Julia herself calls it, "a puddinglike, peasanty dish," put together out of a few good, simple things. As its honest self, it is humbler, less polished, less sharply focused than, say, a cherry pie; yet it is not so generically amorphous as a cherry pudding. It is the French equivalent of a pandowdy or a fruit crumble—which is to say that the identity of a clafoutis is partly fixed and partly a product of circumstance.

This fruitful confusion ties all the disparate threads of this piece together: the October Maine morning, the wild mountain cranberries, the good citizens of Limoges, the disarray of definitions. It explains the trajectory of circumstances that first brought the clafoutis into our kitchen and the reason it persuaded us finally to keep it there—as opposed to the many other, equally good-tasting dishes that were made, enjoyed, and then forgotten. Because it isn't by accident that a dish finds a place—a permanent place—in any particular kitchen.

I got interested in the clafoutis because of cherries. I love them, and when they are in season I yearn to do something with them other than eat them out of hand. Sweet cherries don't bake all that well, at least into pies; cook them too much and they begin to taste like prunes. I thought that the quicker-cooking clafoutis might capture that unique meaty sweetness before it slipped away.

I had just met Matt then and the clafoutis was one of the first dishes we worked on together. We simplified the traditional version to accommodate a temperamental stove and limited *batterie de cuisine* by heating the butter in my black cast-iron skillet, rolling the cherries around in it until they were glossy all over, and then pouring the batter over them. The skillet was put straight into the oven and the dish baked for twenty minutes. This was easy to do and the results were good.

Time passed. I moved to Maine; Matt moved up with me; we got married. It has taken us a lot longer to merge our two cuisines than our furniture, but early on we began to notice that we were eating fewer and fewer desserts and more and more enjoying baking something for breakfast together. We began to wonder if our clafoutis wouldn't make a delicious, not-too-caloric morning meal.

The batter of a clafoutis resembles that of a popover, but with this important difference: you can change the proportions of a clafoutis batter quite a bit . . . and still produce a clafoutis. For instance, Anne Willan makes a "Clafoutis Limousin" in *French Regional Cooking* that, proportionally, calls for half as much flour, twice as much milk, and twice as many eggs (plus two additional egg yolks) as the standard formula—say, that given in *Mastering the Art of French Cooking*. Anne Willan makes a very rich and custardy clafoutis, indeed.

Our original research into clafoutis recipes had impressed us with this adaptability, this willingness to accommodate a range of needs. No matter that, up to this point, we had followed the traditional method rather closely. Now, to make it leaner and less sweet, we reduced the amount of sugar, eliminated butter from the batter, and substituted low-fat milk for whole. We also replaced the usual vanilla and booze (cognac, kirsch, rum, etc.) with lemon zest, to give what was now a breakfast dish an uncomplicated morning freshness. Finally, for ease of making with the reduced amount of fat, we replaced the cast-iron frying pan with a nonstick skillet.

During all this, we had no more sense of making a dietetic clafoutis by reducing the sugar and fat in the dish than we do when we make our cornbread with buttermilk and without sugar. You can make a richer, sweeter cornbread if your taste runs in that direction, but a lean one is perhaps even more traditional and just as good. Our clafoutis remained just what it was—a clafoutis—except, perhaps, in this one thing: it was more *our* clafoutis. And something else was about to happen that would heighten this feeling of possession.

It was early summer; the first local fruits and vegetables were arriving at the farmstands. Most people don't think of Down East Maine as plum- or peach-raising country, and they're right. But people do grow them here and I can still remember the intensely luscious aroma of a pint-sized carton of tiny plums for sale at Fairview Farm in North Brooksville. If cherries, why not these?

We began to work the fruits in: first the plums, then raspberries, blueberries, and, later still, apples and cranberries. Our success prompted us to take a more considered look at the not-very-inviting offerings at the local supermarket. Peaches, when we could find half-decent ones, made a spectacular clafoutis. Hybrid plums, although almost always rather dense and flavorless when eaten out of hand, softened and sweetened during the short cooking time to make a very good one—the best use we've ever found for that fruit.

Not that this dish is mindlessly accommodating—there are better things to do with apples, we discovered, than to make a clafoutis with them, and there were other flops as well. But these failures helped us better understand what we were doing: a clafoutis responds best to juicy, intensely flavored, slightly sour fruit. The flavor of strawberries is too evanescent; that of bananas, too bland. Blueberries teetered on the edge. Apples pushed us to consider pears (more tender and juicier); bananas, by tropical association, canned pineapple.

We haven't tried pears or pineapple yet, but we will. Winter has set in since I started writing, and the only strictly local fruit still available is a few forlorn apples clinging to the bare boughs of the apple trees, bright, rare spots of color in a world of spruce and snow. What would breakfast be these mornings without the occasional promise of a clafoutis?

That is how this dish has found a place in our lives. Of course we know that we're not the first to make a clafoutis with other fruit besides cherries, even with cranberries. Brooke Dojny and Melanie Barnard, for example, have a cranberry clafoutis in *Let's Eat In*. Our clafoutis is ours because, like a comfortable shirt, it has managed to shape itself to our particular fit. Neither well-fitting shirts nor recipes arrive that often in anyone's life, which is why we've been a little skittish about sharing this one. Not because it's so good—although it is—but because it's become so personal.

By now you can see how this clafoutis is connected to our lives, but you'd have to watch us actually make it to understand how it connects us to each other. The oven heats; Matt puts together the batter at one counter and I cut up the fruit on the other. I put the fruit into the skillet in the melted butter and stir it around. As soon as it softens and begins to release its juice, Matt comes and stands beside me to sprinkle in the sugar. She watches as I stir some more. The chunks of plum or tiny cranberries simmer in their delicately colored syrup.

She pours the batter over the fruit, puts the skillet in the oven, and goes upstairs for a shower. I grind beans and drip-brew the coffee. Twenty minutes later—only about a half hour since we began—the clafoutis, puffed, brown-crusted, fruit-studded, emerges from the stove. I divide it into two large flat soup bowls while Matt, still glowing from the towel, pours the coffee and then sprinkles the servings of clafoutis with a little powdered sugar. We eat it with a large spoonful of sour cream. It is delicious and flavorful but neither too rich nor too sweet —just what a breakfast clafoutis should be.

BREAKFAST CLAFOUTIS
(SERVES 2 TO 4)

Fruit (prepared weight): 4 to 6 ounces blueberries, raspberries, or cranberries, or 12 ounces (approximately) cherries, peaches, or plums
Zest from 1 small lemon, grated
2 tablespoons granulated sugar, plus additional to sweeten fruit

½ cup unbleached all-purpose flour
¼ teaspoon salt
2 eggs, any size
1 cup milk (low-fat, if wished)
1 tablespoon unsalted butter
Confectioners' sugar
Sour cream (optional)

Preheat the oven to 425°F. Wash and prepare the fruit. Cherries should be stemmed and, if desired, pitted. Plums or peaches should be pitted and cut into bite-sized pieces; commercial cranberries should be cut in half; small wild cranberries, blue-berries, or raspberries need only be picked over to remove stem pieces and debris.

Make lemon sugar by mixing the lemon zest with the 2 tablespoons sugar in a small dish. In a large bowl (one with a pouring spout makes things easier), sift together the flour and salt. In a small bowl, beat the eggs gently and whisk in the milk. Add the wet to the dry ingredients a little at a time, whisking smooth. Stir in the lemon sugar. Let the batter rest while the fruit is being cooked.

In a 10-inch nonstick skillet, melt the butter over medium heat, coating the bottom and the sides halfway to the rim. When the butter is bubbling, add the fruit. Stir until each piece has softened and is coated with butter, about 2 to 3 minutes. Then sprinkle in sugar to sweeten. We use about 2 tablespoons of granulated sugar for all fruit except cranberries (which require about twice as much) and peaches (where we prefer brown sugar). When this sugar has dissolved and turned into a syrup—about 2 minutes—stir up the batter and scrape it carefully into the pan over the fruit. Put the skillet into the oven to bake for about 20 minutes. At this point the clafoutis will be set, golden brown, and puffed up at the edges. Divide into warmed bowls, sift a little confectioners' sugar over each, and top if you like with a spoonful of sour cream.

COOK'S NOTE: In the original version the cherries are left whole, to keep in the flavor and aroma of what is really a very fragile fruit. This, of course, is impractical with several of the fruits we use, but it is always a consideration, which is why we like to cut our plums or peaches in large, bite-sized chunks rather than thin slices. We do pit our cherries, but otherwise —as we do with our mountain cranberries and other small berries—we leave them whole.

PERFECT PECAN PIE

✧ ✧ ✧

The use of pecans in cakes, pies, and candies is very much an American habit. Pecan pie, with loads of cream, will be part of the American-built heaven.
—Tom Stobart, *The Cook's Encyclopedia*

Perfect pecan pie: the very phrase causes the tongue to quiver with pleasurable expectation—if every tongue to a slightly different savor. Is your quintessential pecan pie dense, chewy, and chock-full of pecans? Or is it custardy soft, with the nuts few and large, to be savored one by one? Is it a dark pie that your taste buds envision, full of the deep flavor notes of molasses? Or one silky light and faintly caramel, with just enough of a taste of sugar to offset the rich, clean flavor of the pecans?

Because a pecan pie is so simple to make and because its major ingredients—sugar and nuts—can be combined in so many various ways, a pecan pie can be uniquely honed to a razor's edge of perfection against a particular palate: unlike almost any dessert, it is amenable to infinite variation. But all that freedom demands that you know yourself; otherwise you will constantly be seduced by other people's notion of perfect and never realize your own.

I know this, because it happened to me. Searching for my own perfect pecan pie, I kept running aground on what others insisted was *the* pecan pie recipe: only for me it never was.

Those whose first battercakes were sweetened with sorghum molasses insist that *that* homespun syrup, with its deep, grassy overtones, is the sugar of choice for pecan pie; for me it was a complete nonstarter. On the other hand, New Orleans cooks still make my mouth water with their descriptions of a praline pecan pie, as mouth-melting creamy-rich as that confection ought to be. But the result was so sweet that it made my teeth ache and my head spin. Sadly I had to put aside their recipes, too.

Most Southern cooks insist that perfect pecan pie is made with corn syrup and not too many pecans—a mellow caramel custard in a crust with the pecan halves laid neatly out on top. But there's something about corn syrup that leaves my mouth feeling dry and cheated; none of it—dark or light—goes into my pie at all. In fact, because most pecan pie recipes are based on corn syrup, I originally never cared much for pecan pie— until a chance encounter sent me in search of my own Holy Grail.

This happened one afternoon almost fifteen years ago, when some friends and I dropped in for dessert and coffee at our local country inn. On the waitress's enthusiastic recommendation, I tried their pecan pie. And it was a revelation: served still warm from its baking pan, heaped with a mound of thickly whipped cream, it was dark and chewy and packed with nuts, full of flavor and yet somehow still ethereal, each mouthful so freshly good that the pleasure of that first bite never dimmed.

I made it a point to return as often as my meager budget would allow, enough to make that pecan pie the eternal standard against which all other versions have since been measured. But, more to the point, since I'm painfully shy about asking for recipes, I knew I would somehow have to re-create this experience with nothing to go on but memory once the inn was no longer a pleasant bicycle ride away.

❖ ❖ ❖

Alas, that day came along very soon after. And it was ten years before I encountered the first clue that would lead me to *my* perfect pecan pie—when I encountered the following quote in

Karen Hess's notes to her splendid edition of Mary Randolph's *Virginia House-Wife*:

> SUGAR HOUSE SYRUP—This amber syrup "from the West Indies" recommended by Mrs. Randolph for preserving is, for all practical purposes, unavailable today. I understand that this was the original base for pecan pie and that the modern versions are nothing as good as the traditional one.

A soft-flavored amber cane syrup—that seemed just the subtle flavor touch I wanted but hadn't yet found in any recipe. Freshly fired with enthusiasm (and enticed with the lure of a pecan pie good beyond modern imagining), I scurried off to do some research, both in the library stacks and in the kitchen. In the former, I hoped to dig up some pecan pie recipes that dated B.C.—"before corn syrup"; in the latter, to find the ingredient that best approximated sugar-house syrup—and then see what sort of pie I could make from it.

So far as the library was concerned, the results were more surprising than helpful. Although several modern food writers talk of pecan pies being around in the last century, I failed to turn up a single recipe dating earlier than the 1920s. In that decade they started cropping up all over the place, just the way carrot cake recipes suddenly start appearing in the 1950s.

What I did find in old Southern cookbooks, however, was what was obviously pecan pie's direct antecedent: sugar, or "chess," pie—an egg-and-sugar custard, sometimes with a piquant edge of lemon, baked in a crust. *These* pies do have a venerable history, since the word "chess" is very likely a corruption or misreading of "chese," a then common variant spelling of "cheese." And a "chese pie" is what in England is still called "cheesecake": that same egg-and-sugar custard in a puff-paste crust. Called cheesecakes because of their cheeselike texture, they first appeared in British cookbooks in the early part of the seventeenth century.

While I'd be the last to assert that pecan pies were unknown in the South in the last century, I'd willingly bet that their current popularity is directly connected with the mass production of corn syrup in this one, and then only because that sweetener does not make a superior chess pie. Some cook or other realized that the slightly oily flavor of pecan meat made the perfect foil for corn syrup's drying aftertaste—and the pecan pie as we know it was born. By the 1940s, a generation later, it had become a grand old Southern dessert.

While they didn't give me my perfect pecan pie, those old chess pie recipes did get me thinking about *sugar*—brown sugar, anyway—and how much actual taste it used to have before they figured out how to make it more cheaply by putting some molasses back into white sugar, instead of just leaving in those natural cane flavors, the same subtle tones you can still discern in fine old rum. That's what made those old sugar pies so good. So even while hunting for my ideal syrup, I began to sample different natural brown sugars—Mexican *piloncillo*, Guyanan Demerara, Barbados brown—each of which delighted me more than the next, but none more than a dark muscovado sugar from Malawi, made directly from the freshly pressed juices of the cane, a soft and rich sugar with a sweetly clean taste.

The syrup, meanwhile, had been waiting for me all the while, quietly sitting on the local grocer's shelf. This was Lyle's Golden Syrup, a British sugarcane syrup, thick as molasses, but with a delicate flavor and a luscious, tongue-coating texture that reminded me of the much loved barley-sugar lollipops of my childhood.

The obscure brands of Southern cane syrup I had been hunting out in the Louisiana bayous, though lighter and sweeter-tasting than molasses, still bore its potent blackstrap flavor. Lyle's Golden Syrup, on the other hand, while it hasn't been around long enough to be the real thing (it dates back only to the 1880s), possesses the same amber color and the same preserving qualities for which Mary Randolph had commended the original sugar-house syrup. And, more important, at last I had a focus around which my own perfect pecan pie could begin to take shape: the taste of sugar without its mouth-deadening sweetness; the rich, thick syrupy texture of molasses without its coarse pungency. Lyle's Golden Syrup in combination with natural raw cane muscovado gave me the perfect match to the suave, rich taste of pecan. I had my pie!

There were only a few further adjustments: I decided to highlight the sugar flavors still further with a splash of a very dark and mellow Haitian rum. And because I wanted a slightly denser texture than the usual pecan pie, I boiled the sugar and syrup together for a minute before blending in the other ingredients—not nearly enough to reach a soft-ball stage, but enough to enhance the moisture reduction that takes place during the regular baking process. (If this step is omitted, the pie simply has a softer texture. Some recipes achieve this by starting the pie off for a few minutes in a 450°F oven, but in my experience that leads to a burnt crust.)

The results were all I hoped: a pie that evoked all the pleasure that I remembered from that first, inspirational pecan pie. It may even surpass it; my palate is a lot more knowledgeable and opinionated than it was then. In fact, I wouldn't be surprised if I learned that the original pie was made with corn syrup, that it was the rich, dense, pecan-stuffed *nature* of the pie that so beguiled me . . . and that memory has since distorted, refined, and improved the raw data my palate provided. Better then that I never did have that pie's recipe, for now I have both the inspiration—and a recipe whose slow evolving has enriched *my* perfect pecan pie with the flavors of memories that are very much its own.

❖ ❖ ❖

And *your* perfect pecan pie? I hope less that my solution proves to be yours, too, than that this account has whetted your appetite to go find it—and has conveyed some of the fun and excitement you may well encounter along the way. In the meantime, here are three of my favorite sugar-and-nut pies, plus some hints that may help you fine-tune your own version a few small steps closer to perfection.

• Other sugars, other nuts: once I realized that what I was searching for was the right sugar/syrup combination to match the taste and texture of pecans, I saw that different balances led to different pies: maple syrup, for example, though way too sweet on my tongue for pecans, would match perfectly against sharper-tasting black walnut meats. Similarly, I could easily imagine a molasses peanut pie or a cane-syrup cashew pie, built on the very same lines as the pecan one.

• A little cream (about one-fourth to one-half cup) mixed into a pecan pie filling before baking gives it a richer, lighter texture: especially nice when the pie is a very sweet one (as is the maple syrup pie).

• For a sweeter, lighter pie: add more sugar and use fewer pecans; for a denser, less sweet pie: add more pecans and use less sugar. One of the virtues of a sweet-potato pecan pie is that it is much less sweet and still very light.

• The buttery flavor and the lard-induced flakiness of a butter-and-lard crust make it the perfect one for a perfect pecan pie. And a Southern pecan-pie authority I know suggests that you roll out the dough a little thicker than usual; a thick, richly shortened crust provides an appetizing balance to the sweetness of the filling—as, in quite another direction, does that mandatory topping of whipped cream.

MY PECAN PIE

1 well-packed cup full-flavored brown sugar	3 eggs
Scant ⅔ cup Lyle's Golden Syrup	¼ teaspoon salt
2 tablespoons premium dark rum	2 cups broken pecan meats
4 tablespoons butter	9-inch unbaked pie shell
	Whipped cream for topping

Preheat the oven to 350°F. In a large saucepan, heat the brown sugar, Lyle's Golden Syrup, rum, and butter to the boiling point. Stirring constantly and scraping back any foam that clings to the side of the pan, let this mixture boil for about 1 minute. Remove from the heat and let cool while, in a separate bowl, you beat the eggs until creamy.

When the boiled syrup has cooled, beat in the eggs, salt, and the broken pecan meats. Pour the mixture into the unbaked pie shell. Bake for about 50 minutes, or until a skewer inserted into the center of the pie comes out clean. Cool the pie on a rack. Serve at room temperature with plenty of unsweetened whipped cream.

COOK'S NOTE: Since I originally wrote this piece, I've found it harder and harder to lay hands on the primitively refined brown sugars discussed in the foregoing pages. However, a new product ideally suited for this pecan pie recipe is now widely available in natural food stores. Called Sucanat, it is made entirely from the evaporated juices of organically grown sugar cane, and although the label doesn't say so (preferring to call it "evaporated cane juice") this is, in fact, a very simply processed, rich-tasting brown sugar, with all those complex, rummy flavor notes. And Sucanat's one flaw as a cooking ingredient—it lacks ordinary sugar's intense sweetness—is more than compensated for by the Lyle's syrup.

Finally, these days, the rum I pour into my pecan pie is Bacardi black.

SWEET-POTATO PECAN PIE
(ADAPTED FROM *800 PROVED PECAN RECIPES*)

For the pie

1 cup cooked sweet potatoes	¼ teaspoon cinnamon
4 tablespoons unsalted butter, softened	½ teaspoon ginger
½ cup packed dark brown sugar	½ teaspoon salt
3 eggs	½ cup chopped pecans
¾ cup top milk (half-and-half)	9-inch unbaked pie shell

For the topping

4 tablespoons unsalted butter, softened	4 tablespoons packed brown sugar
	4 tablespoons flour

Preheat the oven to 350°F. Put the sweet potatoes through a vegetable ricer. Cream the butter and sugar together and then beat in the eggs until the mixture is smooth and light. Beat in the top milk, the sweet potatoes, the seasonings, and the pecans. Turn into the pastry shell.

Make the topping by blending the ingredients together. Sprinkle over pie filling. Bake until the top is golden brown and the filling firm, about 40 minutes (a skewer inserted in the center of the pie should emerge clean). Serve, if desired, with unsweetened whipped cream.

MAPLE WALNUT PIE

2 tablespoons unsalted butter, softened
½ cup packed dark brown sugar
3 slightly beaten eggs
1 cup pure maple syrup
½ cup light cream
1 teaspoon vanilla
⅛ teaspoon salt
2 tablespoons flour
1 cup chopped walnuts
9-inch unbaked pie shell
Whipped cream for topping

Preheat the oven to 350°F. Cream the butter and brown sugar together. Beat in the eggs, maple syrup, cream, vanilla, salt, and flour. When this mixture is well blended, fold in the chopped walnuts.

Scrape the completed filling into the pie shell and bake for 45 to 55 minutes, or until a skewer inserted into the center of the pie comes out clean. Cool the pie on a rack. Serve at room temperature with plenty of unsweetened whipped cream.

A Note on Sources. Lyle's Golden Syrup is available in the imported grocery section of most supermarkets, but can be ordered from G. B. Ratto's, 821 Washington Street, Oakland, CA 94607. A good source for well-priced fresh pecans is Sunnyland Farms, P.O. Box 549, Albany, GA 31703.

THE
BAKER'S
APPRENTICE

AN ARTISANAL
LOAF

✦ ✦ ✦

1

Truly good white bread satisfies, I think, like no other loaf, really like no other food at all. It is the one thing we eat that has been wholly shaped to comfort human hunger. Bringing it to the table, wrapped in a linen napkin, is not unlike holding a small baby—the same hand-filling size, glowing warmth, yielding firmness, and salt-and-sour scent. Here, however, the relationship is exactly inverted: it is the infant who is entirely nurturing—and entirely eaten up.

In this fullness of giving, at least, white bread is different from whole-grain bread. For these, whether made of wheat, rye, oats, or any other grain, retain something of the seed's stubborn unwillingness to be digested. They remain a kind of aerated gruel, filling but not ultimately satisfying. Bakers, of course, have learned to manipulate such breads—to make them dark or light, sweet or sour—so that each has its special occasion when nothing else will do. But a meal can be made of good white bread, if need be, three times a day without exhausting expectation.

I knew this by eating such bread but not by making it. I've been baking bread, off and on, since I was twenty, but until recently I never made a loaf like that—a loaf that truly fed me. It might beguile the mouth and fill the stomach, but it left the self still hungry. No matter how promising the recipe, the result had a certain sameness to it, an inherent insipidity. I never escaped the feeling that I wasn't really making bread at all—just playing at it.

Other people liked my bread but, ultimately, even that was not enough. There comes a critical moment in learning a craft when the pleasure taken in the *idea* of doing something ("Look, Ma—I'm baking bread") is replaced by a total absorption in the thing made: suddenly it has become strong enough to sustain interest all by itself. The thing you have been patiently nourishing begins to nourish you.

I didn't understand this at the time, but I now see that I wanted to make a loaf that would totally absorb my attention in a way that might allow me to forget who was making it in the struggle to make it well: a loaf that would keep drawing me back because I had other questions to ask it, new dissatisfactions with what had only last month, last week, seemed completely right.

In other words, I wanted to be serious about my bread making in ways that were beyond me. I needed instruction, but I wasn't willing to make the commitment necessary to find it. Nothing meaningful is ever learned that hasn't first thrown the learner against the limits of his character, and one big limitation to my character has always been this: teachers scare me.

I needed a real baker to advise me. But shying away from such instruction, I still struggled to convince myself that I could solve this problem once I laid hands on some as-yet-unrevealed secret, some ever-elusive clue. Surely this was something I could find in a book. Elizabeth David's *English Bread and Yeast Cookery*, *Beard on Bread*, Bernard Clayton's *Complete Book of Breads*, the Time-Life volume *Breads* in the Good Cook series, Edward Espe Brown's *The Tassajara Bread Book*—from them I squeezed out every hint and followed up every casual aside. Different ways of kneading, special proofing boxes, genuine baker's yeast, French-made bread pans, oven bricks—each was tried, each left me as confused and ignorant as before.

Finally, after reading Lise Boily and Jean-François Blanchette's *The Bread Ovens of Quebec*, I became convinced that I could not make good bread because I did not have the right *oven*. As we shall see, there was some truth to this. At the time, however, I lived in the outskirts of Boston on the second floor of a two-family house. A bread oven, whether indoors or out, was an impossibility. And there, for several years, the matter had to rest.

2

> The good baguette . . . is made using old-fashioned methods, the way the French did during the 1930s. The good loaf contains nothing but high quality wheat flour, water and sea salt. The dough is kneaded . . . slowly, so the dough and the flavor aren't killed by overwork. The dough rises slowly, several times, with plenty of rest between kneadings.
> —Patricia Wells, "Vive la Baguette: As French as Paris," *The New York Times*, October 9, 1983

If I had not been afraid of teachers, I might, in 1983, when I had come into a little money from my grandfather and quit my job to write about food, have gone to France. Patricia Wells had begun to write from Paris about a small tribe of dedicated artisanal bakers (who also existed here and there in Germany, the Netherlands, Belgium, and Italy, as well as other parts of France) making what for lack of a better word I shall call an *artisanal* loaf of bread.

The methods they were adopting were centuries old, but the understanding they brought to them was relatively new. Just as winemakers had begun to use the growing body of knowledge on the nature of fermentation to produce completely natural wines, so were these bakers perfecting ways to naturally ferment flour to produce a leavened bread out of nothing but three essential ingredients: flour, water, salt.

I had been to Paris as a teenager, had eaten French bread. I knew that there was a fundamental difference between the way such loaves were made and how I was trying to make my own, and I had already spent a lot of time trying to discover what that difference was. Recipes, of course, existed—most notably Julia Child's famous version in the second volume of

Mastering the Art of French Cooking. But these bakers did not bake from a recipe; thus, no recipe could teach me what I wanted to know.

This, I understand in retrospect, was the source of my profound disappointment in Bernard Clayton's *The Breads of France.* I was ecstatic when it appeared in 1978: here was someone who had actually toured France to observe its *boulangers* at work. But in a crucial way, Clayton saw nothing at all. Describing his visit to the Poilâne bakery, he devotes three pages to a drinking session with Poilâne *père*, two paragraphs to a cluster of grapes—made of bread dough—that graces their specialty harvest loaf, but *not a single line* to the actual making of the bread.

Clayton's concern, after all, was to translate what he saw into recipes, and a recipe is nothing if it doesn't work. Consequently, almost every one of his depends on the automatic effects of commercial baking yeast—even his version of *pain Poilâne,* which in reality is made without any such ingredient at all. Lionel Poilâne might just as easily have been speaking about recipe-writing when, as quoted by Joanne Kates in *The Taste of Things,* he disavowed the use of commercial yeast because it was "without surprises . . . definite and calibrated, not so delicate."

These bakers were prepared to let go of what Clayton could not: an approach to bread making that could be captured in a prescriptive formula and replicated by rote. By utilizing the rich mix of wild yeasts that filled the air of their own bakeries to activate an essentially free-form leavening process, they sacrificed a large measure of control in exchange for the chance of active participation in every aspect of the development of the loaf. "Don't confuse the baker with the pharmacist," Poilâne is quoted as saying, this time in Narsai David and Doris Muscatine's *Monday Night at Narsai's.* "The pharmacist weighs the ingredients, but the baker really doesn't; he uses measures only as guidelines. . . . The best way to succeed in bread making is to do things as empirically as possible and trust one's senses."

By doing so, however, they were taking a risk: the same factors that now allowed them to manipulate the loaf made the loaf susceptible to other variables that are not under the baker's control—most notoriously, sudden shifts in the weather. "People complain that it's uneven, but . . . that's the name of the game," says Poilâne to Patricia Wells (in *The Food Lover's Guide to Paris*). "No two batches are ever the same; a simple storm can ruin an entire baking."* If even Poilâne himself cannot guarantee the quality of his bread from one day to the next, there is no safety net for anyone. Success cannot be guaranteed.

Why, then, would anyone *prefer* a natural leavening? In response, it might be argued that at the very center of the artisanal process is not so much insistence on fine ingredients nor mastery of any particular method, but rather a willingness to assume personal responsibility for the thing made. Paradoxically, this means surrendering control, for there can be no responsibility without risk of failure. But willingness to assume that risk restores the baker's artisanal status even as it offers the possibility of creating an incomparably crusty and full-flavored loaf.

It also makes possible a different relationship with the customer as well. Each artisanal loaf expresses an opinion about those who buy it, for this is the bread the baker not only wants to make but must trust us to want as well. Thus, the baker cannot challenge himself without also challenging us—asking, for example, that we accept the risk of imperfect bread one day for the chance to buy, on some other, a loaf that is good beyond belief.

The artisanal baker, then, lives in a very different world from the baker who depends on conditioners, foolproof shortcuts, and automated machinery to produce a reliable but essentially silent loaf. Such a loaf is able to speak of nothing much—even flavor. For that becomes a mumble, albeit a sometimes pleasing mumble, of not-quite-distinguishable flavors: citric acid, malted barley, sugar, powdered milk, yeast.

Cookbooks, however, are rarely about responsibility—and almost always about control. At the time of which I write, still entirely under their tutelage, this was a distinction I couldn't

---

* Noel Comess, an American artisanal baker, says that he never understood why farmers talked interminably about the weather—until he began baking bread (as reported by Stephen Lewis in *Gourmet*, October 1990).

understand. Instead, I remained obsessed with the idea that such bread depended for its success on secrets that those who wrote about it either were not privy to or would not share. I yearned for some *real* French bread flour . . . or even a scrap of Poilâne's own *levain*. But above all, I wanted a wood-fired bread oven.

3

For a long time it seemed that I would never get one. But then I moved to Maine and, at about the same time, learned about Alan Scott, a California-based ovencrafter, who was producing small precast cement cores, based on a seventeenth-century English design, for what might prove a movable (if hardly *portable*) outdoor wood-fired bread oven. We contacted him, purchased one, and helped some abler friends install it in our yard (see pages 224–27). I was in business—*real* bread baking could now begin.

The bread oven, however, proved to be a teacher out of my worst nightmares. It made immediate, huge demands on my small understanding. It not only refused to tolerate mistakes but cruelly punished them with burns and ruined bread. It expected me to know everything and explained nothing. Worst of all, it constantly shifted positions, so what might satisfy it —at least partially—on one day cut no ice the next.

Each time I fired it up, its needs were different. The wind came from a different quarter; the wood burned unevenly; the day turned cool. Nor did anything about it work like an ordinary stove. There was no thermostat, no average heating time. Oven temperature was gauged by holding a hand inside and considering the pain.

A constantly recurring problem, however, was that the bread would be ready, or the oven, but almost never both at once. And since the oven had final say, this meant that I was going to have to relearn how to make my bread. I needed a loaf that could rise and wait awhile without becoming gassy and frail —but that also could go into the oven too early and still find the resilience for one last, compensatory spring. Finally, most important, it had to be a bread that was worth all this work.

For the time being, I simply gave the bread oven up. In a sense, it had done its work already, for it had, more than I then understood, helped clear my head.

What was going on? Well, take the, for me, magical phrase, *pane pugliese*. Before, all I had to do was to see the recipe for this classic country Italian loaf and a few hours later a splendid replication would be emerging from my kitchen stove. The bread oven, however, had no patience with that kind of cookbook romance. It kept me square in my own back yard, covered with sweat, reaching into its scorching interior to shift about the recalcitrant lumps of dough. There was no pretending *here* that because a certain recipe originated in Puglia I was somehow hobnobbing with Pugliese bakers—might even be one myself!

No, if I wanted to romanticize the matter, the best face I could put on was that of a lowly apprentice, sent back to the kneading board with a cuff on the head to learn what I had pretended to know but had been just thoroughly exposed as *not* knowing: how to make a loaf of bread. Before, it had only been appetite that was passing judgment on my bread, and appetite has a limited span of attention . . . and an insatiable need to be entertained. This time around I had a teacher with a very different set of demands. Here, it said, is the flour, the water, the salt—now *get to work*.

4

At about this time I happened to read an article on organic gardening, "Healthy Harvest," in *Harrowsmith* magazine. In it, Doug Whynott distinguishes between what Stuart Hill, one of the experts he interviewed, called "deep organics" and "shallow organics." The shallow-organic farmer

> proceeds much like the conventional farmer. Both look to outside experts to provide external solutions to their problems . . . the shallow-organic farmer substituting natural controls for synthetic ones. But the deep-organic farmer . . . comes to un-

derstand natural processes. "He substitutes knowledge and skill for inputs," thereby lessening his reliance on others, like chemical companies, and thus growing in power.

I realized that I was right then passing through the transitional period from being what might be called a shallow artisanal baker toward becoming a deep artisanal baker, and that the catalyst of this transition was the collapse of my blind faith in commercial yeast. I didn't like it, but I was dependent on it—both the yeast itself and the mind-set that came with it. In baking bread, always, the first step had been activating the yeast in its sweet hot little bath. Once it foamed, that was that: the rest was automatic. All *I* had to do was to follow the recipe.

I had made "naturally leavened" bread before, but the methods I was following had been designed to replicate the action of commercial yeast (often using it as well), so as to guarantee the same flawless performance—and thus guaranteeing as well the perpetuity of old, dependent expectations.

Now for the first time I was experiencing the yeast action as an actual ripening of the dough, not as a separate force exerted on a passive and inert mass. This difference may seem one of emphasis only, but it was an important emphasis. Until then, I had thought that you made different breads by following different recipes and—especially—by adding interesting ingredients to the dough: buttermilk, herbs, cheese, and so on. But as I gained a basic understanding of the variables involved in controlling a natural leavening, I found that I could produce subtly—sometimes even dramatically—different bread out of the same basic ingredients.

This is the loaf I imagine a baker once learned to make as an apprentice, mastered under the different conditions encountered as a journeyman, and finally brought to perfection in his own shop. Such a bread was made less from a recipe than from an ever-adapting strategy, flexible enough to cope with flours of constantly varying quality and strength, with temperamental ovens—and even more temperamental help.

My own loaf is artisanal in at least this sense: *there is no recipe for it*. Each time I make it, I build it out of simple blocks of experience that have accrued as the result of a constant conversation between hand and mind, the one making the dough, the other observing and reflecting. Although I bring questions from previous bakings or my reading, the actual experience of making resides in the hands. In a new situation, I literally *feel* my way.

For example, I usually make my bread with a hard-wheat flour from Great Valley Mills. One day, however, out of curiosity, I substituted Gold Medal all-purpose unbleached flour. The resulting dough was entirely different from what I was used to; for the first few minutes, especially, everything felt completely wrong. But my fingers were already tentatively finding their way with it, and once they had, the dough immediately began to respond. Confidence returned, and I ultimately produced a loaf that, while lacking some of the flavor and loft of my regular loaf, was clearly its cousin.

Of still more interest have been the effects that intentional changes in method have had on the bread I ordinarily make. By changing the proportions of the ingredients and the fermentation times, I have learned to make three distinctly different loaves—each delicious, each with merits entirely its own, all showing, at the same time, their common origin, for they are brothers and sisters in the same small family.

I've come to care for each member of this family, and so I've become that much more cautious about expanding it. There are only so many loaves I can hope to properly cherish—and the goodness of any loaf is directly related to the amount of individual attention I can give it as I make it. A bread now interests me to the extent that I see how to draw it into the family, link it in its making to the rest. I've forsworn new recipes along with yeast packets, so that each loaf might depend entirely on me.

Paradoxically, firing the bread oven has now become more an event than a normal part of our routine. It makes the best bread of all, but a cloche in the kitchen stove makes loaves that are also mine, are also good, and represent a kind of bread making that someone who is, finally, a writer, not a baker, can better attend to.

Bread is important to me in a way that other foods that I love are not. It isn't by accident that I went to such lengths to get a bread oven, where I haven't yet built a smokehouse or even planted a kitchen garden. I'm not sure why this is—except perhaps for the reasons given at the beginning of this piece. Bread nurtures me as no other food.

And now *my* bread nurtures me. It wasn't some special ingredient or piece of equipment I had needed but the courage to accept responsibility for each individual loaf. Doing that has finally brought me to that point familiar to all artisans, the moment when the craft that has been patiently fed for so long begins, in return, to feed the self.

Afterword. Master baker Brother Peter Reinhart, in his thoughtful and often slyly funny book on bread baking, *Brother Juniper's Bread Book: Slow Rise as Method and Metaphor*, devotes several pages of the chapter entitled "The Artisanal Loaf" to this piece. The essence of his discussion can be found in the following lines:

> John Thorne's concerns . . . represent a desire to restore balance, order, and perspective into our daily lives and to counter the shallowness of the assembly-line mentality. The danger, though, is the demeaning of other perspectives that may fall well between the two extremes of artisanal and assembly-line bread. Few, after all, can sustain the effort of firing a brick oven and tending it for hours, in order to make four loaves of bread. I applaud those who do, but what about the average householder who already has a gas or electric oven and no desire or ability to build and fire a brick oven?

Ironically, at the very moment Brother Peter wrote me for permission to quote from "An Artisanal Loaf," Matt and I were preparing to move from Castine and to leave our outdoor bread oven behind. We decided, not without reluctance, that until we have our own home and the time to commit to a wood-fired oven, we would bake bread in the kitchen oven like any other average householder. Consequently, by the time Brother Peter's book was published, I was again without a bread oven, and found myself involuntarily instancing his point.

Even so, I still don't believe that it's an elitist position to insist that the best bread is baked in such ovens. After all, very few people are privileged to eat free-range chickens, and yet it remains a matter of fact that such chickens taste better than battery-raised poultry. To know the substance of that truth, however, one has actually to *taste* a free-range chicken, which for many of us would mean having to raise it ourselves.

Until I built my own bread oven and baked bread in it, I didn't truly understand the issues involved in making good bread because I didn't know what good bread was—nor the price that must be paid to have it. Afterward, I understood that as good as this bread was, the effort involved in making it was too much for most amateur bakers. But given the exemplary quality of this bread, I began to ask myself more seriously why so many professional bakers also refuse to accept its challenge. And, rather confusingly, Brother Peter never deals directly with this issue in his book.

After all, I probably would never have bothered to construct a bread oven at all if I had been able to go to a local bakery and purchase a freshly baked basic loaf of white bread that (forget wood-fired ovens!) tasted simply of good wheat, salt, and yeast, without any overtones of dough conditioner, ascorbic acid, sugar, or shortening. Living near Boston, I could find such a loaf if I was willing to travel about two hours to get it; in Maine, it proved almost out of the question.

As it happens, there are small bakeries a short trip from both Castine and Steuben, the town where we now live. Unfortunately, neither produces what I consider an acceptable loaf of bread. I suspect that these bakers simply do not know how to judge their bread. Because our ordinary bread is so terribly bad, a mediocre loaf, freshly baked, will probably receive enthusiastic and near-universal praise.

This doesn't mean, however, that that bread will necessarily be *bought*. An acid test of the quality of a bakery's bread is whether customers come primarily for the basic loaf or instead for the cranberry muffins, the "French" bread, or the oat-bran, raisin, sunflower-seed loaf. In my own experience, bakers who find that their customers are not willing to buy their basic loaf simply assume that what is wanted is special breads, laden with special ingredients. And so their solution to the problem is: "Let them eat cake."

The fact that customers prefer a bread with flavor, even if it isn't the flavor of bread, is a clue that these bakers are no longer able to make a basic loaf so good that their customers won't want anything else. This ability has been taken away from the bakers by the companies that sell them their ovens, their baking supplies, and their flours—because to a large extent their standard loaf, especially, is determined by these products.

These professional bakers are in a not very much better place than the home bread baker who purchases a patent bread flour and patent yeast and follows a patent recipe. Indeed, the people who run both of these Maine bakeries could be more accurately described as running a kind of franchise operation. They think of their bread as made from scratch, but the ingredients they use are not only highly processed but formulated to produce a particular product as well. Control is almost entirely taken from the baker's hands.

Shortly after the passage I have quoted, Brother Peter writes: "I do not feel diminished nor is my finished loaf diminished because I use instant yeast and a regular oven." This may very well be true, but where—once such predetermined limitations have been embraced—does the baker then turn for continued inspiration, for the necessary challenge to keep his or her skills sharply honed?

For Brother Peter, the answer to this question, as can be seen in the subtitle of his book, is to recommend that we allow our dough a slow rise to fully develop its flavor and character. This is a good strategy, but it is not a sufficient answer to our problem. For if I apply the same acid test to his book that I apply to bakeries, I discover that while he does pay warm homage to a simple, plain loaf made of nothing but flour, salt, yeast, and water, he does not linger in its company for long. He is obviously excited about the *idea* of such bread, but when it comes to *real* loaves, his enthusiasm is directed instead toward such breads as struan, his imaginative—but also fantastical—re-creation of a Scottish harvest loaf. This contains, apart from the essential four, eight other ingredients: polenta, rolled oats, brown sugar, wheat bran, brown rice, honey, buttermilk, and sesame seeds . . . and, tellingly, it is not given a slow rise.

Brother Peter writes: "The brick oven is John Thorne's teacher and apprentice master. The loaf itself is mine." The loaf, however, as I learned myself, can be a devious instructor. That this is also so for Brother Peter can be seen from how quickly he abandons not only the simple loaf but also, where necessary, the slow-rise method in order to concoct such ingredient-laden fantasy breads as struan, roasted three-seed bread, wild-rice and onion bread, and Cajun three-pepper bread—loaves that have become, by his own account, the mainstays of his bakery.

I have no quarrel with such breads, but I also have no interest in eating them. I want to eat a very simple, basic loaf, and I want that loaf to be extraordinary. How does the ordinary become extraordinary? Brother Peter ends up, despite himself, finding the extraordinary in the extraordinary. This is understandable, but it's not the miracle I need.

I don't mean to imply that Brother Peter's own basic white loaf is not a good one, but that his book, despite its apparent enthusiasm for such bread, never truly examples what might challenge a baker—with undiminished involvement and enthusiasm—to continually produce it. Our culture, so imaginative in finding ways to innovate, is not so inspired in finding a way to sustain a commitment to providing excellence in humble necessities. Indeed, sometimes it seems to conspire against it.

I, too, required the extraordinary to accomplish the extraordinary. I needed the discipline of the wood-fired bread oven to break away from the conventional perspective where patent-yeast-risen breads are the norm. As soon as I began baking in earnest with my wood-fired oven, the naturally leavened loaf became completely ordinary . . . because, in that situation, *it was what made sense.*

Brother Peter is right to ask how this same sense might be made in a simpler way: that is, one more appropriate to the way we live. But to ask a question is not the same as to answer it. His book ultimately serves to reconcile the baker to a world of patent flours and yeasts and hi-tech bakery ovens . . . and the loaves that they best produce. So the question remains: How in our contemporary world can the making of a simple loaf of bread be made into what is at once an ordinary *and* an extraordinary event?

Notes on Building and Using an Outdoor Wood-Fired Bread Oven

Alan Scott, a lanky, soft-spoken Australian, first encountered naturally fermented whole-grain bread at the Blue Mountain Center for Meditation, where Laurel Robertson wrote *The Laurel's Kitchen Bread Book*. He helped design and create the center's ovens, an experience that changed the direction of his life. Interviewed in the Food & Drink supplement of the *Pacific Sun* for September 6–15, 1985, Alan Scott said, "I am a blacksmith by trade, and fire is one of my tools. But little did I suspect what was opening up for me once a halfway decent oven was built, and I tasted bread baked in the way it is supposed to be."

The immediate result was his founding OvenCrafters in 1984, to design, build, and promote the use of small, heat-retaining ovens in both private homes and artisanal bakeries. Alan Scott travels around the country building these ovens and leading workshops on both building and operating them. He has also been involved with the Aprovecho Institute of Oregon in developing larger ovens to supplement open-fire cooking in Third World countries where fuel is scarce.

In his continuing search for appropriate ovens for various situations and locales, he has researched and written practical plans for building Quebec clay and Southwest adobe outdoor ovens, an indoor brick pizza/bread oven, and concrete ovens that can be used inside or out.

However, the particular oven that originally drew me to write him was his replica of a ceramic oven liner that had once been manufactured in North Devon and imported into this country in the early 1600s. But where the original version had been made of gravel-tempered clay fired like pottery, his was mold-cast of high-temperature calcium aluminite cement. Consequently, it no longer needs to be built into the masonry of a fireplace, possessing sufficient mass to hold heat for most baking needs, even with walls that are only two inches thick.

We ordered the oven shell in late March of 1988 and drove into Bangor to pick it up on May 16. Although the shell is only two feet wide and a little over a foot high, it weighs a hundred and fifty pounds, and we were a little nervous as to whether we could fit it ourselves into the back of our tiny Honda Civic. Our faces fell when we arrived at the truck depot and discovered a crate almost as large as the car. But one of the freight men, noticing our dismay, produced a crowbar and helped us free the shell and then shoehorn it through the hatchback.

Two friends, Bob Black and Joyce Cambron, who do home renovation work, volunteered to assemble the oven, guided by a set of instructions provided by OvenCrafters. Because of the small size of the oven and its narrow opening, we decided to place it on a wooden platform—essentially a square, sturdy table—built strong enough for an elephant to tap dance on it. The top of this table had raised wooden sides, allowing concrete to be poured into it to a depth of one inch. On this foundation, while still wet, we set precast concrete slabs, and on these laid three rows of bricks. These provided the platform on which we set the actual shell. We then covered that with a concrete/vermiculite mixture for added insulation (necessary in Maine, even in summer).

An oven door was fashioned from a ten-by-ten-inch square of two-inch-thick board, protected from the oven heat by a tacked-on piece of aluminum cookie sheet, trimmed to fit with tin snips. A handle was then attached to the other side. Finally, to protect the whole structure from rain, we covered it with a cedar-shingled roof.

Thus, for the cost of the shell ($150), plus shipping (another $125) and some auxiliary construction costs, we owned an operating wood-fired oven for less than $400.

Once finished, the oven required a breaking-in period of about two weeks and then some further getting used to. The method itself, however, is an easily explained three-step process:

Step one (about ninety minutes). A small hardwood fire is set in the mouth of the oven. When burning freely, it is pushed inside and more wood added. When this larger fire has burnt down to charcoal, which takes about an hour, that is broken into chunks and carefully spread over the entire surface of the oven floor. It is allowed to burn there for about fifteen minutes to heat the floor as thoroughly and evenly as possible.

Step two (about fifteen minutes). The burning cinders are raked out into a small zinc-lined trash can. The oven is swept out with a long-handled brush and then mopped clean with a string mop, which fills the oven with steam. The oven temperature is checked with an ungloved hand by counting slowly until the heat becomes too much to bear. Practice will tell what count produces the best loaf. A too-hot oven can be cooled with a second mopping; a too-cool oven must be refired.

Step three (about sixty minutes). If all is well, the clean oven bottom is sprinkled with cornmeal. The prepared dough is put in place quickly with a bread peel (or a slab of cardboard or shingle). The oven is then closed off with the tin-lined wooden door and the bread left to bake (with an occasional check)—a process that takes from forty to fifty minutes. Success, however, is signaled much earlier, for when all goes well the yard soon fills with the salty-sweet scent of dough becoming loaf.

❖ ❖ ❖

Experience teaches all, so far as this oven goes, and there is much to learn. The dough, for example, will not bake where the floor has not directly absorbed heat, thus creating a loaf that is half dough, half bread if it has not been checked and shifted in time. Also, a not-quite-hot-enough oven produces loaves that are baked through but pale as a tombstone, which can be quite disconcerting. However, by the third attempt I produced bread not only fit to eat (at least *en famille*) but possessing all the right distinguishing marks: the thin, crisp crust, the exuberant plumpness, the delicate savor of wood smoke. It is simply astonishingly good bread.

The small size of this oven is actually quite sensible, for it holds four ordinary-sized loaves without problem. However, nothing has reconciled me to its small mouth. At its narrowest, a mere eight-by-eight inches, it prohibits pizzas and other flat hearth breads and accepts only the smallest vessels for the slow baking of beans or stews. A doorway at least a foot wide and ten inches high would be an enormous improvement. So would a small, pluggable vent in the rear of the shell to help promote the initial burning (which is otherwise very much at the mercy of the day's prevailing winds).

For more information about this and his other ovens, contact: Alan Scott, OvenCrafters, P.O. Box 24, Tomales, CA 94971; (707) 878-2028.

BAKING NOTES:
A READING LIST

• Edward Behr, *The Art of Eating*. Edward Behr writes searchingly and well on topics of concern to all serious bread makers, as can be seen from such essays as: "Millstones, Old Mills, and the Taste of Bread," "Of Wild Yeast, Rhode Island Rye, and Indian Corn," and "The Pursuit of the Fundamental Loaf." His food letter, *The Art of Eating*, is $22 for four quarterly issues from Box 242, Peacham, VT 05862. Back issues are available.

• Paul Bertolli (with Alice Waters), *Chez Panisse Cooking* (New York: Random House, 1988). The chapter on bread is a perceptive, thorough, and sensitively written account of natural fermentation methods, including one that nicely points up the affinity of baker to winemaker through the use of wine-grape must as a leavening agent.

• Roland Bilheux, Alain Escoffier, Daniel Hervé, and Jean-Marie Pouradier, *Special and Decorative Breads* (translated by Rhona

Poritzky-Lauvand and James Peterson; New York: Van Nostrand Reinhold, 1989). Four professional French bakers show how informative and helpful an instructional manual can be. Here, at last, are closeup photographs showing depth and color of crust, the texture of the crumb, the size and distribution of air holes in standard French loaves. Such meticulous attention to detail characterizes the text as well, which starts with a useful glossary of French baking terms and then provides a technical but clear explanation of the mechanics of French bread baking. Expensive as it is ($59.95), technical as it is, and as full as it is of breads you'll never make and techniques you'll never employ, I can't imagine anyone seriously interested in baking French bread not wanting to get hold of this book.

• Lise Boily and Jean-François Blanchette, *The Bread Ovens of Quebec* (Ottawa: National Museum of Man/National Museums of Canada, 1979). An enchanting account of the role of the bread oven in rural Quebec, with a series of photographs that show one being built and then being used. There are instructions for making the bread traditionally baked in these ovens, and of the folktales and songs that have grown up around them. A unique portrait of the central role that bread and bread making play in this culture.

• Elizabeth David, *English Bread and Yeast Cookery* (American edition, with notes by Karen Hess; New York: Viking, 1980). Still by far the most thoughtful book on the baking of bread written in the English language.

• Carol Field, *The Italian Baker* (New York: Harper & Row, 1985). See my essay on this work in my first book, *Simple Cooking*. Because she learned the way Italian bakers actually go about their task before translating their methods into a recipe-oriented format, some working backward is possible to those willing to read between the lines.

• Karen Hess, "The American Loaf: A Historical View," *The Journal of Gastronomy* (Winter 1987–88, pp. 2–23). Karen Hess weaves a fascinating exegesis of the American loaf, starting from an 1824 recipe of Mary Randolph's and drawing together many disparate strands of farming and baking practice. Central to the piece is a persuasive case—accompanied by her very instructive method—for the soft-wheat-flour loaf.

• Tom Jaine, *The Three Course Newsletter*. Until it suspended publication, this British food journal regularly published—as its "third course"—*The Barefoot Baker*, a compendium of practical bread-baking information, historical documents, and detailed reports on European artisanal bakeries. The back issues are still invaluable but rapidly dating: we need a similar publication from a similarly literate, practicing artisanal baker to take its place.

• Thom Leonard, *The Bread Book* (Brookline, MA: East-West Health Books, 1990). Thom Leonard brings to this book the unique bifocal perspective of an organic wheat farmer and an artisanal bread baker. After explaining that the home gardener can produce enough wheat in a ten-by-ten-foot plot to make twenty-five intensely wheat-flavored loaves, he devotes the first part of the book to explaining how to grow, thresh, and winnow this grain, and then mill it into flour. In the second half, he details the baking of several types of naturally leavened bread (including rye, pita, and several different kinds of pizza), and rounds things off with instructions for building a back-yard wood-fired bread oven.

• Lionel Poilâne, *Faire Son Pain* (Paris: Manu Presse/Dessain & Tolra, 1982). Even those who don't read French will find the photographs an education in themselves. Otherwise—until that crisply intelligent text finds its translator—turn to the careful presentation of his method by Patricia Wells in *The Food Lover's Guide to Paris* (New York: Workman, 1984).

• Laurel Robertson (with Carol Flinders and Bronwen Godfrey), *The Laurel's Kitchen Bread Book* (New York: Random House, 1984). Although the weight of good advice lies rather heavily on its pages, this book contains a clear presentation of the mystical *desem* natural whole-grain fermentation method, originated in Belgium by Omer Gevaert and practiced here by such bakers as Hy Lerner at Baldwin Hill.

• Jeffrey Steingarten, *Vogue* (November 1990). His account of making a naturally leavened loaf in his New York City apartment will amuse, reassure, inform, and inspire any beginning amateur artisanal baker.

ONE LOAF THREE WAYS

✦ ✦ ✦

Even before I left my bread oven behind me in Castine, I knew that I would have to learn how to transfer its most important lesson to our ordinary kitchen stove, where I was already doing most of our bread baking. It wasn't enough to find the loaf I wanted to eat; I also wanted the act of baking this same loaf—no matter how many times I made it—to remain a continual challenge.

It's the difference between finding the companion you want to spend the rest of your life with and then learning how to make that relationship work. I already knew that breads made of unbleached stone-ground white flour, water, and salt were the ones I wanted to devote myself to making—and I had begun to learn how to make them. Now I had to learn a way of not taking them for granted, to keep alive the seductive luster that originally fascinated me.

I found the key to this process in an evocative thought of Tom Jaine's: "Making different sorts of bread is not a question of thinking up outlandish ingredients and flavourings but rather changing the manipulation and cooking of flour, salt, and water." For me, progress as a baker would mean coming up with more and more interesting questions to ask the same ingredients . . . instead of devoting myself to finding a continual source of new ingredients to which I would continue to relate as to an endless series of one-night stands.

In a certain sense, this was merely making a virtue out of a necessity. I had already discovered that working with a natural leavening process forced me to adapt to different baking conditions and even to small variations in the composition of my flour or leavening. Now I was learning that it also permitted me to vary the kneading, rising, and baking processes to produce related but still distinctly different loaves of bread. For the purposes of this essay, I have defined these loaves as three. All are made from the same basic dough of flour, water, and salt, worked differently to achieve different effects.

What follows is not a recipe. I'm not yet able to provide infallible directions for producing a successful replication of my own artisanal loaf. Instead, I have tried to explain as clearly as I can how I go about making it, so that the reader can first discern the single method that links these loaves and then notice the changes in that method that make each one distinct. I've tried to provide enough information so that an inexperienced baker can understand what is happening, but to someone in this situation, the following text can serve at best only as a guide. Sources of more comprehensive instruction can be found in the reading list that precedes this chapter.

The Equipment. Since we left Castine, my bread has been baked indoors in a bread cloche or, when that is not suitable, on a baking stone. These are described on pages 239–41. Other essential equipment includes a large bowl, a steel dough scraper (a plastic one is also handy), a firm (heatproof) rubber spatula, and a few other ordinary kitchen items. I also suggest, for ease of cleanup, slipping plastic sandwich bags over the faucet handles on the kitchen sink when mixing and kneading the dough, so that these can be operated with flour-paste-covered fingers.

The Ingredients. I use the unbleached hard-wheat white flour sold by The Great Valley Mills (687 Mill Road, Telford, PA 18969). The resulting loaf has a better flavor and rises higher than bread made from a good unbleached all-purpose flour like King Arthur. However, this is also a matter of taste: a loaf made with a blend of softer flour has a drier, more delicate texture; my first loaf, especially, is moister and chewier and often tastes best a day or so after baking. I use pure sea salt and the water from our well. (I don't write this to make you envious; our well water isn't especially choice. But it is free from chlorine, which can have a deleterious effect on the yeast and synergistic bacteria in your leaven—as, of course, chlorine is meant to do. If you use treated water, I suggest that at least your starter be made from natural spring water.)

The Leaven. See the discussion of natural leavens in the following chapter. My own is based on the *levain* used by Lionel Poilâne for his natural sourdough loaf and is made as follows: Pour half a cup of water into a bowl. Work into it sufficient flour to make a moist but cohering dough, kneading it just enough to form a smooth, elastic ball. This is the starter, or, as French bakers sweetly call it, the *chef.* Put this in a small bowl, cover with a damp dish towel secured with a rubber band, and let sit on a draft-free kitchen shelf for three days, removing and remoistening the towel periodically. Once the starter begins to swell and give off a tangy scent, it is activated and can be either used at once or kept in the refrigerator for a week or so.* A piece of dough—a new *chef*—is removed from each subsequent loaf and held to provide the leavening for the next one, regardless of which of the three different loaves I am attempting.

The Method. All three loaves have the same round shape, contain the same ingredients, are baked for approximately the same amount of time, and are made following what is, essentially, the same method. It begins with 1¼ cups of water. *This is my basic measure.* Experience has taught me that a loaf made with just this amount of water is satisfyingly large but still sized right to be handily manipulated and to fit the baking

---

* If, despite your best efforts, either no rising takes place or the result is flaccid, smelly, and wholly untrustworthy-seeming, dispose of it and purchase a bag of dehydrated sourdough starter from a reliable source such as Walnut Acres (Penns Creek, PA 17862) or Sourdoughs International (see pages 247–50 below). Then proceed to make any of the loaves as directed, substituting a small quantity of the powdered starter for the activated dough in the sponge. Be sure to save a small piece of *this* dough as the starter (or *chef*) for the next batch.

cloche. Because after the sponge is made I work in flour by the handful, I adjust the amount added in response to the way the dough is developing. Except in the most casual way, I do not measure it. Nor, usually, do I make more than one loaf at a time. At this point, I still make bread best when I give a single loaf my full attention.

I begin just before bedtime, pouring the 1¼ cups of *cold* water into a large bowl. I put the *chef* in this and squeeze it with my hands until it dissolves entirely away. (The water is cold partly because at this point I don't want to encourage rapid yeast development, and partly because the gluten in the *chef* otherwise becomes rubbery and hard to dissolve.) Using a firm rubber spatula, I work in twice as much flour as water (another basic proportion) and ½ tablespoon of sea salt. This is stirred and turned over until it forms a coarse, wet mass. With well-floured hands, I coax this free from the sides of the bowl and work it into a ball, which is generously dusted with flour and turned out onto the counter. It is much too slack to hold its round shape for long, but enough maybe for me to wash, dry, and flour the bowl, and put the dough back in. This is covered first with a damp dish towel and then with a piece of plastic wrap, the two of them, one on top of the other, secured to the bowl rim with a rubber band.

This lump of flour is the sponge, which, once ripened and mellowed, will become the foundation of the dough. Hard flour requires this aging time to develop its full flavor and best texture. To accomplish this, it needs a cool environment (about 60°F); I use the top of the cellar stairs. To take full advantage of this ripening process, the sponge must be aged longer (as it is with the Poilâne-style country sourdough loaf, discussed later). Aged overnight, it produces changes that are more subtly attractive, and immediately noticeable in the feel of the dough.

By morning, it will be showing signs of life. Some days it will have shot up to the top of the bowl; on others only a practiced eye can discern that it has done anything but collapse into a flaccid puddle. However, on days when the bread will be the best, it will simply have risen—gotten itself up, as it were, just as I have—a little groggy-looking, perhaps, but ready to face the day.

1

The first loaf is the least complex of the loaves I make. After its night of slumber, I turn the sponge out onto a floured board and begin to knead into it as much flour as it can absorb, without any effort to force-feed it. I work it in by the handful, adding more each time the dough gets sticky during the course of a thorough kneading. This takes about 12 to 15 minutes; by then the dough is satin-smooth and robustly muscular, and my hands, my instincts, tell me: Stop.

There is much good advice written on how to knead bread.* The essential thing to remember is that kneading serves two functions in making naturally leavened bread: to align the molecules in the flour so that they can link up into a complex network of gluten and to trap pockets of oxygen in the dough to assist with the fermentation. This means that the dough must be stretched and folded over on itself, again and again and again—the stretching develops the gluten; the folding captures air bubbles in the dough which, with each fold, become progressively tinier.

The kneaded dough is lightly dusted with flour and set into a large bowl, covered with a damp cloth, and let rise to double its bulk, this time in a rather warm (80°F) and draft-free environment. There is no timing this (or the following) rise except by observing the resiliency of the sponge to gauge the vigor of the yeast. It can take from one to three hours, but usually no more than two.

Then the dough is gently but thoroughly deflated with floured fingers and briefly rekneaded to ensure that all the air bubbles have been worked out. This is the point at which an egg-sized piece of dough is reserved to serve as the *chef* for the next baking. For the second rise, the dough is set face down

---

* My favorite moment after reading much of it comes from Tom Jaine, who speaks of the pleasure of—every once in a while—grasping the dough by its throat, lifting it over the head, and slamming it down onto the counter with a resounding thump. This act is not only rich in symbolism and catharsis, it also accomplishes the two necessary parts of kneading in one dramatic *geste*.

into an impromptu *banneton*, made by generously flouring a dish towel, draping this in a medium-sized colander, and securing it with a rubber band—an arrangement that makes it easier to transfer the risen dough to the baking cloche.

In my experience, the extent of the second rise must be left to instinct, or at least instinct honed by practice. The well-timed loaf should reach its maximum size during the first several minutes of baking; this last, desperate thrust is called "oven spring." To prevent an overinflated loaf, the dough should be put in the oven before it reaches the point where its stretched-gluten walls are no longer able to support it; otherwise the loaf might actually sag down onto itself while baking. Using your observations of the dough during its first rise, try to get the loaf into the oven a little before the dough has risen as high as it can while still remaining taut and firm. Actually getting the loaf into the oven without deflating it is a matter of pure skill and still a heart-stopping moment for me (especially with the more delicate, *pane pugliese*-style loaf that follows).

I bake the loaf in the bread cloche, the base of which has been sprinkled with cornmeal and preheated. A quick deft shake turns the loaf out of the makeshift *banneton*, so that it now sits rounded side up on the hot base. Then two or three half-inch-deep slashes are made on its surface with a small, sharp knife. It is baked at 450°F for 15 minutes, and then at 400°F for another 30, with the top of the cloche removed for the final 10 minutes or so to let the crust brown. It's done when it gives off a hollow sound when tapped on the bottom. The resulting loaf is tightly textured and chewy, with a thick but crisp crust and excellent keeping qualities.

The advice about how to keep bread is contradictory. One camp—led by James Beard—says to wrap the cooled loaf in plastic and store it in the refrigerator. The other—led by Elizabeth David—rejects this method and suggests instead that you wrap the cooled loaf in a clean dry cloth or invert a *porous* earthenware bowl (like a flowerpot) over it as it sits on the cutting board. This reflects, I think, the difference between those who want to keep the loaf "fresh" as long as possible and those who think that bread should be allowed to gently stale, evolving toward better toast and perfect bread crumbs.

These two stands represent attitudes that are as much about reality—philosophical positions, if you like—as they are about bread, and so cannot be easily mediated. We keep our own loaf in a tightly closed brown paper bag.

2

The second loaf, based on the recipe for *pane pugliese* in Carol Field's *The Italian Baker,* is more difficult to make. It uses the same sponge as the first loaf, but this time I work this into a dough using as *little* additional flour as possible. The resulting dough is sticky and difficult to handle, but it produces a re-markably light, open-textured loaf with an especially thin, crisp crust. My strategy is to keep hands and counter well floured and to less knead the dough than stretch and fold it. I tug it out as if making a pizza, then roll it up, flatten it down, and repeat the process. After about eight or so minutes of such manipulation, a yielding but still resilient dough emerges—not unlike a baby's bottom minus the baby.

This dough is given the same first and second rising as the previous loaf, with some extra precaution because of the stickiness. (Don't despair if after the first rising you think you have a pudding, not a dough—the surface becomes silken again once it is worked down and refloured.)

Both cloche and base should be preheated for this baking, with extra care being taken to avoid burns. Again, the base should be sprinkled with cornmeal and the dough gently turned onto it. This time, before you make the knife slashes, the dough should be firmly dimpled with the tip of the index finger to deflate surface air bubbles—which would otherwise burst through the crust or else form a large air pocket just below it. The bread should be covered with the cloche and baked following the same procedure and timing sequence as the first loaf.

The advantage of a wet dough is that it encourages rapid gas expansion; given a moist oven environment and high initial heat, it can triple in size. The cloche, by containing escaped vapor, automatically provides the first of these factors—I've found that actually wetting the cloche overdoes this, resulting in a crust so thin and brittle that it shatters as the loaf cools.*

This bread is best eaten the same day it is baked, although if there is any left over, you'll find that it also makes a particularly fine toast.

3

The third loaf is my translation of *pain Poilâne au levain naturel*. It is also somewhat complicated to make, this time because the long aging of the dough seems to mute the responses intuition depends on to get things right. Until it comes out of the oven, I'm never quite sure where I stand. This loaf, too, is built up out of the basic sponge, but this time the sponge is ripened for two full days. By then, it has become so malleable as to seem already half-kneaded. The dough is then prepared and set to its first rising *the night before* it is to be baked.

Although much of what I've read about Poilâne's method suggests he uses a ripe dough not unlike a fermented version of my second, *pane pugliese*–style loaf, my own attempts in this direction left me with a dough so flaccid that even after two risings it poured onto the baking stone and barely rose to a three-inch height. Consequently, I prepare and knead the dough as I do the first loaf, finding that the ripening has reduced its capacity to absorb as much flour. The resulting dough is notably soft and pliable, but still firm enough to spring back when prodded with a finger. I put it in a draft-free place to rise overnight at room temperature, and in the morning I briefly reknead it (and reserve the new *chef*) before setting the dough in the *banneton* for a much shorter second rise.

This is the one loaf I bake on the baking stone, because for

---

* The crackling crisp crust that is the hallmark of the French *boule* or *baguette* is created in professional ovens by introducing bursts of hot steam through jets at crucial moments in the baking process. Using the moisture from a moist dough in the confined space of the bread cloche has an elegant simplicity that I find much preferable to such melodramatic and (to me) scary tricks as throwing ice cubes onto the oven floor or dropping a red-hot bar of iron into a pan of water beneath the baking loaf.

reasons I don't understand it doesn't do well in the cloche. The oven and stone are both preheated to 450°F. Then the stone is sprinkled with cornmeal and the loaf turned onto it and slashed as described above. However, before I shut the door, I use a plant mister to spray the interior of the oven— directing the spray away from the bread itself. I do this again twice, at five-minute intervals, to promote oven spring and a tenderer crust. As soon as the oven is shut, the heat is reduced to 350°F and the bread baked for about an hour. The resulting loaf has the distinctly sweet, nutty savor and tangy aroma of a fully fermented sourdough.

BAKING NOTES:
THE BREAD CLOCHE

Nothing, really, can compare with bread made in a wood-fired bread oven, where the sheer intensity of the radiant heat and superheated steam produce a loaf with incomparable depth of crust and fullness of flavor. But, for the home baker, at least, the bread cloche—Sassafras Enterprises' Superstone LaCloche—comes the closest, and comes closer still to replicating the professionally made French-style loaves baked in imported French commercial gas ovens.

The original Superstone LaCloche consists of a dome (the "cloche") and a fitted two-inch-deep base, both made of natural stoneware fired at over 2000°F. The design is based on an ancient Greek bread oven, in which the dome was set over the bread and then surrounded with smoldering embers—much as chuck-wagon and other frontier cooks baked bread in cast-iron Dutch ovens with campfire coals heaped on the lid.

Ceramic radiates heat more evenly than cast iron, however, and so the stoneware cloche even better reproduces the radiant qualities of a true wood-fired bread oven. The combined effect of such heat and the moisture-retaining enclosed baking space encourages maximum oven spring and good crust—producing a loaf with a golden, crackly exterior and a tender, good-textured crumb.

The bread cloche comes with complete baking instructions, but every baker will alter these as experience directs (for example, in a convection oven). Carol Field, in *The Italian Baker*, suggests preheating the cloche base at 450°F before baking, which gives the baker more control over the baking process. She also soaks the cloche itself in water prior to baking, but since the high-fired clay has almost no absorptive capacity, soaking it serves little purpose. Instead, if you wish to try this method, heat the base but not the cloche itself, and then, just before you put in the bread, wet the *unheated* cloche under the kitchen faucet, letting all excess water run into the sink. Put the dough onto the preheated base, cover with the damp cloche, and put into the oven to bake.

The bread cloche has been criticized because it can bake only a single loaf of bread. This is true, but that can be a very large loaf indeed, and I have not found this a problem. Sassafras has met the other criticism of the cloche—that it is limited to making round loaves (or small rolls)—by producing a rectangular model for making a single baguette. This produces an even smaller loaf—made from about 1 cup of water and 3½ cups of flour—but it does so in about half the time of the standard round cloche.

Thus, in the same time, the baker can produce two baguette-shaped loaves of the same weight as the single round loaf. (Since two of these cloches will fit in a standard oven, ambitious bakers could produce four loaves during this time.) Sassafras calls this cloche a "covered baker" because it is, essentially, a somewhat specially shaped, unglazed clay baker, and, indeed, they also provide recipes for baking a beef tenderloin and a cut-up fryer in this one. (It makes one wonder how a whole roaster would turn out baked in the round cloche.)

The bread cloche—of whatever shape—has its limitations. Some bread just doesn't do well in it, at least in my experience. This includes loaves made of soft flour and, as described above, my Poilâne-style loaf. For these, I suggest using either ceramic baking tiles (also made by Sassafras) or one of the single round or square ceramic pizza-baking stones. (Another firm, Pizza Gourmet, makes an impressively heavy, 14-by-16-inch rectangular stone that is perfect for this purpose.) These stones, although they don't provide the enclosed atmosphere of the cloche, produce excellent pizza and focaccia.

Bread cloches retail in the vicinity of $40 and are carried by many good kitchenware stores and by such mail-order enterprises as the King Arthur Flour Baker's Catalogue (which also offers a wide range of good-quality baking supplies and equipment). The address is Rural Route 2, Box 56, Norwich, VT 05055; (800) 827-6836. Sassafras Enterprises can be contacted directly at P.O. Box 1366, Evanston, IL 60204.

NATURAL LEAVENS: SORTING OUT SOURDOUGH

❖ ❖ ❖

Sourdough bread is much overrated and is difficult to perfect at home.   —James Beard, *Beard on Bread*

T he problem with sourdough bread is not that it is overrated but that too much nonsense has been written about it—
starting with James Beard's own wrong-headed account in
Beard on Bread. In the space of two pages he perpetrates so
many confusions and outright untruths that his text serves as
a handy benchmark for assessing anything else on the subject:
the more in agreement with Beard, the more wrong.

Beard's recipe begins with a starter made of flour, sugar,
milk, water, and a package of commercial yeast. This is allowed
to ferment for a week, until, as Beard himself says: it "smells
to high heaven . . . if it really takes, it can drive you right out
of the room." Some of this is then used to start a sponge to
which still more sugar is added. After an overnight rising,
another package of yeast is mixed in, with sufficient flour to
make two loaves.

This bread, made from overfermented starter and enough
commercial yeast to levitate a bakery, is no honest sourdough.
The smelly fermentation that Beard at once insists on and
loudly bemoans is merely to provide a lactic acid *tang*. It's this
and nothing else that most people now associate with the word

"sourdough"—and, sadly, the more the bread tastes of it, the more they're convinced they are eating the real thing.

Because of Beard's reputation—and the book's sheer charm—his perverse misrepresentation of sourdough has had an influence in inverse proportion to its worth. Elizabeth David leaned on it too heavily for her comments on "American sourdough bread" in *English Bread and Yeast Cookery*, thus making them something of an embarrassment in an otherwise masterful book. Nor is she alone.

Let's begin, then, by setting the record straight. Noel Comess, who bakes artisanal, naturally leavened sourdough bread at the Tom Cat Bakery in Long Island City, nicely characterized himself to Stephen Lewis (in *Gourmet*, October 1990) as a "micro-farmer": "Bakers plant yeast in fields of dough." Yeasts are microscopic fungi that live in profusion all about us, waiting for the right conditions to multiply. Those most useful in leavening bread produce enzymes that turn starch into sugar, digesting this so completely that the only waste, besides carbon dioxide, is water (unlike wine or beer yeasts, which produce alcohol instead). Then, *lactobacilli*, or lactic-acid-producing bacteria, feed on this sugar and work with the yeast to produce the gases and flavoring agents that make sourdough bread the distinctive thing that it is.*

Commercial bakers use hybrid yeasts developed for their capacity to quickly balloon the dough with gas, especially when primed with sugar and milk. These yeasts die in the oven before they have a chance to digest much of the actual starch, producing a loaf that inevitably tastes of them and raw flour—something bakers attempt to mitigate by sweetening the bread with malted barley. However, when yeast is given time to digest this starch, the result is a more nutritious loaf (additional protein and B vitamins) and one with superior texture and richer, sweeter flavor.

Although some bakers utilize these same commercial yeast strains in combination with a slow-rise method to attain a

---

* Interested readers should consult Harold McGee's comments on yeast throughout *On Food and Cooking* and Edward Behr's essay "Of Wild Yeast, Rhode Island Rye, and Indian Corn" in the Spring 1989 issue of *The Art of Eating*.

better-tasting loaf, more and more artisanal bread makers are finding the challenge of either letting nature sow wild yeasts in their dough or obtaining "heirloom" strains from other similarly minded bakers worth the inherent risks for the complexity and uniqueness of the ultimate product.

In the hands of a master baker, the natural synergistic leavening properties of wild yeasts and *lactobacilli* can produce from a simple dough of flour, salt, and water a whole range of genuine, naturally leavened loaves. Some possess only the faintest whisper of fermentation; others are allowed to develop a full, nutty-sweet flavor and distinctive sourdough tang. Indeed, Old World bakeries have cultivated specialized combinations of local wild yeasts and bacteria for centuries that produce rye loaves with a distinctively emphatic sourness, and they are as careful as French cheesemakers to ensure that their environs remain hospitable to the benign organisms necessary to the proper ripening of their dough.

However, there is none of the boozy harshness that characterizes Jim Beard's yeast-milk-and-sugar formula, clearly meant to encourage a drunken orgy of *lactobacilli*, thus producing as much lactic-acid tang as possible, quite separately from any consideration of the flour-enhancing process that occurs during a legitimate sourdough fermentation.

❖ ❖ ❖

The beginning micro-farmer's task, then, is first to initiate such a fermentation from propitious yeasts and next to learn to utilize it successfully as a leaven. Unfortunately, the strategies that best encourage this—what temperatures, what composition and consistency of starters and sponges, etc.—are still far from being sorted out, mostly because the instincts of the baker are essential—and incalculable—components. The result: what seem like frustratingly conflicting instructions or the usual painful dissonance between confidently asserted "facts" and personal experience.

My first encounter with naturally leavened bread was with a commercial whole-grain loaf made after Omer Gevaert's *desem* method. In essence, this is a leaven (the meaning of the Flemish word *desem*) made out of a pap of organic grain soaked until soft in spring water and then buried away inside dry grain until it ferments. (Those interested in this method should consult *The Laurel's Kitchen Bread Book*—and the Summer 1987 issue of Tom Jaine's *The Three Course Newsletter*, which contains an explanatory text by Omer Gevaert himself.)

Desem advocates insist that this method requires natural whole grains (or their flours). Perhaps because of the moral edge that purity gave their argument, I became convinced that a dough made of plain white flour could not spontaneously ferment. Later on, when I read in *Faire Son Pain* Lionel Poilâne's instructions for a loaf with just such a starter, instead of responding with joy, I persuaded myself that it only worked for him because his bakery was already a rich repository of the right yeasts . . . and that Patricia Wells had gotten his method to work in her own Paris kitchen because she had inadvertently brought these home on her clothing!

Even the success of my own first tentative trials was likewise explained away: *our* kitchen must be permeated with yeasts from the vigorous Walnut Acres starter that I had previously been using. Only after Matt fermented a simple dough of water and patent white flour in her parents' suburban home (where, presumably, wild bread yeast did *not* run rampant) was I able to set *desem* doctrine aside for good.

This is why the beginning baker must bear in mind that sourdough methods spring from quite separate vernacular traditions, each with its own terminology, assumptions, and different needs. The lumber-camp or chuck-wagon cook who produced a perpetual supply of hot biscuits, flapjacks, and cobblers kept a sourdough batter endlessly fermenting in a small cask, replenishing it as fast as he ladled it out. The farm housewife, once she had turned to commercial baking powder to make her quick breads, used "salt-rising" for the yeast-leavened ones—because this technique essentially allowed her to start a fresh fermentation with each new batch of dough.

The artisanal baker, on the other hand, used some of each day's batch to start a fresh sponge that would ferment overnight or else held back a small piece of dough to be kneaded into the new dough in the morning. Hence the similar but slightly differing traditions of the French *levain*, the Belgian *desem*, and the Italian *biga*.

❖ ❖ ❖

Because we bake weekly, retaining a small piece of dough has proven a practical method for maintaining our starter. I kept ours going, loaf to loaf, until last April, when we moved up the coast from Castine to Steuben, another, but smaller, coastal town. Then I let it die out, partly because I knew it would be several weeks before I would be ready to resume bread baking in our new house and partly because I was looking forward to creating a new *levain* in this new, pristine environment, buried away in a pine woods far from the everyday pollution we experienced in Castine, where a state highway ran right beside our house.

Ironically, this new bosky locale, deemed ideal in *desem* mythology, proved inimical to the right strains of yeast; in try after try I activated starters with a chronic inability to leaven, producing, one after the other, flattish, dense, unappetizing loaves, no matter how much time they were allowed to proof. Obviously, if I had started my bread-baking adventures in Steuben instead of Castine (a distance, as the crow flies, of about fifty miles), my attitude toward natural leavening would have been very different. Now, having seen it flourish under all sorts of conditions and with various ingredients in one place and give a listless performance under what seem exemplary conditions in another, I better appreciate the ambivalent attitude many bread bakers have toward it. Making bread is an involving, emotional business, and a lethargic starter can stir up the complex feeling of rage, confusion, and guilt usually reserved for parents with chronically apathetic children.

At least with a starter, there need be no anguish over whether the cause is nature or nurture. Just discard the failure and order a packet of "heirloom" wild yeasts and their properly synergistic lactic bacteria from a reputable supplier. For the micro-farmer-baker, at least, a fallow batch of dough is always at hand, ready for fresh planting, any time of year.

And the good news is that your *chef*, once started, is virtually inextinguishable—if, at least, you remember, as I sometimes have not, to retrieve a new one at some point before the rest of the dough goes into the oven. Slipped into a small Ball jar with a perforated top and kept in the refrigerator, ours stays fresh for intervals of—at the very least—a week.

Still, if I made bread only once a month or so, I'd master salt-rising bread rather than wait out the three days necessary to start a new *chef*. Now that I've worked with starters in the form of a batter, a sponge, and a piece of dough, I find their difference lies in means, not in the loaf they finally help make.

In other words, all methods have the same aim: to encourage the yeast that is right for the task and then help it to get on with it. A simple truth, but one I learned the hard way. The secret of success with a naturally fermented leavening is to find the method that works for you and then to persist in questioning it—the better the questions, the better the bread.

BAKING NOTES: :
SOURDOUGHS INTERNATIONAL

"There's something alive in your kitchen and it's ten thousand years old!" This—to my ear—rather ambivalent-sounding slogan is the battle cry of Ed Wood, retired pathologist, home bread baker, and man with a mission. The something is wild yeast, and he's spent many years traveling around the world, collecting local strains from bakeries that still use it to give their breads a special character and taste.

Although he himself baked bread for years using a starter that originated during the California Gold Rush of 1849, he came by this sense of mission relatively recently. In 1983, he was in Saudi Arabia, organizing the pathology laboratory for a new hospital fifteen miles from Riyadh. A radiologist at the hospital turned out to be a medical school classmate, and as they renewed their friendship they discovered they had sourdough in common. The friend's ninety-year-old father had a starter given him by one of the original "sourdoughs," an old Yukon gold prospector.

California Gold Rush versus Klondike sourdough: a bake-off was clearly called for. Ed Wood had brought his starter with him; the radiologist wrote to his father, asking him to dry a little and send it along to Saudi Arabia. Several weeks later an envelope arrived with a tiny bit of the culture tucked inside. Loaves of bread were made from the two starters, and Ed Wood was intrigued to discover how distinct in texture and flavor the breads from these two sourdough starters were.

This isn't surprising: over fifty-nine distinct strains of wild yeast and two hundred and thirty-eight strains of bacteria have been identified in sourdough, offering the potential of radically different flavor and performance characteristics in any particular batch. Yeast-leavened bread baking had begun in Egypt ten thousand years ago, utilizing a sourdough starter. Ed Wood began to wonder if, by tracking down bakeries still making bread in the old manner, he could find a yeast culture that had survived from antiquity, handed down—as his friend's had been—from father to son . . . perhaps the culture that produced man's first loaf of bread?

A bold idea, but Ed Wood was a pathologist, used to calculating such odds. In a recent letter he explains: "Farfetched? Well, maybe. It's pretty well known that certain wild yeasts and some *lactobacilli* form a strong symbiotic relationship resulting in a very stable combination. Such cultures resist contamination by other organisms and survive almost indefinitely. In the Middle East and Europe the professions are passed down through the family for generations and this is especially true of bakers. So we looked for the oldest, most ethnic bakeries in the world in the search for a sourdough that had passed from father to son for century after century."

In Egypt, Ed Wood and his wife, Jean, found several such bakeries. Again, the comparison between the loaves of bread made from these ancient starters delighted his palate and stimulated his imagination. If yeast from the village of Hurghada on the shore of the Red Sea produced a very different-tasting loaf from the one made at a tiny bakery in Giza, what about others from Saudi Arabia? Bahrain? France? Austria? Even Russia?

For two years we scrabbled down medieval streets and back alleys over two continents looking for village bakeries that had outlived history. When we found one, it was an experience beyond words! Gaining access was always a challenge, sometimes a rewarding challenge. Rewarding because it meant overcoming language barriers and suspicions to become acquainted with the people who "live" bread. Rewarding because those bakers still nurture sourdoughs that are stepping-stones in the history of man. Each success was a triumph; each sourdough a treasure of unmeasured value.

These adventures are recounted in greater detail in his book, *World of Sourdoughs from Antiquity*, which also contains directions for making many of the breads he encountered abroad. The section on the Middle East is especially noteworthy, containing several unusual and appealing Egyptian and Arabic breads. There are, of course, plenty of recipes for various American sourdough loaves, as well as such specialties as Yukon buttermilk waffles, greenhorn biscuits, forty-niner pancakes, and camp muffins.

The most fascinating part of this story, however, is Ed Wood's decision to make the most interesting of his sourdough cultures available to the American home baker. Through Sourdoughs International, Inc., he now offers nine different cultures, including those from the Red Sea and Giza; another from a 150-year-old bakery on the outskirts of Paris; still another, especially suitable for rye flours, from an Austrian bakery founded in 1795. Also available are his friend's Yukon starter and his own San Francisco one.

The most recent culture is from Russia, obtained from bakeries in Tarusa, a small town south of Moscow near the Oka River, and in Paleck, a village in Vladimir-Suzdal. About his work with these Soviet yeasts, Ed writes: "We're just starting to bake with them, but they look great. Leavening time for heavy loaves of whole wheat and rye is two to two-and-a-half hours and the breads are surprisingly moist and light."

Ed Wood generously sent us several of his cultures to experiment with, but since our bread baking is following its own mysterious course, we've not been able to do them full justice—especially since this would require a side-by-side comparison of loaves made from the different cultures. Even so, we did find that the most complexly interesting flavor came from the Saudi Arabian culture; the California one produced the familiar "San Francisco sourdough" taste—delicately tangy and sweet.

Bakers requiring a special culture tailored to a particular need—fast- or slow-working; especially sour, tangy, or mild— or who bake with particular flours such as whole wheat or rye will discover what they need among the starters of Sourdoughs International; any sourdough buff will find romance and adventure aplenty.

As this book went into galleys, Ed Wood wrote to say that he has temporarily suspended publication of *World of Sourdoughs from Antiquity* while he revises it to incorporate recipes, information, and baking techniques that have come his way since the book was first published. In the meantime, however, his cultures, with complete directions and recipes, are still available for $10.50 each: these include Red Sea Egypt, Giza Egypt, Bahrain, Saudia Arabia, France, Austria, Yukon, San Francisco, and Russia. Write to Sourdoughs International, Inc., P.O. Box 1440, Cascade, ID 83611.

IRISH SODA BREAD

✧ ✧ ✧

1

What we liked best in those far-off days were the loaves
of the wife who cooked them in her Irish pot-oven. These
had a thin skin-like crust, a brownness and flavour all their
own, a perfection achieved by no written rules but by years
of practice. The dough was put into the heated, floured
pot with room left for rising, the upturned lid was put on
and a few hot turfs set in it, then the pot was set in the
hot ash at the side of the fire.

—*The Constance Spry Cookery Book*

I rish soda bread, *real* Irish soda bread, whatever else it might
be made of, must have the whisper of peat smoke about it to
be genuine, even if that taste is only a memory in the mouth
of the eater. For soda bread, even more than the potato, rep-
resents what is best about Irish cuisine—true hearth cooking,
the love for things simple and good and made on the very fire
that warms the cook and keeps her or him company.

Indeed, there is no sense to be made of soda bread except
as hearth bread: without the aura of the fireplace behind it, it
does nothing that a batch of biscuits can't do better. It is a
bread meant to be baked in a cast-iron pot (or bastable or pot

oven, as the Irish call it) over a fire, the lid inverted and heaped
with coals to give the loaf within a brown and crusty top. Or
to be patted flat and set out to bake on a thick iron griddle
. . . or simply put in a steep-sided cake tin and shoved among
the coals. It might be made from white flour or brown, oat- or
cornmeal, plain or dotted with sultanas or caraway seeds—but
always, always with the hint of sod fire as its last, lingering
savor.

This is not mere sentiment speaking. Because peat, Ireland's
cheapest and most readily available fuel, is not ideal for firing
cookstoves, it is only in living memory in rural Ireland that the
hearth lost its central place in the home to the television and
the electric range. Traditionally, the Irish farmhouse was a
single room and the fireplace its heart, for the slow but steady
peat fire in that hearth cast out warmth continually, day and
night, the year round. It was let go out only on the first of
May, to be ceremoniously rekindled as hopeful emblem of the
burgeoning fecundity of the fields outside. Without a source
of drying heat, Ireland's damp climate would otherwise rot the
thatch, stain the walls, mildew the linen, and fill the bones
with chill. To the Irish, a house without a fire is a dead thing,
the presence of one a pledge of warmth and conviviality.

It was on those same coals that the baking and cooking were
done, and it is from this hearth cookery that what is so special
about Irish cooking comes: simplicity, insistence on freshness,
and implicit hospitality. For that single farmhouse room was
—in every meaning of the word—a *living* room: kitchen, dining, and front room all rolled into one. Only the bedrooms
were separate (and the privy, of course, which was a shed in
the back). There, the cook was not shunted off to some separate
place: the cooking was done in full view and the cook included
in the general sociality. Except on formal occasions, family and
guests ate not at the table but before the hearth, balancing their
plates on their knees and setting their mugs on a floor kept
scrupulously clean for that purpose.

The appeal of such a cuisine lies in its informal linking of
cooking, eating, talking, and relaxing before the fire into a
single seamless pleasure. Here the smell of the cooking food
was as present and vivid as the conversation—which, as likely

as not, was about that very thing, for the Irish are as pleased to talk about their food as to eat it.

Even the limitations of this cooking, which is necessarily simple and quickly done, are virtues in a culture that places a premium on hospitality, for a passerby can then be assured of place, plate, and welcome, with none of the sense of interruption that comes from squeezing in another chair around an already crowded table. Since the meal itself is no more than cabbage or potatoes, the guest is encouraged to eat to satiety, and because those vegetables are freshly dug, sweet of flavor, and served with good country butter and hot baked bread, the host need feel nothing but pride and happiness in being able to provide such satisfaction.

Understanding all this, I think, gives back to soda bread some of the character and flavor that it possessed when it truly was a child of the hearth. Unlike yeast bread, it can be mixed in a minute, set to bake on a stone or in a pot, and be done and ready to slice within the hour—at which point, hot from the oven, it will never taste better. Inexpensive to make, readily adapting to ingredients at hand and a peat fire's slow burn, it was a bread that could easily be taught that uniquely Irish language of open hospitality: to work great generosity from small means.

And, like that hospitality, if you will learn to love it for what it can give, you won't hold against it what it cannot. Irish soda bread is the artisanal quick bread. While it lacks the tangy savor of yeast bread, it has a soft, delicate, dairy sweetness to it that makes it the ideal match to good butter, a jar of marmalade or strawberry jam, and a pot of Earl Grey. If your pleasure is a loaf made from scratch, baked in the instant, and the perfect thing to serve for tea, then soda bread will do for you—and it will come from your oven (or off your griddle) with the faint, fine rumor of peat fire and good company.

2

Soda bread is artisanal, too, in being more complicated to make than its seeming simplicity might make you think. Oh, it is easy enough once you have the knack—it's the learning that's the trick. Even Irish cooks are humbled by the thing, as the legendary Myrtle Allen confesses in *Cooking at Ballymaloe House*:

> I was many years married before I triumphantly put a really good brown soda loaf on the tea table. Of course, this brought me no praise, only a disillusioned grunt about the pity it was I had taken so long to learn the art!

Because of this, most recipes for it simply don't work, and for the same reason that verbatim instructions from experienced makers are so maddeningly vague.* Neither can give you the thing you truly need: a pair of practiced and sympathetic hands.

As with all breads leavened with baking soda, speed and deftness are required to get the bread into the oven before the gas released by the chemical interaction of the soda and the acid in the soured milk has all bubbled away. Unlike yeast bread, which loves a rough and leisurely knead, the ingredients of soda bread must be quickly worked into a cohesive dough and slipped into the oven still quivering from the final pat.

The skill is not simply a matter of speed, however, but in correctly gauging the amount of liquid the dough will need to pull together: too little and the dough will not adhere; too much and it becomes gummy, and the bread it produces will be a leaden lump. This is a point, especially, where many recipes will lead you astray, at least those that share the perverse notion that a pound of flour (the standard Irish measure) equals 4 cups of the same (in our measure) when 3 cups is a far closer approximation. A more sensible approach is to expect the flour to absorb from *a third to a half* its weight in liquid and to mix in most of it quickly and steadily, adding the last bit with careful attention to the needs of the dough and not to measurement.

But certainly approach your first few loaves of soda bread

---

* "Just take the full of the little blue jug of milk, as much as you think of flour, a taste of salt and a suspicion of bread soda. And then you mix it—but you don't want to wet it, if you know what I mean," says Laura Feeney in Maura Laverty's charming *Full and Plenty*.

as practice material, not becoming discouraged if they emerge from their baking soggy and sour. Most likely you did nothing wrong, only did what was right too slowly. After the first two or three loaves, you'll have the pleasure of producing a traditional loaf that is distinctly homemade, rich with crust and flavor, and different entirely from yeast and biscuit breads.

THE INGREDIENTS

The Flour. Irish flour is soft flour, which helps make the bread tender and light-textured, not dense and chewy—"cake bread," the Irish also call it, to distinguish it from "loaf" or yeast bread. Happily, good soft white flour can be found here, as can the nutty-tasting organic stone-ground whole-wheat pastry flour necessary for making an authentic version of Ireland's celebrated "brown bread"—really a whole-wheat soda bread. Not surprisingly, an oat version is made from Irish oatmeal, which is among the best there is. Unexpected, however, is the cornmeal soda bread, which is an obvious first cousin to our own cornbread. In Ireland it is called many things, among them "pike" or "paca" bread, after—it is said—the ship *Alpaca* that brought a shipment of cornmeal to Ireland during the great potato famine of 1846.

The Liquid. The traditional acidic liquid used to moisten the flour and react to the baking soda was real buttermilk, the sour liquid left over from butter-making. For the dairy country that it is, Ireland's farmers traditionally have had little to do with cheese. Milk and cream are used fresh or else allowed to go sour and churned into a tangy butter (see the comments of Liz Jeffries on page 257), with the buttermilk being used in baking and drunk as a famous summer thirst-quencher and forever hangover cure.

This true buttermilk is not the same as our store-bought cultured product, which almost never has the thickness that

Vera Young describes in Rosalind Cole's *Of Soda Bread and Guinness:*

> Well, I think the whole secret to making Irish bread is to have the sour milk just the right thickness. You must have the milk like yogurt—thick and almost solid—to get the brown bread and scones really fluffy.

Consequently, many Irish cooks prefer to sour their own milk, mixing a half-teaspoon of strained fresh lemon juice per cup (or two teaspoons per quart) of sweet milk. This is allowed to sit in a warm place for a day or two until it thickens, then refrigerated until used (soon—it does not keep long). Although the clabbered product this method produces is called sour milk, it has a mild, sweet, delicate flavor, producing a fine-textured soda bread.

Leavening. This should be baking soda and only baking soda. Some recipes call for the addition of cream of tartar (the other half of old-fashioned baking powder) as well, or even baking powder itself, as insurance, but the action of the buttermilk and soda should be the only leavening the bread needs—it is, after all, *soda* bread.

The Salt. Sea salt, in as fine a grain as possible, so as to mix cleanly into the batter.

Et Cetera. Favored Irish flavorings include raisins and/or caraway seeds. No shortening is used in traditional recipes; however, a tablespoon of butter, cut into the flour before the liquid is added, is said to help the loaf to keep.

THE METHOD

Although you may not care to bake your soda bread in the fireplace, you will find your best success duplicating as nearly as possible the implements with which it was originally made. Soda bread was traditionally baked in a large flat-bottomed cast-iron pot, and is hence formulated (as biscuits also are) to rise best in a tightly enclosed space. This can be replicated by using a cookie sheet with a large ovenproof mixing bowl inverted over it, but this is very awkward to manage when hot. I find the round bread cloche ideal for baking soda bread, perhaps even an improvement over the traditional cast-iron pot oven. The bottom of the cooking surface should be dusted lightly with flour to prevent the bread from sticking, which gives it a characteristic floury look. However, a metal baking pot or cookie sheet can be greased with butter if you prefer instead.

If the bread is to be baked on a heavy griddle on top of the stove, that implement should also be dusted with flour (or greased) and preheated over a moderate flame. Since the crust will burn before the bread is baked if the griddle is too hot, the flame should not be turned too high—the griddle is just hot enough if it takes three minutes for the dusting of flour to lightly brown.

It is best to make the dough while the griddle or pot and oven are preheating, so that the finished dough can be turned immediately onto a hot baking surface. The ingredients should be fresh—especially the baking soda, which has surely gone flat if the box has been hanging around for a year or so—often the case with baking soda. Stir the dry ingredients together well, breaking up any lumps. Then, using the handle of a wooden spoon, quickly beat in the liquid, which should be poured into the bowl in a steady stream until the crumbly mass begins to adhere: "While you put your buttermilk in with your left hand, you worked it in with your right—you didn't want a too-sticky dough, you see."* With floured hands, gently form

* Liz Jeffries, speaking to Rosalind Cole in, again, *Of Soda Bread and Guinness.* This is a book rich in soda-bread lore (see, for instance, the contribution by Brian McMahon) and good advice. Here's another comment from Liz Jeffries: "We made griddle bread, too, baked on a flat griddle. We would use sour milk, at least a week old, and sour butter. Butter is much better when it's made from sour cream; the sourer the butter, the better the bread, I'd say. Good butter is what's needed for good food." Amen to that.

it into a single ball, soft to the touch and slightly coarse in texture. Don't expect it to have the velvety flesh of biscuit dough or the resiliency of yeast bread.

To bake it in the oven. Pat the dough into a round loaf. I happen to like the jagged crevices that appear when the bread is allowed to expand in the oven at its own violent whim, but for a neater, traditional-looking loaf you'll want to cut a deep cross into it, from one side right to the other. And for a bit of gloss to the loaf, brush it with sweet milk before setting it to bake.

Set it in the preheated cooking pot, cover, and return to the oven. Popular wisdom has it that a done loaf sounds hollow when rapped on the bottom—which is a load of codswallop. Insert a cake tester or stiff broom straw into the loaf. It is done if the straw or tester comes out clean. Richard Olney, among others, advises—in the Time-Life volume *Breads* in the Good Cook series—that you remove the top of the baking pot for the last ten minutes or so of baking, so that the crust will brown. My own experience is that the crust browns and crisps perfectly with the pot left unopened.

To bake it on the griddle. Pat the dough flat to a cake about one to one-and-one-half inches thick and cut this into four quarters or farls. Set these on a hot and floured griddle (see above) and cook for the same time as given in the recipe, turning each farl over about halfway through the cooking process. Don't expect these to rise as high as the oven-baked bread, but they will have a deliciously thick, double-sided crust—and on soda bread, the crust is a truly wonderful thing.

Let cool and set, then slice thin and serve with plenty of sweet butter and your best marmalade or preserve.

IRISH SODA BREAD
(1 LOAF)

3 cups soft white flour
1 teaspoon baking soda
½ teaspoon salt

Enough buttermilk to form a coherent but not sticky dough (about 1¼ to 1½ cups)

Preheat the oven and baking pot to 425°F or heat a griddle over medium heat. Combine the ingredients and prepare the dough as directed in the general instructions above. Bake for 45 minutes or until the crust is golden and the bread baked through. Serve as soon as it is cool enough to eat, or wrap it in a clean dish towel to keep it soft until it can be served.

COOK'S NOTE: A sweeter tea bread can be produced by adding 1 tablespoon of sugar and about ¼ cup of raisins or currants. Or, instead, *treacle bread* can be made: warm the buttermilk just enough to dissolve ¼ cup of unsulfured molasses. Mix 2 teaspoons of brown sugar and ¼ cup of raisins into the dry ingredients, otherwise preparing as directed above. Finally, for *seedy bread*, mix 1 tablespoon of white sugar and 2 teaspoons of caraway seeds into the dry ingredients, then rub 4 tablespoons of fresh lard or vegetable shortening into the flour before mixing in the buttermilk.

IRISH BROWN BREAD
(1 LOAF)

2 cups stone-ground whole-wheat flour
1 cup soft white flour
1 teaspoon baking soda
½ teaspoon salt
Enough buttermilk to form a coherent but not sticky dough (about 1¼ to 1½ cups)

Preheat the oven and baking pot to 425°F or heat a griddle over medium heat. Combine the ingredients and prepare the dough as directed in the general instructions above. Bake for 50 minutes or until the bread is baked through. Set to cool on a wire rack.

COOK'S NOTE: While some cooks do insist that this bread should be sliced and eaten hot, most Irish ones say that it must be allowed to cool and "set" for about 4 to 6 hours. Also, the proportions of white to whole wheat can be reversed for a lighter bread, or the white flour can be omitted entirely, using 3 cups of the whole-wheat flour to produce a darker, thicker one. Maura Laverty suggests throwing a handful of rolled oats into the recipe to give it a "lovely nutty texture."

IRISH INDIAN-MEAL (OR PACA, PIKE, OR YALLA MALE ["YELLOW MEAL"?]) BREAD
(1 LOAF)

1½ cups soft white flour
1½ cups stone-ground cornmeal
1 teaspoon baking soda
½ teaspoon salt

Enough buttermilk to form a coherent dough (about 1¼ to 1½
cups)

Preheat the oven and baking pot to 425°F or heat a griddle over medium heat. Mix the ingredients and prepare the dough as directed in the general instructions above. Bake for 55 minutes or until the bread is baked through.

OATEN SODA BREAD
(4 FARLS)

1¼ cups oat flour
1¾ cups soft white flour
1 teaspoon baking soda
½ teaspoon salt

A handful of rolled oats
Enough buttermilk to form a coherent dough (about 1¼ to 1½
cups)

Preheat the oven to 425°F or heat a griddle over medium heat. Mix the two flours, soda, salt, and handful of rolled oats together well, adding enough buttermilk to make a stiff, coarse, but not sticky dough. Pat and poke into a flat round about 1½ inches thick and with a sharp knife cut this into quarters or farls. Set these on a greased or floured baking sheet and bake for about 30 minutes, or until the crust is golden and the dough baked through.

COOK'S NOTE: Oat flour is available at most natural food stores.

To make *oaten honey bread*, whisk 1 tablespoon of honey, 1 egg, and 2 tablespoons of melted butter into a little of the buttermilk (about ¼ cup) and use this as part of the total amount of liquid.

Nà mól an t-arán go mbruithtèar é.
(Don't praise the bread until it is baked.)

THE
CULINARY
SCENE

MARTHA STEWART

❖ ❖ ❖

Of all dinners . . . the impromptu one is ranked the most
infallibly successful; the enjoyment therein is proportioned
to the absence of ceremony, and to the cordial feeling each
guest brings with him.
                —Charles Pierce, *The Household Manager* (1857)

You've never heard of Martha Stewart? Well, that's all right,
she's easy enough to describe. First of all, fall asleep . . . now
I'll tell you what to dream. *You're a slender, attractive woman
looking years younger than your age. You live in a beautiful old country
house in Connecticut, where everything is as glossy as a color photograph: the honey-golden wood floors, the charming patchwork quilts,
the hand-rubbed antique furniture.*

*Step into the kitchen. The sun streams in, glinting off the French
copper cookware, the shelves full of turn-of-the-century stoneware
bowls, the collections of fine old stemware . . . hand-woven farm baskets
. . . mix-and-match china plates . . . the half-dozen different stoves.*

*And everywhere you look, every surface in the kitchen—the dining
room, the house, it seems—is covered with food. Brilliant-colored pastries oozing fresh fruit crowd against whole roast geese . . . racks of
lamb . . . spectacular loaves of bread plump as chef's toques . . . salad
bowls brimming with unusual greens.*

*Guests must be coming for an intimate dinner for six . . . a Chinese
banquet . . . a Sunday omelet brunch . . . a pie party . . . a clambake*

. . . a whole country weekend. Relax, you're ready for them. Your expensive frock is attractive and becoming, your skin glows with perfect health, not one golden hair is out of place. How at ease you feel, knowing how glad they'll be to see you—the sort of pretty, winsome woman that every other woman wants as a best friend, every man wants to cosset and gently tease.

Wake up! wake up! You're only dreaming! Or, if you prefer, dream on. You'll be joining the millions of others enraptured with the same fantasy: a world where entertaining holds no terror, perfect taste sets no pratfalls, and cooking makes all things good.

As well as attracting a horde of fans and do-alikes, Martha Stewart has drawn a surprising amount of vituperation from other food writers (sheer jealousy) and social commentators in general (who ought to know better). Most of the people susceptible to Martha Stewart's fantasy of entertaining belong to a world where that activity is not only a social obligation but a professional one: promotion depending as much on commitment to a corporate-sanctioned social life as it does on raw business skill. For many people, this is the occasion of sheer terror, and if Martha Stewart psychs some of them through it, more power to her.

The interesting thing, really, is how she gets away with it. This isn't the same thing as how she does it, which is easy to explain. Martha Stewart markets on a massive scale the same idea that she once sold person-to-person as a caterer: "Use my help, my expertise, and my good taste," her books all say, "and entertaining can be a breeze. You too can be a guest at your own party, as I so manifestly am at mine."

So far, so good. But anyone who has ever known a caterer knows that in order to create this illusion of ease, they themselves must work like dogs. Buy a copy of Martha Stewart's *Entertaining* (over 700,000 copies sold), and you get some enchanting pictures and some useful tips, but after you put it down *you* still have to do all the work yourself. And having read this book (or one of its many clones), you ought now to realize that entertaining is work—more work, really, than you ever even imagined.

This is the crux of the matter. Even the most flattering portraits of Martha Stewart show her to be a driven, extremely ambitious woman who has used her enviable capacity to devote enormous amounts of energy to an infinite number of details as a means of squeezing every profitable drop out of her luck, looks, and near-infallible instinct for conspicuous consumption. Perhaps all her millions of readers are the same. But somehow I doubt it. And this being so, why don't they catch the obvious subtext of her oeuvre—if you *have* to have people over, for God's sake, hire a caterer—instead of falling, over and over again, for the same subliminal message: Buy this book, and this one, and this one, and this one, *and* the videotape, and, while you're at it, subscribe to my magazine.

If on the evidence of Martha Stewart's books I had to compose a generic portrait of her readers, I would describe them as female, relatively well-off (maybe even extremely well-off), but newly come by this money and rather insecure about the position it has purchased. I say this because of two noteworthy facts about the photographs in Martha Stewart's books: the absence of actual people (apart from her) in most of them and the overwhelming emphasis on *things*.

Now, if I understand anything about entertaining, it is about people having a good time with other people. I imagine good food and attractive surroundings—why not?—but mostly I imagine rapport—and the kind of good, witty, interesting interaction that brings rapport about. To the extent that entertaining is not about social obligation, it is about socializing, which means, at bottom, about talk.

Those of us who at social gatherings are too shy to interact tend to walk around and, nervous of catching anyone's eye, stare at things—pluck books out from the shelf, examine the pictures on the wall, peer at the *objets d'art* on the étagère. If you know this feeling you can easily visualize a hostess, experiencing this same unease, finding her eyes compulsively drawn, again and again, to the various decorations and canapés set out to enhance the evening, to make sure that they are really all right. Now, by one more leap of imagination, you can understand the powerful narcotizing effect of a book like *Entertaining*: it soothes the anxiety by reenacting this behavior under conditions of complete tranquillity.

The nervous hostess-to-be is shown, over and over, through a unique reversal of perspective, not the frightening guests she is setting out to entertain but what she means the guests themselves to see. The photographs that fill Martha Stewart's books create a series of compelling illusions. They use the artful arrangement of foods and festive-seeming objects to craft a façade of tasteful opulence, a simulacrum of welcoming generosity. Her "signature"—an antique gardening basket heaped full-to-tumbling with several pounds of ripe strawberries—is just one example of what can be done by bringing the right few things together. No matter that the berries won't be eaten; it's enough that there are so many and that they are a fruit everyone loves. The gesture is meaningless but the effect is guaranteed . . . especially on the hostess herself. What does it matter how nervous she is if all the objects in her house radiate that arranged marriage of the two most contradictory human impulses: wealth-display and generosity?

Martha Stewart herself, although she radiates WASP-y self-assurance (the Federalist colonial home in Westport, the Barnard College degree, the long blond hair, and the casual *haute*-preppie outfitting), was actually born in Jersey City of second-generation Polish parents. Her father, a pharmaceuticals salesman, was, according to one man who knew him, "a very handsome, very driven, and very frustrated man." According to Jeanie Kasindorf,* "Martha was his favorite, and although she will never say it, it doesn't take long to realize that the main thing he taught her was how to be a salesman."

She was arranging children's parties for pay at the age of

---

* "Living with Martha," *New York* magazine, January 28, 1991. All the following biographical material is drawn from that profile, and from Nancy Harmon Jenkins's "Viewing Women's Lives through a Martha Stewart Fantasy," *The Boston Sunday Globe*, April 28, 1991, and Frank Lovece's "Lady of the House," *Trump's*, June 1990.

ten; she was modeling before she turned sixteen. It would be only a matter of time before she put the two together. In the meantime, she modeled to help pay for her Barnard education (she graduated with a degree in European and architectural history); met and married Andy Stewart; had a daughter, Alexis, her only child; and tried out a career as a stockbroker, but ended up hating it. "I liked the sales part of it, the human contact," she told Jeanie Kasindorf. "But I wanted to sell things that were fun to sell." Meanwhile, she and her husband had found their 1805 rambling colonial in Westport, completely remodeled it, and called it "Turkey Hill."

In the mid-1970s, she went into the catering business with Norma Collier, whom she met when each was picked to be one of *Glamour*'s Ten Best-Dressed College Girls. The partnership lasted less than a year. According to Norma, this was partly because Martha Stewart "was resentful that I wasn't willing to work 128 hours a week." The final straw came when she overheard Martha telling Andy that "I deserve to keep more because I work harder and I'm more talented." Norma quit; the catering business was renamed "Martha Stewart, Inc."; it acquired a sheaf of corporate clients and in ten years grew into a million-dollar business. Then there was the book contract for *Entertaining*, repeated bestsellerdom, the videos, the magazine, history.

Telling the story so briefly, one can almost feel the different parts of "Martha Stewart" coming together. If you can be born to succeed, she was born to succeed at this. If Martha Stewart were a man, her drive, her success, her obvious relish of its accoutrements, even the breakup of her "ideal" marriage, would be reported without any edge of sneer; as it is, you often feel that one is just barely being suppressed. Attractive women who are also aggressive, demanding, smart, and driven make men nervous, if not hostile, and bring out complicated feelings of envy, admiration, and self-doubt in other women.

Ironically, fascinatingly, her career, her genius has found its *raison d'être* in disarming them all. For Martha Stewart, the salesman's first commandment—sell yourself—has taken on an overwhelming, even poignant, totality; her life has become her sales pitch, an act of persuasion. How can you hate someone so eager to bring you into her home, to welcome and entertain you? This—the need to be loved—is the real subject of her books, and, consequently, it's almost impossible to leaf through their pages (the videos are a different matter) without suspending, for the moment, the sneer, the suspicious hostility.

The successful salesman puts himself into your place only to better persuade you to put yourself in his, to cajole some part of you to help him with his sale. For most of us, I think, Martha Stewart's books succeed in having us want not to be entertained by her but, in some deep, analogous way, to help her. Even as she makes us envy her, she has also learned to make us feel sorry for her—want, even, to become her friend.

Most of her readers, I think, confuse this feeling—or enrich it—with sheer identification; they, pure and simple, want to *be* her. But this is only fantasy: even they must know that *that* Martha Stewart is an illusion—although they would perhaps be the last to understand that her books gain their peculiar power from a strong undercurrent of self-pity, both in her and in themselves.

Poor little me. Self-pity, like irony, is a slippery concept, least obvious when it is most compelling, especially in ourselves. If I find self-pity in Martha Stewart's books, it is because of a suspicious sweetness that I feel inside myself when I leaf through them—a feeling, despite myself, of how desirable what she portrays there really is, and which resists all effort to look at its cost. I don't even want to own these things, but some part of me can't help but yearn for the protection that they promise.

You can't look at the objects that fill all the many interiors of Turkey Hill without realizing that she has recently bought almost everything in them. You're *meant* to notice this; just as you are meant to feel, as you turn the pages of her books, that she is reaching out and offering all this to you. "All this" is not the things themselves; there is nothing here of that tacky feeling you get in the homes of antique dealers where everything you see is up for sale. Martha Stewart would say that what she offers is a form of aesthetic self-improvement, but the bottom line is not knowledge but the release that comes from spending money. This not only gets you nice things, it also provides security from the probing, critical eyes of others, who, in these books, bear the euphemistic name of "guest." Surround yourself with things that these people want and their warm feelings about them rub off on you. We might call this the Scrooge McDuck effect. Donald's uncle is an irascible old pill, but everyone loves him; even in the comics, cash is the irrefutable aphrodisiac.

Martha Stewart uses antique pots instead of piles of cash; this is where aesthetics, taste, comes in. The effect, however, is the same. If you take your house and remove from view everything that is quirky, ugly, or difficult, and heap the polished shelves with unthreatening, desirable objects coveted by your neighbors, surface becomes everything: an impenetrable, calculated, and intensely desirable veneer. The idea isn't to invite people over to see these things but to invite them over to see *you*. In most homes, the contents are a mirror of the selves that live there; in this home, the mirror reflects nothing but desire. We don't look into it; we look at it and murmur: "I love it—where can I get one like it for myself?"

Martha Stewart shows us that if you can't buy happiness, you can certainly sell it . . . and, I suspect, feel it constantly brush up against you as you do. If we did not so greatly desire what Martha Stewart has, would she desire it herself? Could she maintain the sweetness that first drew her to these things—the copper pudding molds, drabware, creamware, yellowware, Depression glass, antique linens—if she weren't continually offering them to us, keeping them lustrous with the ache of our desire?

Food writers have accused her of appropriating their recipes without due credit. This, whatever the truth to it, is a peculiar charge, for apart from her gala pastries they're rarely of much interest. This, too, I think, is by intent. It is a truism of catered food that it can only appear unique—caterers know that what their clients want is risk-free originality: arresting dishes that never fail to please.

All too often, in fact, her solution is simply a knee-jerk recourse to richness. In *Martha Stewart's Quick Cook*, she gives a menu for four that starts with a salad dressed with one-half cup of blue cheese and two-thirds cup of olive oil, features thick-cut pork chops served with a side dish of turnips into which a quarter cup of butter and one-and-a-half cups of heavy cream have been mixed. Dessert is vanilla ice cream over which is poured a chocolate sauce made of twelve ounces of melted chocolate and three-quarters cup of heavy cream.

Our reaction to all this might be different if we could imagine Martha Stewart herself digging into such a meal, but there is something disquieting about the killing richness of such food and the slender appearance of the person who insists we take some. To do so is to feel as if, on accepting an invitation for a piece of pie, your hostess cuts you a slice and then sits down to watch you eat it . . . all too eager to serve you more.

"I made this to make you happy," her books all say, not "I made this for us to share." I would suggest that one word for what separates those two phrases is self-pity. In Martha Stewart's books, possessions seem to exist only to give her power over others; to maintain the absolute distance between her and us. Become Martha Stewart's guest and—if you lack the self-protection of her determined will—you'll find yourself coming home gorged with food that you didn't mean to eat . . . just as, under the influence of her books, you may find yourself with armloads of stuff that when you come back to your senses you won't be able to imagine why you bought.

❖ ❖ ❖

The danger with all "self-catered" parties, hers included, is forgetting that a good time isn't a gift but a joint conspiracy. Fortunately, guests have a way of protecting themselves against hosts and hostesses who forget this. Consider Thomas Carlyle's account of tea with the very different but equally self-absorbed family of Leigh Hunt:

> Hunt's household in Cheyne Row, Chelsea. Nondescript, un-utterable! Mrs. Hunt asleep on cushions. Four or five beautiful, strange, gypsy-looking children running about in undress, whom the lady ordered to get us tea. The eldest boy, a sallow,

black-haired youth of sixteen, with a kind of dark cotton night-gown on, who, whirling around like a familiar, providing every-thing. An indescribable, dream-like household.

We guests are adept at working up much less conspicuous self-centeredness than this into our *own* entertainment, as Martha Stewart has, in fact, discovered to her discomfort. After all, when Laura Shapiro called Martha Stewart in *Newsweek* "the Barbara Cartland of entertaining," she was only saying in print what we might mutter in our companion's ear on our boozy way back home. There are some things a fine old country house and all the stoneware bowls in the world can't protect you from . . . but being yourself just might.

STRANGER IN A
STRANGE LAND

❖ ❖ ❖

MYTHOLOGY & MEATBALLS:
A GREEK ISLAND DIARY/COOKBOOK
Daniel Spoerri

In 1967, the artist Daniel Spoerri, his companion, Kichka, and five cats spent eight months on Symi, a tiny Greek island off the coast of Turkey. This remarkable book is an account of that stay, the food eaten, the people encountered, and the thoughts that all of these (but especially the food) inspired. However, even though it is about food and cooking and is full of recipes, it is not a cookbook; and while it also records much about the people and the history of Symi, it is not really a travel book either.

It is, in fact, what the title claims—a *diary*, written from a diary's special perspective, the daily recording of the tremors on that fault line where self (European writer and artist with an unusually fertile and eclectic mind) and world (Greek island, picturesque but also self-absorbed, austere, and untouristed) rub together.

Also in true diary fashion, the book volleys from the events it records to the associations they evoke, then back to the events again, with the connections personal and often tangential. The latter is especially the case here, because Spoerri's mind is a potpourri of fascinating, obscure, sometimes shocking bits of knowledge—much of it culinary. And giving free rein to a kind of whimsical, unfettered free association, he weaves it all, events and facts together, into a fabric that he then cuts to a distinctly personal fit:

> Our pepper mill being broken, I afforded myself the luxury of a brass Turkish coffee grinder, very pretty, but my assertion that I wanted to use it for *piperi* astonished, and intrigued, the merchant, who would never have imagined it possible to use it for anything but grinding coffee [*here a footnote about the peppercorn that wanders off into a cure for hemlock poisoning*]. I also drank a bottle of vintage *retsina* with Dimitri Antonoglou at the *taverna* of his cousin, Mitzo Antonoglou [*here a footnote on that cousin's infallible (and disgusting) remedy for foot scratches, given in the original Symian dialect (a pidgin mixture of Italian, Greek, and Turkish: the publisher has generously provided a section of entertaining and illuminating notes by the culinary scholar Charles Perry, who explains Spoerri's allusions and translates his polyglot quotations)*], a wine that, after you are accustomed to "real" *retsina*, has no taste. But the surprise again was the *meze*: small, deep-fried pieces of shark. (Kichka's comment: "*Merde alors*, I missed the shark!" But to console her I quote from the *Larousse Gastronomique*: "The flesh of the shark, though very tough, is used as a foodstuff by the Lapps and by some Negro people who are very partial to it.")

Not, I think you'll agree, the usual culinary travelogue. Even so, it's not difficult to figure out what's going on. If you have ever, on your own or with a friend, gone to live in an entirely foreign place, you'll know that this experience—exciting as it is—requires incredible stamina, since you are bombarded with a never-ending flood of stimuli that must be somehow absorbed and placed. Even familiar acts become new and strange: using the phone, taking a bath, cooking on the stove. After a certain point, this constant intake becomes exhausting, disorienting—you feel like an oversaturated sponge, longing only to be wrung out. Shirley Hazzard said it best: "Intimacy with another country is ripened by pleasures but also by loneliness and error." What she didn't say is that the pleasure, loneliness, and error can happen simultaneously . . . almost too much for the system to bear.

This is when most people pack up and go home. For those who survive it, something shifts inside. The stranger no longer wanders around with mouth, eyes, and ears helplessly agape but instead begins to impose a kind of order on the landscape, working the torrent of sensory impression into a comprehensible, personal design. It isn't that you suddenly become "Greek" (or whatever) but that the place begins to seem like home. One day—somehow—it also becomes *yours.*

This personal appropriation of Symi is what *Mythology & Meatballs* is all about, and Spoerri accomplishes it on what is the most difficult turf of all, that of cuisine. For, a thousand glossy travel books to the contrary, it is the cooking and eating habits of another culture that are the hardest to come to terms with—they affect us where we are both most vulnerable and most insistent on clinging to our ways.

For example, trying to buy some steak in Symi, Spoerri discovers that its two butchers

> are savage brutes, worse than cannibals anywhere. They don't sell meat but leftovers from a massacre. . . . The pound (of meat) you ask for ends up almost double that, and in this pile —you can't call it anything else—you find bones, fat, tendons, and, if you're lucky, even a minute piece of meat you might call steak, all strewn with splinters of crushed bone.

Most, faced with these revolting scraps, would simply give up meat for the duration of the visit. Spoerri, however, grapples with the experience—first wrestling an insight from it and then working that insight into a means of appropriating the experience as his own.

The insight is an explanation as to why, even though the sale of ground meat is forbidden in Greece, meatballs (*keftedes*) are so popular. The reason is that Greek butchers feel it their prerogative to include in your order (and charge you for) scraps of meat that are useless for anything else. So Spoerri gets a meat grinder—and, more important, spins this insight into the richly entertaining speculations on *keftedes* that fill a third of the book. Despite the title of the section, these are less a dissertation than the cranking of this experience through his own mental meat grinder until he (and we, too) can happily digest it.

It's important to note, however, that this act of appropriation is not the same thing as assimilation: Spoerri is not interested in becoming a Symiote. What makes this book unique is that he does *not* set out to master Greek or even Symiotic cooking, but continues to be his own cook, while learning to take advantage of what Symi has to offer. His Greek friends are as puzzled as they are appreciative of his efforts, for he takes their ingredients and their dishes and works them to his own taste, after his own manner.

This act of heresy must also have shocked American reviewers, given the muted reception they gave this book. But, when you think about it, what he is doing is exactly right. We don't travel to a foreign country to adopt its morals or language or customs, but to set our own into a heady ferment out of which we hope to change and grow. Better to come back from Greece with a new depth to our own cooking, with an appreciation for new flavors and ideas, than with a mastery of a few token souvenir dishes we can never hope to prepare with the same authority as an ordinary Greek cook.

In the same way, since this is a faithful record of his everyday cuisine, the recipes are not usually scintillating on their own —like our own cooking, his gains its interest through the context of the everyday life in which it takes part. Here are recorded the small successes, the lessons of the failures, learning to live within the limitations of what Symi cannot supply, even while gaining appreciation for what it can—eggs laid daily by his hens, fish caught only a few hours before purchase, lamb flavored by the fragrant herbs on which it browsed on the rocky cliffs, soft-shelled oysters gathered for him by spongefishers, succulent woodcock and quail. The taste of all this and more is to be found in these pages.

I first encountered this book in 1971, when it had just been published by Something Else Press (whose address was "in New York City, by the Parking Lot of the Chelsea Hotel"), as *The Mythological Travels of a Modern Sir John Mandeville, being an account of the Magic, Meatballs and other Monkey Business Peculiar to the Sojourn of Daniel Spoerri upon the Isle of Symi, together with divers speculations thereon.*

This Aris reprint excises the entire first section of the original, a record of obsessional artifacts made from *objets trouvés*, Spoerri unraveling their menacing meanings in accompanying texts. There is no doubt this abridgment weakens the effect of the book (although it does not especially affect the travelogue), because if titles are ever hints, surely this one suggests that these pages be read as a modern variation on the theme of *The Tempest*, with Daniel Spoerri playing the role of Prospero and the texts being records of the various spells he conjures up to take possession of the magic isle, tease Ariel, and torment Caliban. Still, enough of the original remains for a sympathetic reader to experience the effect of the subsequent enchantment.

THE SPICE SELLERS

❖ ❖ ❖

Today, however much we love our work, it is still a mental coat we put on when we take up our tools and remove when we set them down. Artists are another thing, of course, but most of us no longer see our craft as a prism through which to view the world—the way a cabinetmaker might once have seen it—as an act of jointure, as neatly and finely put together as a chair.

Consider the following passage from Patrick Süskind's *Perfume*:

> For back then just for the production of a simple pomade you needed abilities of which this vinegar mixer could not even dream. You had to be able not merely to distill, but also to act as maker of salves, apothecary, alchemist, and craftsman, merchant, humanist, and gardener all in one. You had to be able to distinguish sheep suet from calves' suet, a victoria violet from a parma violet. You had to be fluent in Latin. You had to know when heliotrope is harvested, and when pelargonium blooms, and that the jasmine blossom loses its scent at sunrise.

Long after the War of Independence, America possessed a proud class of artisan merchants to whom neither the designation blue- nor white-collar could be neatly applied. Their work was done equally by hand and brain, the one inseparable from the other. This was because for certain tasks the mind *thought* with the hands, or nose, mouth, or ears . . . and the experience so acquired produced a mode of thought that was not only uniquely revelatory to its possessors but, made into sayings and proverbs, became coin for all.

Ruth and Bill Penzey are such merchants; to correspond with them after having purchased their wares is to experience a pleasant confusion between the subtle but still assertive redolence of their own character and that of the herbs and spices they sell.

Indeed, at times the whole Spice House enterprise seems a colloquy of rare aromas orchestrated by two beings sprung straight from the imagination of Giuseppe Arcimboldo—benevolent avatars made up of laurel sprays, lavender sprigs, saffron threads, nutmegs, cardamom berries, and caper buds, and, for that matter, packets of cream of tartar and jars of pure beef extract.

This is, of course, mere fancy, but as a metaphor it is accurate enough. The difference between the simple knowledge of a craft and its mastery is the difference between ingestion and a very long period of digestion. The Penzeys have so absorbed the spice trade that I suspect the mere whiff of their astonishing Tung Hing cassia cinnamon brings them back not only to the ancient groves in China that produce it but to the intense, perfumed brightness of that piece of bark when it was still sweet of its particular tree.

The road to such an understanding is complex, demanding, and ultimately fascinating. Bill Penzey learned the trade from his father, who himself was taught it in Russia at age eleven by an Indian spice merchant named Alladiya. Thus, the knowledge Bill is now passing on to his children is already generations deep:

> We sit for two hours at a time going over an attempt to buy a certain spice, and I try to teach them why they must elevate the level of their dealing in order to elevate the level of their purchases. This gets into the fine art of bargaining with men from different cultures, men with different world views—who have to be paid not only in money, but also in another, higher way. The nature of this payment, of course, is something the

kids must learn for themselves. I can't tell them what it is, only
that it is there to be paid. Other buyers will come with the same
amount of money, and there is only so much of a certain spice
to be had of a certain quality. So, they have to learn first what
the best *is* and then—a very different thing—how to *get* it.

The most obvious result of this devotion to craft is the exquisite quality of the goods they sell. The firm but delicate
presence of the Provençal lavender; the aroma of fresh juice
that still clings to the dried, cracked Chinese ginger; the nose-
filling spiciness of the hand-milled Penang cloves . . . the list
is a long one, with, for me at least, much still to be explored.

But the Penzeys also believe that understanding is to be
shared. They are genuinely curious about their customers and
not at all above learning from anyone who enters their shop.
Several of their special blends were given to them by strangers,
perhaps because such unaffected interest is itself a kind of
generosity that is surprisingly often met in kind.

When I first wrote them, it was partially because I was seeking a source for Mexican vanilla beans, supposedly as excellent
as they are difficult to obtain. They responded by sending me
several of them, plus some Tahitian and Madagascar beans for
the sake of comparison. And this was not the last of their
kindnesses.

Not that such generosity doesn't sometimes exact its price.
They delight in presenting you with some unexpected bit of
pungency—and then asking not only what you like about it
but also what you don't. They know that we sometimes live
closer to our dislikes than to what we think we love, and thus
have as much to learn from our prejudices as from our pleasures. All teachers should be so crafty; all craftspeople so wise.

Although the Spice House itself is easy to find—it's located
on Milwaukee's historic Old World Third Street—the exact lo-
cus of the Penzey family spice business is harder to pinpoint.
All three Penzey children have been called to the trade, and
each has chosen to follow it via a separate path.

Ruth and Bill, after thirty-three years, have retired to the
smaller Kavanaugh Hill Spice Shop in nearby Wauwatosa,
where they continue to pursue their interest in exceptional

grades of spices. Their daughter Patty, with her husband, Tom, has taken over the Spice House proper. Pam, the younger daughter, is to open a branch in nearby Madison, in conjunction with a restaurant she's planning with her own husband, Brian. Son Bill Jr. has transformed the mail-order operation into a successful business in its own right (catalogue is $2 from P.O. Box 1633, Milwaukee, WI 53201). That he is also a chip off the old block can be seen from the following abridged text from a recent catalogue:

> I remember working in my parents' store in my early teens. At that time we had many Indian customers who were new to the U.S. They would come to the store in small groups, wearing their saris, and us kids would run and hide in the back. When my mother was working, she would let us hide, but when my father was there he and I would wait on them together. If the store was busy, I would have to wait on them myself. He felt that there are customers where the role of the sales clerk is to be a teacher, and customers where the role of the clerk is to be a student. These Indian customers were the best teachers. To this day I look at spices through their eyes. Still, at the time, I did not enjoy waiting on them, because unlike most of our customers, they did not smile at us or tell us what a unique and exciting store we had.
>
> Instead, the Indian women would always smell the spices and in most cases look at each other, shake their heads, and murmur something in their native tongue. A few would tell us what was wrong, in English, pointing out the characteristics of really good spices. As time wore on our spices improved. Sometimes an Indian woman would chew a cumin seed or a cardamom pod and not say anything at all. When we first got Ceylon cloves, I actually saw one woman smile. Finally we even received a compliment. An older Indian gentleman told us—through his son, who was acting as translator—"With spices like these, you will have many snakes on your street."

ACETARIA

❖ ❖ ❖

THE FRUIT, HERBS, & VEGETABLES OF ITALY
Giacomo Castelvetro, translated with an introduction
by Gillian Riley, and with a foreword by Jane Grigson

I remember reading, several years ago—I no longer remember where—that Elizabeth David was engaged in writing a book about Italian cooking before the introduction of the tomato. I'm sorry that it never appeared, but some sense of the riches it might contain can be found in this fascinating volume, written in 1614 by Giacomo Castelvetro, an Italian refugee residing in England.*

This was a time when the English were, as Jane Grigson notes in her foreword to this book, "building Italianate houses, planning Italian gardens, visiting Italy, speaking Italian, reading Italian writers, wearing Italian clothes." The young noblemen who as part of their education toured what was then a hodgepodge of separate republics returned with, among other things, an awareness that the center of the cultural universe

* The information on which this review is based has been gleaned from the book's introductory material and from K. T. Butler's seminal essay on Castelvetro, An Italian's Message to England in 1614: "Eat More Fruit and Vegetables." Italian Studies, II, no. 5 (1938), pp. 1–18.

perceived them as gross and unimaginative trenchermen, wed-
ded to huge slabs of beef, to tables laden with every sort of
fruit tart and sweetmeat, and to sitting down to such food
several times a day, from breakfast to "rear-supper."

English cooking, even as early as the beginning of the seventeenth century, was already on the defensive. In 1617, Fynes
Moryson wrote that "our longe sitting and discoursing at tables
makes men unawares eate more than the Italians can at their
solitary tables," and went on to explain:

> The Italians esteeme basely of those who live at other men's
> trenchers, calling them vulgarly *Scoccatori di pasti*—shifters of
> meals. . . . They think it best to cherish and increase friendship
> by meetings in Gardens and Market-Places, but hold the table
> and bed unfit for conversation, where men should come to eate
> quickly and sleep soundly.*

But Italians were not only solitary eaters: their meals were (and
still are) made up out of a much greater proportion of vegetables and starch. Whereas the English, Moryson wrote, "might
have a Pullet and some flesh prepared for us, eating it with a
moderate proportion of bread," an Italian would more likely
sit down to a "Charger full of hearbs for Sallet, and with rootes
and like meates of small price [and] . . . two or three-penny-
worth of bread."†

Although the English were learning, partly as a result of the
influx of French and Italian political and religious refugees, to
grow and eat more vegetables and fruit, Castelvetro continued
to marvel at how many they were still ignorant of and how
much they still had to learn about growing the ones they had.
It was his hope that his treatise—*Brieve racconto di tutte le radici,*

---

* An Itinerary: 1617 (Glasgow, 1907), Vol. IV, p. 99. (Quoted from K. T.
Butler, *op. cit.*, p. 3.) Patience Gray suggests, sensibly I think, that the
word Fynes Moryson heard—or remembered—as *scoccatori* was really
scocciatori—i.e., not "shifters" but "disturbers" of meals.
† Ibid., Vol. IV, p. 173. (Quoted from Butler, p. 4.)

di tutte l'herbe et di tutti i frutti, che crudi o cotti in Italia si mangiano*—might change all this.

If the art of persuasion alone could have accomplished the task, Castelvetro might have managed it, for he was a charming writer who also knew his beans. At the age of seventeen, he became the traveling companion of his uncle Ludovico Castelvetro, famed humanist and literary theorist whose own violent Protestantism had forced him to flee Italy. Ludovico had suffered serious illness as a youth, which saved him from a career in the law but ruined his digestion; he lived on a diet of simple vegetable dishes, eschewing both meat and wine. Giacomo developed an appreciation not only for his uncle's politics but also for his diet. Although he never became a vegetarian, his interest in botany expanded to include the culinary uses of the fruits and vegetables of the various European countries he visited—which included Spain, Germany, Switzerland, Austria, Sweden, and, for an extended stay, England.

In 1611, at the age of fifty-five, Giacomo Castelvetro was saved from the clutches of the Inquisition in Venice through the intervention of the British Ambassador, Sir Dudley Carleton. Castelvetro then fled Italy, and had he gone straight to England, his story might have had a happier ending, for he became for a short time there a political celebrity. But he dawdled, visiting a round of friends on the Continent, and he arrived in London in 1613 to find he had become yesterday's news. He was forced to piece together a precarious existence as Italian tutor (and companion) in the household of Sir Adam Newton at Eltham. There he died, poor, ill, and sad, only a few years later in 1616.

During this brief time, Castelvetro pinned his hopes on gaining patronage from the dazzling—beautiful, intelligent, and

---

* Translated literally: "A brief account of all the roots, herbs and fruit that are eaten raw or cooked in Italy"—the category "herbs" here embraces what we might call greens, and this, added to the "roots," subsumes the whole category of vegetables, for which in Italian there is no single, all-embracing word. Herbs, as we know them—basil, thyme, rosemary, etc.—although they are mentioned, are not, in fact, given separate entries, a misleading aspect of the English title.

wealthy—Lucy Russell, Countess of Bedford. It was his luck that she had just suffered a crippling (although well-hidden) financial blow that almost completely ended her previous generosity to writers and poets. It was for her that Castelvetro wrote his treatise, knowing her to be a keen amateur gardener, and it is because of such an intended reader, speculates Gillian Riley, the book's translator, that he wrote it in the manner that he did: simply and charmingly, seasoned generously with observation and anecdote and more lightly with botanical and metaphysical theory.

A sympathetic reader will suspect that it was also meant to assuage the homesickness of an Italian expatriate who sorely missed the warmth and gaiety of his native land. The tone of gentle melancholy that pervades its pages (echoed in its own way in Jane Grigson's touching foreword—one of her last, and nicest, pieces of writing) is the first of this book's many pleasures.

If the English were, at this date, enchanted with Italian literature, music, manners, and art, Castelvetro saw no reason why they might not be charmed as well by Italian produce and especially the delicately simple manner in which it could be prepared. He takes his reader through the seasons, introducing his subjects—mulberries, elderflowers, eggplants, purslane, etc.—one by one, describing each, providing, as he feels it necessary, hints as to its successful cultivation, the benefits of eating it, and often the way in which it might be best prepared.

It seems even today an embarrassment of riches, perhaps because for all our Italian cookbooks we still do not understand the pleasure Italians take in the simplest of vegetable preparations. After noting that "most of the salads we eat in summer are made of *capucina* (head lettuce)," Castelvetro explains how it might also be cooked: "Cut the solid heart into four parts, each well oiled and salted and peppered, and roast them on a grid over hot charcoal (not burning embers) and eat them sprinkled with [bitter] orange juice. They are delicious, almost as good as asparagus." Another recipe, this time for zucchini: "Boil them in salted water, and when they are almost done, add a decent amount of sweet herbs, finely chopped spring onions, olive oil, and at least a ladleful of unripe grapes or *agresto.''**

In essence, he offers two basic preparations: a cooked salad in which the vegetable is briefly cooked and seasoned with salt, sour, and savor; and a *minestra*, or soup (whether wet or dry), which can be exampled by his recipe for preparing turnip: "We make [them into] an excellent dish, different from the way you do here; they are first peeled, then cut into thin slices and cooked into good broth, and served with grated cheese and pepper." Here is another version, this time for artichokes, which is about as elaborate as he cares to get:

> If you do not feel like eating artichokes raw, select some small ones and cut off the tips of the pointed outer leaves. Boil them first in fresh water to take away the bitterness, and then finish cooking them in rich beef or chicken broth. Serve them in a shallow dish on slices of bread moistened with just a little of the broth, sprinkled with grated mature cheese and pepper to bring out their goodness. We love these tasty morsels; just writing about them makes my mouth water.

If what interested me most about the book was Castelvetro's approach to the vegetables and fruits I know, as opposed to those that are strange to me, it is for two reasons, the first of which I raise only as a question. It is hard not to wonder, given the rich abundance of foodstuffs and culinary strategies developed over the centuries to use them, whether the culinary gifts of the New World—tomato, maize, sweet and hot peppers, potato, etc.—ultimately did more to enrich or to impoverish Italian cooking. This seems especially true in the case of the tomato, which provided a single, simpleminded culinary solution to what before had been a subtle, wide-ranging medley of sweet-sour saucing. Change it these new foods certainly did; improve it—well, at least one starts to wonder.

The second reason is that Castelvetro made me realize that

* That is, the slightly fermented juice of unripe sour grapes. Since it is unavailable here, it's worth noting that Castelvetro sometimes just squeezes a handful of unripe grapes into a stew or over a salad instead.

it is not a lack of variety that characterizes the poverty of our vegetable cooking but a lack of . . . I want to write *intensity* . . . of attention. There were only a few fruits and vegetables in this book that were completely new to me, but many I have never considered eating, from dogwood berries to elderflower blossoms. Castelvetro makes me feel as if I were eleven years old and regarding a pretty girl in the company of an older brother. His interest agitates me because I partly feel it and partly don't understand it. After all, when you come right down to it, it's just a *girl*.

So if I am any kind of test case, Castelvetro's message is as appropriate today as it was four centuries ago. And unlike most manuals of sensual appreciation, it is a joy to read. Not only do many of his recipes still have immediate appeal, so does his company. He traveled much and observed keenly, which allowed him to enliven his text with vivid anecdotes: the children learning to swim in the Brenta canals, kept buoyant by huge dried pumpkins used as water wings; the Venetian ladies ogling passersby behind curtains of verdant beanstalks; the attack of constipation that "was so bad that I went for ten or eleven days without relief, which when it came caused such intense pain that I do not believe a woman in childbirth could have suffered more than I."

To write about Castelvetro is to long to quote him. Here he is on a subject as mundane as the making of a cabbage salad:

> I once happened to be in France in the company of a group of ladies and gentlemen, and we came one afternoon to a large village with a good inn, where we proposed to dine. One of the ladies, sitting in the window-seat in the dining room, which overlooked an orchard, said to me, "Let's go into the garden and pick a salad!" to which I replied, "Yes, indeed!" When we got there we found nothing but cabbages, so the young lady picked one of these saying, "Well, if there's nothing else, I'll make you a nice salad out of this."
>
> Having never seen or eaten anything like this before, I kept silent and waited for the outcome. First she removed the green outer leaves until she came to the white part, which she proceeded to slice very finely with a razor-sharp knife. She then salted and dressed it in the usual way, and brought it to the

table, where it was pronounced excellent, and her ingenuity was much admired by the entire company.

There are very few culinary works of this age that have the ability to reach so effortlessly across the years (even through what reads as a rather pedestrian translation) and win our hearts. The publisher has given us all this in an attractively designed and profusely illustrated edition that is, to my mind, simply one of the best books about food and cooking I have read all year.

Afterword. This review is—obviously, I hope—the product of an enthusiast, not an authority; I know nothing of seventeenth-century Italian culinary writings, nor can I read Renaissance Italian. Consequently, I was rather discomfited to receive, in response to an earlier review of this book, a letter from Patience Gray—who *is* conversant in both those areas—taking me to task for unknowingly praising a mountebank, snob, sycophant, and, very possibly, plagiarist.

In brief, the author of *Honey from a Weed* and *Plats du Jour* (see pages 326–37 below) and a translator of a previous edition of the *Larousse Gastronomique* accuses Castelvetro, whom she characterizes as a man who "never went into a kitchen except to pinch a cook's bottom,"* of working up much of his "brief account" out of an earlier work by Costanzo Felici da Piobbico, entitled *Lettera sulle Insalate*, written in 1566–67. According to her, Castelvetro took bits and pieces of this work, rearranged them, intermixed Felici's anecdotes with some of his own, and hurriedly produced what he hoped would prove to be the equivalent of today's trendy culinary best-seller.

After the shock subsided, I decided that even if these charges were true, they would have little effect on my feelings about the *book*, since what most interested me about it was its portrait of the Italian relationship with vegetables and fruit. My opinion about Castelvetro would, of course, become more complex . . . but not necessarily be lowered. I actually liked him a bit

---

* This and all following quotations from Patience Gray are from a personal letter sent to me and reprinted with her express permission. Of course, I take all responsibility for the paraphrases.

better with a touch of the rogue brushed onto his rather pathetic lifelong predilection for sucking up to the titled rich.

In her introduction to the book, Gillian Riley does mention the possibility that Castelvetro might have come across a copy of *Lettera sulle Insalate*, admits that there are some similarities between the two texts, and then makes what seems the rather strange assertion that "we should not assume from this that Castelvetro took the idea for his own essay from Felici's manuscript"—which rather dodges the question of how much *material* he might have taken from it.*

I can only bring the matter up; others will have to resolve it. Until they do, we should bear in mind that the reasons we have this book at all are due mostly to sheer contingency: Castelvetro's relationship with England and English nobility; his references to the English and their way of eating; and the romance of the manuscript, buried for so long at Trinity College. It is all that, not intrinsic worth, that made the translation of this manuscript a project for Penguin, a commercial publisher, whereas Felici remains ignored even by scholarly ones. And there is no more point in being surprised at this than at the fact that the first American cookbook to be translated into French was *The Silver Palate Cookbook* and not, say, *James Beard's American Cookery*.

Still, Patience Gray's brief description of *Lettera sulle Insalate* does make it sound like an extraordinary piece of writing:

> This doctor, Felici, living in the wilds of Le Marche, had a wonderful feeling for plant life, which he collected, studied, and introduced to botanical gardens in Urbino, Rimini, and Bologna.
>
> The edible plants, hidden in this wonderfully disorganized Salad Letter, form a chain beginning with bulbs, roots, then on to shoots, leaves, fruits, flowers, seeds, grains. Nothing to do with the tables of the rich, but with his knowledge of wild plants and their uses as food, as medicine, derived from centuries-old practices of mountain peasants and confirmed by the Ancients —Dioscorides, Theophrastus, etc.
>
> He passes all this on to his friend Aldrovandi, the letter trav-

* See pages 41–42 of the book for the translator's complete discussion of this matter.

elling precariously on muleback to Bologna. And, in his many other letters* which take the same course—often accompanied by specimens, dead birds, dried plants, seeds, dried fish, rocks—we can witness the *rebirth* of Natural History (pioneered by the Elder Pliny), and also return to an unspoiled beautiful world in the great solitudes of the mountains of Le Marche.

Perhaps now that attention has been called to it, a publisher might even be persuaded to issue *Lettera sulle Insalate* (perhaps translated by Patience Gray herself). That would be a bit of irony, both bitter and sweet—*agrodolce*—a flavor that both of those seventeenth-century Italians would have recognized.

* *Lettere all'Aldrovandi*, Costanzo Felici da Piobbico (Giorgio Nonni, ed. Urbino: Quattro Venti, 1982).

MONET À TABLE

✦ ✦ ✦

MONET'S TABLE: THE COOKING JOURNALS
OF CLAUDE MONET
**Text by Claire Joyes, photographs by Jean-Bernard Naudin,
recipes adapted by Joël Robuchon**

Giverny is a small town along the Seine between Paris and
Rouen. For most who recognize the name, however, the word
means simply one house within that town, the final home of
Claude Monet. A man who loved company almost as much as
he loved escaping from it, Monet was that strange creature, a
gregarious recluse. He used Giverny as he would a canvas to
create his own vision of a living place, a contradictory mixture
of privacy and display whose seductive intimacy has enchanted
visitors ever since.

The two most important rooms in the house were the studio
and the kitchen, and these were created first: the studio in the
barn and the kitchen elevated from the basement and walled
with blue and white Rouen tiles. Any other kitchen would be
dominated by the formidable Briffaut stove, with its several
ovens, brass towel-drying rack, and hot-water faucets rising
out and up. But this kitchen gets its aura from the windows
that open out onto the balcony, letting in the flower garden
and a flood of air and light.

The dining room, right next door, is likewise full of color.

Its pale yellow walls are trimmed with glossy chrome yellow, hung with Japanese prints, and punctuated with a huge tile-lined fireplace and two French doors. The chairs match the trim; the formal dining service is yellow edged with blue. Monet mixed the colors and picked the plates.

He also devised the menus. Painting, gardens, and food were Monet's passions, and as he grew older he devoted himself almost entirely to them. He rose at dawn, had a cold bath beneath the bemused stare of Cézanne's "Nègre," which hung in his dressing room, and came down to eat a huge, eclectic breakfast—eggs and bacon, grilled tripe sausages, Dutch or Stilton cheese, toast and marmalade, Kardomah tea. If the light was right that day, he would then retire to his studio and paint.

Lunch, served at eleven, was the day's convivial center. It was the meal to which guests were invited and where conversation flowed, but never in a way to impede his eating—slow eaters drove him crazy. Monet had a hearty but picky appetite; as much as possible, he liked to produce what he ate. The foie gras might be from Alsace and the truffles from Périgord, but the vegetables and fruit came from the garden, the pike from his own pond, and the ducks and chickens from his own carefully selected stock.

All this was prepared in the rich, unstinting manner of the French Belle Époque: the chicken with crayfish butter; the duck in red wine sauce or made into a pie with cognac, sausage, and veal; the pike simmered in a court bouillon of white wine and served in a sauce of butter and shallots. Afterward there was coffee in the studio drawing room, a sip of homemade plum brandy, and a return to painting, Monet working until the gong summoned him to supper. Bedtime followed, inexorably, at nine-thirty.

Still, life was not *all* painting and eating. The book contains a delightful picture of Monet perched in the back seat of the family Panhard-Levassor, waiting to be driven to market. He also found time to discuss the daily menu, harass poultry breeders, and design and supervise the two-and-a-half-acre walled kitchen garden. There, pear trees were espaliered along the sunny walls and other fruit trees planted: cherry, quince, a special russet for making *tarte Tatin*, and greengage plum for the homemade brandy.

As for the rest . . .

> One could stroll along paths lined with climbing vegetables, along avenues of Milan cabbages, Brussels sprouts, or broccoli, beside rows of romaine lettuces, celery, pale endives or Paresseux de Castillon spinach. One crossroads, marked by a rosemary bush, was bordered with thyme, chives, and savory for the lima beans, and even Belleville garlic for the *sauce verte*.

And on and on.

A wonderful place; in many ways, an idyllic life. The charm of both conspires to lull the critical faculties: this, alas, is not the book it might have been. The photographs are too artful to capture the *feel* of the house, especially its interior (the flowers come across better, but the book is not about them); we are shown only parts of the kitchen and dining room, and nothing of the cellars, the storeroom, the huge Régence-style cupboard that held the precious preserves, the Provençal olive oil, and the many spices. Claire Joyes, who lives at Giverny, conveys all this in a prose that, while stiffly translated, has its moments of charm—although she might have told us more about Marguerite, the family cook, whom she knew personally but never quite manages to bring to life.

A third of the text is devoted to chef Joël Robuchon's re-creation of the contents of the journals—dishes Monet encountered in his travels, at favorite restaurants, or at the homes of friends—into workable recipes. Here are Cézanne's salt-cod bouillabaisse, Millet's recipe for *petits pains*, Sacha Guitry's boiled pork shoulder, and Monet's own creation, *cèpes* baked in garlic and olive oil. These dishes are for the most part attractive, and many are within the reach of the interested (and experienced) home cook.

But how explain the book's near silence regarding its supposed subject, the cooking journals themselves? We are not told how closely these recipes approximate Monet's, how much of the journals are replicated here, or—most important—*who originally kept them*. Are these the "Monet family recipes," or are the pages actually written in Monet's own hand? Given the fact that the book implies just that provenance, such reticence can only provoke suspicion—especially since Jane Grigson, in her chapter about Monet's culinary passions in *Food with the Famous*, doesn't mention them at all.

Counter Revolution

❖ ❖ ❖

THE TASTE OF CHINA
Ken Hom, with photographs by Leong Ka Tai

Even the best foreign cookbooks tend to present the cuisines they explain as static, unchanging entities, although cooking in many countries today is in a state of accelerating change. When culinary commentators do notice this situation, their tone is often one of nostalgia, if not outright lamentation—a cry of "Let me have one more taste before they take my favorite dish away."

On mainland China, however, for most of its occupants these dishes already have been taken away. For decades, an oppressive and puritanical regime enforced a policy known colloquially as the "iron rice bowl." Fine eating was suspect, culinary traditions were abandoned and talented cooks actively discouraged from developing their skills. The state-run restaurants were

> often noisy, not very clean, poorly lighted, aesthetically repellent, and in general badly managed. . . . After waiting in line to get in, I was usually seated at a table still heaped with the debris from the previous diners. Employees were often lackadaisical, discourteous, and even surly to travelers as well as local patrons . . . [because the policy of the "iron rice bowl" pre-

sumed] that public institutions, including state restaurants, exist not to serve people but to provide income and security for the employees.

This policy has since been relaxed, and Ken Hom, followed by photographer Leong Ka Tai, has gone into mainland-China home kitchens, small-town bazaars, big-city markets, and all sizes and sorts of public eating places to report on the enormous culinary sea change that is now taking place.

These particular chapters (others recount the general history of Chinese cuisine, with a special emphasis on Cantonese cooking) are the best in the book, starting with "Family Traditions" and continuing through "City and Country Fare," "Restaurant Cooking," "Snacks and Street Foods," and "Food for the Body and Soul." For all the good things this book has accomplished, the best may be its testimony that appetite has its ways of revivifying what perverse necessity has torn down. Here is a classic cuisine being reconstructed not from the top down by innovative chefs but from the bottom up by peasants, cooking stalls, and home cooks, all enthusiastically embracing the opportunity to bring new life to what in some respects was on the way to becoming, even before the Revolution, a moribund cuisine.

To understand something of the paradoxical nature in this far-from-programmatic counterrevolution, turn to the full-page photograph of the young man in his early twenties, standing in the middle of a country road, herding a flock of several hundred ducklings with a long bamboo switch. Other pictures in this book have more inherent drama (a mother huddled intently over a bowl of noodles as her child sobs behind her), compelling fascination (the wholesale duck market in Hunan, where countless ducks lie passively on the pavement awaiting their fate), or sheer loveliness (sunshine pouring down from a skylight over the primitive straw-fueled, brick-and-concrete-slab Hom family cookstove), but the one of the duck herder tells a more interesting story, and in a subtler, less theatrical way.

It takes a minute to put it all together: his age, his intelligent and cheerful demeanor, the touches of Western style about his dress, the macadam on the road, the electric pylons in the background. The eye is presented with an equation whose parts don't quite balance out . . . as they would have had the road been dirt, the herder a boy or an old woman, or the garb that of peasant dress. But here everything is modern except the *event*: in today's world, ducks are raised in wire enclosures and young men are put to (or find for themselves) more profitable employment.

You can find photographs like this of Italian youths, equally unself-conscious (and unresentful) of such an occupation, but these were taken in the 1920s, not the 1980s. This young Chinese stands at the cusp of modernity: a place where human labor, and hence food, is still cheap but where modern production techniques and commercial ingenuity mean an influx of cash—a chance, at least for the moment, for poorer peasants to enjoy themselves as they never have before (and may never again).

In urban areas, this culinary revolution is given further momentum by the government's policy of keeping rents artificially far beneath market value. But without financial return, there has been no impetus to build new housing—with the result that the average living space in the smaller Chinese cities (it is even less in the larger ones) is one small room for every two people. However, low rents also mean that more than half the average urban household budget can be spent on food, and much of it is street food . . . which is not surprising, when you consider that everyone who can, from Grandfather on down, spends as much time outdoors as possible, thronging "the tea shops, the public squares, the streets, the food stalls, and restaurants—conversing, playing mahjong and cards, walking, and, above all, eating."

Until these were banned by the government, a feature of the Chinese urban scene was a prolific number of "small eats," both ordinary street stalls and night markets (food stalls that feed night-shift workers and—especially in the summer, when many flee their hot, airless apartments—casual idlers). Hom describes the effect of the recent rescinding of the government ban in Beijing, which is famous for its street food:

I was struck by the carnival atmosphere of the street scenes, crowded with people sampling the assortment of local and regional favorites. . . . That one eats better at the sidewalk food stalls in Beijing than at most of the fancy tourist restaurants is an opinion with which I concur. Freshly made pulled noodles are boiled and served, as are homemade *jiaozi* dumplings, Beijing sausage, Sichuan cold noodles, Tianjin turnovers, Lanzhou noodles, Wenzhou fishball soup, and Xinjiang mutton barbecues—I sampled *all* of these at the Wangfujing street market in Beijing.

For poor Chinese, these are exciting culinary times.

However, options have also increased for functionaries, academics, and other professionals with what in Communist China might be called a middle-class income. The relaxation of rules regarding private plots has allowed a rebirth of market gardening, giving shoppers greater choice and better quality. These options, along with a more positive attitude toward culinary indulgence, have brought about a renaissance in home cooking for those families with the time and income (and kitchen space) to pursue it.

Because these changes are erratic and take place at wildly disparate tempos, the cuisine of mainland China defies easy categorization. Fresh bean sprouts, now available in most American supermarkets, there remain a luxury; restaurant cooking, at which the Chinese have always excelled, is in China itself still very uneven at all levels of society. This is partly because of lost talents and partly because a good restaurant is a complex organism, and those don't evolve overnight.

All this in good time . . . or so we can hope. But whatever other shape culinary modernity assumes in China we can be sure that it will not be a simple clone of Coca-Cola drinkers and TV-dinner eaters. This is, after all, a country where, on the one hand, the height of sophistication is to own an electric rice cooker and, on the other, a fifth of all arable land in some sections is devoted to raising traditional medicinal herbs. The Chinese still make no clear distinction between the medicinal and culinary properties in the foods they eat, regarding eating as not only a way to keep the body healthy but the primary way to make it so.*

Nor, given the Chinese passion for many-course banquets (Hom attended one in Kunming consisting of fifty-four dishes, all made with goat!), will there be an end to their delight in culinary pomp. What Chinese cooks do seem to be up to is re-creating what was once a rather rigidly formal cuisine into one which features—at all levels of Chinese society—simpler, earthier, and more easily prepared food.

At least that seems to be the leitmotif that threads its way through the chapters of this excellent book, linking together its many unusual—and unusually well-chosen—recipes. In the opening chapter, "A Personal Odyssey," Ken Hom tells of returning with his mother to his ancestral village, Kaiping, in Canton. They were greeted with a special eleven-course banquet made up almost entirely of just this type of food: simple but elegant-sounding preparations like Chinese water spinach cooked with fermented bean curd, bitter melon stir-fried with lean pork, soybean sprouts also stir-fried with lean pork (the dish is authentically made with pig's intestines, but, Hom writes, "unsure of my cultural adaptability, they had substituted lean pork"), long beans prepared with silk squash and crispy cloud ear fungus, a stew of dried oysters, a braised goose dish, and platters of roast duck and roast pig that had been purchased already prepared. The beverage served throughout the meal? Not, as you might think, tea . . . but instead a clear rabbit broth, laced with spices and medicinal herbs.

---

* Hom devotes the penultimate chapter of *The Taste of China*—"Food for the Body and Soul"—to Chinese medicinal foodstuffs and the vegetarian cooking of Daoists and Buddhists. In Sichuan province, he visits a famous herbal market, which first appeared "to be one huge spice market, but closer inspection revealed . . . vendors, both wholesalers and retailers, haggling amid dried carcasses of snakes and skeletons of monkeys, cattle, and goats. All around were mounds of dried citrus fruits, wasp hives, dried starfish and sea cucumber, dried crab and scallop shells. I began counting the various mounds and sacks of plants, roots, and herbs but stopped when I reached two hundred."

RICHARD OLNEY,
ENCORE UNE FOIS

❖ ❖ ❖

THE FRENCH MENU COOKBOOK
Richard Olney

Richard Olney's *Simple French Food* is one of our great cookbooks, a match of sensibility and subject so perfect that even when we go to it for no more than a recipe, it is impossible not to linger awhile in its company . . . the prose inviting, the author's love and mastery of his subject endlessly compelling.

His earlier *French Menu Cookbook* has been overshadowed by this triumph, for while it is a very good cookbook, it is not a great one. Consulting this book, unlike *Simple French Food*, is an act of stealth—we sneak into the kitchen, peek over the author's shoulder, and then steal away.

Not that we aren't meant to feel welcome. On the contrary, the author is eager to share a wealth of information. Unfortunately, however, when he claps his hand on our shoulder, we feel much like the unfortunate wedding guest cornered by the Ancient Mariner. His flood of advice tends ultimately to dominate, not help, and it is a supremely self-confident cook who, after such an encounter with Olney, can then set him firmly aside and go cook.

In *Simple French Food*, this obsessive seriousness was touching and involving, because it was set in contrast to ordinary dishes, which were enriched and made desirable by it. But in this book,

with its elegant menus and high tone, he often risks transforming himself into the sort of snob who will impatiently wave
away a compliment, completely absorbed in stripping a mouthful of Béarnaise sauce down to its component parts to find that
traitorous little ingredient which kept it from achieving total
perfection.

Consequently, I was both surprised and delighted when
David R. Godine's revised, updated, and handsomely produced reissue of that book (the original was published by Simon
& Schuster) brought about some very happy and informative
hours of reading and thinking about food . . . although perhaps
not entirely in the way his new publisher intended. For I read
with *both* editions open in front of me—comparing recipe to
recipe, page after page.

The new edition is in many ways an improvement over the
older one. But even better is the opportunity they offer together
to set up a tension between two carefully worked-out versions
of the same recipe, versions that are almost identical, but not
quite. This tension makes Olney seem not quite so difficult a
kitchen companion: two quibbling recipes for the same dish
give a very different impression than either does when read
alone, where it appears as some perfect thing, immutably set
in stone. Now, as we watch him tug them here and adjust
them there, they suddenly become fragile, volatile acts of a
creative culinary imagination.

This isn't to imply that there are radical changes in the
recipes—when Olney wrote the first version of this book in
1970, he had lived in France for almost twenty years and had
been producing menu-oriented recipes for *Cuisine et Vins de
France* for the last four of them. He already knew his mind as
regards these dishes and he has changed it only in small ways.
But it is easy enough to consult several cooks when we want
bold contrast between versions of the same recipe: here we get
to watch a strongly opinionated cook shift in those opinions,
a very different sort of thing.

Consider, for example, his change of tack in the making of
boeuf à la bourguignonne. The dish is essentially a stew—cheap,
gelatinous cuts of beef marinated in red wine and then sim-

mered in it for hours. He still follows the general lines set forth in the first book, but the dish is tightened up. American substitutes are no longer mentioned; now the chunks of beef are larded with fresh pork fat and the dish garnished with crispy bits of *pancetta*, where before salt pork did duty for both. Likewise, vegetable oil is excised from the new recipe as a possible sautéing medium. At the same time, he is even more meticulous in removing every possible amount of excess fat.

But if he is stricter in some areas he is more permissive in others: before, he called for a bottle of "good red Burgundy" for the marinade and cooking; now, he only asks for a "robust, deeply colored young wine." As is generally the case throughout the book, the amounts of butter and oil are reduced and those of the seasonings increased, especially if one takes advantage of his hints as to the composition of the bouquet garni and adds some aromatic wine essence to the final sauce.

It's important to note that this is a wine book (and still pretty emphatically a *French* wine book): Mr. Olney may not go so far as to brush his teeth with a light Sauternes, but after reading his collected oeuvre you may well wonder if water or even beer has ever crossed his lips except under duress. Read, for example, his comments on fresh coriander (or cilantro): "[It] is repellent in the presence of wine [and thus] of lesser interest for the purposes of this book. . . ." It would be enough, you would think, to simply note that the French don't do much with it.

He is almost as dismissive of rosemary, which he now considers a "vehement" herb, and corrects the younger Olney on its use throughout. On the other hand, hyssop, once relegated to beguile the occasional "erudite curiosity seeker," has since been put to much good use:

It is easy to grow and most interesting fresh, its finely chopped leaves, delicately bitter and refreshing, adding liveliness to many a salad or marinated raw fish. The tiny, lacy, labiate flowers of hyssop, clear ultramarine, are ravishing scattered over a salad accented by the yellow of hard-boiled egg yolks, or atop thinly sliced raw salmon or the silver sheen of very fresh filleted fish of the sardine-herring family, the one and the other marinated in a bit of lemon juice and olive oil.

The wealth of such small contrasts lets us know the cook. If you own the first version of this book, the revised one *is* worth buying, or if you begin with the new one and come to love it, you will find it equally worth your while to scour the second-hand market for the earlier one. They are both excellent books, but together they make a whole superior to either part.

If choosing between the one or the other, however, I would opt for the new one: as far as design and production are concerned, David R. Godine has done Olney proud, and the introductory material is greatly enhanced. It is also much more accommodating to the novice cook, as the recipe directions are both better thought out and more concise (thanks, perhaps, to the author's editorial direction of the Time-Life series The Good Cook).

Even so, there are pleasures in the earlier edition missing in the new one, including much helpful, interesting information that once prefaced the recipes. (A little of it is still there, but in abbreviated form, with other parts worked into the introductory material. Still, the former edition ran to 446 pages; the new one has 295. While the page size is larger, it is obvious that substantial cutting has taken place.)

The most notable absence—since it was the part of the book I remember most fondly—is the preface, in which Olney describes his home in Provence: "The house, perched halfway up a hillside, its only access from below a somewhat precarious footpath . . . was a total ruin. Stretching above, the several acres of stone-walled terraces planted to olive trees, once meticulously cared for, are grown wild to all those herbs—rosemary, wild thyme and savory, oregano, fennel, lavender, and mint—whose names are poetry and whose mingled perfumes scent the air of Provençal kitchens and hillside alike."

Instead of updating this passage, Olney omitted it entirely. Perhaps the effort to redo it seemed too autumnal . . . the first edition is dedicated to Georges Carin, "a great chef and friend"; this edition is dedicated to his memory (and to that of two other French friends who have also since died).

So it is that these two volumes together share the changing flavors of a life as well as of a palate. I can think of no more pleasant way to spend a quiet evening, if you are lucky enough to own—or at least get hold of—both these books, than to leaf through them together, listening to this gifted cook as he argues with himself over the stove in his kitchen in Solliès-Toucas.

THE TASTE OF
THE PAST

❖ ❖ ❖

THE ROMAN COOKERY OF APICIUS: A TREASURY
OF GOURMET RECIPES AND HERBAL COOKERY,
TRANSLATED FOR THE MODERN KITCHEN
John Edwards

"Latin Lives Today" was the motto of my tenth-grade Latin class, and Miss North, our teacher, had us regularly scour the newspapers and popular magazines to unearth evidence of its truth. If she's still out there pounding declensions into stubborn adolescent brains, she'll be making an event of *The Roman Cooking of Apicius*. Here is a whole book of modern recipes worked up from the very sketchy accounts of the Roman dishes described in various works attributed to Apicius, that legendary Roman glutton, but especially *De Re Coquinaria*.

To comment first on the road not taken: There is yet an untouched culinary lode to be mined by some knowledgeable author who, using these (and other Latin) texts as guides, sets out to discover what remnants of the cooking of ancient Rome still linger on in Italy, despite both modernity and the tomato—such, for example, as Horace's *porri et ciceris refero laganique catinum* (*Satire I.6*), a casserole of leeks, chickpeas, and seedcake that can, according to Patience Gray in *Honey from a Weed*, still be recognized in such Apulian dishes as *cece e lasagna*.

This, however, the author did not do. Instead, he has translated the extant Latin texts and, on facing pages—after those eighteenth-century English imitations of Horatian odes and Virgilian eclogues—composed recipes "in the manner of Apicius." Mr. Edwards is himself a British poet (although currently living on an island off the coast of British Columbia) and cannot but be aware of the irony inherent in this comparison. Just as those poems, despite their swains with Latin names and mythological beasties, were unmistakably English, so are his own recipes. For all their being highly flavored with myrtle berries, honey, lovage, and boiled wine, they are utterly contemporary in nature and not truly Roman at all.

This distinction needs emphasizing if only because the publisher has attempted to convince us otherwise, especially in the "revised" paperback edition, which deletes not only almost all of the author's translation of the Roman original but also the name "Apicius" from the title—in order to convince us that by following the book's recipes we are preparing "delectable, poetic dishes from classical Rome, from simple snacks to complete dinners" and that the book makes "Roman cooking completely accessible to us in our day."

Of course, nothing could be further from the truth. Here is a simple sausage dish from *De Re Coquinaria*:

> Forcemeats in a Ring. Fill an intestine with seasoned forcemeats and form it into a circle. Smoke it. When it has turned cinnabar red, roast it a little. Arrange attractively on a serving dish. Last, pour wine sauce for pheasant dumplings over it, but [remember to] add cumin.

The information we still need to complete this dish would fill a book. What seasonings would turn a sausage bright red when smoked? Roast it for how long? What did Roman wine taste like? What stock was used in the wine sauce and how was it seasoned? The list goes on and on.

To grasp the problems the author/translator faces in attempting to solve these puzzles, imagine some writer two thousand years hence attempting to resurrect twentieth-century French cuisine with nothing to go on but a badly mutilated copy of the *Code Culinaire*. This book, a menu reference for French chefs, gives a brief description of specific dishes and their major ingredients, but expects the cook to know the methods, the nature of the ingredients, and the amounts of seasoning each requires to be properly prepared.

Thus, for example, it assumes knowledge of what sort of duck is appropriate for *caneton aux nouilles à l'alsacienne*, the exact vegetables on which it is to be nested, and the quantity of each seasoning needed to flavor it, as well as how to make the veal stock with which the dish is sprinkled and the very *nouilles à l'alsacienne* themselves, for the *Code* is no more specific about such particulars than any of the directions in Apicius.

(This comparison is all the more apt because it is most likely that the texts attributed to Apicius—who was not one but three famous gluttons of the same name who lived in different periods of Roman history—are no more than a collection of dishes of the sort that would, and perhaps did, please one or another "Apicius." The lack in both books of a single guiding palate makes the difficulties to be resolved even more insurmountable.)

It's also worth noting that the Apicius texts and the *Code* both describe dishes most usually eaten by the wealthy: neither is a source of information about the cuisine of *hoi polloi*. When Edwards writes that the Romans "customarily took three meals a day" (a simple breakfast of bread and fruit; a lunch of fish, eggs, cold meats, vegetables, and fruit; and a supper that began at four in the afternoon and continued into the evening "or even into the night"), he is writing not about all or even most Romans but about the wealthy. The cuisine of Apicius may be typically Roman, but how typical was the Roman who ate it?

The author further and unnecessarily complicates this issue by insisting that salt, because it is so rarely mentioned by name in the Latin text, was sparingly used in ancient Rome (in fact, although it is not advertised as such, this is a salt-free cookbook), where it is far more likely that the original compiler(s) took seasoning with salt for granted and simply didn't bother to specify it (as often happens in the *Code Culinaire*).

This perverse position leads to some fast and loose playing with the spirit of the Latin text, and even with the letter: the author's recipe for *garum*, the omnipresent Roman fish sauce (their equivalent of catsup), has no salt—but he directs that it must be kept refrigerated. This was not an option open to the Romans: as the original text makes clear (and the author notes elsewhere), it was heavily salted instead.

Nor is it only in their saltlessness that his recipes distort the originals. Given the then-primitive conditions for keeping meat, it is most likely that the Romans had a taste for eating it "high" (i.e., smelly), and their love of pungent and complex seasoning was in part necessary, not to mask that taste (for nothing can), but to *complement* it—whereas such intense flavoring interacts with our own bland-tasting viands to a quite different effect. Furthermore, hung meat has a different texture as well as a different taste to it, something else his recipes do not take into account . . . as they fail to note that rabbit and hare are not interchangeable—the one being a white-meated, tender-flavored animal and the other a red-meated, gamier-tasting one.

Lastly, it should be noted that Edwards's recipes understandably sidestep dishes that might turn a contemporary stomach, but whose omission or down-playing distorts our understanding of the balance of Latin cuisine. Given the number of recipes for them, it's probable that the Romans had something of a taste for sterile sow's womb (*vulvae steriles*), as well as dormice (basted with honey and poppy seeds) and various songbirds (which the Italians still eat with relish). And the conceit of filling each ear of a suckling pig with stuffing before roasting it shows a very different attitude as to what food play was permitted and what forbidden.

As with any such attempt at imaginative reconstruction, the accumulation of misplaced emphases and unrealized gaps of understanding means that the best we can hope for is to be brought to the doorway of this cuisine and there allowed to smell the appealing scent of spices being pounded and the heady aroma of meat turning on a spit—and to catch brief, uncertain glimpses of steaming platters being quickly carried by. Somewhere in the house there is feasting and merriment, but it is a party we will never join.

That understood, we are better placed to enjoy what John

Edwards actually has accomplished. For he has lingered on the stoop of this house much longer than we, and his best guesses about the contents of those trays have been transformed into a series of carefully imagined dishes that are appetizing, interesting, and not without wit.

While contemporary poets rarely pen georgics and eclogues, classics scholars at Oxford University are still given examination questions that require them to translate, say, some lines of Virgil in the manner of Dryden or Pope. It is easy to imagine an examiner with a culinary bent setting the challenge in a slightly different arena:

> IUS IN ELIXAM OMNAM. *Sauce for all boiled meats.* [Mix] pepper, lovage, oregano, rue, silphium, dried onion, wine, boiled wine, honey, vinegar, and a little olive oil. Dry [the boiled meats] and then wrap in a linen cloth [and press out the remaining moisture]. Pour the sauce over the boiled meats." *De Re Coquinaria*: VII.vi.i.
>
> *Create a recipe in the manner of Elizabeth David from the preceding that (a) utilizes these same ingredients, (b) resembles as closely as possible what Latin scholars assume this dish to be, (c) can be prepared in a modern kitchen, and (d) your friends will happily if astonishedly devour.*

Sound like fun? If so, you'll very much enjoy *The Roman Cooking of Apicius.* Set aside all this book's donnishness and what you have left is a scholar-poet at play in the kitchen with fresh herbs, sweet spices, honeyed vinegar, and spiced wine. His is the sort of intellectual larking that makes us think, even as we enjoy the game—and, more often than not, the results.

My Paula
Wolfert Problem

❖ ❖ ❖

COUSCOUS AND OTHER GOOD FOOD FROM MOROCCO

MEDITERRANEAN COOKING

THE COOKING OF SOUTH-WEST FRANCE

PAULA WOLFERT'S WORLD OF FOOD

1

In the opening lines of *World of Food*, Paula Wolfert declares that her passion is the search for great bread. On her trips to France, Italy, and elsewhere, the most important questions on her mind are " 'Where can I find the best bread around here?' 'Who is the best baker?' And nearly always, as soon as I ask, the eyes of my respondent will light up. He or she will utter a name and an address. And then I am off upon the hunt."

So begins the account of how she tracked down one such loaf in a small town in Sicily near Palermo. She had heard tales of this bread, she tells us, even before she left the States, and a Sicilian friend in New York insisted that he make arrangements so that she might get to taste it.

She demurred at his taking such trouble, but he insisted . . . and so not long thereafter she found herself being driven out of Palermo in a tiny car to a spring near the town of Monreale, where two women in their eighties—"their eyes twinkling with pleasure at my arrival"—had a bakery in a tiny shack. Their bread was made of wheat grown on nearby farms and the water from their spring, where the neighbors still came to fill their jugs. The old women kneaded the dough for forty-five long minutes, and then baked it in a bread oven fired by twigs gathered from olive and lemon trees. The result was a sublime loaf with a chewy texture, crackling crust, and the delicious flavor of wheat.

Our mouth watering, we reach out for a taste for ourselves —only to have our hand pushed away. "No, I cannot tell you how to find the place," she says, floating away from us, as if in a dream. "And, no," she continues, "I cannot give you a recipe. . . ."

This passage, no matter that it is a depiction of a real event, is also a romance. I mean by this both that the experiences it describes are charged with drama and emotion and that our response to them is so much like the narrator's that we are clearly being asked to identify with her.

After all, is not great bread *our* passion? Would we not also love the task of searching Europe for the very best loaf of it . . . and many other good things as well? And were we not so shy—so sure that our interlocutors would look at us as if we were idiots—wouldn't we, too, demand of every pass-erby: "Take us to your best bakery, confectionery, cheese-monger . . ."?

In Paula Wolfert's world, eyes light up at such commands, addresses are shoved into her hand, strangers spring into automobiles to take her to them . . . and, never, when she arrives, is the shop closed, the bread all sold, the baker silent and surly. Instead, eyes gleam with pleasure that she has bothered to come at all.

In our world, travel is exhausting and ofttimes defeating. Meals do not live up to their advance billing. Strangers are indifferent to our curiosity and sometimes even hostile to our desire to appropriate their best things for ourselves—especially when we have nothing more to exchange for them than the cheap coin of a moment's appreciation.

Nor do we—you and I—have friends who not only have news of such remarkable things but are willing to go out of their way to make sure we actually get our hands on them, who impatiently shrug off our protests as they place the necessary transcontinental calls. Paula Wolfert, it seems, does have such friends—people, like her, passionate about food. Yet this passage—and, as we shall see, other passages like it—says that she has no similar desire to be that kind of friend to *us*. Not, of course, that she puts this in so many words.

Instead, she says that she does not really know the way (although she knows someone who could draw a map). She says that, without the local ingredients, the recipe for that bread would be useless (but she gives a recipe for Sicilian semolina bread without explaining why that loaf, made in our oven, would be any more authentic).

Again and again in Paula Wolfert's writing, we experience this same ritual denial: we are brought to the secret source of some perfect dish; we share her thrill at finding it, her delight in tasting it, her love for the people who have made it; and then we are pushed away. The excuses are different, the message always the same. We, her readers, are not yet—somehow—serious enough to be invited to join the table.

This seriousness is the single recurrent theme of her four major cookbooks, each still in print: *Couscous and Other Good Food from Morocco* (1973); *Mediterranean Cooking* (1977); *The Cooking of South-West France* (1983); and, most recently, *Paula Wolfert's World of Food* (1988). It is the subject of her narratives and the subtext of the near-obsessive definitiveness that has become the characteristic trademark of her recipes. Not only does each dish have an impeccable regional pedigree but each is also distilled in the alembic of her perfectionism—without regard to cost or effort—until flavor can be intensified and structure refined no more.

This is true especially of the recipes in her last two books, the ones on which her reputation rests. For as it happens—and certainly in no small part because of the influence she herself has exerted—the making of certain signature regional dishes has become the kind of cooking most desirable to America's new breed of knowledgeable, ambitious, very earnest amateur cooks. They are drawn to Paula Wolfert, more than to almost any other food writer, because they crave to possess not only her recipes but the deep culinary seriousness that such cooking is made to reflect.

2

In the summer of 1959, Paula Wolfert and her then husband, Michael, both in their early twenties, boarded a Yugoslav freighter and set sail for Morocco. At that time, her acquaintance with foreign food was limited to what she had learned when she had dropped out of college to attend the Dione Lucas Cordon Bleu Cooking School.

Moroccan food—much as she would later come to love it— was not what drew this young acolyte of haute cuisine. That country was just being discovered as the ideal refuge—at once cosmopolitan and picturesque, tolerant and affordable—by young expatriate writers and artists, American and otherwise, who sought to escape the stifling conformity of the fifties.

This young couple was in the vanguard of a shift in cultural tastes that would soon have graduate students decorating their college apartments not with Utrillo or Bernard Buffet posters but with colorful wall hangings and terra-cotta pottery—acquired with the Peace Corps in Guatemala . . . on a shoestring trek through Nepal . . . or during a summer spent on a tiny island in the Cyclades.

Then, and especially to us, the young, these were places that seemed fresh and new, unexplored cultures our imaginations might be among the first to inhabit and possess. And for those with any literary or artistic pretensions, that private itinerary was most likely plotted from one spot to another around the Mediterranean . . . from Robert Graves's Majorca to Lawrence Durrell's Corfu to Paul and Jane Bowles's Tangiers. What we hoped to imbibe in these cells of Prospero was not only the wine of genius but that even stronger intoxicant—spiritual enlightenment.

Paula Wolfert was among the first of her generation to get there, and her books should be read, at least in part, as authored by a participant in an Age of Aquarius voyage of self-discovery—a search less for recipes than a culinary way of knowledge. The counterculture figures who briefly appear in her earlier books serve only to accentuate how much of Carlos Castaneda, the naïve but serious seeker, there is in her own self-portrait—and even more of Don Juan, the trickster shaman, in her cooks.

> My visit to the kitchen of a restaurant [in Marrakesh] would be an unprecedented invasion into a world of jealousy and intrigue. . . . When I came in [the women] stopped and looked me up and down with a small measure of scorn. . . . Three of them gave me shy smiles, but one, who was huge, fat, and black, expressed her derision with an outraged sniff. . . . I knew—I could *feel*—that the Queen Bee was the best cook, and I wanted her to like me so she would tell me some of her culinary secrets.

In Paula Wolfert's world, there is an essential difference between such cooks and the rest of us—qualities whose specific characteristics depend on whether the cook in question is a man or a woman.

Her women cooks possess—like witches—a capacity to enchant food through potions whispered down the ages by mothers into the ears of the deserving daughters. These women, like the Queen Bee, are often described as wise, sly, secretive: "[Madame X] was obsessed with the notion that she must guard her 'culinary secrets,' suspicious of my interest in her knowledge, and totally confident in her ability to deceive."

On the other hand, her men—almost all chefs—form a kind of mystical brotherhood of *illuminati*, willing to reveal their secrets to all who truly appreciate them. More numerous but less interesting than her women, they can be epitomized by Lucien Vanel of Toulouse, who opened to her "the kitchen of his restaurant and all the 'secrets' of his mother's famous *cuisine Quercynoise*"—something his mother surely would *not* have done.

This transfer of understanding, with its accompanying—if only temporary—ticket of admission into the circle of the elect, is a constant motif in her writing. Only in *Mediterranean Cooking* is it missing, for that is a collection of recipes almost without any explanatory narrative—which may be why it is the least satisfying of her works, a collection of spells without the requisite cast of magicians.

Early into *The Cooking of South-West France*, Paula Wolfert travels to a half-abandoned town in Lot-et-Garonne to interview a Gascon *restaurateuse*. They talk food late into the day, and so a call is made to the local château to see if there is a bed to spare. There is, and the count himself invites her to dinner—a feast, really, with wine flowing freely, regional delicacies spread on a groaning board, and guests eating, drinking, and making merry:

> This delirium went on for hours. I felt myself entranced. At one point a young man turned to me. "You want to know about the South-West?" he asked. I looked up at him and nodded. "Welcome," he said, gesturing with his hand. "You are here. This is it."

Implicit in this gesture is the unspoken recognition: "You are one of us." Equally implicit is its corollary as regards the reader . . . but that anxious-making exclusion is left for each reader to deduce for herself.

3

Here is another example of the primal Wolfert scene, this time to be found in *Paula Wolfert's World of Food*:

> Alice Waters . . . gave me the name of an old friend in Bandol. "Lulu makes the best bouillabaisse I've ever eaten. Of course you won't be able to send your readers to her, but still you should watch her cook."
> Lulu (who has asked that I not give her full name) is the owner of an important vineyard. . . .

Again, three witch-cooks whisper secretively together, slyly glancing at us out of the corners of their eyes. "Of course you won't be able to send your readers to her," murmurs one of them, and another assents, "Yes, nor even give them my full name. . . ."

Familiar, yes—but there is also a difference worth remarking between the language of this encounter (and the others like it in her last two books) and that describing the visit to the Queen Bee in Marrakesh in her first. That earlier account conveyed the sense of an actual confrontation—of genuine learning, genuine risk.

The prose above, with its stresses on quality and exclusivity, suggests something entirely different. Accompanying Paula Wolfert into the mysterious Lulu's Provençal home is a thrill much more like accompanying a home decorator past the discreet sign posted at the door of certain off-limit shops: TO THE TRADE ONLY.

This is all the more true since the anonymity-seeking Lulu is none other than Lulu Peyraud, whose cooking skills are, if anything, an open secret in the culinary world—and who, with her husband, Lucien, is proprietor of the vineyard Domaine A. Tempier in Le Plan, easily found on any wine map of Provence. In fact, despite all this talk of anonymity, Paula Wolfert prints Lulu's full name in the book's acknowledgment section and, in her account of her visit, gives what is practically the vineyard's complete address. It is, after all, already available to anyone with a need for it; the Peyrauds have professional reasons to welcome strangers to their door. The coyness about her identity means to convince the reader of Lulu Peyraud's status and, by extension, that of the select few for whom she consents to cook.

In the same way, an interior decorator would never pretend that it was greater sensitivity to home decor that opened doors closed to the rest of us—but would certainly encourage us to believe that it was just this, not a mere card, that caused the proprietor to come running up, beaming, with *"Mais c'est Paula!"* forming ecstatically on his lips.

"My friend Lucien Vanel . . . ," "my friend Michel Bras . . . ," "my friend the chef Roger Duffour . . . ," "my friend André Daguin . . ."—the persona may be still that of the humble seeker, but the prose conveys someone with the food world's most prestigious credentials suddenly appearing in the foyer of an important French restaurant.

Paula Wolfert is not the same woman she was when she set out to write about Moroccan cooking, but she doesn't seem to notice how much she has changed. Her search for culinary knowledge has succeeded—she is now a noted author and cooking authority—but success has also revealed a core of self-absorption at the center of her quest, a confusion between such status and the dedication required to set it aside so as to remain genuinely open to new experiences, fresh encounters.

This is why her best book is still her first: it is the only one of her narratives to capture a sense of true conversion . . . a young visitor culinarily transformed, despite her Cordon Bleu training, by the complex and various beauties of that mysterious cuisine. Not that she has forgotten how to look, listen, and learn. But the prose of her recent books strains too much to convey an image that her life is no longer able to sustain.

Though each of her last two books took five years to write, there is more of a feeling of excursion to them than of immersion. The experiences they relate seem plucked from a tiny stock of actual events and plumped into significance. Like holiday snapshots, each is different and yet all somehow the same: the author posed before the predictably picturesque, as she is here in *Paula Wolfert's World of Food*:

> It wasn't until I went to Sicily and tasted the luscious salted capers of the islands of Pantelleria and Lipari that I understood the appeal of these extraordinary capers.

> The building had been converted into a private restaurant with no name on its door. I was about to have lunch at what the French call "a precious address."

This is the language of the tourist, intent on making every second of the vacation count. Her followers have not noticed the change because this is how they want her to write. Tourists themselves, they do not wish to plunge after her into another foreign cuisine. Better that she should skim the cream away and give them that, so they can play at concocting their own personal "worlds of food." They love Paula Wolfert because she tells them they can have it all—and proves it by hurrying off to Périgord . . . Corfu . . . Sicily . . . Catalonia, to search out the very best of those regions' dishes and bring them back alive.

4

> [It is] the best of the recent "terrines," a jewel-like mosaic of bright fresh fruits arranged in an airy almond cream. The whole is enclosed in a thin casing of Génoise. It is served with two sauces, a thin raspberry sauce and a light Crème Anglaise. . . . This dessert is not complicated, but you should begin two to three days before serving. . . .
> —*The Cooking of South-West France*

It is no accident that we have come this far into Paula Wolfert's world of food before considering her recipes. For these require the context of her narratives—journeys taken, cooks approached, ingredients found and savored—for us to understand their appeal . . . or at least their appeal to those who undertake to make them.

Not, of course, that they are not good: it is that their goodness can carry a steep price. One of the more renowned recipes in *Paula Wolfert's World of Food* is the delicious-sounding "Duck You Can Eat with a Spoon," in which that fowl is

> marinated in *cooked* red wine. . . . The cooked . . . pieces, soft and succulent, are boned and garnished with rich caramelized baby onions, crisp lardons, mushrooms, and garlic-parsleyed croutons. The sauce resonates with the dark, musky perfume of bitter cocoa and Cognac. . . .

In truth, the duck is marinated in a mixture of twelve ingredients, including orange slices, aged red wine vinegar, ruby Port wine, and one-and-a-half bottles of Bordeaux. The sauce (called an "enrichment" in the recipe) "resonates" with several other ingredients besides the cocoa and Cognac, including juniper berries, shallots, and duck liver. In total, over two dozen ingredients are required, not counting the marinade ingredients or the duck. Two pages of complex instruction are prefaced by an introductory plea: "Please don't be put off by the length of this recipe, for it is really an easy step-by-step procedure. . . ."

There is something disingenuous about such an entreaty from an author who well knows she is famous for the daunting nature of her recipes. The number of hours required to make them has become so notorious she no longer provides total cooking times. "I felt it was turning people off," she told *The New York Times*, "that people were making jokes about me."

Not all her dishes are equally difficult, but the simplest can require exotic or pricey ingredients—and all of them are so intensely reworked in her kitchen that no honest cook could ever imagine making Paula Wolfert's version of even a simple French bistro dish without giving her the credit.

Nevertheless, many good cooks are willing to give that to her, and gladly. They, too, joke about her fanatical complexity—but fondly, for it is exactly what draws them to her books. They willingly face days of work and endless kitchen mess to replicate these dishes, knowing that at the end of this labor they will be able to produce for their guests (as is most often the case) a culinary triumph . . . unmistakably stamped PAULA WOLFERT⒯⒨, with its accompanying "Big Taste" guarantee.

Most of us can establish our reputation as "serious" cooks without such effort: our neighbors, after all, are rarely much interested in such cooking at all. We do not need to see ourselves as competitive with them, because no overt competition is required. But when our next-door neighbor tastes our extravirgin olive oil and pronounces it unbelievably delicious, it isn't the small grower in Tuscany who suddenly feels all warm inside. Anyway, wasn't it *we* who noticed the bottle at Williams-Sonoma, bought it, brought it home, tried it, and knew it to be good?

Paula Wolfert's readers, upscale professionals almost all, live in a different world. Knowledge of cuisine has become culturally fashionable, and their friends already know all about the ingredients we think make our kitchen special, are already bored with dishes we think unique and new. To keep pace with such expertise, cooks who set out to impress need someone like Paula Wolfert at their elbow, enabling them to prepare food of stunning complexity and sophistication without a stumble and then to bring it to the table with proof of pedigree.

Such readers are willing to accept their lowly place in Paula Wolfert's world of food because they have no interest at all in competing with *her*. Instead, they mean simply to borrow her status for the night. For them, Paula Wolfert's exclusive "seriousness" is more a product for sale than a genuine way of knowledge. It certifies her as an acceptable arbiter of culinary taste, providing her readers with the cues they need and the necessary authentication of the results.

By buying her book, her followers purchase the right to replace her at the bottom of this culinary hierarchy. As their friends savor their food and listen to the account of its making—this double braising, that double degreasing, the requisite confit prepared months before the dish could ever hope to be made—the cook slips into Paula Wolfert's role: intermediary between the humble eater and the world of secret knowledge whence this dish has come.

The author herself then becomes the honored tutelary whose twinkling eyes beam down upon the feast. And André Daguin and Lucien Vanel and Madame Lulu—who, after all, are known to no one present—quietly fade away into the mists of myth.

5

I have always been drawn to what I call the Mediterranean Myth . . . a robust, simple, and sensual life far from the madding crowds of our competitive North Atlantic culture.
—*Paula Wolfert's World of Food*

I admire Paula Wolfert for being her own person, for her superb palate, for having more culinary smarts than almost anyone else writing about food today. I admire her for her generosity to other food writers, for the way she gives forthright credit where credit is due, for preferring to scout out new dishes, new cuisines, taking new risks instead of resting on her laurels. And I think her sense of how dishes work—and how they can be made to work better—is often astonishingly right.

It's because of this admiration that, reading through her work, I find it so hard to understand why, with each new book, she seems more at home in the world of Mr. Kenneth than in that of Elizabeth David. Why all the fuss over celebrity chefs, why the self-hype, the big taste, the trademark dishes? Some observers of the food scene feel that all this is built into the system—that's what you have to do if you want to climb to the top. And it's true that these elements have not always been a part of Paula Wolfert's writing; but if my reading is right, the competitiveness that brought them into being has, always.

From her first book on, it played sun to her appetite's moon, illuminating the landscape of her world of food with Mediterranean brightness. It is the single common denominator—apart from talent—of her secretive old women and her ambitious young chefs; as much as her palate, it is what draws her to the ultimate ingredient, the consummate flavor, the irrefutable version of a famous dish.

In this, she is more the child of her times than the victim of food-world celebrity-making; either way, the end result is a confusion between means and ends—a confusion as to what, exactly, her books are about. *The Cooking of South-West France* is not at all a bad book, but in twenty years or so, readers will open it to find less Périgord staring out of its pages than Paula Wolfert herself. The translation of cuisine follows the same rules as the translation of poetry: to the extent that its success depends on the stylistic mannerisms of the translator, as persuasive as these may be to the readers who are dazzled by them at the time, they will grate more and more on those who come later and find them dated and unpersuasive.

This is why—no matter her claim that she prefers to acquire a dish standing next to the original maker, asking questions and taking notes—we should not mistake her version as replicating what she actually tasted at the time. Even if a recipe points as its source to some dish first eaten outside her own kitchen, none leaves her hands without having been first trans-muted into her very personal property.

Consequently, despite lip service to the contrary, there is little in Paula Wolfert's recent writings that attempts to preserve original ways of making and thus to increase the wealth of our shared culinary commons. If you should want the original ver-sion of a particular dish—the way she herself found it—you must go, say, to Zakinthos in the Ionian Sea and ask Maria Lykouresis for it yourself.

What Paula Wolfert has perfected instead is a method of lifting dishes *out* of the public domain and patenting them as her own. Such a trademark cuisine delights her followers because it provides them with a series of exclusive possessions . . . a Paula Wolfert cassoulet to set next to their Lexus sedan, their Movado watch. But it does this by impoverishing the rest of us, and not least because every dish so patented weakens the very concept of such a commons—a pool of dishes shared by all members of a culture.

We already live in a time that more and more denies good foodstuffs to all but the most advantaged. There is good food out there, but it has to be found and paid for, and this requires both leisure and money. Paula Wolfert's world of cooking takes place almost entirely within this privileged place, even as, para-doxically, its subject is often food that, historically at least, belonged to the less advantaged who can now no longer afford to eat it.

Such an approach can only confuse our perception of what gives cooking its vitality and life. We have already seen how her "seriousness" has had the ultimate effect of transforming her readers from cooks into customers; now it is time to notice that it also awards possession of a dish to the person who can give it the most exquisite flavor . . . ignoring the fact that history is littered with delicious dishes that lost connection with their roots and thus withered and died.

Dishes, too, have souls: they owe their character to the local ingredients out of which they are made, to the hands that have long and familiarly made them, and to the company of other local dishes that time has honed as their best accompaniments. And this is especially true of those quintessential regional dishes whose every element speaks intimately to their native eaters of shared place, produce, history.

Paula Wolfert once knew this; her book on Morocco is tempered throughout with feeling for the vulnerability of this elegant cuisine. Her sensitivity has faded as her livelihood has come more and more to depend on convincing herself and her readers that the souvenirs she has uprooted from such slowly evanescing worlds might survive hydroponically in the corner of her Manhattan kitchen.

Even her famous pages on cassoulet in *The Cooking of South-West France* ring hollow, for they are absent any meaningful recognition that the ground on which this dish once found its footing is melting away into the air. The dish fades as the world that made it is itself evaporating: the need to preserve meat for which confit was the epicurean solution; the flocks of geese whose feathers were as prized as their meat; the pig waiting outside each door for the daily ration of slop—the list goes on and on.

If these are fast vanishing even in France, what chance has such a dish to find a foothold here? Cassoulet's caloric content alone, double degreasing or no, says very different things to us than it did to frugal eaters who preferred to heat their bodies with fat and beans than their homes with coal and wood.

For us, confit and cassoulet are only flavors—and, as flavors, we will eventually tire of them, so long as they are presences without meaning in our lives. What cassoulet needs is not a few gourmet cooks who can make it to perfection but a whole nation of home cooks enough reminded of the consolation of slowly simmered meats and beans to regularly work up such a dish from a country ham bone and the local butcher's garlic sausages.

In other words, cassoulet, if it is to strike root here, must be made somehow to feel at home. That is what the French did when they came: they turned it into red beans and rice. Paula Wolfert's world of food has no room for such a welcoming . . . or for such a dish. Choice, rare ingredients, complex methods of flavor enhancement—apply these to it and the dish wouldn't even *be* red beans and rice anymore. "Honey," we can hear the cooks who make it saying, "it tastes so good already—why go gild the goose?"

What sort of cooks have we become if our answer to them is: "To take the dish away from you and copyright it—so that it belongs to us alone"?

MEDITERRANEAN ODYSSEY

✦ ✦ ✦

HONEY FROM A WEED: FASTING AND FEASTING IN
TUSCANY, CATALONIA, THE CYCLADES, AND APULIA
Patience Gray

Early into this truly astonishing book, Patience Gray describes her "cookstove" in Apollona, a tiny village on the island of Naxos in the Greek Cyclades:

> Outside the dwelling . . . was an outdoor hearth constructed on a stone shelf at waist level against a wall, roofed over with an escape hole for the smoke. The bricks were cemented at the precise distance to support a large black pot over a twig fire, and there was room below the shelf for stacking driftwood. This was ideal for summer, and as the sea was at the door, I was able to light a fire, start the pot with its contents cooking, plunge into the sea at mid-day and by the time I had swum across the bay and back, the lunch was ready and the fire a heap of ashes.

Here in a short compass we have almost everything that is most wonderful about this author: her awareness of the evocative nature of place and her ability, in order to open herself to it, to cheerfully and unself-consciously adapt herself to the most primitive kinds of cooking. And while she may be very serious about the food she makes, she is refreshingly free of hubris about herself as its maker.*

All that is missing in that passage is her great relish for the various indigenous foodstuffs that have come her way during her stays in the four very different and yet remarkably similar areas of the Mediterranean littoral—Tuscany, Catalonia, the Cyclades, and Apulia—a relish compounded with curiosity and a sure sense of their place in her kitchen and her life.

In fact, her surety is such that she can share her tenderness for the simplest of weeds without a hint of sentimentality— that is, without condescending to them. She everywhere insists that these foods earn the right to be taken seriously by her, but she also knows she herself has dues to pay if she is to earn their friendship in return:

> Most of these [edible weeds] were gathered by cutting a section of the root, thus preserving the plant entire. Washed at the fountain, they were boiled and served with oil and lemon juice, the lemons picked from neighboring groves. During the Lenten fast they were eaten in quantity like vegetable spaghettini, but without the olive oil.
>
> Filling my water jar at the spring, I had a daily opportunity to examine these weeds and ask advice, and began to gather them myself, but at first always offering them for inspection. At the time I was reading the landscape and its flora with as much attention as one gives to an absorbing book.

She has earned it because she is a practiced cook whose knowledge comes not only from the kitchen and learned texts in several languages, but from an ongoing conversation with the landscape and those who cultivated it; because she is a

---

* Another entertaining example of this: a Greek friend gives her a lesson in the proper cooking of fresh haricot beans, which instruction produces a great and delicious-sounding stew of olive oil, beans, onions, tomatoes, and aromatics. There is so much of it that the author generously decides to share these beans with an elderly neighbor—who, "brought up with prejudice and believing them to be cooked by me and foreign in consequence, later threw them to the pig."

jewelry maker who has learned to articulate the sensual immediacy of all the raw materials from which she works; and, most important—although this may seem an entirely irrelevant consideration—because she decided twenty and more years ago to share the gypsy life of a wandering sculptor.

He, Norman Mommens—referred to in these pages solely as "the Sculptor"—drew her after him to those parts of southern Europe where there are still small marble quarries where inexpensive slabs of stone are to be had and affordable space (if only outdoors) in which to work them. These places are, almost by definition, both primitive and poor, and their existence was stripped down to the bare essentials (for this day and age) in order to afford the luxury of a life that was entirely their own.

Therefore, although their poverty was of a different order from that of their neighbors, neither was there any great gulf of possession to separate them. While they might be able to afford a two-burner gas stove on Naxos to supplement the outdoor fireplace in inclement weather, or to purchase from the local fisherman one of the larger, tastier fishes that would otherwise be taken elsewhere for sale (the local populace contenting themselves with what they considered their destiny: the tiny, bony fish that were cheap and plentiful) . . . even so, as the above passage informs us, they drew their drinking water from the same spring, cooked in the same sort of pots, ate much the same food, and—also like their neighbors—when that food became scarce, went without.

This is the fasting to which the author refers in her subtitle, and whose presence as a major theme in this book is one good reason why it stands alone among the many Mediterranean cookbooks published in the last several years—or, for that matter, almost any other food book at all. Other descriptions of traditional peasant fare have all concentrated on the feasting and have given the fasting short shrift: what Patience Gray conveys with grace and power in these pages is that fasting is a necessary component of any appetite desiring the full measure of experience that eating has to offer. This is not the willful, self-mortifying fasting that is dieting, but a patient matching of one's hunger to the rhythms of earth and season:

Once we lose touch with the spendthrift aspect of nature's provisions epitomized in the raising of a crop, we are in danger of losing touch with life itself. When Providence supplies the means, the preparation and sharing of food takes on a sacred aspect. The fact that every crop is of short duration promotes a spirit of making the best of it while it lasts and conserving a part of it for future use.

That hunger sauces the plainest fare will seem no news—until this book arouses in you that deeper, more compelling hunger that comes of riding life's pulse from fast to feast, and evokes the feeling of how that rhythm connects us to the world in a way no other action, however attentive or loving, can ever hope to do.

During the summer . . . we would be pressed to visit a fig or mulberry tree in the next valley and were expected to eat our fill on the spot. The island Greek has a habit of going for long periods, in the fields or on foot or muleback, on a crust of home-baked bread, a hunk of hard goat's cheese and wild pears, honey sweet, stuffed inside his shirt. He then makes the most of a providential event, a ripe fruit tree, a sudden haul of fish, or the killing of a pig. This is a fundamental attitude, and only underlined by Greek Orthodox practice, whose solemn four week Advent fast and six week Lenten one, in fact, corresponded to moments when on Naxos there was hardly anything to eat. Fasting is therefore in the nature of things and feasting punctuates it with a joyful excess.

The sweetness of the fig plucked from the tree, so ripe that nectar beads at its tip, tasting of honey—or, as some do, of raspberry jam—in the mouth of one whose only meal that long hot day has been a crust of bread . . . how the mouth surrenders to that sweet and sticky profligacy. This is an appetite whose contours shape it to the source of its pleasure, just as the tongue voluptuously enfolds the sticky finger and sucks it dry.

❖ ❖ ❖

Poverty, of course, can be a desperate thing, and this book makes no attempt to romanticize desperation; but poverty no more means desperation than vulnerability means being victimized. We are so used to thinking of hunger as the antithesis of appetite, of fasting as a moral purgative, that we have lost the ability to understand it as the underside of the feast, the background that gives it definition and depth. If there is no scarcity, there is no real having, either: it is not hunger that makes men greedy but fear of hunger. Those who accept it as a needful condition earn that true fastidiousness that is attentive, not to what they eat, but to what they truly want to eat.

In this same way, it is hunger that shapes the intimacy established between the cultivator and his or her small plot. A piece of land upon which all hope of sustenance rests, a mode of planting and tending and harvesting that is accomplished by a ceaseless laying on of hands, creates a union of aggressive and robustly physical intimacy. And through her own participation in these acts, as neighbor, friend, and fellow hungerer, Patience Gray has made that connection real in her own life.

This relationship between feasting and fasting, which naturally occurs in any deep relationship between small producers and the plots of land that sustain them, is so palpable in this work that she takes only two short passages to set the argument out; then she is content to let it rest. What makes this book so affecting and ultimately convincing is the way this relationship between fasting and feasting is articulated into a constantly renewing source of insight and sensual pleasure; because of it her narrative bursts with life.

In this regard, it is interesting to compare her account of an olive harvest with a similar description of grape picking recounted in Mary Taylor Simeti's journal of life on Sicily, *On Persephone's Island*. Ms. Simeti is a talented writer and her book is full of evocative description, as in this passage where she recounts assisting with the grape harvest:

> Harvesting grapes is hard work: one must bend double to liberate the low-growing bunches from the clutch of the vine, and the bucket, light at first, gets heavier and heavier as you drag it along the row from vine to vine until, full up, you leave it where it stands (feminine prerogative) and start in on another

one. The ripe grapes burst in the picking and the sticky must runs down your arms and gets wiped on your forehead and into clothes and hair, attracting flies and wasps and vinegar gnats that buzz around your temples and down your bare arms.

Now compare this to Patience Gray, busy picking olives:

Like the pains of childbirth, one quickly forgets the olive-picking pains. In childbirth you are on your own, while in the olive field the ordeal is endured in good company. What you need ideally is short thighs and a long back. Adopting a martial attitude—like the bronze Zeus discovered at Ugento, now in the Taranto Museum—but bending from the hips and keeping the head permanently down, with an extraordinary rapidity you pick up the olives with both hands, the endless olives. The women are on the ground, the men are in the trees.

A casual glance might discern no great difference between these two passages, at least until one considers which of the two one would hire as a harvester. For while the Simeti passage flows from work to discomfort, the motion in Patience Gray is from discomfort to work. We feel Mary Simeti's interest in grape picking fade in the course of only a few sentences, and not only her physical interest but her intellectual interest as well. The demands of the work distance her from the activity around her: as she becomes tired, she quickly draws into herself . . . and into a privileged distance.

The passage by Patience Gray, however, is dominated by her delight in the sheer physical act of olive picking: discomfort is mentioned only to be dismissed. That opening sentence is but a girding of the loins; we soon feel the muscles flexing, the body assuming the shape of the olive picker. This first paragraph is a gathering of strength, a drawing in of wind. In the following ones, she plunges to work, and we scurry with her from tree to tree, picking up the olives before the men can lay their nets and hurrying back to gather the olives knocked down into nets already laid.

This pleasure in the sheer physicality of olive picking can

only come from one who shares a hunger for its results: at the beginning is the pain but at the end is the fragrant, fresh-pressed olive oil, darkly golden in its bottles, triumphantly borne home. With it also comes the rich sense of fellowship that a genuine sharing of labor entails, an act accomplished at no one's expense and to everyone's benefit. As she herself says, describing another wine harvest:

> Once a man has leapt into the wine-pit and sweated a whole morning treading the lustrous grapes, friendship declares itself with as generous a flow as the fiery liquid poured from the pit into the bloated goatskins for transport on muleback to the village.

If I quote these not strictly culinary passages to make my point, it is because there are many writers who can write evocatively and well on food: her own previous (1957) *Plats du Jour* is a small triumph of that genre. But there is nothing in that (or any other food book I can think of) that conveys the sheer animal satisfaction of earning appetite as does *Honey from a Weed*.

And, outside of food writing, only D. H. Lawrence—in such works as *Twilight in Italy*—comes to mind as her equal in conveying the rich physical sensuality of Mediterranean life without ever flinching at its salt-and-bitter taste. But in Lawrence it is quickly drowned in a rush of dark thought—like those alpine railway trains that burst onto sunlit mountain meadows and as quickly out of them again into the darkest imaginable tunnels. Lawrence is the better writer, but Patience Gray has found the better balance.

❖ ❖ ❖

A few words remain to be said about how to read this book. Like many cookbooks it is set out into chapters, each of which is given its separate culinary subject—beans, peas, and rustic soups; fish, shellfish, crustaceans; smoked and salt fish; edible weeds—followed by the recipes that relate to it. At least on first encounter, however, I think it is a mistake to read the book straight through. The narrative is one of intricate connection, with one dish . . . place . . . person evoking the thought or memory—and hence description—of another. Each of these should be seen as the stroke of a brush at work at a single picture—a brush that is often at work on many parts of the canvas at once.

Early in the book, writing about basil, she notes—rightly—that it is impossible to put up for winter eating, for that wonderful spice-edged aroma soon fades whether the leaf be dried or preserved in oil. "The best way to recall the perfume in winter," she concludes, "is to immure some sprigs at the last moment in a cauldron of peach or quince jam"; and refers us to her recipe for *kydóni glikó*, some three hundred pages on. Who would not, tempted by such a suggestion—and a proffered page number—skip ahead? As it turns out, the jam is made by Kyría Erynni (the same woman who had tossed the author's haricot stew to the pigs), who dips fragrant sprigs of basil into the boiling conserve and then shakes off the drops onto the rosy chunks of quince that float on the surface.

This not only sounds delicious but arouses our interest in quinces, and the author helpfully refers us on to yet another page for her comments on them. And so we turn on—only to discover we have completely lost track of the thought that started us on this journey. No matter—we have merely to turn back a page to discover how the Japanese eat persimmons . . . or turn ahead to see how the Italians eat figs . . . or just browse at random, for long before you exhaust this last chapter's treasures, you will catch up another strand that will take you somewhere else.

But, if the book is studded with fascinating bits of information, the argument itself does not so much develop as present itself in an ever-changing guise: once you grasp it, understanding becomes an act not of progression but of absorption. It is as if what you held in your hand was a ripening piece of fruit. It starts out seeming hard and sour and not much worth eating, but as you wait, watching, it softens and sweetens, filling the air with a delicate scent and letting its juices spill onto your hand:

Turning a corner I came upon an open doorway and the stooping form of a very old peasant carrying a large curved and blackened frying-pan in which were a heap of fungi.

I greeted her and asked how she was going to cook them. "In the usual way," she replied reprovingly. She invited me into the kitchen, a space so bare it reminded me of Naxian rooms. All it contained was a small table, two broken chairs and a black cast-iron stove with pipe in the centre of the room, a pile of sawn-up chestnut wood beside it. She began to slice up the boletus heads.

She sliced them fine like tripe, simmered them in oil with garlic, mountain savory, thyme, parsley, seasoned them with salt and black pepper, added a spoonful or two of tomato sauce she had bottled and a little stock from boiling the carcase of a scraggy hen. This was simmered and reduced. When fairly dense, some grated *pecorino* was added—her lunch, eaten with some slices of rough bread.

Coming upon this scene on opening the book, you might well notice only its poverty: the bare room, the broken chairs, the carcass of the scraggy hen, the coarse loaf. But now, having read even this review, you find the image ripening before you: a feast is about to be served.

Again and again in these pages you are brought back to this same place. Like a Zen koan, all is put in a single enigmatic nut: the locale, the person, the dish. You are given everything except what you want most, a mouthful of the meal . . . or, more even than that, the way to taste it with that old woman's tongue. So, after her fashion, does the author lead us to hunger: the fruit in our hand is ripe, but we do not yet know how to eat.

No book since Richard Olney's *Simple French Food* was published in 1974 has revealed more of the sheer possibilities inherent in food writing—the ability of an apprehending appetite to work place, time, and the stuff of eating itself into a sensually pleasing, intellectually stimulating, morally sustaining whole. Brilliantly written and stunningly designed, not only is *Honey from a Weed* the best food book written in English in this decade; it has already attained the status of a classic. For all of us, it has opened an important door.

PLATS DU JOUR
Patience Gray and Primrose Boyd,
with illustrations by David Gentleman*

Sometime in the early 1980s, browsing among the cookbooks in a dingy used-book store near Boston's South Station, I came across a paperback I had never seen or heard of before. It was practically falling apart—and why not, having been published in 1957!—but I had only to pull it from the shelf to know that I was going to take it home. The faded pink cover showed an illustration of a family—French? Greek? Italian?—sitting down to supper. Grandfather dandles his favorite granddaughter on his knee, Father and Uncle pull corks, Grandmother strokes her cat, and Mother, still in her apron, looks—despite a table heaped with platters—as if she were about to dash back to the kitchen for one dish more.

This attractively homey foreign air pervades *Plats du Jour*. I was astonished to learn in Alan Davidson's introduction to this lovingly produced hardcover facsimile edition that though the original was published only in paperback, it sold 50,000 copies during its first ten months of publication. Still, I could understand why. Until *Simple French Food*, there was really nothing like it—a clearly written, informative guide to good, mostly simple, mostly French supper dishes—each feeling as if it were part of these authors' ordinary daily cooking.

This approach was unusual enough in the fifties; depressingly, it is even more unusual today. I can think of only a handful of American writers—Edna Lewis, Miriam Ungerer, Laurie Colwin, Sylvia Vaughn Thompson—whose cookbooks have the air of sharing a part of the writer's actual life, rather than dishes (no matter how good) that were called up for the occasion of the book. Having written this, I also ought to add that this impression is partly an illusion, since at least a portion

* Available in the U.S.A. from Books International, 3950 Park Center Road, Herndon, VA 22071. Write or call (703) 435-7064 for current price and shipping charges.

of *Plats du Jour* was worked up straight from other cookbooks —which perhaps explains why, although I love this book, I don't much cook from it. Its genius lies not in its recipes but somewhere else.

It resides, most of all, in the genuine hunger the two authors felt for the food they write about. Food rationing had ended in England only in 1954, and both women were eager to revivify a kind of eating that they had learned to love in prewar explorations of the Continent. Theirs were not the usual destinations. Patience Gray had hitchhiked with her sister to Budapest in 1937; then, in 1938, they had both vanished into Romania on a student travel grant. Primrose Boyd was exploring France, Spain, and Holland. A deluxe dinner was a rare treat during these excursions, and both women acquired a taste for the humble, hearty dishes that these pages share.

But what really drew them to this way of cooking was not any particular dish but a previously unexperienced attitude toward eating. In simple meals, they discovered that "attention is given not only to the *vin du pays*, but to the kind of bread, the choice of cheese, and the crispness of the salad, as well as to the preparation of the principal dish."

How does one convey the spirit of this kind of attention in a cookbook? Patience Gray admits in her brief but illuminating new prefatory note that she and Primrose Boyd were too quick to assume their readers knew how to make a good simple green salad; she might have included the ability to find (or make) a decent loaf of bread. There is a chapter on cheese and another on decent *vin ordinaire*, but really, the nettle was not grasped. The book preaches what its authors could not yet example, only wished might be.

The result? A very practical, matter-of-fact collection of recipes on the one hand and, on the other, an enchanted dream—captured by David Gentleman in his evocative, gentle drawings. I wrote above that *Plats du Jour* anticipates *Simple French Food*, a book—or something like it—that Patience Gray might herself have gone on to write, had she chosen to lead a more ordinary life. However, she didn't; she made a much bolder leap and gave us instead something without antecedent, *Honey from a Weed*. There, desire and reality form a coherent whole, providing an answer to what, in this, her first book, she could set out only as a vexing puzzle:

> Contemplating . . . a preparation as ancient and simple as *cotriade à la bretonne* . . . in which a variety of fish are poached with onions, potatoes, and herbs, and daily served in the cottages of Breton villages not a stone's throw from the sea, it must be clear that the natural qualities which give this dish its flavour are with us partially absent; besides, the air we eat it in, the stove we cook it on, and the pot we cook it in are different. This is a dish which involves only fresh fish, waxy yellow potatoes, and Breton onions; how much more variation enters the picture when the oil used comes in question, or the wine added to a casserole, or the herbs that we include.

A final word perhaps ought to be said about why I would encourage any serious cook to obtain this book, after I have made it plain that I don't very often consult it and have never actually made anything from it. For me, at least, there is a category of cookbooks to treasure not for what they do but for what they are. This is because the personality of the author somehow gives you the courage to sustain your own culinary persona against the prevailing trends. The very last books that I would let go from my cookbook collection are the ones that —like Ann Rogers's *A Cookbook for Poor Poets (and Others)* and Miriam Ungerer's *Good Cheap Food*—fall into this category. *Plats du Jour* belongs on the same shelf. As soon as I opened it I knew that I very much liked Patience Gray and Primrose Boyd, I liked the way they wanted to cook, and their book made me—as well as happy—think. My other cookbooks, however useful, are just cookbooks; these three books are friends.

CUISINE MÉCANIQUE

✤ ✤ ✤

1

I first encountered the food processor and the microwave oven in the mid-1970s. This didn't happen on the same day or even in the same week or month, but it did happen in close enough proximity to my own newly acquired self-identity as a food enthusiast for the two machines to become forever firmly linked in my mind. At the time, of course, I didn't think of them as twins, or even near relations, although they were impressive in the same way. Both were on the breaking edge of cooking technology; both were designed to make work shorter and easier. Even so, to me—and to others as well— they initially appeared, as kitchen appliances, exactly opposite in *virtu*. While one was opening whole new culinary horizons, the other was fast becoming the boon tool of the I-hate-to-cook crowd, a hyped-up gadget that did things incredibly fast at the cost of not doing them well.

Upwardly mobile *nouveau cuisinier* that I was quickly becoming, there was simply no question in my mind as to which was which—even though I knew the attraction I felt for the food processor was not universally shared. Debates about its merits still raged in the food magazines, fueled by complaints from those of the culinary old guard who had so far refused to join the stampede.

Not me. I read their opinions with interest, but distantly. I knew that no matter how convincing the case against the machine might be, I *had* to have one. All it had taken was a department-store demonstration: the moment I saw that ball of brioche dough take form and leap up onto the whirring blades, I knew, for me, cooking would never be the same. I couldn't afford an actual Cuisinart—not everyone gets a Volvo in life—but I did purchase their own short-lived bargain-basement brand, the quite adequate Omnichef.

If you were there then, you'll remember the feeling. The food processor was different from other appliances: it compelled belief. Supper guests actually came into the kitchen after dinner to feed it carrots. It was the next best thing to having Paul Bocuse himself come out with the coffee for introductions and acclaim.

As time went on, most serious cooks gave in and got one; the scoffing now came from somewhere else. The food processor has found such a secure place in our kitchen that it seems hard to believe that fifteen years ago it was the same sort of contempt-generating machine that, until very recently, the microwave oven was for us. Cultural critics of the time coined the phrase "Cuisinart liberal" to convey what was wrong with suburbanite reformers: they adopted all the correct positions without having to pay any of the requisite dues.

They were wrong—cultural critics always are—but they do know how to hurt. The phrase stung because we already knew that our culinary titularies—Elizabeth David, Diana Kennedy, Jane Grigson—didn't own Cuisinarts. Nor did we want them to. The thought of hearing the machine's high-pitched keening in Richard Olney's Provençal kitchen would have filled most of us with genuine grief.

The truth was that we felt that we had come too late to pay our dues. We were only just discovering true French cuisine at the very moment it had started to fade away. Now that its ingredients were available and gifted cooks were coming back home to explain it, few of us could imagine devoting ourselves to the time-consuming, meticulous preparation it demanded. Many of us were, after all, young professionals whose careers were just then getting into gear.

If the food processor had not been right there, we might

have paused, might have asked how the French themselves
were managing this. We knew that food and its preparation
played a different role in their lives than it did in ours, but our
understanding of this was, for all our enthusiasm, essentially
shallow.

For centuries, they had been on to a good thing, and now
—almost too late—we were being let in on it. At last, what
they could buy, we could buy; what they could do, we could,
too—but *only* because of this machine. What luck for us it was
the very same one that, in Roy Andries de Groot's words, had
in France "already brought about the major gastronomic revolution of the past twenty years,"* the style of cooking that
was becoming known as *nouvelle cuisine*.

If Carl Sontheimer, the entrepreneur who adapted and mar-
keted the machine in America, is a genius, it is for knowing
that the time was ripe for this machine and exactly which cooks
it was ripe *for*: those of us who took our cooking *seriously*.
Other manufacturers copied the machine but missed the mark.
They colored it pink, softened its formidable lines, and advertised it as another kitchen work-saver, a kind of turbo-blender.

In truth, the food processor is a work-*maker*. The sort of
things you are drawn to do with it you wouldn't even think
of trying without it: shredding your own rillettes, sieving your
own quenelles, hand-mounting your own mayonnaise.

If you had no interest in that sort of thing, a food processor
was a mistaken purchase. The Dad who bought one as a surprise for Mom to help her out with the kitchen chores was in
for a rude surprise: if Mom didn't own at least one French
cookbook, she most likely put the machine away under the
counter after the first exploratory spin.

But to the fledgling serious cook, the Cuisinart, dressed in
its spotless kitchen whites, presented itself not only as a tool
of professional chefs (which it was) but as a professionalizing
one, the one essential shortcut to chefdom. We had only to
follow instructions to be jumped straight from *commis* to *gros
bonnet* . . . at least in our own kitchen. Or so we thought.

---

* Roy Andries de Groot, *Revolutionizing French Cooking* (New York:
McGraw-Hill, 1975), p. 74.

2

Before we can begin to understand what the food processor has done to our cooking, we first need to take account of the impact of a tool from an earlier stage of kitchen technology: the cookbook. My generation (by which I mean those who came of age under the lingering aura of the Kennedy presidency) did, I still think, bring a breath of fresh air into the American kitchen. College education had made our minds hungry for new experiences; now our mouths were catching up. We were open to a new kind of culinary adventuring—we wanted to be exposed to the connoisseurship of food as well as the eating of it.

However, our strength was also our weakness. We had learned to think in the classroom; the printed page brought what was, for most of us, our first real interactions with culture. Hence, it was also via the printed page that we expected to master French cooking—just as we had done French literature. We might attend cooking classes to polish the edges, but mostly we accumulated cookbooks.

These first food books had an enormous influence over our sensation-starved sensibilities, and we unconsciously imbued them—and still do imbue them—with a luster that made them seem the equal of other texts that had similarly been transformed into inspirational touchstones. Unfortunately, few cookbooks, then or now, are of the intellectual caliber of the books from which we received what was best about our education. Our understanding of English literature, for example, would have been quite different if it had never gotten beyond anthologies of "best" or "favorite" poems, prefaced with little potted biographies of the authors.

This is the way food writing still is. Its great shameful secret is its utter intellectual poverty: it may sometimes tell you things you never knew, but nowhere does it make you think. The contents may have a twentieth-century cast to them, but the mind-set is definitely nineteenth-century. I doubt if there has been a cookbook written in this century that would not be understood by Isabella Beeton (although she might not approve of it); some of them are very fine, but they are so in an increasingly out-of-date way.

The Elizabeth David of *French Provincial Cooking* and *Italian Food* and the Jane Grigson of *The Art of Charcuterie* are best understood as among the last of the breed of those sensitive, diligent collectors who throughout the last century tramped rustic Britain to transcribe folk songs, one variant after the other, filling up notebooks as others filled museum cases with specimen songbirds.

What food writers collect is recipes; like folk songs or stuffed birds, these are considered end enough in themselves. The recipe collection—the cookbook—is the original kitchen machine. If it did not exist, there could be no food processor, no microwave oven . . . probably no cooking at all as we now know it. Recipes collapse the fullness of lived experience into a mechanical succession of steps that—once parsed small enough—can be followed by anyone. But the result—the made dish—is only a copy, a simulacrum, whose true meaning lies somewhere else.

This does not much matter in a cuisine whose coherency resides in a complex amalgam of tradition, prejudice, shared skills, and that ultimate common denominator—available ingredients. What is dangerous is when the use of recipes becomes so prevalent that this coherency is lost—because recipe cooking cannot bring it back. Even if a cook internalizes enough familiar recipes so as not to need often to consult her cookbooks, this explains nothing about a cuisine in which all recipes are essentially beside the point.

A food writer writing within a recipe-based cuisine likewise has no choice but to reduce all culinary experience into recipe. Even our best culinary writers present French cuisine as a standard repertoire of recipes, provincial and classical, that all French cooks prepare, some better and some worse than others.

Recipes do play their role in French cooking, without a doubt, but that cuisine is much better explained as a complexly interacting network of artisanal skills. From such a perspective, we might have been brought to understand the French housewife's reluctance to become her own *boulanger*, *patissier*, or *charcutier*

—the very tasks that we were ourselves enthusiastically considering embracing.

A trained craftsperson, she knew the skills of such tasks well enough to realize that she simply did not possess the necessary time—even if she did have the talent—to master them. But she was well able to appreciate and judge the execution of those skills by others.

Because the language of recipe writing cannot capture the fragile ecology of such relationships in an artisanal culture, there is an inevitable rupture between the experience the French have of their cooking and the way that cookbook writers attempt to capture it.

This rupture can literally rend a book in two: sometimes comically, as in Bernard Clayton's *Breads of France*, where every artisanal baking procedure the author encounters is blindly translated into the mechanical rote of recipe bread baking; sometimes ironically, as in Madeleine Kamman's *When French Women Cook*, where the honest, evocative prose convinces any careful reader that the cuisine she describes lives only in the hands of the women who have long nurtured it—directly countermanding the recipes that follow after. Most French cookbooks, however, follow a discreet middle course so that it is not always easy to see where the cracks have been papered over.

This was especially true with *nouvelle cuisine*. Its originators, although they had been trained in the traditional methods, had created a cooking that, in part because of its break with tradition and in part because of its ostensible simplicity, seemed especially suited for a recipe-oriented cooking—and for a *food processor*-oriented cooking.

3

In any case, the problem was not easily discernible in any individual recipe, and it was on individual recipes that we tended to concentrate. We treated each one the way we had been taught to read a poem, intensely, producing from each an ingenious personal reading, a kind of edible explication. How we got from the one to the other was of no great moment as long as the results showed brilliance. We were willing to learn ad hoc the necessary skills but even more willing to see them, as opportunity arose, relegated to a machine.

Until the food processor, this did not matter all that much. Most machines assist the cook without disrupting or denying that hard-earned repository of manual experience whose density gives depth and meaning to the dishes it produces. Just as one electric motor can help turn a steering wheel without robbing the driver of all feel for the road, so can another crank an eggbeater without denying the tactile mastery gained from working a whisk in batter.

The food processor is different. It is not an electric knife (which had already been invented, only to prove itself nothing much) but a cutting *machine*. It pushes the cook's hands aside, for it works far too quickly for the body to directly control it. Our responses are simply not fast enough; we learn to count seconds instead.

Set the steel blade in place, fill the container with basil, pine nuts, garlic, and chunks of Parmesan, and switch the motor on. The machine begins to sauce the ingredients so immediately that they seem to flow together; for its operator, there is a genuine sensual delight in the way, so quickly, so smoothly, it pulps the basil, grinds the cheese, and, as the olive oil starts dribbling down the feeding tube, plumps it all into a thick and unctuous cream.

Sensual it truly is, but it is the sensuality of observing, not participating. The food processor does not enhance the cook's experience. Instead, that work is divided between the mind, which directs it, and the machine, which performs it. The body's part is reduced to setting out and—mostly—cleaning up afterward.

In short, no matter what the mind learns, the hand remains as ignorant as ever. And as time passes, the ease by which the machine accomplishes its tasks makes the hands seem awkward when we *do* put them to use. Anyone who has tried to make pesto in a mortar and pestle after years of concocting it in a food processor knows that the experience can quickly turn into one of helpless frustration. The body just does not know how to go about it: the pestle feels clumsy and ineffectual in the hand, and as the minutes tick by and the contents of the mortar refuse to meld into a sauce, one feels increasingly foolish. Although one knows, from having read books, that this is how it was always done, it doesn't *feel* right. It simply takes too long.

No other kitchen appliance makes the body feel so impotent because no other dissolves away so much hands-on kitchen work. A blender may whir at an equally incomprehensible speed, but it remains a gadget, its niche in our cooking small. The food processor, on the other hand, is capable of assuming almost the entire repertoire of kitchen prep.

The cost of this usurpation was not only the loss of kitchen work by which the body had formerly refreshed itself, exercising genuinely demanding skills and shaping work to the tempo of personal rhythms. There were two other unexpected consequences.

The first was that, by strength of example, the food processor began to corrode the meaning of *all* kitchen work. This was true not only of the homes that already had a food processor, for once a kind of kitchen work becomes identified as a tiresome chore by enough cooks, it begins to lie heavy and sullen in the hands of all of them. What could not now be done effortlessly, cleanly, perfectly, became by comparison drudgery, all the more susceptible to replacement by some other, cleverer machine.

The second consequence was one to which we *nouveaux cuisiniers* were especially vulnerable. The product of a wealthy, acquisitive culture that could pick the ingredients of its meals almost at will, we had now been given a machine that allowed us to prepare an almost unlimited number of complex dishes without any kind of physical restraint.

For the same reason, we were equally enticed by any and all new recipes that came our way. The less that cooking comes from hands-on kitchen experience, the harder it is for a cook to gauge the desirability of a newly encountered dish. A cook who makes all chicken broth from scratch will cast a more discriminating eye on a recipe that calls for it than the cook who pours it from the can. The cook who does all her own cutting, chopping, and sieving immediately knows the appropriateness of a new recipe: it must fit the hands.

On the contrary, freed of the necessity of such choices, *our* only way of judging a dish's rightness was becoming the wanton appreciation of the tongue and the riot of culinary fad. Appetite has always had a hard time saying no; it needs guidance we were no longer in a position to provide.

None of this, of course, was the food processor's fault. But just as the automobile changed the landscape of America in ways that no one had expected or prepared for, the food processor shifted the nature of culinary reality . . . more slowly for the culture at large, but almost immediately in the microculture that was beginning to take food seriously. As it proliferated, it began raising the stakes for all, even for those who did not yet possess one. And it is this effect—in an equally unexpected way—that we have just begun to experience with the microwave.

4

Unlike the food processor, the microwave has no French ancestry, or even—until relatively recently—any influential food-world friends. It lacks the assertively simple high-tech styling and the haute-cuisine associations that might have provided it with Cuisinart-like cachet. In fact, with its buttons, buzzers, and revolving carousels, the microwave, from the very start, has seemed irredeemably prole—right down to the reason for owning one. For no matter the culinary arguments voiced in its favor, the only truly compelling reason to own a microwave is still the first: it is the best medium yet devised for the almost instant reheating of cooked food.

Even so, what made the microwave seem irresistible to *its* original purchasers is not all that different from what made the food processor seem so desirable to us. Both fed a fantasy of participating in a cuisine whose rationale had already evaporated, no matter how delicious its dishes. For the first microwave owners, however, that cuisine was the familiar American supper. With its assistance, a family could dispense with a regular cook and even a common dinnertime—and still sit down to the familiar trinity of meat, starch, and vegetable, courtesy of Swanson's LeMenu, served piping hot on a premium plastic plate—no more the TV-dinner tripart, tinfoil, cafeteria-style serving tray.

The price was the same: the cook was obliged to surrender involvement for convenience. Microwave energy offers no equivalent experience to replace our intuitive understanding of heat; indeed, the body's inability to respond or protect itself means the cooking food must be locked away out of reach. Because microwaves cook food from the inside out, they are unable to provide us with any of radiant heat's familiar, helpful clues. As with the Cuisinart, the cook must count seconds instead.

Food processor, microwave oven . . . the one speeds preparation by removing it from human hands and human time; the other does the same to the actual process of cooking. As the food processor devours the experience of knife and cutting board, whisk and bowl, the other eats away at an even more primal experience: the putting of food to fire.

That we *nouveaux cuisiniers* originally missed the connection is not surprising; we put a very different weight on the meaning of the two types of experience. Our inspiration was, after all, the chef; if there was any experience in cooking that remained crucial to us, it was dexterity before the flame.

What we never expected was that as kitchen experience in its entirety became progressively devalued, the aura that still clung to the stove would also necessarily fade. Unnoticed by us, the image of the chef before his range, sweat dripping down his face as hot fat shimmered in his sauté pan, was undergoing as radical a change for microwave users as the role of scullion had for us.

As more and more cooks began to learn how to use their microwave, the conventional oven was progressively being found too hot, too time-consuming, too wasteful of energy, and, above all, too *greasy* . . . literally, but figuratively, too, for the description began to embrace as well the meals that it was used to prepare.

Unlike traditional cuisines, recipe-based cooking has never allowed the home cook to shape a meal by reworking the same dish from day to day in response to what her family needs to eat—adding or eliminating meat, throwing in a smaller or larger proportion of chopped greens or a larger or smaller handful of rice. The amounts and the ingredients of recipe dishes are already determined forever by someone else who knows none of the eaters—or their needs or appetites.

There is something relentless about recipes in this regard: they create a condition not unlike the air temperature in a large office building, where it is always too hot in the winter and too cold in the summer—but if no one is really happy, neither can anyone complain. Recipe cooking likewise gives us too much; whether in the guise of fattening us up or slimming us down, somehow things are always being waved in front of our mouths. This is the purpose of recipes, after all: to arouse appetite. Like central heating, food writing's only task is to make us "comfortable"; it might be establishing a climate of self-indulgence or self-denial, but it is still busy making us feel hungry—the only question being what we are to become hungry *for*.

So far as reheating was concerned, of course, no food writing was needed to get microwave owners to turn the appetite thermostat up. Because of its original audience, much of pre-packaged microwave food was already laden with calories. Turning the thermostat down, however, was quite another matter. Microwave cooking, because it required that all recipes be recast for its peculiar way of heating, offered a glorious opportunity for cookbook writers to play not only on their readers' increasingly compulsive need for cooking to be made easy, but also upon their terror of fat.

The microwave's chief handicap—that it cooks best what is best cooked inside out—suddenly became a plus. No need to apologize that it can't crisp the fat when there's no fat to crisp—especially when you can harp on the fact that it can steam broccoli in its own moisture to tender doneness before the exterior has a chance to dry out—with not a calorie added or a vitamin lost.

"An odd thing happened a few years ago as I began to cook

a great deal in the microwave oven," writes Barbara Kafka in the introduction to her *Microwave Gourmet Healthstyle Cookbook.* "It was less hard to lose weight when it started to go up, and it was easier to keep it off. . . . After a while, I figured it out. The microwave oven doesn't need fat to cook."

Neither, of course, do many conventional cooking techniques, and those that do don't always add that many calories to the completed dish. But such language sells microwaves— just as it once sold food processors. As Henri Gault (of *Le Nouveau Guide de Gault-Millau*) told Roy Andries de Groot in *Revolutionizing French Cooking:* "Our French *Robot Coupe* [the original Cuisinart] . . . is a precious tool for the easy preparation of the new low-fat, low-starch, low-sugar, yet high-pleasure cuisine. With it, you can emulsify and thicken the sauces . . . with no use whatsoever of butter or flour." All you need is the machine—and some new recipes.

5

The fact is, neither can do anything beyond what its user asks of it, but this has not prevented that untampered-with stalk of broccoli from becoming the emblem of the increasingly neur-asthenic cuisine of a new, post-gourmet generation of cooks who, unsettled by the preceding generation's inability to come to terms with unbridled consumption, are increasingly shrink-ing not merely from the conspicuous display of appetite, but even from appetite itself. Harbingers of a new Age of Prohi-bition, they are at least their parents' children in this: a love of convenience. For them, too, time spent in the kitchen is wasted time.

Consequently, the food processor is no stranger to their kitchen, either—they use it to shred their salads and emulsify their cottage-cheese spreads. But the irony is more poignant in their embrace of a device that in our minds has always meant greasy fast food and the general collapse of cooking into TV-dinnerdom. Because we despised it, they embraced it—as a means of becoming cooks like us. Welcome to the macrobiotic microwave: a work-free, fat-free way of cooking.

Perhaps the clearest display yet of the forces that have brought about this unexpected conjunction is to be found in a piece that appeared in the December 1987 issue of *The Atlantic*, written by Corby Kummer, an editor of the magazine and its regular food columnist. His account of his conversion to microwave cooking begins with the frank assertion that—despite initial resistance—he now uses that device "more than any other appliance in my kitchen, including the stove."

To explain how this has come about, he describes in detail how the microwave has completely changed his attitude toward cooking fish. These comments are worth quoting at some length, for they neatly tie together the whole bundle of post-oven cooking attitudes:

> Fish cooked in a microwave oven is the single best example of how owning one can change your life. . . . You take it out of the wrapping paper and put it on the plate you plan to serve it on. It needs nothing to make it taste good: no oil, no court bouillon to poach it in, no herbs you forgot to buy. Even a fish as bland as sole reveals itself to be much more interesting than it was when poached in a liquid that drew off its flavor or baked at a heat that dried it out. The inside and the outside of the fish cook at the same time . . . eliminating the problem of a raw center and a dry exterior. . . . I used to buy fish only rarely, despite my great fondness for it, out of reluctance to take the time to figure out how best to cook it and for how long. Now I buy any fish that I can find, knowing that I will taste it at its best after a few minutes. And I'll have only the plate to wash.

No one asked for the emotional gist of this passage would say that it resides in a heartfelt passion for fish. If anything, these words reflect an active resentment at having to cook. In less than a paragraph, that activity is portrayed as one strewn with annoyances, from having to remember to buy the parsley at the one end to having to clean up the frypan at the other . . . and in between, of having to think, smell, taste, and pay attention to what you're doing.

Here is a culinary voice in which the promise of the food processor has been so completely interiorized that it can state without ironic inflection that "microwave ovens can't eliminate preparation time. I will admit that as obvious as this lesson seems, it came as an unpleasant surprise. The vegetables still have to be peeled, the onions chopped, the spices retrieved from the back of the cabinet."

At first glance, even given that this attitude might be felt as liberating by readers of *The Atlantic*, it would still seem that *fish* would not be the first food with which to justify conversion to microwave cooking. After all, a whole sole can be broiled in a conventional oven in five minutes, a fillet in less. Pan frying takes no longer (and a not-too-fussy cook can usually clean the pan with a wipe of a paper towel).

However, precisely because fish cooks quickly and its flesh is so fragile, preparing it by conventional means does require concerted attention—although really no more than is required to not overcook a steak. Unlike steak, however, fish does not possess sufficient prestige with most of us to command such care. Overcook the steak and the cook blames himself; overcook the fish and the cook blames *it*.

Fish cookery, then, is a good index of our culture's resentment at having to cook, which would explain why it is currently available in far greater abundance precooked and prepackaged in the supermarket's freezer case than fresh in the seafood section (if the supermarket has a seafood section at all).

Frozen fish is also preferred because there is no chance that it might stink. Although Corby Kummer does not mention this, one might be forgiven for suspecting a subtext to his thrice-repeated relief at having nothing to wash but his plate: that the microwave owner can buy, cook, and eat fresh fish *without ever having to touch it.*

Contrast such "great fondness" for fish with the sentiments of Jeffrey Steingarten, in an essay on the same subject that appeared a few months afterward in *HG*. Steingarten's feelings about microwave fish cookery were mixed, something that could be anticipated from moments such as this one, when he realized that his pleasure in some medallions of salmon

came from the marinade of mustard, olive oil, and lemon, which was so good that, having grown weary of steamed fish, I broke the rules and grilled a salmon steak smeared with the marinade in my powerful salamander broiler. The results, I regret, were wonderful. . . .

Were this an actual debate, one could imagine the *nouveaux cuisiniers* in the audience leaping to their feet and cheering— here, at last, a moment where new-fashioned restraint gives way to old-fashioned indulgence. Steingarten's prose is studded with such verbal whets—and their implicit permissiveness.

Readers whose expectations of food prose turn on such points of sensual enhancement will find little pleasure in Corby Kummer's article, which evidences no similar moment of appetite in all its paragraphs of instruction. But an increasing number of others will be happy to at last encounter a food writer not given to compulsive lip-smacking, a prose in which culinary temptation is conspicuously absent.

Instead, it is a prose that knows the price of pleasure and is willing to pay for it only with carefully counted nickels and dimes. His basic fish recipe is *fish*: no herbs, no court bouillon, no oil. "You can nearly always eliminate fat from any recipe you want to adapt to the microwave oven. If you *do* want to add it, a *spoonful* of olive oil or melted butter . . . drizzled over the fish just before it is served will taste fresher and stronger than if cooked." The emphases are mine.

In the world where this kind of cooking takes place, "fish" is a code word. We all know that it is good for us; we all hate to cook it. Frozen fish fingers are one answer, but how much more pleasant, how much more guilt-free, instead to stick a fresh fillet into the microwave, *tout nu*, and, in a matter of mere seconds, be able—be *allowed*—to lick our platter clean.

6

What the proponents of this new cuisine do not understand —and what we seem to be in no position to teach them—is that the impoverishment that cooking has undergone in our hands has left them even less able than we to imagine a cuisine not based on the promiscuous use of recipes or the necessary convenience of machines.

We too are still convinced that by following recipes and using devices like food processors and microwave ovens we are saving time, when what is happening instead is that we are being made more efficient—at the price of a whole realm of experience.

The argument that these machines are time-saving depends on our own refusal to notice how short-lived is the space that some new technology frees up for us before it is taken away. Otherwise, we would have a huge reservoir of free time, given all that we've supposedly been banking away. But the truth is quite different.

Once, not so long ago, we were allowed some of the evening to cook supper. Even in the seventies, when Pierre Franey began his "60-Minute Gourmet" column for *The New York Times*, to make a complete dinner within an hour seemed quite a feat. Now it seems an extravagance. Today, twenty minutes is more like it: hence the *Times*'s food editor Marian Burros's column, "20-Minute Menus." Corby Kummer's five-minute fish bake will soon be eating into that.

The reason we still believe we possess this free time is that we have been persuaded to externalize the experience of cooking into a series of unwanted chores. Whatever the user of the microwave is doing with his or her freed-up time, it is obviously not *cooking*—and to that very limited extent, he or she has been set free. But for what?

To understand what has really happened to us, imagine attempting to reverse the process. Imagine *wanting* to take a whole afternoon to leisurely prepare supper—without food processor, microwave oven, or cookbook. To live, after all, is to experience things, and every time we mince an onion, lower the flame under a simmering pot, shape the idea and substance of a meal, we actually gain rather than lose lived time. Such minutes are not only full and rich in themselves, but they brush a lasting patina of lived experience onto our memory.

Anyone who has seriously attempted to do such cooking knows that it requires more concentrated physical attention than most of us can spare. This kind of commitment is one we are no longer able to give our regularly lived lives, for it has become too dear for casual expenditure.

The devices making more and more demands on our actual lived time do not themselves provide experience in kind to what they have taken away. What they usually provide instead is a kind of compressed, fictive experience that does not take place in genuinely lived time.

What I mean by fictive experience can be compared to the act of watching television. While we view it, it fills us up with an experience of events taking place, but, unlike actually lived experience, this feeling of enrichment soon evaporates when we pull our attention away. This is because, in terms of experience, all we have been doing is sitting on a couch and staring at a machine that, at bottom, we do not take very seriously.

As cooking has progressively taken on much of this same character—the mind kept busy, the body left essentially uninvolved—it has forced onto our eating the same fictive quality, the living of a pretend life. A frozen microwave entrée like Armour's Classic or Swanson's LeMenu dinner might in this sense be viewed as a cookbook brought to its ultimate consummation: a food book that can be opened and its contents devoured.

Like cookbooks, these food packages arouse appetite through glossy photographs, enticing prose, and that sense—conveyed through the general design and pricing—that we are being given the metaphorical equivalent of a good home-cooked meal.

The mind can feed on metaphors, and it becomes progressively hungry for them the less our own lives are able to provide them. For the mind, it is of little matter that the actual experience of eating the dish has a blank sameness to it, even if for our mouth it is just another frozen dinner. Instead, the mind simply becomes less inclined to consult a dulled tongue when offered an appealing fantasy. It lingers over the fading image of the wrapper and insists it is having a good time.

Invert this insight, and the cookbook reveals itself to us as a kind of pretechnological TV dinner. It, too, stimulates appetite by end-running actual sensual experience and appealing directly to the mind. It, too, wraps endless sameness in metaphors that the brain hungers for, steadily blurring the distinction between actual and fictive experience. "Look," it says to the tongue, "stop complaining. Tonight we're going to France to have *moussaka provençale* with Mireille Johnston." But the tongue doesn't reply; it has long since stopped paying attention.

All recipes are built on the belief that somewhere at the beginning of the chain there is a cook who does not use them. This is the great nostalgia of our cuisine, ever invoking an absent mother-cook who once laid her hands on the body of the world and worked it into food for us. The promise of every cookbook is that it offers a way back into her lap.

She's long gone, that lady. But without the fantasy of her none of this would be bearable. Our cuisine has become a Borges fable or an Escher print, a universe crammed with cookbook writers all passing the same recipes around and around. And each time one passes through their hands, they manage to find a way to make it faster and faster, leaner and leaner— until everything fuses together into a little black box. You put in a piece of fish on a clean plate; a minute later, you take it out cooked, and eat it. You can call that progress, if you want, but you can't call it Mommy.

BIBLIOGRAPHY

✣ ✣ ✣

Abdennour, Samia. *Egyptian Cooking: A Practical Guide.* Cairo, Egypt: The American University in Cairo, 1984.

Adam, H. Pearl. *Kitchen Ranging.* New York: Jonathan Cape and Harrison Smith, 1929.

Allen, Myrtle. *Cooking at Ballymaloe House.* New York: Stewart, Tabori and Chang, 1990.

Anderson, Jean. *The Food of Portugal.* New York: Morrow, 1986.

Andrews, Colman. *Catalan Cuisine.* New York: Atheneum, 1988.

Arora, David. *Mushrooms Demystified.* Berkeley: Ten Speed Press, 1986.

Batcheller, Barbara. *Lilies of the Kitchen.* New York: St. Martin's Press, 1986.

Bateman, Michael, and Heather Maisner. *The Sunday Times Book of Real Bread.* Aylesbury, U.K.: Rodale Press, 1982.

Beard, James. *American Cookery.* Boston: Little, Brown, 1972.

———. *Beard on Bread.* New York: Knopf, 1973.

Beck, Simone, Louisette Bertholle, and Julia Child. *Mastering the Art of French Cooking,* Vol. I. New York: Knopf, 1961.

———, and Julia Child. *Mastering the Art of French Cooking,* Vol. II. New York: Knopf, 1970.

Behr, Edward. *The Artful Eater.* New York: Atlantic Monthly Press, 1992.

Bentley, James. *Life and Food in the Dordogne.* New York: New Amsterdam, 1986.

Bertolli, Paul (with Alice Waters). *Chez Panisse Cooking.* New York: Random House, 1988.

Bilheux, Roland, Alain Escoffier, Daniel Hervé, and Jean-Marie Pouradier. *Special and Decorative Breads* (trans. Rhona Poritzky-Lauvand and James Peterson). New York: Van Nostrand Reinhold, 1989.

Boily, Lise, and Jean-François Blanchette. *The Bread Ovens of Quebec.* Ottawa: National Museum of Man/National Museums of Canada, 1979.

Boni, Ada. *Italian Regional Cooking.* New York: E. P. Dutton, 1969.

Boxer, Arabella. *Mediterranean Cookbook.* London: J. M. Dent & Sons, 1981.

Brown, Edward Espe. *The Tassajara Bread Book.* Berkeley: Shambala, 1970.

Bugialli, Giuliano. *Bugialli on Pasta.* New York: Simon & Schuster, 1988.

———. *The Fine Art of Italian Cooking.* New York: Quadrangle, 1977.

Buonassisi, Vincenzo. *Pasta.* Wilton, CT: Lyceum Books, 1973.

Burros, Marian. *20-Minute Menus.* New York: Simon & Schuster, 1989.

Calingaert, Efrem Funghi, and Jacquelyn Days Serwer. *Pasta and Rice Italian Style.* New York: Scribners, 1983.

Campbell, Helen. *In Foreign Kitchens.* Boston: Roberts Brothers, 1893.

Carluccio, Antonio. *A Passion for Mushrooms.* Topsfield, MA: Salem House, 1989.

Castelvetro, Giacomo. *The Fruit, Herbs & Vegetables of Italy,* trans. Gillian Riley. New York: Viking, 1989.

Chamberlain, Lesley. *The Food and Cooking of Russia.* London: Allen Lane, 1982.

Chelminski, Rudolph. *The French at Table.* New York: Morrow, 1985.

Chen, Joyce. *Joyce Chen Cook Book.* Philadelphia: Lippincott, 1963.

Child, Julia. *The Way to Cook.* New York: Knopf, 1989.

Clark, Sydney. *All the Best in Italy.* New York: Dodd, Mead & Co., 1968.

Clayton, Bernard, Jr. *The Breads of France.* Indianapolis: Bobbs-Merrill, 1978.

———. *The Complete Book of Breads.* New York: Simon & Schuster, 1973.

Cole, Rosalind. *Of Soda Bread and Guinness.* Indianapolis: Bobbs-Merrill, 1973.

Courtine, Robert. *Real French Cooking.* London: Faber & Faber, 1956.

Daguin, André, and Anne de Ravel. *Foie Gras, Magret, and Other Good Food from Gascony.* New York: Random House, 1988.

David, Elizabeth (Introduction and Notes for the American Cook by Karen Hess). *English Bread and Yeast Cookery.* New York: Viking, 1980.

———. *Italian Food.* New York: Harper & Row, 1987.

———. *An Omelette and a Glass of Wine.* New York: Viking, 1985.

———. *Spices, Salt and Aromatics in the English Kitchen.* Harmondsworth, Middlesex: Penguin Books, 1975.

David, Narsai M., and Doris Muscatine. *Monday Night at Narsai's.* New York: Simon & Schuster, 1987.

de Groot, Roy Andries. *Revolutionizing French Cooking.* New York: McGraw-Hill, 1975.

Del Conte, Anna. *Pasta Perfect.* New York: Doubleday, 1987.

———. *Portrait of Pasta.* New York: Paddington Press, 1976.

della Croce, Julia. *Pasta Classica.* San Francisco: Chronicle Books, 1987.

de' Medici, Lorenza. *The Renaissance of Italian Cooking.* New York: Fawcett, 1989.

der Haroutunian, Arto. *Middle Eastern Cookery.* London: Century Publishing, 1982.

Dojny, Brooke, and Melanie Barnard. *Let's Eat In.* New York: Prentice Hall, 1989.

Edwards, John. *The Roman Cookery of Apicius: A Treasury of Gourmet Recipes and Herbal Cookery, Translated for the Modern Kitchen.* Point Roberts, WA: Hartley & Marks, 1984.

Escudier, Jean-Noël, and Peta J. Fuller. *The Wonderful Food of Provence.* Boston: Houghton Mifflin, 1968.

Field, Carol. *The Italian Baker.* New York: Harper & Row, 1985.

FitzGibbon, Theodora. *A Taste of Ireland in Food and Pictures.* London: Pan Books, 1968.

Fu Pei-Mei. *Chinese Snacks & Desserts.* Taipei: Fu Pei-Mei (no date).

Glasse, Hannah. *The Art of Cooking Made Plain and Easy.* (Facsimile of the first [1747] edition.) London: Prospect Books, 1983.

Goldstein, Darra. *A La Russe.* New York: Random House, 1983.

Gray, Patience. *Honey from a Weed.* New York: Harper & Row, 1987.

————, and Primrose Boyd. *Plats du Jour.* (Facsimile edition of the 1957 Penguin Books original.) London: Prospect Books, 1990.

Grierson, E. *Things Seen in Florence.* London: Seeley, Service & Co., Ltd., 1928.

Grigson, Jane. *Food with the Famous.* London: Michael Joseph, 1979.

Haim, Nadine. *The Artist's Palate.* New York: Harry N. Abrams, 1988.

Hambro, Nathalie. *Particular Delights: Cooking for All the Senses.* London: Jill Norman & Hobhouse, Ltd., 1981.

Harris, Jessica B. *Iron Pots and Wooden Spoons.* New York: Atheneum, 1989.

Hazan, Marcella. *Marcella's Italian Kitchen.* New York: Knopf, 1987.

Hazelton, Nika. *The Regional Italian Kitchen.* New York: Evans, 1978.

Heatter, Maida. *Maida Heatter's Book of Great Desserts.* New York: Knopf, 1974.

Hibben, Sheila. *American Regional Cookery.* Boston: Little, Brown, 1946.

Holt, Geraldene. *French Country Kitchen.* London: Penguin Books, 1987.

Hom, Ken. *The Taste of China.* New York: Simon & Schuster, 1990.

Howe, Robin. *The Mediterranean Diet.* London: Weidenfeld and Nicolson, 1985.

Jarratt, Enrica and Vernon. *The Complete Book of Pasta.* New York: Dover, 1977.

Johnston, Mireille. *The Cuisine of the Sun.* New York: Random House, 1976.

Joyes, Claire. *Monet's Table: The Cooking Journals of Claude Monet.* New York: Simon & Schuster, 1989.

Kafka, Barbara. *Food for Friends.* New York: Harper & Row, 1984.

————. *Microwave Gourmet Healthstyle Cookbook.* New York: Morrow, 1989.

Kamman, Madeleine. *When French Women Cook.* New York: Atheneum, 1976.

Kates, Joanne. *The Taste of Things.* Toronto: Oxford University Press, 1987.

Keys, Ancel and Margaret. *How to Eat Well and Stay Well the Mediterranean Way.* New York: Doubleday, 1975.

Kummer, Corby. "Fast Fish." *The Atlantic,* December 1987.

——. "Pasta." *The Atlantic,* July 1986.

Lang, Jenifer Harvey (ed). *Larousse Gastronomique.* New York: Crown, 1988.

Laverty, Maura. *Full and Plenty.* Dublin: The Irish Flour Millers Association, 1960.

Leonard, Thom. *The Bread Book.* Brookline, MA: East-West Health Books, 1990.

Létoile, Valérie-Anne, Monique Maine, and Madeleine Peter. (English-language editor, Jill Norman.) *La Cuisine: The Complete Book of French Cooking.* New York: Galley Press, 1985.

Leung, Mai. *The Chinese People's Cookbook.* New York: Harper & Row, 1979.

Lewis, Edna, and Evangeline Peterson. *The Edna Lewis Cookbook.* Indianapolis: Bobbs-Merrill, 1972.

Lewis, Stephen. "High Bold Loaves." *Gourmet,* October 1990.

Liebling, A. J. *Between Meals: An Appetite for Paris.* New York: Simon & Schuster, 1962.

Luard, Elisabeth. *European Peasant Cookery.* London: Bantam Press, 1986.

McGee, Harold. *On Food and Cooking.* New York: Scribners, 1984.

McLucas, Suzanne. *A Provençal Kitchen in America.* Boulder: Johnson Books, 1982.

Martini, Anna. *The Mondadori Regional Italian Cookbook.* New York: Harmony Books, 1983.

——. *Pasta & Pizza.* New York: St. Martin's Press, 1976.

Mickler, Ernest Matthew. *White Trash Cooking.* Winston-Salem, NC: The Jargon Society, 1986.

Middione, Carlo. *The Food of Southern Italy.* New York: Morrow, 1987.

Mintz, Sidney. *Sweetness and Power.* New York: Viking, 1985.

Muffoletto, Anna. *The Art of Sicilian Cooking.* New York: Doubleday, 1971.

Olney, Richard. *The French Menu Cookbook.* New York: Simon & Schuster, 1970; rev. ed. Boston: David R. Godine, 1985.

——. *Simple French Food.* New York: Atheneum, 1974.

Ortiz, Elisabeth Lambert. *Caribbean Cooking.* Harmondsworth, Middlesex: Penguin Books, 1977.

——. *The Food of Spain and Portugal.* New York: Atheneum, 1989.

Paddleford, Clementine. *How America Eats.* New York: Scribners, 1960.

Pearson, Haydn S. *The Countryman's Cookbook.* New York: Whittlesey House (McGraw-Hill), 1946.

The Pecan Institute. *800 Proved Pecan Recipes.* Philadelphia: Macrae, 1925.

Pellegrini, Angelo. *The Unprejudiced Palate.* New York: Macmillan, 1948.

Pépin, Jacques. *The Art of Cooking,* Vol. 2. New York: Knopf, 1988.

The Picayune's Creole Cook Book. 2d ed. (1901). New York: Dover, 1971.

Plotkin, Fred. *The Authentic Pasta Book.* New York: Simon & Schuster, 1985.

Randolph, Mary. *The Virginia House-Wife*. (Facsimile of the first edition, 1824, with additional material from the editions of 1825 and 1826 to present a complete text, with historical notes and commentaries by Karen Hess.) Columbia, S.C.: University of South Carolina, 1984.

Redwood, Jean. *Russian Food: All the Peoples, All the Republics*. Felixstowe, Suffolk, England: Oldwicks Press Ltd., 1989.

Reinhart, Br. Peter. *Brother Juniper's Bread Book: Slow Rise as Method and Metaphor*. New York: Aris/Addison Wesley, 1991.

Robertson, Laurel (with Carol Flinders and Bronwen Godfrey). *The Laurel's Kitchen Bread Book*. New York: Random House, 1984.

Roden, Claudia. *A Book of Middle Eastern Food*. New York: Knopf, 1972.

Rogers, Ann. *A Cookbook for Poor Poets (and Others)*. New York: Scribner, 1966.

Root, Waverley (and the Editors of Time-Life Books). *The Cooking of Italy*. New York: Time-Life Books, 1968.

Rorer, Sarah Tyson. *Mrs. Rorer's New Cook Book*. Philadelphia: Arnold, 1902.

Ross, Janet, and Michael Waterfield. *Leaves from Our Tuscan Kitchen*. New York: Atheneum, 1974.

Sakamoto, Nabuko. *The People's Republic of China Cookbook*. New York: Random House, 1977.

Schrecker, Ellen (with John Schrecker). *Mrs. Chiang's Szechwan Cookbook*. New York: Harper & Row, 1976.

Scott, Jack Denton. *The Complete Book of Pasta*. New York: Morrow, 1968.

Scott, Natalie, and Caroline Merrick Jones. *Gourmet's Guide to New Orleans*. New Orleans: Scott & Jones, 1951.

Seed, Diane. *The Top One Hundred Pasta Sauces*. Berkeley: Ten Speed Press, 1987.

Seymour, John. *Gardener's Delight*. New York: Harmony Books, 1979.

Sheraton, Mimi. *The German Cookbook*. New York: Random House, 1965.

Siegel, F. (translator). *Russian Cooking*. Moscow: Mir Publishers, 1974.

Simeti, Mary Taylor. *On Persephone's Island*. New York: Knopf, 1986.

———. *Pomp and Sustenance: Twenty-Five Centuries of Sicilian Food*. New York: Knopf, 1989.

Simonds, Nina. *Classic Chinese Cuisine*. Boston: Houghton Mifflin, 1982.

Spoerri, Daniel. *Mythology & Meatballs: A Greek Island Diary/Cookbook*. Berkeley: Aris, 1982.

Spry, Constance, and Rosemary Hume. *The Constance Spry Cookery Book*. London: J. M. Dent, 1956.

Standard, Stella. *Stella Standard's Soup Book*. New York: Taplinger, 1978.

Steingarten, Jeffrey. "Fish without Fire." *HG*, March 1988.

Stewart, Martha. *Martha Stewart's Quick Cook*. New York: Crown, 1983.

———, with Elizabeth Hawes. *Entertaining*. New York: Clarkson N. Potter, 1982.

Stobart, Tom. *The Cook's Encyclopedia*. New York: Harper & Row, 1981.

Thorne, John. *Simple Cooking*. New York: Viking, 1987.

Thubron, Colin. *Where Nights Are Longest: Travels by Car Through Western Russia*. New York: Random House, 1984.

Time-Life, Editors of. *Breads* (The Good Cook, Techniques and Recipes). Alexandria, VA: Time-Life Books, 1981.

Torres, Marimar. *The Spanish Table*. New York: Doubleday, 1986.

Tropp, Barbara. *The Modern Art of Chinese Cooking*. New York: Morrow, 1982.

Ungerer, Miriam. *Good Cheap Food*. New York: Viking, 1973.

Vada, Simonetta Lupi. *Step by Step Pasta Cookbook*. Secaucus, NJ: Chartwell Books, 1984.

Visson, Lynn. *The Complete Russian Cookbook*. Ann Arbor, MI: Ardis, 1982.

Volokh, Anne, with Mavis Manus. *The Art of Russian Cuisine*. New York: Macmillan, 1983.

von Bremzen, Anya, and John Welchman. *Please to the Table: The Russian Cookbook*. New York: Workman, 1990.

Wasson, Valentina Pavlovna, and R. Gordon Wasson. *Mushrooms, Russia, & History*. New York: Pantheon, 1957.

Wells, Patricia. *Bistro Cooking*. New York: Workman, 1989.

———. *The Food Lover's Guide to Paris*. New York: Workman, 1984.

Whynott, Doug. "Healthy Harvest." *Harrowsmith*, September/October 1989.

Willan, Anne. *French Regional Cooking*. New York: Morrow, 1981.

Wolfert, Paula. *The Cooking of South-West France*. New York: The Dial Press, 1983.

———. *Couscous and Other Good Food from Morocco*. New York: Harper & Row, 1973.

———. *Mediterranean Cooking*. New York: Quadrangle/New York Times, 1977.

———. *Paula Wolfert's World of Food*. New York: Harper & Row, 1988.

Wood, Ed. *World of Sourdoughs from Antiquity*. Cascade, ID: Sinclair Publishing, 1989.

Wretman, Tore. *The Swedish Smörgåsbord*. Helsingbord, Sweden: Forum, 1983.

Zanger, Mark. "Stock." *The Real Paper*, January 21, 1978.

INDEX

❖ ❖ ❖

CPSIA information can be obtained
at www.ICGtesting.com
Printed in the USA
LVHW020550261218
601646LV00002BA/342/P